HENRIK IBSEN was born of well-to-do parents in Skien, a small Norwegian coastal town, on 20 March 1828. In 1836, his father went bankrupt, and the family was reduced to near poverty. At the age of fifteen, he was apprenticed to an apothecary in Grimstad. In 1850, Ibsen ventured to Christiania—present-day Oslo—as a student, with the hope of becoming a doctor. On the strength of his first two plays, he was appointed "theater-poet" to the new Bergen National Theater, where he wrote five conventional romantic and historical dramas and absorbed the elements of his craft. In 1857, he was called to the directorship of the financially unsound Christiania Norwegian Theater, which failed in 1862. In 1864, exhausted and enraged by the frustration of his efforts toward a national drama and theater, he quit Norway for what became twenty-seven years of voluntary exile abroad. In Italy, he wrote the volcanic *Brand* (1866), which made his reputation and secured him a poet's stipend from the government. Its companion piece, the phantasmagoric *Peer Gynt*, followed in 1867, then the immense double play *Emperor and Galilean* (1873), expressing his philosophy of civilization. Meanwhile, having moved to Germany, Ibsen had been searching for a new style. With *The Pillars of Society* he found it; this became the first of twelve plays, appearing at two-year intervals, that confirmed his international standing as the foremost dramatist of his age. In 1900, Ibsen suffered the first of several strokes that incapacitated him. He died in Oslo on 23 May 1906.

TERRY OTTEN is a Professor of English and Kenneth E. Wray Professor in the Humanities at Wittenberg University. He has published three books about the stage and contemporary literature, and has also written more than fifty essays for a variety of journals, including essays on Ibsen in *Modern Drama, Comparative Drama,* and *Mosaic.* Professor Otten was named Ohio Professor of the Year and National Bronze Medalists by the Council for the Advancement and Support of Education in 1988. He is currently working on a book about Arthur Miller.

HENRIK IBSEN

FOUR MAJOR PLAYS
VOLUME II

Ghosts

An Enemy of the People

The Lady from the Sea

John Gabriel Borkman

Translated by Rolf Fjelde

With a New Afterword by Terry Otten

A SIGNET CLASSIC

SIGNET CLASSIC
Published by New American Library, a division of
Penguin Putnam Inc., 375 Hudson Street, New York, New York 10014, U.S.A.
Penguin Books Ltd, 27 Wrights Lane, London W8 5TZ, England
Penguin Books Australia Ltd, Ringwood, Victoria, Australia
Penguin Books Canada Ltd, 10 Alcorn Avenue, Toronto, Ontario, Canada M4V 3B2
Penguin Books (N.Z.) Ltd, 182–190 Wairau Road, Auckland 10, New Zealand

Penguin Books Ltd, Registered Offices: Harmondsworth, Middlesex, England

Published by Signet Classic, an imprint of New American Library,
a division of Penguin Putnam Inc.

First Signet Classic Printing, July 1970
First Signet Classic Printing (Otten Afterword), August 2001
10 9 8 7 6 5 4 3 2 1

Ⓒ REGISTERED TRADEMARK—MARCA REGISTRADA

Library of Congress Catalog Card Number: 65001031

Printed in the United States of America

To Christel

CONTENTS

FOREWORD

People want only special revolutions,
in externals, in politics, and so on.
But that's just tinkering. What really
is called for is a revolution of the
human mind. . . .
      IBSEN, *letter to Brandes, 1871*

Both literally and literarily, Henrik Ibsen came of age in
the troubled aftermath of the year of revolutions, 1848.
Today many would find it difficult to summon any firm
image of that time of spontaneous combustion that leapt
like crown fire across the capitals of Europe. Compared
with 1789 in France or 1917 in Russia, with their now
legendary leaders, their Marats and Robespierres, Trot-
skys and Lenins, their wide international reverberations
and their legacies of a shaken and altered world scene,
1848 has come to seem a revolution for specialists: a
brief, faceless tumult in the streets, followed by the opu-
lencies of the Second Empire. Yet more than 1917 and
—at least for the arts—perhaps even more than 1789, the
year 1848 extinguishes one era in Europe and initiates
another. And correspondingly for Ibsen, the impact of that
general crisis was decisive for the whole of his later development; Brian Downs has observed that its events
marked him so deeply that those who regard him above
all as "the apologist of revolt might attribute the most
vital part of his genius to the germ that was here im-
planted."

In 1848 Ibsen was a half-starved, overworked pharma-
cist's assistant, aspiring determinedly toward a university
education. Physically tough and tireless, immensely hard-
working, irrepressibly and irreverently humorous, he was
well equipped and accustomed through his caricature
drawings, his satiric verses and sharp-tongued conversation
to ridicule the better class of citizens, the merchant oligarchy that ran the little shipping port of Grimstad, so similar

to those first families of his birthplace, Skien, who had excluded him coldly and completely after his father's bankruptcy twelve years before. Now this same favored class suddenly felt themselves in peril of their own fortunes and lives as the status quo disintegrated everywhere on the Continent.

For more than thirty years, since the end of the Napoleonic Wars, the social order of Europe had been held together by the so-called Metternich System, identified with the influential Austrian foreign minister whose name was synonymous with reaction. That system was an effective antidote to the pervasive fears of "the Revolution" that continued to haunt the titled and propertied after Waterloo; it consisted of a practice of armed intervention abroad by the major powers wherever insurrection threatened, reinforced by intensive police surveillance and repression of free speech, press, and assembly at home. The Austrian policy of *Regiere und verändere nichts* ("Govern and change nothing"), widely imitated or paralleled elsewhere, provided a favorable laissez-faire environment for the steady accumulation of capital, the extension of the factory system, and the rise of bourgeois affluence into, finally, the classic unstable antithesis of the exploiters and the exploited soon to be analyzed with such consequence by Karl Marx.

If wealth was increasingly concentrating in the hands of the few, the instance of Ibsen in the Grimstad apothecary shop could be multiplied into the hundreds of thousands: dissident students, penniless apprentices, craft workers displaced by new machines, peasant farmers appealing crop failures to indifferent bureaucracies, artists and intellectuals of the urban, educated class whose resentment of the absolutist state was matched by a burning idealism for causes—a united Germany, an Italy purged of foreign oppressors, a France where more than one adult male in thirty might vote, an Austria free of omnipresent spies and censors. The first breach in the system occurred, however, not in that citadel of arch-conservatism, Vienna, but, repeating history, in Paris. The issue was trivial: a banquet planned by the opposition was canceled by Louis-Philippe's minister, Guizot. Once again barricades materialized in the streets, mobs formed, demonstrators marched; and in the space of three late February days the king had abdicated and fled to England, and a republic led by a bourgeois-socialist coalition was declared.

The startling success of the Paris uprising sent a shock wave of revolt through Europe. Within weeks the university students of Vienna rioted, insurgents demanded political and economic reforms, and Metternich was forced into exile. The Hungarians claimed autonomy within the Austrian Empire; the young Czechs followed suit and seized Prague. Revolutionists took to the streets in Berlin, exacting a constitution from the King of Prussia; the lesser German principalities capitulated in turn, while the duchies of Schleswig and Holstein, attached to the Danish crown, broke away and sought to join the German Confederation. All Italy seethed with nationalistic fervor; Lombardy and Venice rose against their Austrian overlords, as supporting armies swarmed northward from Tuscany, Naples, and the Papal States. In country after country constitutions were wrested from stunned monarchs, committees met to draft governmental revisions, new nations were proclaimed, serfdom was abolished, habitual police controls dissolved in a clamor for civil liberties, public jury trials, and vastly extended voting rights. For one intoxicating and unforgettable moment, liberalism seemed everywhere triumphant.

But only for a moment. The urban radicals had misjudged the sentiments of the more populous and conservative provinces. The middle-class and lower-class revolutionists grew increasingly suspicious of each others' aims. Nationalism, which originally had provided a powerful impetus to rebellion, deteriorated into skirmishes among rival ethnic groups for domination. Capitalizing on these divisive factors, the Austrian general Windischgrätz besieged Prague, subjugated the city, and dispersed the dissension-wracked Slav congress in session there. With exemplary timing, Radetsky, leader of the Austrian troops in Italy, let discords ripen among the republican forces, then shattered them at Custozza. These threats to the Empire dispelled, the Hapsburg monarchy ruthlessly suppressed the Hungarians. Meanwhile, the constitutional convention at Frankfurt found itself powerless to impose its ideal of democratic union on the jealous German states. Nowhere were the early hopes of the revolution more grimly betrayed than where they were born, in Paris. A Constituent Assembly, elected by all France, unseated the

socialist members of the ruling coalition. The Paris workers, foreseeing a return to their normal exclusion from
power, occupied the Assembly, proclaiming a new pro-
visional government and a social as well as a political revolution. When the National Guard restored the original
members, the middle-class and lower-class revolutionaries
were split into hostile camps; and after disorders erupted
throughout Paris, what rapidly became class war was sav-
agely resolved by General Cavaignac and the regular army
in the infamous "Bloody June Days," in which tens of
thousands of workers and unemployed were killed or im-
prisoned for deportation, and a chain of circumstances
was prepared leading directly to the accession and virtual
dictatorship of Emperor Napoleon III.

No abbreviated montage of the events of 1848 can do
justice to their turbulent amplitude, their pace and con-
tagion, and the intensity of feeling they stirred in all who
lived deeply through them, either by immediate participa-
tion or, like Ibsen, the inveterate reader of newspapers,
through columns of print and a vivid imagination. Something of the transforming impact of the experience is
caught in the words of the young expatriate Russian
liberal, Alexander Hertzen, who witnessed the "June
Days" in Paris:

> It is enough to kill you or drive you mad to have to sit in
> a room with arms folded, without being able to go outside,
> and yet to hear everywhere, near and far, gunshots, cannon-
> ades, cries, the roll of drums, and to know that somewhere
> nearby blood is being shed, the people are being knifed,
> bayoneted—dying. I did not die, but I have aged. . . . No
> living man can remain the same after such a blow. . . . I
> shall make my way, a spiritual beggar, through the world,
> my childish hopes and adolescent aspirations uprooted. Let
> them all appear before the court of incorruptible reason.*

In remote Norway, Ibsen likewise resembled a man
sitting with arms folded in an outwardly peaceful room,
hearing the cries of the dying from all over Europe. He
responded first in poetry: a sonnet sequence addressed to
the king of the dual monarchy of Sweden and Norway,
imploring his intervention to aid the Danes in Schleswig,
along with verses exhorting the Hungarians to stand
against tyranny. Later came a more important and endur-

---

* *Realism, Naturalism and Symbolism*, ed. by Roland N. Strom-
berg (New York: Harper Torchbooks, 1968), pp. 2 ff.

ing response, the writing of his first play, which Ibsen re-
called in calmer perspective years after, in a preface to
its second edition:

> *Catiline,* the play with which I began my literary career, was
> written in the winter of 1848-49, that is, during my twenty-
> first year. . . . Those were immensely stirring times. The
> February Revolution, the rebellions in Hungary and else-
> where, the Prusso-Danish War over Schleswig—all these
> meshed powerfully and formatively with my own develop-
> ment, as unfinished as that remained for a long time there-
> after.

The last phrase carries particular weight, with its impli-
cation that years, even decades, passed before Ibsen had
assimilated all the lessons of 1848 into his work. Indeed, it
was the long-range response to those lessons generally, as
interpreted in innumerable lives, that permanently altered
the course of the nineteenth century. For all their confusion, the events of the several revolutions can be distinguished into two main aspects, each of which had a
penetrating effect: an initial expansive phase, in which
habitual or imposed restraints gave way in a common
fervor of possibility, and long deferred dreams of freedom
seemed at last capable of realization; followed by a constrictive phase, a time of crushed hopes and restored
controls, when society's complex resistance to change had
to be painfully re-approached and examined. If the keynote of the first phase was liberation, that of the second
was realism. Among the intelligentsia, who played so
prominent a role in 1848, some responded primarily to the
former and intensified their efforts to bring down a system
that had demonstrated itself so close to collapse: Marx,
for example. The majority of the revolutionists, however,
being more romantic and less committed, succumbed to
disillusionment, abandoning political action altogether for
business, for finance, for scholarship, science, or the arts.
One can, in fact, trace from this point on the revolutionary spirit deflected from politics to aesthetics in the unprecedented phenomenon of the avant-garde that emerges
to provide wave upon wave of radical artistic innovation.
The first of these waves, reflecting the prevalent devalua-
tion of all forms of idealism, was shortly announced, again
aptly in Paris, by Courbet's *Pavillon du Réalisme* at the
Exposition of 1855, and in literature the next year by
Edmond Duranty's polemical review, *Réalisme.*

If, as Downs suggests, the most vital part of Ibsen's genius germinated in the climate of 1848, then its long cultivation through a half century of plays must be seen as rooted in, not one, but both of these divergent responses. It encompassed, on one hand, an apocalyptic sense that a new era in world history was nearing birth, a Third Empire, as Ibsen came to call it, which would arise out of the present time of disintegration, and toward which the liberation of each individual self would contribute; and, on the other hand, a gradually evolved realism of style and outlook that would uncompromisingly examine the failures of individuals, and of society at large, to live up to their human potentialities. The theme of liberation and the techniques of realism acquired, in their wavering growth through the successive early works, a substrate of enriching and modifying ideas, to flower at last as "the spirit of freedom and the spirit of truth," the fundamental guiding principles affirmed by Lona Hessel in the closing lines of *Pillars of Society*. These principles are of the essence of Ibsen's mature art and, as well, of his changed perspective on revolution, which had brought him to regard as special, limited, and inadequate all that he had welcomed with unqualified enthusiasm in 1848. The latter is nowhere so plainly and surely and exuberantly expressed as in *An Enemy of the People*, wherein the solid majority confronts the spirit of truth and freedom in the embattled figure of Dr. Thomas Stockmann.

Perhaps the most productive approach to the structure and significance of this play would be to begin with that often remarked buoyancy that pervades it throughout, in such contrast to the popular image of its author as the darkly brooding Sphinx of the North. Its tone has been explained in some quarters as stemming simply from Ibsen's love of a good fight, an argument diminished somewhat by the record of his letters reacting to the earlier hostile criticisms of *Peer Gynt*, which project not élan but rather a bewildered, impotent rage at those who cannot or will not recognize artistic quality. Eric Bentley suggests another explanation when he scores the play as "inferior Ibsen" by reason of its didacticism; we are here, he writes, not the playwright's companions on a search into the unknown, but instead a lecture audience being indoctrinated in what has already been thought. From this standpoint one is free to see Ibsen, relaxed from his customary rigor of exploration, enjoying a brief, genial holiday of admonishment, resulting in the prevailing atmosphere, not of martyrdom, but of celebration. Though the play is perhaps less didactic and more ironic than it first appears, Mr. Bentley's stricture points directly to the underlying cause of the play's distinctive exuberance, namely, that the synthesis of elements toward which Ibsen had long been moving seems here to have been triumphantly confirmed to his own satisfaction as a fulfilling medium of personal expression and as an accurate mirror to the age. The ingredients of that synthesis had provisionally cohered in *A Doll House* three years before, they had been pressed and tested to an extreme through the harrowing of Mrs. Alving to the edge of sanity in *Ghosts,* and now, fused, supple, and obedient, they lay ready and waiting for anything further Ibsen might wish to say, a source of confidence that could not fail to make *An Enemy of the People,* for all its serious content, in several senses a *jeu d'esprit.*

The more accessible if less vital of the ingredients is that matured repertory of realistic techniques that had found prototypal form in *The League of Youth* and lasting commitment with *Pillars of Society,* to become the moving authenticity of art in *A Doll House.* The gist of Ibsen's realistic style could be termed the method of reductive analysis. The playwright creates a setting which is partially localized ("a coastal town in southern Norway") and, in most cases, seemingly constrictive; and then, within this area of controlled inquiry, he sets in motion minutely individualized characters in a limited action that by no stretch of Brechtean imagination could be considered epic. The sense of larger dimensions that all great drama must evoke is achieved, nevertheless, through the fact that setting, character, and action are shaped to correspond at significant points with the deepest tendencies and conflicts of the age, against a background of the entire history of Western civilization. In *Enemy,* this pattern of equivalents receives a glancing reference in Act I, when Dr. Stockmann parallels the ferment of activity in the provincial seaport setting with a bustling metropolis in the great world, adding, as if to stress the analogy: "Oh, I'm well aware this is small scale compared with a lot of other places." Thus the mayor's assertion, moments later, that the individual must learn to subordinate himself to the whole, and the doctor's response throughout the play, countering that thesis to the utmost, together mirror a conflict polarizing that century of ascendant nationalism, one which culminates in the totalitarian coercions of the present age. (Brian Johnston has noted several respects in which Stockmann resembles a diminished contemporary version of Socrates, the unwelcome gadfly of his community. One might additionally observe that Ibsen's means of examining the failure of human possibility, his method of reductive analysis, is appropriately the reverse of the one identified with Socrates in *The Republic:* instead of discovering the fundamental moral traits of the individual writ large in the ideal state, Ibsen discovers the fundamental moral deficiencies of his civilization writ small in the unidealized individuals of his symptomatic community.)

The second, weightier ingredient, one of substance more than style, comes in focus with the recognition that *An Enemy of the People* conducts an inquiry, through Ibsen's reductive method, into the emerging conflict between two kinds of revolution—what might be called the traditional or conventional conception, and the new or modern conception. Traditional revolution has been the prevailing form on countless occasions throughout the past, from the insurrections of 1848 back to earliest classic antiquity. The scenario for this conception pits a champion of the oppressed masses, or a party of the people, against the repressive force of irrational authority vested in an individual tyrant or a small, self-perpetuating power elite. The traditional conception, holding the deprived majority to be right and the ruling minority to be wrong, adopts for its remedy the drastic expedient whereby Fortune's wheel, given a half turn, paradoxically yields a full revolution: the outs are swept in, the ups are brought down—but beyond a redistribution of material goods, nothing further is won. The new establishment, in fact, immediately generates a new underground, plotting *its* program for the next half turn of the wheel. Insecure in this knowledge, and aware of the self-interest behind his own rhetoric, the traditional revolutionist may betray a secret fear and guilt, which must be stifled under ever more vehement assertions of preemptive right, in terms of the rationalizations of his ideology. Conventional revolution, the outgrowth of an autocratic system, is at one with a world-view that conceives history as repetitive or cyclical, a concept typical of classic antiquity, the Middle Ages, and the Renaissance. Ibsen had portrayed a romanticized version of just such a traditional champion of the people in the classic Roman setting of his first play, derived from the Latin historian Sallust's *Conspiracy of Catiline*. There, in that source, were the impassioned speeches that any rebel of 1848 would have felt to be the echo of his own experience, as when Catiline berates a Rome fallen "under the jurisdiction and control of a powerful oligarchy" wherein "the rest of us, however energetic and virtuous we may be" are nothing but "a crowd of nobodies without influence or authority, subservient to men who in a soundly governed state would stand in awe of us."* Now, after more than three decades of reconsidering the nature of revolt in the perspectives of realism, Ibsen, in returning to the theme, assigned the traditional revolutionary role to the two journalists of the play, Hovstad and Billing.

The first impressions they give in Act I are deceiving, since they come filtered through the warm conviviality that radiates from the doctor's personality to dominate the scene. Only later, in Act III, is it revealed that they share the doctor's table, not for his company, but for Petra's, and less for her sake than for the sizable inheritance they calculate will be settled on her by Morten Kiil. Thus when Hovstad presents Stockmann with his plans to overthrow the incompetent leadership of the town, we still (Act II) have no grounds for doubting his utter sincerity. The clique of the rich and established who have built the prosperity of the community have done so, he states, at the cost of one disastrous and inexcusable mistake, the pollution which the doctor has discovered; they must accordingly be stripped of their power, not only for reason of that blunder, but also to demonstrate an ideological point that will advance the liberation of the oppressed masses, namely, by demolishing the myth of the infallibility of the ruling class. Yet even as Stockmann is nodding in agreement, unexpectedly the guilt hidden in the traditional revolutionist breaks through the vehemence of Hovstad's argument. "You mustn't think badly of me," he abruptly interjects. "I'm no more self-seeking or power-

* Sallust, *Conspiracy of Catiline*, tr. by S. A. Handford (Baltimore, Md.: Penguin Books, 1963), p. 189.

hungry than most people." "But—whoever said you were?" replies the bewildered doctor. In this momentary disclosure, the end is foreshadowed: Hovstad's program for liberation will fail, not because he lacks a cause and an issue (the generation of 1848 had both), but because his commitment is compromised from the start, and, more-over, because, as Ibsen will shortly suggest, the conven-tional conception of revolution is no longer adequate to the changing reality of the times. By Act IV Hovstad has conformed his possibilities to his situation sufficiently to become the willing apologist of his publisher, Aslaksen, who in turn is the chosen spokesman for that well-greased axle of the wheels that run the town, Mayor Peter Stock-mann. Thus, by several telescoped stages, Hovstad tra-verses a summation of what Ibsen must have witnessed of the radical's progress as a journey of accommodation, one terminated already by Billing, who cynically bids for a job on the municipal payroll of the government he pro-poses to overthrow. As the two factions of the majority learn their common interests and solidify in the turbulent public meeting, the process of reductive analysis reveals its larger conclusion: the traditional revolutionist proves in-distinguishable from the established order he ostensibly at-tacks—if he fails, he joins it; if he succeeds, he supplants it and, after some ideological redecoration of the premises, finds himself in time practicing the same uses and abuses of power he had once protested.

Both the leaders of the community and its conventional rebels are self-proclaimed friends of the people; the bearer of the new conception of revolution is, of course, the man they jointly brand as an enemy of the people, Dr. Stock-mann. If one asks what the difference is, at the core, between the old and new conceptions, the answer given by the play and supported elsewhere in Ibsen's writings would be, succinctly, if not simply: ideas. The traditional ins and outs, molding their lives to the expediencies of power, are essentially identical in character, whereas Stockmann is an outsider of another kind altogether, being obstinately com-mitted to a new, unpopular truth that the majority will have to learn to live with.

But how novel, after all, is this notion of ideas as the critical element? Surely as far back as Plato, they have been granted that distinction. Ideas in the Platonic tradi-tion are fixed and timeless, however, whereas those described in this play are conspicuously mortal: gestating, growing into full potency, becoming senile, dying, having meanwhile bred their successors. Dr. Stockmann sets their life-spans, with a dramatically arbitrary brevity that need not be taken too literally, as "some seventeen, eighteen, at the most twenty years." A Platonic idea might abstractly fix the eternal archetype of truth or honor; by contrast, an Ibsenist idea might find it tantamount to criminal negligence, under such and such circumstances (*Ghosts*), to teach a child to honor his father and mother and not to tell the truth about them, and find equal criminal negligence, under other circumstances (*The Wild Duck*), in telling the truth about a child's mother and father and not sustaining an illusion, a "life-lie" about them. The Ibsenist idea is more concrete, more dialectical and, being adapted to instances, is infinite in its versions and shadings. It may even give the appearance of pure relativism, but always is saved from that extreme by the elusive, indispensable spirit that shapes and guides it. That inward, restlessly inventive spirit of truth and freedom thus becomes the prime agent of revolt against the tyranny of fixed abstractions on one hand, and of constricting naturalistic circumstance on the other. It proves to be the crucial ingredient both of the entire final twelve-play cycle, and of the new conception of revolution, liberating and transforming the human mind, which is passionately advocated by Dr. Stockmann.

The obvious source for spirit regarded as the principal means of liberation is the Bible. The influence of Ibsen's early absorption in scripture, especially in childhood and during the hard years that culminated in *Brand*, persists throughout the final cycle from *Pillars of Society* to *When We Dead Awaken,* reinforcing Shaw's insight that "there is not one of Ibsen's characters who is not, in the old phrase, the temple of the Holy Ghost, and who does not move you at moments by the sense of that mystery." To consider the spirit of freedom and the spirit of truth, however, as simply a paraphrased reversion to the words of Christ to the woman at the well, that "God is a Spirit: and they that worship him must worship him in spirit and in truth," would be to ignore the clear insistence in *An Enemy of the People* that the truth must be perpetually restated and made new. It would vitiate what, again, Shaw aptly observes about the prophetic content of these plays:

"He that does not believe that revelation is continuous does not believe in revelation at all." The record is gapingly incomplete without mention of two latter-day interpreters of spirit reigning in Ibsen's immediate background, namely, Hegel and Kierkegaard.

The cultural climate of the northern countries was suffused with Hegelian idealism during Ibsen's formative years, as specimens of his earliest theater criticism attest. More recently, in *Emperor and Galilean*, he had prefaced the realistic cycle with a vast and searching study of the nature of historical forces, conceived along Hegelian lines. And, as the epigraph to this Foreword suggests, he could hardly have been inattentive later that same year when, in the opening lecture of the series on *Main Currents in Nineteenth Century Literature*, which Ibsen declared to have changed the course of his writing, Georg Brandes quoted Hegel with approval to the effect that:

> As long as the sun stood in the firmament, and as long as the planets revolved around it, no one noticed that man [in the French Revolution] was standing on the principle of pure thought—one might say, standing on his head—and was trying to reshape and rebuild the universe according to his own point of view. All the earlier revolutions had had limited aims; this was the first that wished to re-create mankind.*

Hegel's eminently dramatic view of history is one whereby Pure Thought (or Mind, or Spirit), the animating principle of all reality, evolves through a sequence of clashes spearheaded by "world-historical" heroes, from a rudimentary, common-sense, unenlightened world-view into ever higher and more expansive stages of consciousness. (It should be stressed here that the Norwegian word *ånd*, like *Geist* in German, merges in one term what English keeps separate and distinct: "spirit," and "mind" or "intellect.") Disengaged from its exceedingly difficult philosophical language, the Hegelian vision of history would see man as spirit steadily graduating (with intermittent dialectical reversals) from a fixed bondage to nature, and a mode of awareness wherein, among other things, revolutionary struggle has been directed toward securing material goods and power, into higher and freer planes

---

* Georg Brandes, "Inaugural Lecture, 1871," *The Theory of the Modern Stage*, ed. by Eric Bentley (Baltimore: Penguin Books, 1968), p. 385.

where man will increasingly live in an environment of his own ideas, not merely through leisured meditation, but more tangibly through those ideas as concretized in revolutionary technology, in artifacts of the human mind that generate new, more liberated patterns of living. The unprecedented decisions called for in the modern phase of world history require the expertise of those who have attained the most inclusive stage of consciousness, hence the doctor's angry assertion that the intelligent and informed minority alone can be trusted to rule. (The specific new idea integral to *Enemy* is, incidentally, often missed, this being Pasteur's demonstration two decades earlier, in 1862, of the relationship of bacteria, contamination, and disease. Old Morten Kiil's function in the action is, in part, to dramatize comically the incapacity, in the given circumstances, of a mind whose mold has set well before this new item of consciousness materialized.)

Although Ibsen had joined in the study and discussion of a number of Kierkegaard's works as early as his late teens in Grimstad, the Danish existentialist's thought did not figure importantly in his drama until *Love's Comedy* some fifteen years after. From that point on, however, the Kierkegaardian outlook was never wholly absent from his writings. Shortly before the composition of *Enemy,* that outlook was strengthened by the publication of two volumes of Gottshed's edition of Kierkegaard's *Posthumous Papers,* 1848-50 and 1851-55; as Harald Beyer observes, Ibsen seems quite likely to have examined these, so numerous are the parallels that abound. The *Posthumous Papers* cover the period of Kierkegaard's fiercest battles with the newspaper, the *Corsair,* and with the Established Danish Lutheran Church; *Enemy* appropriately depicts one Stockmann brother, Thomas, the Doubter, driven into battle against the other, Peter, the rock that upholds orthodoxy, in alliance with the *People's Courier.* The doctor asserts that "the minority is always right," that truths sicken and decay when their minority becomes a majority; Kierkegaard states that "the truth is in the minority" and that when the truth becomes recognized by the majority, it nonetheless is "nonsensical to have numbers and the crowd on your side, since the truth is in a new minority once again." The evidence of these and other parallels in no way detracts from Ibsen's achievement; it merely indicates that certain tenets of Kierkegaardian (and Hegelian)

thought function as vitally in his dramatic universe as do
the medieval ideas of order drawn from the church homi-
lies in Shakespeare's.

"One single individual is the highest power," in Kierkegaard's words: or, as Dr. Stockmann has it, "the strongest man in the world is the one who stands most alone"—
on these two interchangeable paradoxes the central structure of *Enemy* is built. Under the democratic, rather than
autocratic, system that increasingly prevails in the nineteenth century, it is now, for Stockmann, the majority that
tends to be wrong, and the minority right—since only a
tiny knowledgeable minority, "holding their positions like
outposts," can comprehend in perspective the accelerating
changes of a historical process that shows itself to be more
and more evolutionary, or at least genuinely innovative,
rather than cyclical and repetitive. The true guardian of
society is thus no longer the good prince, like Edgar or
Fortinbras, restoring a static but healing order to the sick
kingdom, but in Hegel's terms a world-historical hero with
the spirit of the changing age at his fingertips. This new
hero must, however, not only contain, but also surmount
the time-spirit; otherwise, he risks becoming a mere fol-
lower of fashions—like Peer Gynt in North Africa, always scrambling to be with the moment. He must rather
be one who, in Stockmann's words, has mastered all the
new truths that have been germinating. That effort neces-
sitates his remaining clear-sightedly independent—a matter
of becoming the Individual, for Kierkegaard a category
the same as existing as man, rather than only the dormant,
dreaming possibility of man. For "man is spirit," he states.
"But what is spirit? Spirit is the self. But what is the self?
The self is a relation which relates itself to itself"—that is,
through an act of existential choice, a decision so basic
that the whole of one's being is staked and defined in the
outcome.

In *Enemy*, Dr. Stockmann is depicted in the throes of
just such a decision. Without entering too extensively into
the rich design of the play, one can see first that the action
carries the protagonist through that same emotional curve
identified with the events of 1848: expansive optimism,
prompting dreams of liberation, followed by disillusion
and a sharper realism about society. More significant than
the emotional response, though, is the protagonist's education in the claims of spirit. In Act I Dr. Stockmann is

shown pleasurably immersed in a benign materialism—
eating, drinking, smoking his pipe, admiring new pieces of
furniture for which he has overspent his income. By Act
V all these creature comforts have yielded their attractions to the empty rooms of a borrowed house where the
doctor plans to teach—without pay, after the Socratic
model- a dozen young disciples, drawn from the deprived
poor, to become free-spirited individuals like himself. Reductively detailed between these two points is all the
turmoil of a failed revolution, not of the conventional
kind, but one turning upon an idea that becomes, in its
expansive phase, Dr. Stockmann's "great discovery,"
namely that the polluted water system of the town is directly analogous to that other, larger system that is not
about to be changed by those who control it, even though
it circulates the waters of the spirit dangerously contaminated by vested interests, by willful egotism, by indiffer-
ence to the quality of life, and all the other common
betrayals and compromises of the truth. More auspicious-
ly, his great discovery proves simultaneously to be a self-
discovery. Although he forefeits his warmly sustaining
sense of community to become a solitary, persecuted individual (Kierkegaard), who nonetheless is fighting in the
vanguard of the world's evolving consciousness (Hegel),
Dr. Stockmann discovers at the end that, inwardly, he has
not lost in losing. By briefly associating Stockmann with
the figure of Christ at the conclusions of Acts IV and V,
Ibsen intimates that the "enemy of the people" may in fact
be the redeemer of society. For the traditional revolutionist with his limited goal must fail, even if he succeeds;
whereas the new revolutionist, even if he fails, can succeed,
by releasing the new idea to a larger, future destiny. At
the heart of the buoyancy of the play is the Christian
paradox: the knowledge that the redemptive hero dies to
the world and yet brings, through dying, life, and through
defeat, victory.

An Enemy of the People warrants a disproportionate
share of attention here by virtue of its presentation, in a
positive and conveniently accessible form, of that quint-
essential spirit of freedom and truth more frequently
conspicuous by its absence in Ibsen's realistic drama. It is,
for example, exactly what Mrs. Alving has betrayed some
twenty years before her play begins; that remote fall away

from her true spiritual being is the actual point of origin for the catastrophe of *Ghosts*. Mrs. Alving's tragic flaw, which no circumstance can extenuate, was one of failing to live the truth at a critical moment—specifically the "new truth" adumbrated more fully in *Enemy*, one which will reject both "abstract demands claiming absolute validity and all codes and social norms making similar claims for conformity." F. W. Kaufmann, who draws these distinctions, goes on to define this new truth admirably as

> more than a mere logical agreement of thought and fact; it is rooted much deeper, since it originates in the interpenetration of life and thought and involves the total personality. Consciousness of truth in this organic sense can be derived neither from reason nor from emotional reaction alone. It has its source in the undefinable depth of the personality, and only when this is realized may it be elucidated by reason; that which is emotionally perceived becomes true only when it has been so elucidated and manifests itself in meaningful action. Ultimately, such organic truth is to be found in the appropriate response to a given situation, based on an intelligent and sympathetic examination of all factors involved and carried out with the will to assume fullest responsibility for the decision.*

In the dramatic world of *Ghosts* the equivocal purveyor both of abstract demands categorically imposed and of codes and norms surrendering to conformity is Pastor Manders. The situation calling for appropriate response occurred two decades previous: the marriage with young Lieutenant Alving. The intelligent and sympathetic examination of all the factors involved thus takes place after long delay and constitutes the retrospective action of the drama, the recovery of the lost reality of the past. And the burden of the play's lament, cumulatively achieved through the brooding scenic images, the subtly nuanced language, the slow sacrifice of its ritual victim, Osvald, is: "What worth have truth and freedom, realized twenty years too late?"

Francis Fergusson, in his justly famed interpretation of *Ghosts*, has defined its binding action, through a Stanislavskian infinitive phrase, as "to control the Alving heri-

---

* F. W. Kaufmann, "Ibsen's Conception of Truth," *Ibsen: A Collection of Critical Essays*, ed. by Rolf Fjelde (Englewood Cliffs, N. J.: Prentice-Hall, 1965), p. 19.

tage for my own life." But this formulation, as he observes, confines the action chiefly to the plane of maneuver for material or social advantage, a motive shared by only three of the five characters. Helene Alving, however, is seeking a nobler objective, namely, a true and free human life, an ideal for which her artist son, Osvald, stands as the incarnation. Thus her action, on a higher plane, could be rephrased as "to regain my son" and all he ideally is, as a symbol of the fulfillment of her quest. This motivation has as well a negative corollary: "to repudiate Captain Alving" and all *he* really was, under that cloak of respectability she wove to conceal him, blessed and abetted by Pastor Manders. Toward this end the orphanage has been built, to absorb every last trace of the Alving inheritance. The ceremony of dedication is now at hand; the maltreated wife, the solicitous mother hopes then to be as free as the son. Except that Osvald, in the grippingly theatrical conclusion of Act I, proves to be inhabited by a ghost. Mrs. Alving is thrust into a paralyzing impasse, able neither to regain nor repudiate, having discovered to her horror the hated father subsisting in the loved son.

Nothing has prepared her for this revelation. Before and during her marriage, she had been conventionally devout, oriented toward duty, easily subject to direction by her relatives and pastor. In the ten years since her husband's death, she has arduously made herself over into a model of enlightenment, a liberal, a rationalist, a freethinker—without, however, confronting the ultimate truth that arises out of the indefinable depth of the personality, determining the profound ambiguities in all human relationships, including her own complicity in the wasted possibilities of Captain Alving. "I can't stand it!" she cries out at one point, in belated recognition of default. "I've got to work my way out to freedom." The great, the moving spiritual action of the drama then commences, when "to regain my son" gradually becomes "to regain my husband, young Lieutenant Alving," and all he *really* was. Inga-Stina Ewbank has shown how delicately Mrs. Alving's deepening perception of the truth is conveyed, even to the thematic repetition of the tiny modal verb "had to." In Act I it expresses a litany of self-centered complaint: *because* Alving was thus-and-so, "I *had to* become his drinking companion . . . I *had to* sit alone with him . . . I *had to* pull the whole load . . ." The rankling resentment

in the phrase, the certitude of its premise are both reflexes
of the diminished consciousness instilled by Manders' rigidly codified view of morality. By Act III the subject has
shifted from "I" to "he." The underlying content of the
litany has altered to a recognition that "this child [Alving]
. . . *had to* make his life here . . . he *had to* get along
with no real goal in life," and so on. The little phrase is
now resonant with Mrs. Alving's new, intensely felt awareness of human limitation and suffering, of the pathos of
irreplaceable gifts stifled by enveloping mediocrity and by
misunderstanding, not the least of which has been her
own.

On the reduced stage of Ibsen's realism, Mrs. Alving's
spiritual struggle, her anguished expansion of consciousness into the truth of an antithetical human being's existence gives the play a heroically sustained impetus toward
self-liberation that moves counter to Osvald's gathering
despair and disintegration. But as with *Enemy*, that move-
ment implies larger parallels as well. The ghosts of the
title are also "all kinds of old dead doctrines and opinions
and beliefs." From the initial opposition of the wife's
righteous moralism vs. the husband's joy of life, the play
comes to resemble, as Brian Johnston has brilliantly indicated, an immense séance that raises the essential spirits
of the main "intellectual currents" (*åndelig strømninger*)
that have formed Western civilization. From the Judeo-
Christian tradition, the action is haunted by specters of the
temptation and fall of man, the trinity, the *pietà* (shock-
ingly reenacted at the end), and the millennium of Ibsen's
Second Empire dominated by Pauline religious orthodoxy;
and, from the eclipsed Hellenic tradition, by reminiscences
of a lost paganism, the search for which proved such a
vital element in the historical Enlightenment, as both
reductively paralleled and awesomely reproved for lack of
sufficient depth in the tragic quest for self-recovery by the
woman significantly named Helene. With so large a field
of world-historical forces at work, it might be well as a
final note to reaffirm, echoing Peter Brook, that for all its
seriousness, the play is still play; that it already prefigures,
particularly in the Manders-Engstrand exchanges, the sly
and buoyant humor that will burst forth shortly in *Enemy;*
and that any stage production is remiss if it neglects a
comic lightness of touch that, in its intermittent way, is as

amusing as anything in James Joyce's delightfully racy verse "Epilogue to Ibsen's *Ghosts*."

If *Ghosts* is intensive, *The Lady from the Sea* is expansive. In the former the single enclosed set confines the accumulating pressures to the point of claustrophobia; in the latter all the characters move about in the open, through a softer, more luminous air. Four of the five acts take place out-of-doors, and the exception stipulates a garden room interpenetrated by the green world of nature. Moreover, with its part-singing and its band concerts, the play is more musical than any other of the cycle, in a manner anticipatory of Chekhov; it is the only Ibsen work that might be called Chekhovian. The constantly shifting scene is, furthermore, enlivened by a crisp medley of colors, in the long summer dresses of the women, the foliage and flowers, the blossoming rose tree, the distant snowcapped mountains, and the changing sky. The director Lugné-Poë displayed a stroke of genius in retaining the impressionist Vuillard as scenic artist for his series of Ibsen productions at the Théâtre de l'Oeuvre; that painter's subdued, mellow palette accords perfectly with the usual sober hues of Ibsen's interiors. For the tonality of this work, however, only Monet or Renoir figures in a landscape could suffice. It undoubtedly is the most ingratiating of all the later plays.

Still, there are furies beneath this charm of surface—two, at least, in Ellida Wangel and the Stranger. Ibsen unaccountably gives the latter faintly ludicrous red hair and beard, with a Scotch tam, in his stage directions; subsequently, however, he described as unsurpassable the characterization by a German actor whose features caught the demonic element in the role: "a long, thin figure with a hawk face, piercing black eyes, and a wonderfully deep and soft voice." The Stranger's name is Johnston, or perhaps Freeman, or perhaps something else altogether— an indication that, like the unindividuated creatures of the ocean depths, his identity subsists somewhere beneath the civilized convention of names. Far more than his forerunner, the young Captain Horster in *Enemy,* he lives detached from the concerns and responsibilities of the land; and his atavistic sea-freedom holds a hypnotic fascination for one of the land's least acclimated inhabitants, the lighthouse keeper's daughter, Ellida. "Haven't you ever noticed," remarks her husband, "that the people who live

out close by the sea are almost like a race to themselves?
It's as though they lived the sea's own life."

For, like the fjord visible in the background, the lure of
the sea reaches deep into the land, exactly as the headlands fling themselves out toward the open ocean; and
where sea and land meet, the freer element works like a
solvent on the more fixed, not merely in the centrally
portrayed longing of Ellida and the Stranger for each
other, but subtly and variously throughout the play at
large. *The Lady from the Sea,* though set in clear summer
light on the stable shore, is infiltrated by the watery
influence of Aquarius: by a yearning for primal oneness, a
loosening of conventional bonds, a dissolution of forms.
Among the land people, this dissolution shows itself chiefly
through a condition that Ibsen calls, in a virtually untrans-
latable Norwegian word, *halvhed*: a kind of inconclu-
siveness that stems from living by half measures. Consider
Ballested, the keynote figure for the drama, as unfocused
in vocation as Ellida is in her personality. At curtain rise,
two of his many scattered occupations are displayed; within moments he has abandoned the role of handyman for
painter, his subject being a mermaid who is neither (and
both) of sea and land, half dead, half alive, artistically
conceived and yet unrealized. The vacillating indetermina-
cy of this opening image introduces a wavering, fluid
world where Dr. Wangel alternates between two zones of
affection, moving back and forth from his daughters on
the veranda to Ellida in the summerhouse; where Lyngstrand and Bolette can discuss whether a husband's being
can flow into and be absorbed by his wife's; where the
eyes of a child can change color with the weather; where
even the boatloads of tourists, coming and going like
birds of passage at the very fringe of the action, express
a continual flux, a restless suspension of commitment.

Above all, Ellida, drawn by the tidal pull of the
Stranger, fluctuates in her divided mind. That part of her
in revolt against the half-life of her marriage presses the
revolutionary impulse to its ultimate conclusion: the demand for absolute, unconditional freedom. And there the
Stranger's claim asserts its compelling validity, for her
earlier "marriage" to him was consecrated by the sea,
symbol of the boundless totality of nature that tallies with
and speaks to the indefinable, unfulfilled depths of her
total personality, in contrast to the limited contractual

bond with her legal husband. Through the contention of these rival claims, Ibsen examines the attraction and the terror of pure freedom, divested from any goal and exalted to the verge of idolatry. And through Dr. Wangel's response to the challenge of the Stranger—the Kierkegaardian hazard of extending an absolutely unqualified free choice—he resolves the drama, not by any relapse into mere conventional wisdom, but by involving a law of the spirit fully as powerful as the personality's urge toward liberation beyond all check or limit.

The Lady from the Sea takes place in the full of summer; *John Gabriel Borkman* at the dead of winter, when the forces of life are withdrawn and frozen, and the bitter season outside accords with all the bitterness stored within. No one would accuse *Borkman* of being an ingratiating play; yet Henry James wrote of its "hard, frugal charm," and it undeniably has a palpable atmosphere and a poetry distinctively its own. In basic structure the play is as starkly simple and as austerely formal as a French neoclassic tragedy. No other work of the final cycle is as tightly unified in time. From beginning to end, act merges into act without the slightest interruption of continuity. Spatially like *The Master Builder*, but to somewhat different effect, the major part of the drama is unfolded in two interiors of the same house, to move then out-of-doors with the concluding act. The action of *Borkman* gains its simple unitary strength from the seemingly divisive fact that its cast comprise cross-sections of two generations—the older one composed of John Gabriel, Gunhild, Ella, and Foldal; the younger, of Erhart and Frida; with Mrs. Fanny Wilton in a necessarily anomalous position that calls for separate discussion. The thematic conflicts are both horizontal and vertical, among various members of the older generation, like Gunhild and Ella, or Borkman and Foldal, but also between several of these and Erhart in the younger generation; so that the tensions and antagonisms that join to propel the action could roughly be diagrammed by the letter T.

In the figure that dominates the older generation, Borkman himself, Ibsen applied his method of reductive analysis to the type that he now could see had, more than any other, shaped the character of the nineteenth century (and thus by extension, one could say, of the twentieth): that of the financier. As a child Ibsen had studied the local entrepreneurs from whose family circles he had been excluded after his father's bankruptcy. As a young man he had been impelled into a lifetime of iconoclastic drama by the spectacle of the secure order of this increasingly affluent class so shaken by the rebels of 1848. In *Peer Gynt* he gave his representative nineteenth-century man, as the pinnacle of his worldly career, the role of empire-building finance capitalist. Now, returning to the subject thirty years later, he depicted it with a difference. For while Peer fails to live up to the possibilities of the role through a defect of personality, in *Borkman* it is the role itself which has failed, through the "unforgivable sin" of killing the capacity to love. The larger parallel implied is that, in this regard, the entire generation of financial empire-builders has failed; the elders are left locked and frozen in their old feuds and rancors, and it is now up to the new generation to revise and improve or to reject the sum of their parents' lives.

Borkman has lived by the investment ethic of deferred satisfactions; and as Maurice Valency points out, Erhart here is the exact opposite of his father: he will sacrifice his whole career for a few years of happiness. But not on his own. Like John Gabriel, waiting in vain for the deputation that will recall him to rightful leadership in his field, Erhart also expects liberation to come to him from outside; and fortuitously it does, in the person of Fanny Wilton, who functions as the catalyst of the action. In the vast wintry landscape of the play, the warming glow of her mature, unconstrained sensuality establishes her as the latest in Ibsen's gallery of studies in eroticism, which would have to include the watchful animal *volupté* of Regina, the yearning languor of Ellida, the precocious perversity that flickers in Hilda Wangel, eventually to destroy Solness, the master builder, and even something unspoken in the trim femininity of Petra Stockmann, above all a creature of scruple and conviction, who nonetheless can draw men in clusters about her. But Mrs. Wilton's hold over Erhart goes beyond the seductive wiles of an experienced divorcée to suggestions of telepathy and witchcraft; and her special powers in the service of eros, acting upon the son, are a fit counterpart to the chthonic powers, the metals under the earth singing to Borkman in the tones of Saint-Saën's *Danse Macabre*, the Dance of Death.

Is Erhart wrong not to stay behind and work to reconstitute the family? Is it weakness or strength in him to break away completely? Such questions must inevitably arise on the realistic plane of the play's action. But, as already intimated, something larger is going on here than problems of character, or even of the appropriate response to a generation's failure, something ancient and archetypal which is confirmed by the ritualistic conclusion of the drama. Out of an indispensably long prelude of inquiry and recrimination, the play climaxes in a dual, quasi-mythic bursting of the bonds of winter and the women: the father into the dark kingdom of death, the son into a freedom which may or may not be specious. That this powerful, desperate resurgence of vitality be experienced as impressively as possible, Act III should be conceived as flowing directly, without pause, into Act IV, conforming with contemporary stage practice as against the more stolid expectation by ninteenth-century audiences of a four-course banquet of separate acts.

John Gabriel Borkman may be a broken man living out the last hours of his quiet desperation; nonetheless, he has resided in a great house, with better than minimal comforts available to him. Similar statements could be made of all the protagonists of the twelve realistic plays. Even the impoverished Ekdals of *The Wild Duck,* in escaping the fiercest, most dehumanizing competition for survival, are relatively well off in life. Yet these protagonists almost invariably feel or demonstrate themselves to have failed. It is too facile to suppose that Ibsen's preoccupation with the condition of failure stemmed simply from some chronic self-pitying morbidity that stands at variance with all we know of his later years. Nor is it sufficient to state that failure is more interesting dramatically than smooth, successful professionalism; involving an audience with compelling material is the *sine qua non* of the playwright's craft, but only its rudiments for the true artist. (The crippling determinism of heredity and environment must also be discounted as a major factor, though the influence of doctrinaire Zolaesque naturalism on Ibsen's art is too broad an issue for consideration here.) One explanation has already been advanced, with respect to Dr. Stockmann's inability to arouse his fellow townspeople out of their institutionalized fear and greed: in worldly failure, the degree of presence or absence of the spirit is most conspicuously revealed in the individual. But also, in a changing, evolving historical situation, what it is objectively that brings the protagonist down is equally significant, by indicating where outworn responses are no longer adequate to new challenges in an increasingly revolutionary age.

The continued bearing of Ibsen's investigations on these concerns today can perhaps best be demonstrated through a comparison with Bertolt Brecht, since the greatest dramatist of the nineteenth century and the greatest, so far, of the twentieth are in many ways complementary figures, the values and hopes of the former being centered in the individual, and those of the latter in the collective. No utterance is more typical of Brecht's outlook than his now familiar *Erst kommt das Fressen, dann kommt die Moral.* In the raw jungle of cities, in a peasant culture of poverty, or a time of severe economic depression, problems of simply getting enough to eat take priority over the principles of morality. Hunger devours the conscience first: Baal, Kragler, Macheath, Mother Courage, the good Shen Te all learn, or have learned, that bitter lesson. Eventually Brecht found a philosophy that correlated positively with his early nihilistic precept; for Marxism, the primary reality is the economic organization of society, the material means of production and distribution, of which all ideas and states of consciousness, including those of morality, are secondary, class-conditioned, rationalized reflections. For Ibsen, however, with his background in Hegel and Kierkegaard, the prime reality is to be found precisely in ideas—or rather in the inherent power of the concrete human spirit unceasingly to evolve them. All valid ideas and theories, not excluding Marxism itself, have objective truth and usefulness *under certain circumstances,* but when they no longer can be validated by those circumstances, or when their doctrines become a constricting tyranny, their life-spans are over, and they must be discarded. Only the spirit, the creative mind, persists.

If Ibsen's ghost were to return today and confront Brecht's maxim, he might well ask, with his usual flair for open-ended questions: *"Ja, Herr Brecht, aber wenn man voll ist, was—?"* What happens when the urban slum jungle is replaced by the bleak slabs of high-rise developments, when the peasants operate efficient collective farms, when recovery and affluence follow depression, and, inevitably, moral and existential questions of the possibilities and the limits of freedom and the claims and the penalties of truth reemerge? Such an imaginary exchange suggests the strengths and deficiencies of both dramatists, and the extent to which they supplement each other. In his mature works Ibsen is too prone to ignore, as irrelevant to the frontiers of human development, the daily bondage of the majority of mankind to the peril of imminent starvation or to immediately felt political and economic oppression. His protagonists always require at least minimum financial resources and the basic guarantees of democracy to grapple with the dilemmas of individual self-realization. On the other hand, Brecht in his mature writings is too prone to discount the individual as an anarchic threat to the whole, the social collective, which must be supported beyond all private reservations as essentially above criticism and deserving only of disciplined loyalty.

But the contrast can be put more affirmatively, in terms of strengths, as well. It has been observed that there are actually two long-range revolutions in process throughout the world. To the first, that material revolution wherein the unjustly deprived are demanding their share of the affluence made possible by modern technological means of production, Brecht is outstandingly relevant. To the second, the ensuing revolution of consciousness wherein the outwardly secure and satisfied grope with basic questions about the truth of their lives and the purposes their freedom should be put to, Ibsen remains equally relevant. The short remove of something under a hundred years has only lent his plays a kind of gratis Brechtean alienation-effect, whereby the relevance of his themes arrives with an air of rediscovery, wearing the slightly foreign costumes and manners of a nearby province in time. On several occasions Ibsen was approached by an actor or actress who, by way of compliment, thanked him for the great roles he had created. His somewhat gruff reply invariably was that he had not sought to create roles, but rather to trace the destinies of living human beings. His half century of dedication to the stage makes clear by this, not that he valued theater less, but rather that he valued life the more, and put the utmost of his genius at the service of the truest artists of the theater in order to join them in paying it mutual reverence. That full, multi-dimensional life—of the mind, of the emotions, of the eros of the flesh and the evolution of the spirit—pulses still in the lines of his dramas, waiting always for new artists to seize it, liberate it, and make it their own.

ROLF FJELDE
Pratt Institute

SELECTED BIBLIOGRAPHY
AND CRITICISM

HENRIK IBSEN: THE PLAYS

Catiline (1850)
The Warrior's Barrow (1850)
Norma (1851)
St John's Eve (1853)
Lady Inger of Oestraat (1855)
The Feast at Solhaug (1856)
Olaf Liljekrans (1857)
The Vikings in Helgeland (1858)
Love's Comedy (1862)
The Prentenders (1863)
Brand (1866)
Peer Gynt (1867)
The League of Youth (1869)
Emperor and Galilean (1873)
The Pillars of Society (1877)
A Doll House (1879)
Ghosts (1881)
An Enemy of the People (1882)
The Wild Duck (1884)
Rosmersholm (1886)
The Lady from the Sea (1888)
Hedda Gabler (1890)
The Master Builder (1892)
Little Eyolf (1894)
John Gabriel Borkman (1896)
When We Dead Awaken (1899)

CRITICISM

Adler, Stella. *On Ibsen, Strindberg, and Chekhov.* Ed. Barry Paris. New York: Alfred A. Knopf, 1999.

Archer, William. *William Archer on Ibsen: The Major Essays, 1889–1919.* Ed. Thomas Postlewait. Westport, Conn.: Greenwood Press, 1984.

Bolckmans, Alex, et al. *The International Ibsen: Contemporary Approaches to Ibsen.* Oslo: Universitetsforlaget, 1966; New York: Humanities Press, 1967.

Bryan, George B. *An Ibsen Companion: A Dictionary-Guide to the Life, Works, and Critical Reception of Henrik Ibsen.* Westport, Conn.: Greenwood Press, 1984.

Downs, Brian W. *Ibsen: The Intellectual Background.* London: Cambridge University Press, 1946; New York: The Macmillan Company, 1947.

Egan, Michael, ed. *Ibsen: The Critical Heritage.* London: Routledge and Kegan Paul, 1972.

Ferguson, Robert, *Henrik Ibsen: A New Biography.* London: R. Cohen, 1996.

Fjelde, Rolf, ed. *Ibsen: A Collection of Critical Essays.* Englewood Cliffs, NJ: Prentice-Hall, 1965.

Goldman, Michael. *Ibsen: The Dramaturgy of Fear.* New York: Columbia University Press, 1999.

Ibsen, Henrik. *Letters and Speeches.* Ed. Evert Sprinchorn. New York: Hill and Wang, 1964.

Jorgenson, Theodore. *Henrik Ibsen: A Study in Art and Personality.* Westport, Conn.: Greenwood Press, 1978.

Knight, G. Wilson. *Henrik Ibsen.* New York: Grove Press, 1963.

Koht, Halvdan. *Life of Ibsen.* 2nd ed. New York: Benjamin Blom, 1970.

McFarlane, James, ed. *The Cambridge Companion to Ibsen.* Cambridge: Cambridge University Press, 1994.

Meyer, Michael. *Ibsen: A Biography.* New York: Doubleday, 1971.

Shafer, Yvonne. *Henrik Ibsen: Life, Work, and Criticism.* Frederiction, N.B., Canada: York Press, 1985.

Shaw, George Bernard. *The Quintessence of Ibsenism.* New York: Hill and Wang, 1957.

Templeton, Joan. *Ibsen's Women.* Cambridge: Cambridge University Press, 1997.

Theoharis, Theoharis Constantine. *Ibsen's Drama: Right Action and Tragic Joy.* New York: St. Martin's Press, 1996.

Weigand, Hermann J. *The Modern Ibsen: A Reconsideration.* New York: Dutton, 1960.

GHOSTS

THE CHARACTERS

MRS. HELENE ALVING, widow of Captain Alving, late
  Court Chamberlain
OSVALD ALVING, her son, a painter
PASTOR MANDERS
ENGSTRAND, a carpenter
REGINA ENGSTRAND, in service with Mrs. Alving

*The action takes place on Mrs. Alving's country estate
by a large fjord in West Norway.*

⌒ ACT ONE ⌒

A large garden room, with a door in the left-hand wall, and two doors in the wall to the right. In the middle of the room a round table with chairs grouped about it; on the table lie books, magazines, and newspapers. In the left foreground, a window, and next to it a small sofa with a sewing table in front of it. In the background, the room is extended into a somewhat smaller greenhouse, whose walls are great panes of glass. From the right side of the greenhouse, a door leads into the garden. Through the glass walls a somber fjord landscape can be glimpsed, half hidden by the steady rain.

ENGSTRAND *is standing by the garden door. His left leg is partly deformed; under his bootsole he has a wooden block.* REGINA, *with an empty garden syringe in her hand, is trying to keep him from entering.*

REGINA (*in a low voice*). What do you want? Just stay where you are. Why, you're dripping wet.

ENGSTRAND. It's God's own rain, my girl.

REGINA. The devil's rain, it is!

ENGSTRAND. Jeez, how you talk, Regina. (*Hobbles a few steps into the room.*) But now, what I wanted to say—

REGINA. Stop stomping about with that foot, will you! The young master's sleeping upstairs.

ENGSTRAND. Still sleeping? In broad daylight?

REGINA. That's none of your business.

41

ENGSTRAND. I was out on a binge last night—

REGINA. I can imagine.

ENGSTRAND. Yes, because we mortals are weak, my girl—

REGINA. Yes, so we are.

ENGSTRAND. And temptations are manifold in this world, you see— But for all of that, I was on the job, so help me God, five thirty this morning early.

REGINA. All right now, get out of here. I'm not going to stand around, having a rendezvous with you.

ENGSTRAND. You're not going to have any what?

REGINA. I'm not going to have anyone meeting you here. So—on your way.

ENGSTRAND (*a few steps closer*). Damned if I'll go before I've had my say with you. This afternoon I'll be done with my work down at the schoolhouse, and then I'll rip right back to town by the night boat.

REGINA (*mutters*). Pleasant trip!

ENGSTRAND. Thank you, my girl. Tomorrow they'll be dedicating the orphanage, and there'll probably be all kinds of carrying-on here, with hard liquor, you know. And nobody's going to say about Jacob Engstrand that he can't put temptation behind him.

REGINA. Ha!

ENGSTRAND. Yes, because you know a lot of the best people'll be here tomorrow. Pastor Manders is expected from town.

REGINA. He's coming today.

ENGSTRAND. There, you see. And I'll be damned if he's going to get anything on me.

REGINA. Ah, so *that's* it!

ENGSTRAND. What do you mean, *that*?

REGINA (*looks knowingly at him*). Just what are you out to trick him into this time?

ENGSTRAND. Shh, are you crazy? Would *I* trick the pastor into anything? Oh no, Pastor Manders, he's been much too good to me for that. But it's what I wanted to talk to you about, see—that I'll be leaving for home then, tonight.

REGINA. The sooner the better.

ENGSTRAND. Yes, but I want you along with me, Regina.

REGINA (*open-mouthed*). You want me along—? What did you say?

ENGSTRAND. I'm saying I want you back home with me.

REGINA (*scornfully*). Back home with you? Never. Not a chance!

ENGSTRAND. Oh, we'll see about that.

REGINA. Yes, you can bet we will, all right. *I*, who've been brought up by Mrs. Alving—? Been taken in like one of the family—? *I* should move back with *you?* To a house like that? Pah!

ENGSTRAND. What the devil is this? You trying to cross your own father, you slut?

REGINA (*mutters, without looking at him*). You've always said I had no part of you.

ENGSTRAND. Ahh, never mind about that—

REGINA. How many times haven't you cursed me and called me a—*fi donc!*

ENGSTRAND. So help me God if I've ever used such a dirty word.

REGINA. Oh, I haven't forgotten the word you used.

ENGSTRAND. Yes, but that was only when I had some drink in me—hm. Temptations are manifold in this world, Regina.

REGINA. Ugh!

ENGSTRAND. And when your mother got nasty, see—then I had to find something to needle her with. Always made herself so refined. (*Mimics.*) "Let go of me, Engstrand! Leave me be! I've been three years in service to Chamberlain Alving at Rosenvold!" (*Laughs.*) Jeez, that was something she never could forget—that the captain was made a chamberlain while she was in service there.

REGINA. Poor mother—you bullied the life out of her soon enough.

ENGSTRAND (*with a shrug*). Yes, that's right; I get the blame for everything.

REGINA (*in an undertone, as she turns away*). Ugh—! And that leg.

ENGSTRAND. What did you say, my girl?

REGINA. *Pied de mouton.*

ENGSTRAND. What's that—German?*

REGINA. Yes.

ENGSTRAND. Oh yes, you got some learning out here, and that's going to come in handy now, Regina.

REGINA (*after a short silence*). And what was it you wanted with me in town?

ENGSTRAND. How can you ask what a father wants with his only child? Aren't I a lonely, forsaken widower?

REGINA. Oh, don't give me that garbage. Why do you want me in town?

ENGSTRAND. All right, I'll tell you—I've been thinking of striking into something new.

REGINA (*with a snort*). You've done that so often, and it always goes wrong.

ENGSTRAND. Ah, but this time, Regina, you wait and see! Hell's bells—!

REGINA (*stamps her foot*). Stop swearing!

ENGSTRAND. Sh, sh! Perfectly right you are, my girl! I only wanted to say—I've put by a nice piece of change out of the work on this new orphanage.

REGINA. Have you? Well, that's good for you.

ENGSTRAND. Because what can you spend your money on here, out in the country?

REGINA. Well, so?

* "English," in the original, which loses meaning in an English translation.

ENGSTRAND. Yes, so you see, I thought I might put the money into something that'd turn a profit. It was going to be a sort of hotel for seamen—

REGINA. Ugh-ah!

ENGSTRAND. A regular, first-class inn, you understand— not just any old pigsty for sailors. No, damn it all—it's going to be for ship captains and mates and—and real fine people, you understand.

REGINA. And how do I—?

ENGSTRAND. You? You get to help, see. Just for the look of things, if you follow me. There wouldn't be so damn much to do. You can have it just like you want it.

REGINA. I'll bet!

ENGSTRAND. But there've got to be women on the premises, that's clear as day. Because we want a little life in the evenings—singing and dancing and that sort of thing. You have to remember, these are wayfaring seamen on the ocean of life. (*Comes nearer.*) Now don't be stupid and hold yourself back, Regina. What can you come to out here? What good can it do you, all this learning Mrs. Alving's paid out for? You're supposed to take care of the children, I hear, in the new orphanage. Is *that* anything for you, uh? Have you such a hunger to run yourself ragged for the sake of those filthy brats?

REGINA. No, if things go the way *I* want, then— And it could happen, all right. Yes, it could!

ENGSTRAND. What could?

REGINA. None of your business. Is it—quite a bit of money you made out here?

ENGSTRAND. Between this and that, I'd say up to seven, eight hundred crowns.

REGINA. That's not so bad.

ENGSTRAND. It's enough for a start, my girl.

REGINA. Don't you think you might give me some of that money?

ENGSTRAND. No, I don't think I might!

REGINA. Don't you think you could send me at least some cloth for a dress?

ENGSTRAND. Just come with me into town, and you'll have dresses to burn.

REGINA. Pah! I can do as well on my own, if I care to.

ENGSTRAND. No, but it goes better, Regina, with a father's guiding hand. There's a nice house I can get now in Little Harbor Street. They don't want too much money down; and it could make some kind of seamen's home, all right.

REGINA. But I don't want to stay with you! I've got no business with you. Get out!

ENGSTRAND. You wouldn't stay so damn long with me, girl. No such luck—if you know how to show off yourself. A wench as good-looking as you've turned out these last two years—

REGINA. Yes—?

ENGSTRAND. It wouldn't be long before some ship's officer—maybe even a captain—

REGINA. I'm not marrying any of those. Sailors don't have any *savoir-vivre*.

ENGSTRAND. They don't have any what?

REGINA. Let me tell you, I know about sailors. They aren't any sort to marry.

ENGSTRAND. Then forget about getting married. That can pay just as well. (*More confidentially.*) Him—the Englishman—the one with the yacht—he gave three hundred dollars, he did—and she was no better looking than you.

REGINA (*advancing on him*). Get out of here!

ENGSTRAND (*steps back*). Easy now, you don't want to hit me.

REGINA. Don't I! Talk about Mother, and you'll find out. Get out of here, I said! (*She forces him back toward the garden door.*) And no slamming doors; young Mr. Alving—

ENGSTRAND. Yes, he's asleep. It's something all right, how you worry about young Mr. Alving— (*Dropping his voice.*) Ho-ho! It just wouldn't be that *he*—?

REGINA. Out of here, quick! You're all mixed up! No

not that way. There's Pastor Manders coming. Down the kitchen stairs.

ENGSTRAND (*moving to the right*). All right, I'm going. But you talk with *him* that's coming in. He's the one who'll tell you what a child owes her father. Because, after all, I *am* your father, you know. I can prove it in the parish register.

(*He goes out by the farther door, which* REGINA *has opened, closing it after him. She hurriedly glances at herself in the mirror, fans herself with her handkerchief and straightens her collar, then busies herself with the flowers.* PASTOR MANDERS, *in an overcoat, carrying an umbrella along with a small traveling bag on a strap over his shoulder, comes through the garden door into the greenhouse.*)

MANDERS. Good morning, Miss Engstrand.

REGINA (*turning with a pleasantly surprised look*). Why, Pastor Manders, good morning! The boat's already come?

MANDERS. It just arrived. (*Entering the room.*) It's certainly tedious weather we've been having these days.

REGINA (*following him*). It's a godsend for the farmers, Pastor.

MANDERS. Yes, you're quite right. That's something we townspeople hardly think of. (*He starts taking his overcoat off.*)

REGINA. Oh, let me help you—that's it. My, how wet it is! I'll just hang it up in the hall. And the umbrella, too —I'll leave it open to dry.

(*She goes off with the things through the farther door on the right.* MANDERS *removes his traveling bag and sets it and his hat down on a chair, as* REGINA *returns.*)

MANDERS. Ah, but it's good to be indoors. So— everything's going well out here?

REGINA. Yes, thank you.

MANDERS. But terribly busy, I suppose, getting ready for tomorrow?

REGINA. Oh yes, there's plenty to do.

MANDERS. And, hopefully, Mrs. Alving's at home?

REGINA. Why, of course. She just went upstairs to bring the young master some hot chocolate.

MANDERS. Yes, tell me—I heard down at the pier that Osvald was supposed to have come.

REGINA. He got in the day before yesterday. We hadn't expected him before today.

MANDERS. In the best of health, I hope?

REGINA. Yes, just fine, thank you. But awfully tired after his trip. He came straight from Paris without a break—I mean, he went the whole route without changing trains. I think he's sleeping a little now, so we should talk just a tiny bit softer.

MANDERS. Shh! We'll be so quiet.

REGINA (*as she moves an armchair up to the table*). Please now, do sit down, Pastor, and make yourself comfortable. (*He sits; she slips a footstool under his feet.*) That's it! Is that all right, Pastor?

MANDERS. Just perfect, thank you. (*Regarding her.*) You know, Miss Engstrand, I .definitely think you've grown since I saw you last.

REGINA. Do you think so, Pastor? Mrs. Alving says that I've filled out, too.

MANDERS. Filled out—? Well, yes, maybe a little—but acceptably. (*A short pause.*)

REGINA. Shall I tell Mrs. Alving you're here?

MANDERS. Oh, thank you, there's no hurry, my dear child—well, uh—but tell me now, Regina, how's it been going for your father out here?

REGINA. Fairly well, Pastor, thank you.

MANDERS. He was in to see me when he was last in town.

REGINA. Really? He's always so happy when he can talk with you.

MANDERS. And you make it your rule, of course, to look in on him daily.

REGINA. I? Oh, yes, of course—whenever I have some time—

MANDERS. Your father is not very strong in character, Miss Engstrand. He's woefully in need of a guiding hand.

REGINA. Yes, I'm sure of that.

MANDERS. He needs to have someone around him that he can love, and whose judgment carries some weight. He confessed as much quite frankly when he was last up to see me.

REGINA. Yes, he said something like that to me. But I don't know if Mrs. Alving could spare me—especially now, when we've got the new orphanage to manage. And then I'd be so awfully unhappy to leave Mrs. Alving—she's always been so kind to me.

MANDERS. But, my dear girl, a daughter's duty— Naturally, we'd first have to obtain Mrs. Alving's consent.

REGINA. But I don't know if it would do for me, at my age, to keep house for a single man.

MANDERS. What! But, my dear Miss Engstrand, this is your own father we're speaking of!

REGINA. Yes, maybe so, but all the same—you see, if it were a *good* house, with a real gentleman—

MANDERS. But, my dear Regina—

REGINA. One I could care for and look up to, almost like a daughter—

MANDERS. Yes, but my dear child—

REGINA. Because I'd like so much to live in town. Out here it's terribly lonely—and you know yourself, Pastor, what it is to stand alone in the world. And I think I can say that I'm both capable and willing. Mr. Manders, don't you know of a place like that for me?

MANDERS. I? No, I don't, for the life of me.

REGINA. But dear, dear Mr. Manders—you will think of me, in any case, if ever—

MANDERS (*getting up*). Yes, I'll remember, Miss Engstrand.

REGINA. Yes, because if I—

MANDERS. Perhaps you'll be good enough to tell Mrs. Alving I've come.

REGINA. I'll go call her right away, Pastor.

(*She goes out left.* MANDERS *paces back and forth in the room a couple of times, then stands for a moment at the far end of the room, hands behind his back, looking out into the garden. He then returns to the table, picks up a book and looks at the title page, starts, and inspects several others.*)

MANDERS. Hm—aha! Well!

(MRS. ALVING *comes in by the door, left. She is followed by* REGINA, *who immediately goes out by the nearer door to the right.*)

MRS. ALVING (*extending her hand*). So good to see you, Mr. Manders.

MANDERS. Good morning, Mrs. Alving. Here I am, just as I promised.

MRS. ALVING. Always on the dot.

MANDERS. But you can imagine, it was touch and go for me, getting away. All those blessed boards and committees—

MRS. ALVING. All the more kind of you to come so promptly. Now we can get our business done before lunch. But where do you have your bags?

MANDERS (*hurriedly*). My things are down at the general store—I took a room there for tonight.

MRS. ALVING (*repressing a smile*). You can't be persuaded even yet to spend the night here in my house?

MANDERS. No, no, really; thank you so much, but I'll stay down there as usual. It's so convenient to the boat.

MRS. ALVING. Well, you do as you wish. But I really thought instead that two old people like us—

MANDERS. Gracious me, the way you joke! Yes, of course you're in rare spirits today. First the celebration tomorrow, and then you've got Osvald home.

MRS ALVING. Yes, can you imagine how happy I am! It's more than two years since he was home last. And then he's promised to stay with me this whole winter.

MANDERS. No, has he really? That's certainly a nice gesture for a son to make—because there must be other, quite different attractions to life in Rome and Paris, I'm sure.

MRS. ALVING. Yes, but he has his mother here at home, you see. Oh, that dear, blessed boy—he still has room in his heart for me!

MANDERS. It would really be tragic if distance and devotion to anything like art should dull his natural feelings.

MRS. ALVING. You're perfectly right. But there's no chance at all of that with him. Oh, I'm going to be so curious to see if you still recognize him. He'll be down shortly; he's just stretched out to rest a little on the sofa upstairs. But now, my dear Mr. Manders—do sit down.

MANDERS. Thank you. It *is* convenient, then—?

MRS. ALVING. Why, of course. (*She sits at the table.*)

MANDERS. Good. Then let's have a look— (*Goes over to the chair where his bag lies, takes out a sheaf of papers, sits at the opposite side of the table, and searches for a space to lay the papers out.*) Now here, first, we have— (*Breaks off.*) Tell me, Mrs. Alving, where did these books come from?

MRS. ALVING. These books? I'm reading them.

MANDERS. You read this sort of thing?

MRS. ALVING. Yes, of course I do.

MANDERS. Do you feel you've grown any better or happier for this kind of reading?

MRS. ALVING. I think it makes me feel more secure.

MANDERS. That's astonishing. What do you mean?

MRS. ALVING. Well, I find it clarifies and reinforces so many ideas I've been thinking out all to myself. Yes, that's the strange part, Mr. Manders—there's actually nothing really new in these books, nothing beyond what most people think and believe. It's simply that most people don't like to face these things, or what they imply.

MANDERS. Oh, my dear God! You don't seriously consider that most people—?

MRS. ALVING. Yes, I certainly do.

MANDERS. Well, but not here in our society? Not among us?

MRS. ALVING. Yes, definitely—among us, too.

MANDERS. Well, I must say, really—!

MRS. ALVING. But what exactly do you object to in these books?

MANDERS. Object to? You surely don't think I waste my time exploring that kind of publication?

MRS. ALVING. In other words, you know nothing of what you're condemning?

MANDERS. I've read quite enough about these writings to disapprove of them.

MRS. ALVING. Yes, but your own opinion—

MANDERS. My dear Mrs. Alving, there are many circumstances in life where one has to entrust oneself to others. That's the condition of this world, and it's all for the best. How else could society function?

MRS. ALVING. That's true; maybe you're right.

MANDERS. Besides, I wouldn't deny that there's a certain fascination about such writings. And I can't blame you either for wanting to become acquainted with the intellectual currents that, I hear, are quite prevalent in the larger world—where you've let your son wander so long. But—

MRS. ALVING. But—?

MANDERS (dropping his voice). But one needn't talk about it, Mrs. Alving. One doesn't have to recount to all and sundry everything one reads and thinks within one's own four walls.

MRS. ALVING. No, of course not. I agree.

MANDERS. Remember your obligations to the orphanage, which you decided to found at a time when your attitude toward things of the mind and spirit was so very different from now—at least as I see it.

MRS. ALVING. Yes, I admit it, completely. But it was about the orphanage—

MANDERS. It was about the orphanage we wanted to

speak, yes. All the same—prudence, my dear Mrs. Alving!
And now, let's turn to business. (*Opens a folder and takes
out some papers.*) You see these?

MRS. ALVING. The deeds?

MANDERS. The whole set—in perfect order. You can
imagine it hasn't been easy to get them in time. I actually
had to apply some pressure. The authorities are almost
painfully scrupulous when it comes to decisions. But here
they are, in any case. (*Leafing through the papers.*) See,
here's the duly recorded conveyance of title of the Solvik
farm, said property being part of the Rosenvold estate,
together with all buildings newly erected thereon, including the schoolhouse, the staff residence, and the chapel.
And here's the official charter for the institution—and the
by-laws governing its operation. You see— (*Reads.*) "By-
laws governing the Captain Alving Memorial Orphan's
Home."

MRS. ALVING (*looking at the papers for a long moment*). So—there it is.

MANDERS. I chose "Captain" for the title, rather than
"Court Chamberlain." "Captain" seems less ostentatious.

MRS. ALVING. Yes, whatever you think.

MANDERS. And here you've got the bankbook showing
interest on capital reserved to cover the running expenses
of the orphanage.

MRS. ALVING. Thank you—but please, won't you hold
onto it, for convenience' sake?

MANDERS. Yes, gladly. I think we can leave the money
in the bank for a time. It's true, the interest rate isn't very
attractive: four percent, with a six-month withdrawal notice. If we could come across a good mortgage later on—
naturally, it would have to be a first mortgage, of unques-
tionable security—then we could reconsider the situation.

MRS. ALVING. Yes, dear Mr. Manders, you know best
about all that.

MANDERS. Anyway, I'll keep an eye out. But now there's
one more thing I've meant several times to ask you.

MRS. ALVING. And what's that?

MANDERS. Should the orphanage be insured or not?

MRS. ALVING. Why, of course, it has to be insured.

MANDERS. Ah, not too fast, Mrs. Alving. Let's study this question a bit.

MRS. ALVING. Everything I own is insured—buildings, furniture, crops, livestock.

MANDERS. Obviously, when it's your own property. I do the same, naturally. But here, you see, it's a very different matter. This orphanage is going to be, so to say, consecrated to a higher calling.

MRS. ALVING. Yes, but if—

MANDERS. From my personal standpoint, I wouldn't find the slightest objection to insuring us against all eventualities—

MRS. ALVING. No, I wouldn't either.

MANDERS. But how would that sit with the public opinion hereabouts? You know better than I.

MRS. ALVING. Public opinion, hm—

MANDERS. Is there any considerable segment of opinion—I mean, really important opinion—that might take offense?

MRS. ALVING. Well, what do you mean, exactly, by important opinion?

MANDERS. I was thinking mainly of people of such independent and influential position that one could hardly avoid giving their opinions a certain weight.

MRS. ALVING. There are a few like that here who might possibly take offense if—

MANDERS. There, you see! In town we have any number of them. The congregations of other churches, for example. It would be the easiest thing in the world for them to construe this as neither you nor I having adequate faith in Divine Providence.

MRS. ALVING. But, my dear Mr. Manders, as long as you know to your own satisfaction—

MANDERS. Yes, I know, I know—I have my own inner conviction, quite so. But the fact remains that we wouldn't be able to counter a false and damaging impression—and that, in turn, could easily hamper the work of the orphanage.

MRS. ALVING. Well, if that's the case, then——

MANDERS. Also, I can hardly ignore the difficult—I might just as well say, painful—position I'd probably be in myself. Among the best circles in town there's a good deal of interest in the orphanage. After all, it's partly being established to benefit the town as well, and hopefully it's going to have a sizable effect in lowering our local public welfare taxes. But since I've been your adviser in this and made all the business arrangements, I'm afraid those bigots would concentrate all their fire on me——

MRS. ALVING. No, you shouldn't be exposed to that.

MANDERS. Not to mention the charges that would doubtless be leveled against me in certain papers and magazines that——

MRS. ALVING. Enough, Mr. Manders; that settles it.

MANDERS. Then you won't want the insurance?

MRS. ALVING. No, we'll let that be.

MANDERS (*leaning back in his chair*). But now, if there *should* be an accident—one never knows, after all—would you be able to make good the losses?

MRS. ALVING. I can tell you right now, I absolutely wouldn't.

MANDERS. Ah, but you know, Mrs. Alving—then it's a grave responsibility we're taking on.

MRS. ALVING. But what else do you see that we *can* do?

MANDERS. No, that's just the thing: we *can't* do anything else. We shouldn't expose ourselves to unfavorable opinion; and we certainly have no right to stir dissension in the community.

MRS. ALVING. Especially you, as a clergyman.

MANDERS. And also I really do believe that we can depend on a project like this carrying some luck along with it—standing, so to say, under a special protection.

MRS. ALVING. Let's hope so, Mr. Manders.

MANDERS. Then we'll leave things as they are?

MRS. ALVING. Yes, of course.

MANDERS. Right. As you wish. (*Jotting a note.*) No insurance.

MRS. ALVING. It's strange you happened to speak about this just today—

MANDERS. I've often thought to ask you about it—

MRS. ALVING. Because yesterday we nearly had a fire down there.

MANDERS. What!

MRS. ALVING. Well, there wasn't anything to it, really. Some shavings caught fire in the carpenter shop.

MANDERS. Where Engstrand works?

MRS. ALVING. Yes. They say he's often so careless with matches.

MANDERS. He has so much on his mind, that man—so many tribulations. Praise be to God, he's now making a real effort to lead a blameless life, I hear.

MRS. ALVING. Oh? Who's been saying that?

MANDERS. He's assured me of it himself. And he's a capable workman, too.

MRS. ALVING. Why, yes, as long as he's sober—

MANDERS. Ah, that distressing weakness! But he tells me he frequently has to resort to it for the sake of his ailing leg. Last time he was in town, I really was quite moved by him. He stopped in and thanked me so sincerely for getting him this work out here, so he could be together with Regina.

MRS. ALVING. But he hardly ever sees her.

MANDERS. No, he speaks with her every day—he told me that himself.

MRS. ALVING. Yes—well, it's possible.

MANDERS. He feels so positively that he needs someone there who can restrain him when temptation looms. That's what's so engaging about Jacob Engstrand, the way he comes to one so utterly helpless and accuses himself and admits his faults. Just this last time that he talked to me—Mrs. Alving, if it became a vital necessity for him to have Regina home with him again—

MRS. ALVING (*rising impulsively*). Regina!

MANDERS. Then you mustn't set yourself against it.

MRS. ALVING. Yes, I'm decidedly set against it. And besides—Regina will have a position at the orphanage.

MANDERS. But remember, he *is* her father—

MRS. ALVING. I know all too well what kind of father he's been to her. No, she'll never have my blessings to go to him.

MANDERS (*rising*). But my dear Mrs. Alving, don't take it so violently. It's such a pity, the way you misjudge Engstrand. Really, it's as if you were somehow afraid—

MRS. ALVING (*more calmly*). Never mind about that. I've taken Regina in here, and she'll stay here with me. (*Listens.*) Shh, now! Dear Mr. Manders, let's not talk of this anymore. (*Her face radiating joy.*) Hear that! Osvald's coming downstairs. Now we'll think only of him.

(OSVALD ALVING, *wearing a light overcoat, hat in hand, and smoking a large meerschaum pipe, comes in through the door to the left.*)

OSVALD (*pausing in the doorway*). Oh, I'm sorry—I thought you were in the study. (*Comes in.*) Good morning, Pastor Manders.

MANDERS (*stares at him*). Ah—! That's amazing—!

MRS. ALVING. Yes, what do you think of him, Mr. Manders?

MANDERS. Well, I must say—no, but—is it really—?

OSVALD. Yes, really—the prodigal son, Pastor.

MANDERS. But my dear boy—

OSVALD. Well, the homecoming son, anyway.

MRS. ALVING. Osvald's thinking of the time when you were so against his becoming a painter.

MANDERS. From our human viewpoint, you know, many a step looks doubtful that later turns out— (*Shaking his hand.*) Ah, welcome, welcome back! Imagine, my dear Osvald—may I still call you by your first name?

OSVALD. What else could you think of calling me?

MANDERS. Good. What I meant to say, my dear Osvald—was that you mustn't suppose that I categorically condemn the artist's life. I assume there are quite a few who keep their inner selves uncorrupted even in those circumstances.

OSVALD. Let's hope so.

MRS. ALVING (*beaming with pleasure*). I know one who's kept both his inner and outer selves incorruptible. You only have to look at him, Mr. Manders.

OSVALD (*pacing about the room*). Yes, all right, Mother dear—that's enough.

MANDERS. Completely so—that's undeniable. And you've already begun to make your name. You're often mentioned in the papers—and most favorably, too. Though lately, I should say, there seems to be less.

OSVALD (*near the greenhouse*). I haven't been painting so much lately.

MRS. ALVING. Even artists need a rest now and then.

MANDERS. That I can understand. A time to prepare oneself and gather strength for the great work to come.

OSVALD. Yes. Mother, are we eating soon?

MRS. ALVING. In just half an hour. He certainly has an appetite, thank goodness.

MANDERS. And likes his tobacco, too.

OSVALD. I found Father's pipe upstairs in the bedroom—

MANDERS. Ah, that explains it!

MRS. ALVING. What?

MANDERS. When Osvald came through the door there with that pipe in his mouth, it was as if I saw his father in the flesh.

OSVALD. Really?

MRS. ALVING. Oh, how can you say that? Osvald takes after me.

MANDERS. Yes, but there's a look around the corners of

the mouth, something about the lips, that's the very picture of Alving—especially now that he's smoking.

MRS. ALVING. No, it's nothing like him, not at all. To me, Osvald has more of a minister's look about the mouth.

MANDERS. Yes. Yes, a number of my colleagues have a similar expression.

MRS. ALVING. But put the pipe down, dear. I don't want smoking in this room.

OSVALD (*sets the pipe down*). All right. I only thought I'd try it because I'd once smoked it as a child.

MRS. ALVING. You?

OSVALD. Yes. I was very small then. And I remember going up to Father's room one evening when he was in such a marvelous humor.

MRS. ALVING. Oh, you don't remember anything from those years.

OSVALD. Oh yes, I distinctly remember him taking me on his knee and letting me smoke his pipe. "Smoke, boy," he said, "smoke it for real!" And I smoked for all I was worth, till I felt myself go pale, and the great drops of sweat stood out on my forehead. Then he shook all over with laughter—

MANDERS. That's most peculiar.

MRS. ALVING. I'm sure it's just something that Osvald dreamed.

OSVALD. No, Mother, it was definitely no dream. Because—don't you remember—then you came in and carried me off to the nursery. I was sick then, and I could see you were crying. Did Father often play such tricks?

MANDERS. When he was young he was always full of life—

OSVALD. And still he got so much accomplished—so much that was good and useful, for all that he died so early.

MANDERS. Yes, Osvald Alving—it's a strong and worthy name you've inherited. Well, let's hope it'll inspire you—

OSVALD. It certainly ought to.

MANDERS. And it was good of you to come home for the ceremonies in his honor.

OSVALD. It's the least I could do for Father.

MRS. ALVING. And that he'll remain with me here so long—that's the best of his goodness.

MANDERS. Yes, I hear you're staying all winter.

OSVALD. I'll be staying on indefinitely, Pastor. Oh, it's wonderful to be home again!

MRS. ALVING (*radiant*). Yes, how true!

MANDERS (*looks sympathetically at him*). You were out in the world quite early, Osvald, weren't you?

OSVALD. Yes. I wonder sometimes if it wasn't too early.

MRS. ALVING. Nonsense! There's nothing better for a healthy boy, especially when he's an only child. He shouldn't be kept home and coddled by his mother and father.

MANDERS. That's a highly debatable proposition, Mrs. Alving. A child's rightful place is and always will be his parental home.

OSVALD. I have to agree with Mr. Manders there.

MANDERS. Now take your own son, for instance. Yes, we can discuss this in front of him. What effect has this had on him? He's grown to age twenty-six or -seven without any chance to experience a normal home life.

OSVALD. Excuse me, Mr. Manders—but you're quite wrong about that.

MANDERS. Really? I thought you'd been moving almost entirely in artistic circles.

OSVALD. I have.

MANDERS. And mainly among the younger artists.

OSVALD. Yes.

MANDERS. But I thought most of those people hadn't the means to start a family and make a home.

OSVALD. It's true that a number of them haven't the means to get married—

MANDERS. Well, that's what I'm saying.

OSVALD. But they can still have a home life. And several of them do—one that's quite normal and pleasant.

(MRS. ALVING, *following attentively, nods but says nothing.*)

MANDERS. But it's not a bachelor life I'm talking about. By home life I mean a family home, where a man lives with his wife and his children.

OSVALD. Yes, or with his children and his children's mother.

MANDERS (*jolted, clasping his hands together*). Merciful God—!

OSVALD. What—?

MANDERS. Lives together with—his children's mother!

OSVALD. Well, would you rather have him abandon her?

MANDERS. But you're talking about illicit relations! About plain, irresponsible free love!

OSVALD. I've never noticed anything particularly irresponsible about the way these people live.

MANDERS. But how is it possible that—that even moderately decent young men or women could accept living in that manner—before the eyes of the world!

OSVALD. But what else can they do? A poor young artist—a poor young girl—and marriage so expensive. What can they do?

MANDERS. What they can do? Well, Mr. Alving, I'll tell you what they can do. They ought to keep each other at a distance right from the start—that's what they ought to do!

OSVALD. You won't get very far with that advice among warm-blooded young people in love.

MRS. ALVING. No, you certainly won't!

MANDERS (*persisting*). And to think the authorities tolerate such things! That it's allowed to go on openly. (*To* MRS. ALVING.) You see what good reason I've had to be concerned about your son. In circles where immorality is flaunted, and even seems to be prized—

OSVALD. Let me tell you something, Pastor. I've been a

frequent Sunday guest in a couple of these so-called unconventional homes—

MANDERS. Sunday, no less!

OSVALD. Yes, the day of rest and relaxation—and yet I've never once heard an offensive word, nor have I ever witnessed anything that could be called immoral. But do you know when and where I *have* met immorality among artists?

MANDERS. No, thank God, I don't!

OSVALD. Well, then let me tell you. I've met it when one or another of our exemplary husbands and fathers—on a trip away from home and out to see a little life—did the artists the honor of dropping in on them in their poor cafés. Then we had our ears opened wide. Those gentlemen could tell us about things and places we never dreamed existed.

MANDERS. What? Are you suggesting that respectable men from here at home would—?

OSVALD. Have you never—when these same respectable men came home from their trips—have you never heard them carrying on about the monstrous immorality abroad?

MANDERS. Why, of course—

MRS. ALVING. I have, too.

OSVALD. Well, you can trust their word for it—they're experts, many of them. (*Clasps his head.*) Oh, that the beautiful freedom of that life—could be made so foul!

MRS. ALVING. You mustn't provoke yourself, Osvald. It's not good for you.

OSVALD. No, you're right, Mother. It's bad for my health. It's this damnable fatigue, you know. Well, I'll go for a little walk now before lunch. I'm sorry, Pastor. You can't share my feelings about this—but it's the way I see it. (*He goes out through the farther door to the right.*)

MRS. ALVING. My poor boy—!

MANDERS. Yes, you can well say that. How far he's strayed! (MRS. ALVING *looks at him, saying nothing.* MANDERS *paces up and down.*) He called himself the prodigal son. Yes, it's sad—sad! (MRS. ALVING *continues to look at him.*) And what do you say to all this?

MRS. ALVING. I say Osvald was right in every word that he said.

MANDERS (*stops short*). Right? Right! With such principles?

MRS. ALVING. Here in my solitude I've come to the same conclusions, Mr. Manders—though I've never dared breathe a word of it. All well and good—my boy can speak for me now.

MANDERS. You're a woman much to be pitied, Mrs. Alving. Now I must talk seriously with you. It's no longer as your business adviser, nor as your and your husband's childhood friend, that I'm standing before you now—but as your priest, exactly as I once did at the most bewildered hour of your life.

MRS. ALVING. And what does my priest have to tell me?

MANDERS. First, let me call up some memories. It's a suitable moment. Tomorrow is the tenth anniversary of your husband's death; tomorrow the memorial will be unveiled in his honor; tomorrow I'll be speaking to all those assembled—but today I want to speak to you alone.

MRS. ALVING. All right, Mr. Manders—speak!

MANDERS. Do you recall how, after barely a year of marriage, you stood on the very edge of the abyss? That you left house and home—deserted your husband—yes, Mrs. Alving, deserted, deserted, and refused to go back to him, for all that he begged and implored you to?

MRS. ALVING. Have you forgotten how unutterably miserable I was that first year?

MANDERS. But this is the very essence of the rebellious spirit, to crave happiness here in this life. What right have we human beings to happiness? No, we must do our duty, Mrs. Alving! And your duty was to stand by that man you once had chosen, and to whom you were joined by a sacred bond.

MRS. ALVING. You know well enough what kind of life Alving led in those days—and the appetites he indulged.

MANDERS. I know quite well the rumors that circulated

about him; and to the extent that those rumors were true, I'd be the last to condone such conduct as his then. But a wife isn't required to be her husband's judge. It was your proper role to bear with a humble heart that cross that a higher will saw fit to lay upon you. But instead, you rebelliously cast away the cross, left the groping soul you should have aided, went off and risked your good name and reputation and—nearly ruined other reputations in the bargain.

MRS. ALVING. Other reputations? Just one, I think you mean.

MANDERS. It was exceedingly thoughtless of you to seek refuge with me.

MRS. ALVING. With our pastor? With an old, close friend?

MANDERS. Yes, for that very reason. You should thank Almighty God that I had the necessary inner strength—that I got you to drop your hysterical plans, and that it was given me to lead you back to the path of duty, and home to your lawful husband.

MRS. ALVING. Yes, Pastor Manders, that certainly was your doing.

MANDERS. I was only a humble instrument directed by a higher power. And that I bent your will to duty and obedience—hasn't that grown as a great blessing, from that time on, in all the days of your life? Didn't it go the way I foretold? Didn't Alving turn away from his depravities, as a man must, and take up a loving and blameless life with you right to the end? Didn't he become a benefactor of the community, and uplift you as well into his own sphere of activities to share them all? And how effectively you shared them, too—that I know, Mrs. Alving; I'll give you *that* credit. But now I come to the next great mistake in your life.

MRS. ALVING. What do you mean?

MANDERS. Just as you once evaded the duties of a wife, you've since evaded those of a mother.

MRS. ALVING. Ah——!

MANDERS. All your life you've been governed by an incorrigible spirit of willfulness. Instinctively you've been drawn to all that's undisciplined and lawless. You never can bear the least constraint. Everything that inconveniences your life you've carelessly and irresponsibly thrown aside—as if it were baggage you could leave behind if you chose. It didn't agree with you to be a wife any longer, so you left your husband. You found it troublesome to be a mother, so you put your child out with strangers.

MRS. ALVING. Yes, it's true—that's what I did.

MANDERS. And for that same reason you've become a stranger to him.

MRS. ALVING. No, no, I'm *not!*

MANDERS. You are. You had to be! And what sort of son have you gotten back? Think well, Mrs. Alving. You were terribly unfair to your husband—you admit as much by raising this monument to him. Now admit as well how unfair you've been to your son; there may still be time to lead him back from the paths of error. Change your ways—and save what's still left to be saved in him. For truly, Mrs. Alving—(*With an admonishing forefinger.*)—you're profoundly guilty as a mother! I've considered it my duty to tell you this.

(*Silence.*)

MRS. ALVING (*deliberately, controlling herself*). You've said your piece, Pastor; and tomorrow you'll be speaking publicly in my husband's memory. Tomorrow I'll make no speeches; but now I want to say something to you, exactly as you've just spoken to me.

MANDERS. Naturally, you want to make excuses for your conduct—

MRS. ALVING. No. Only to tell a few facts.

MANDERS. Well—?

MRS. ALVING. All that you've been saying here about me and my husband and our life together—after, as you put it, you led me back to the path of duty—all this is something you don't know the least thing about at firsthand. From that moment on, you, our dearest friend, never set foot in our house again.

MANDERS. But you and your husband moved out of town right after that.

MRS. ALVING. Yes, and you never came out here to see us while my husband was living. It was business that impelled you to visit me, since you were involved with the orphanage, too.

MANDERS (*in a low, hesitant voice*). Helene—if that's meant as a reproach, then I ask you to consider—

MRS. ALVING. The respect you owed to your calling, yes. And I, after all, was a runaway wife. One can never be careful enough with such reckless women.

MANDERS. Dear—Mrs. Alving, that is a flagrant exaggeration—

MRS. ALVING. Yes, yes, all right, then forget that. I simply wanted to say that when you make judgments on my married life, you're basing them on no more than common gossip.

MANDERS. Granted. Well, what of it?

MRS. ALVING. But now, Mr. Manders, now I'll tell you the truth! I swore to myself that one day you were going to hear it—you alone.

MANDERS. And what, then, is the truth?

MRS. ALVING. The truth is—that my husband died just as dissolute as he'd lived every day of his life.

MANDERS (*groping for a chair*). What did you say?

MRS. ALVING. After nineteen years of marriage, just as dissolute—in his desires, in any case—as he was before you married us.

MANDERS. But these mistakes of his youth, these confusions—dissipations, if you want—you call them a dissolute life?

MRS. ALVING. It's the phrase our doctor used.

MANDERS. I don't understand you.

MRS. ALVING. You don't have to.

MANDERS. It makes my head spin. You mean the whole of your marriage—all those many years together with your husband—were nothing more than a hollow mockery?

MRS. ALVING. Exactly. Now you know.

MANDERS. This—I find this so hard to believe. I can't understand it! It doesn't make sense! But how was it possible to—? How could it be kept a secret?

MRS. ALVING. That was the constant battle I had, day after day. When Osvald was born, I thought things might go better with Alving—but it didn't last long. So then I had to redouble my efforts, fight with a vengeance so no one would know what kind of a man my child's father was. And you know, of course, how charming Alving could be. No one thought anything but good of him. He was one of those people whose lives never detract from their reputations. But then, Mr. Manders—and this you also have to hear—then came the most sickening part of the whole business.

MANDERS. More sickening than what you've told me!

MRS. ALVING. I'd borne with him, even though I knew very well what was going on in secret away from this house. But when the infection came right within our own four walls—

MANDERS. You mean—here!

MRS. ALVING. Yes, here in our own house. In there— (*Pointing to the nearer door on the right.*)—in the dining room, that was where I first discovered it. I had something to get inside, and the door was ajar. I heard the maid come up from the garden with water for the plants—

MANDERS. And—?

MRS. ALVING. A moment later I heard Alving come in after her. I could hear him saying something to her. And then I heard— (*With an abrupt laugh.*) —oh, I can hear it still, as something both so shattering and so ludicrous— my own maid whispering: "Let go of me, Captain Alving! Leave me be!"

MANDERS. How terribly gross and thoughtless of him! Oh, but Mrs. Alving, it was no more than a moment's thoughtlessness, believe me.

MRS. ALVING. I soon learned what to believe. The captain had his way with the girl—and that affair had its after-effects, Pastor Manders.

MANDERS (*as if stunned into stone*). And all that in this house! In this house!

MRS. ALVING. I've endured a lot in this house to keep him home in the evenings—and nights, I had to become his drinking companion as he got sodden over his bottle, holed up in his room. There I had to sit alone with him, forcing myself through his jokes and toasts and all his maundering, abusive talk, and then fight him bare-handed to drag him into bed—

MANDERS (*shaken*). That you were able to bear all that!

MRS. ALVING. I had my little boy, and I bore it for him—at least until that final humiliation, when my own maid—! Then I swore to myself: that was the end! So I took charge of the house—complete charge—over him and everything else. Because now, you see, I had a weapon against him; he couldn't let out a word of protest. It was then I sent Osvald away. He was going on seven and starting to notice things and ask questions, the way children do. All that was too much for me, Manders. I thought the child would be poisoned just breathing this polluted air. That's why I sent him away. And now you can understand, too, why he never set foot in this house as long as his father lived. No one will know what that cost me.

MANDERS. What a trial your life has been!

MRS. ALVING. I could never have gotten through it if it hadn't been for my work. And I *have* worked, I can tell you. All the additions to the property, all the improvements and technical innovations that Alving got fame and credit for—do you think those were *his* doing? *He*, sprawled all day on the sofa, reading old government journals! No, I can tell you as well; it was *I* who got him moving whenever he had his lucid moments; and it was I who had to pull the whole load when he fell back in his old wild ways or collapsed in groveling misery.

MANDERS. And for this man, you're raising a monument!

MRS. ALVING. There's the power of a bad conscience.

MANDERS. A bad—? What do you mean?

MRS. ALVING. It always seemed inevitable to me that the truth would have to come out someday and be believed. So the orphanage was meant to spike all the rumors and dispel the doubts.

MANDERS. Well, you've certainly accomplished that, Mrs. Alving.

MRS. ALVING. And I had still another reason. I didn't want Osvald, my own son, to inherit the least little thing from his father.

MANDERS. Then it's with Alving's money that—?

MRS. ALVING. Yes. The sums I've contributed year after year to the orphanage add up to just the amount—I've figured it out exactly—just the amount that made Lieutenant Alving such a good catch at the time.

MANDERS. Then, if I understand you—

MRS. ALVING. It was my selling price. I don't want that money passing into Osvald's hands. Everything my son inherits will come from me, and no one else.

(OSVALD *enters by the farther door to the right. He has left his hat and overcoat outside.*)

MRS. ALVING (*moving toward him*). You back again, dear?

OSVALD. Yes. What can anyone do outside in this interminable rain? But I hear lunch is ready. That's good news!

(REGINA *enters from the dining room with a package.*)

REGINA. A parcel just came for you, ma'am. (*Handing it to her.*)

MRS. ALVING (*with a quick look at* MANDERS). The choir music for tomorrow, most likely.

MANDERS. Hm—

REGINA. And lunch is served.

MRS. ALVING. Good. We'll be along in a moment; I just want to— (*Starts opening the package.*)

REGINA (*to* OSVALD). Will Mr. Alving have red wine, or white?

OSVALD. Both, Miss Engstrand.

REGINA. *Bien.* Very good, Mr. Alving. (*She goes into the dining room.*)

OSVALD. I better help her uncork the bottles— (*He*

*follows her into the dining room, the door swinging half
shut behind him.)*

MRS. ALVING (*who has unwrapped the package*). Yes,
quite so—it's the choir music, Mr. Manders.

MANDERS (*with folded hands*). How I'll ever be able to
give my speech tomorrow with any conviction—!

MRS. ALVING. Oh, you'll manage all right.

MANDERS (*softly, so as not to be heard in the dining
room*). Yes, we musn't stir up any scandal.

MRS. ALVING (*in a quiet, firm voice*). No. And then this
long, horrible farce will be over. After tomorrow, it will
really seem as if the dead had never lived in this house.
There'll be no one else here but my son and me.

(*From the dining room comes the sound of a chair
knocked over, along with* REGINA's *voice in a sharp whisper.*)

REGINA. Osvald! Are you crazy? Let me go!

MRS. ALVING (*starting in terror*). Ah—!

(*She stares distractedly at the half-open door.* OSVALD *is
heard to cough within and start humming. A bottle is
uncorked.*)

MANDERS (*shaken*). But what happened, Mrs. Alving?
What was that?

MRS. ALVING (*hoarsely*). Ghosts. Those two from the
greenhouse—have come back.

MANDERS. You mean—! Regina—? Is *she*—?

MRS. ALVING. Yes. Come. Not a word—!

(*She grips* PASTOR MANDER's *arm and moves falteringly
toward the dining room.*)

∼❬ ACT TWO ❭∼

The same room. A thick mist still veils the landscape.
MANDERS *and* MRS. ALVING *enter from the dining room.*

MRS. ALVING. Why, you're very welcome, Mr. Manders. (*Speaking into the dining room.*) Aren't you joining us, Osvald?

OSVALD (*from within*). No, thanks; I think I'll go out for a while.

MRS. ALVING. Yes, do that. It's clearing a little now. (*She shuts the dining room door, goes over to the hall door and calls.*) Regina!

REGINA (*from without*). Yes, ma'am.

MRS. ALVING. Go down to the laundry room and help out with the decorations.

REGINA. Very good, ma'am.

(MRS. ALVING *makes certain* REGINA *has gone, then shuts the door.*)

MANDERS. You're sure he can't hear us in there?

MRS. ALVING. Not with the door closed. Anyway, he's going out soon.

MANDERS. I'm still in a daze. I can't understand how I ever managed to devour one morsel of that heavenly meal.

MRS. ALVING (*pacing up and down, suppressing her anxiety*). Nor I, either. But what's to be done?

71

MANDERS. Yes, what's to be done? Believe me, I just don't know; I'm so utterly inexperienced in such matters.

MRS. ALVING. I'm convinced nothing serious has happened so far.

MANDERS. God forbid! But it's still an unsavory business.

MRS. ALVING. It's just a foolish fancy of Osvald's, you can be sure of that.

MANDERS. Well, as I said, I'm not really up on these things; but it definitely seems to me—

MRS. ALVING. She'll have to get out of this house. Immediately. That's clear as day—

MANDERS. Yes, that's obvious.

MRS. ALVING. But where? We can't simply—

MANDERS. Where? Home to her father, of course.

MRS. ALVING. To whom, did you say?

MANDERS. To her—ah, but of course, Engstrand isn't—! Good Lord, Mrs. Alving, how is this possible? You must be mistaken, really.

MRS. ALVING. Unfortunately, I'm not the least bit mistaken. Joanna had to confess everything to me—and Alving couldn't deny it. There was nothing else to do, then, but have the whole thing hushed up.

MANDERS. Yes, that was essential.

MRS. ALVING. The girl was turned out at once and given a fairly sizable amount to keep quiet. She managed the rest for herself when she got back to town. She revived an old friendship with Engstrand—probably dropped a few hints, I would guess, about all the money she had—and spun him some tale of a foreigner on a yacht berthed here for the summer. So she and Engstrand were married straight off—well, you married them yourself.

MANDERS. But I don't see how—? I distinctly remember when Engstrand came to arrange the wedding. He was so woefully penitent, accusing himself so bitterly of the casual ways he and his fiancée had allowed themselves.

MRS. ALVING. Well, naturally he had to take the blame himself.

MANDERS. But the hypocrisy of the man! And with *me!* I absolutely never would have believed that of Jacob Engstrand. Well, I'll have to be very severe with him; he better be ready for that. And the immorality of such a marriage—all for money! How much did the girl get?

MRS. ALVING. Three hundred dollars.

MANDERS. Yes, can you imagine—to go and get married to a fallen woman for a paltry three hundred dollars!

MRS. ALVING. Then what's your opinion of me, who let herself be married to a fallen man?

MANDERS. God of mercy, what are you saying? A fallen man!

MRS. ALVING. Do you think my husband was any better when I went with him to the altar than Joanna when Engstrand married her?

MANDERS. But—there's a world of difference between you and her—

MRS. ALVING. Much less than a world, I think. There was a considerable difference in price—a paltry three hundred dollars as against a whole fortune.

MANDERS. But there's just no comparison here. After all, you'd listened to the counsels of your own heart, and those of your family.

MRS. ALVING (*not looking at him*). I thought you understood where I'd lost what you call my heart at the time.

MANDERS (*withdrawn*). If I'd understood any such thing, I would never have become a regular visitor in your husband's house.

MRS. ALVING. Anyway, one thing is clear: I never really listened to myself.

MANDERS. Well, to your nearest of kin then, as it's ordained you should: your mother and your two aunts.

MRS. ALVING. Yes, how true. The three of them wrote up my bill of sale. Oh, it's amazing how neatly they figured it out, that it would be stark madness to turn down an offer like that. If Mother could come back and see me now, where all those splendors got me.

MANDERS. No one's responsible for the outcome. At least there's this to be said: your marriage was carried through with every respect for law and order.

MRS. ALVING (*at the window*). Yes, always law and order! I often think they're the root of all our miseries on earth.

MANDERS. Mrs. Alving, that's a sinful thought.

MRS. ALVING. Yes, perhaps it is. But I can't stand it any longer, with all these webs of obligation. I can't stand it! I've got to work my way out to freedom.

MANDERS. What do you mean by that?

MRS. ALVING (*drumming on the windowpane*). I never should have covered up Alving's life. It was all I dared do then—not only for Osvald, but to spare myself. What a coward I was!

MANDERS. Coward?

MRS. ALVING. If people had known anything of what went on, they would have said: "Poor man, it's no wonder he strays at times; his wife ran away, you know."

MANDERS. And they could say that with some right, too.

MRS. ALVING (*looking straight at him*). If I were all I should have been, I would have taken Osvald aside and said: "Listen, my boy, your father was a degenerate human being—"

MANDERS. Good Lord—!

MRS. ALVING. Then I ought to have told him everything—word for word as I've told it to you.

MANDERS. I find you almost frightening, Mrs. Alving.

MRS. ALVING. I'm aware of that. Yes, I'm quite aware! I frighten myself by the thought. (*Coming away from the window.*) That's the coward I am.

MANDERS. And you call it cowardice to do your bounden duty? Have you forgotten that a child should love and honor his father and mother?

MRS. ALVING. Oh, don't let's talk abstractions! Why don't we ask, should Osvald love and honor Captain Alving?

MANDERS. Isn't there something that tells you, as a mother, not to destroy your son's ideals?

MRS. ALVING. Yes, but what of the truth—?

MANDERS. Yes, but what of his ideals—?

MRS. ALVING. Oh—ideals, ideals! If I only weren't the coward I am!

MANDERS. Don't demolish ideals, Mrs. Alving—that can have cruel repercussions. And especially now, with Osvald. He hasn't too many ideals, sad to say—but as far as I can make out, his father is some sort of ideal to him.

MRS. ALVING. Yes, you're right about that.

MANDERS. And the impressions he has you've instilled and nourished yourself, through your letters.

MRS. ALVING. Yes, I felt it was my duty and obligation—so year after year, I've gone on lying to my own child. Oh, what a coward—what a coward I've been!

MANDERS. You've built up a beautiful image in your son's imagination—and that's something you mustn't take lightly.

MRS. ALVING. Hm—who knows how good that's been, after all. But, in any case, I'm not going to have any trifling with Regina. He's not going to get that poor girl in trouble.

MANDERS. Good God, that would be dreadful!

MRS. ALVING. If I knew he was serious about it, and that it would make him happy—

MANDERS. Yes? Then what?

MRS. ALVING. But it wouldn't work out. Regina just isn't the type.

MANDERS. How so? What do you mean?

MRS. ALVING. If I weren't such a wretched coward, then I'd say to him: "Marry her, or live any way you like—but just be honest together."

MANDERS. Heavens above—! A legal marriage, no less! That would be barbarous—! It's unheard of—!

MRS. ALVING. Unheard of, you say? Word of honor, Pastor Manders—haven't you heard that, out here in the country, there are numbers of married couples who are just as closely related?

MANDERS. I really don't understand you.

MRS. ALVING. Oh yes you do, very well.

MANDERS. Well, you mean cases where possibly they—? Yes, unfortunately family life isn't always as pure as it ought to be, that's true. But what you're referring to is hardly ever known—at least, not conclusively. But here, instead—you, the mother, are willing to let your own—!

MRS. ALVING. But I'm not willing. I don't want to encourage it for anything in the world—that's just what I was saying.

MANDERS. No, because you're a coward, as you put it. But if you weren't a coward—! Almighty God—what a monstrous union!

MRS. ALVING. Well, as far as that goes, it's been rumored that we're all descended from a similar union. And who was it who thought up that arrangement, Pastor?

MANDERS. I will not discuss such questions with you, Mrs. Alving—because you're not in the proper state of mind. But, that you can dare call it cowardice on your part—!

MRS. ALVING. You have to understand what I mean by that. I'm anxious and fearful because of the ghosts that haunt me, that I can't get rid of.

MANDERS. Because of—what did you say?

MRS. ALVING. Ghosts. When I heard Regina and Osvald in there, it was as if I was seeing ghosts. But I almost believe we *are* ghosts, all of us, Pastor. It's not only what we inherit from our fathers and mothers that keeps on returning in us. It's all kinds of old dead doctrines and opinions and beliefs, that sort of thing. They aren't alive in us; but they hang on all the same, and we can't get rid of them. I just have to pick up a newspaper, and it's as if I could see the ghosts slipping between the lines. They must be haunting our whole country, ghosts everywhere—so many and thick, they're like grains of sand. And there we are, the lot of us, so miserably afraid of the light.

MANDERS. Ah! So this is the outgrowth of all your

reading. Fine fruit, I must say! Oh, these disgusting, insidious freethinking books!

MRS. ALVING. My dear Mr. Manders, you're wrong. It was you yourself who set me to thinking—and for that I'll always be grateful.

MANDERS. *I?*

MRS. ALVING. Yes, when you made me give in to what you called duty and obligation; when you praised as right and proper what I rebelled against heart and soul as something loathsome—that's when I started going over your teachings, seam by seam. I just wanted to pull out a single thread; but after I'd worked it loose, the whole design fell apart. And then I realized it was only basted.

MANDERS (*quietly, with feeling*). Is that all that was won by the hardest battle of my life?

MRS. ALVING. You mean your most shameful defeat.

MANDERS. It was the greatest victory I've known, Helene—victory over myself.

MRS. ALVING. It was a crime against us both.

MANDERS. That I entreated you by saying, "Woman, go home to your lawful husband," when you came to me distracted, crying, "Here I am, take me!" Was that a crime?

MRS. ALVING. Yes, I think so.

MANDERS. We two don't understand each other.

MRS. ALVING. Not anymore, at least.

MANDERS. Never—never, in even my most secret thoughts, have I seen you as anything but another man's wife.

MRS. ALVING. You believe that?

MANDERS. Helene—!

MRS. ALVING. One forgets so easily.

MANDERS. I don't. I'm the same as I always was.

MRS. ALVING (*shifting her tone abruptly*). Yes, yes, well—let's stop talking about the old days. Now you're up to your ears in boards and committees; and I go around here struggling with ghosts, inside me and outside both.

MANDERS. At least I can help you manage the outer ones. After all the disturbing things I've heard from you today, my conscience won't suffer a defenseless young girl to remain in this house.

MRS. ALVING. It would be best, don't you think, if we could see her established? I mean, decently married.

MANDERS. Undoubtedly. I'd say it's desirable for her in every respect. Regina's already at an age when—of course, I'm really no judge of these things, but—

MRS. ALVING. Regina matured quite early.

MANDERS. Yes, didn't she, though? It's my impression she was unusually well developed physically when I was preparing her for confirmation. But temporarily, in all events, she ought to go home, under her father's supervision—ah, but of course, Engstrand isn't—to think that he—that *he* could conceal the truth from me like that!

(*There is a knock at the hall door.*)

MRS. ALVING. Who can that be? Come in!

(ENGSTRAND, *in his Sunday clothes, appears in the doorway.*)

ENGSTRAND. I beg your pardon most humbly, but—

MANDERS. Aha! Hm—

MRS. ALVING. Oh, it's you, Engstrand.

ENGSTRAND. There were none of the maids about, so I made myself so bold as to give a knock.

MRS. ALVING. Well, all right, come in. You want to talk to me about something?

ENGSTRAND (*coming in*). No, thanks all the same. It was the pastor, actually, I wanted to have a little word with.

MANDERS (*walking up and down*). Oh, yes? You want to talk to me? Is that it?

ENGSTRAND. Yes, I'd be grateful no end—

MANDERS (*stopping in front of him*). Well, may I ask what this is about?

ENGSTRAND. See, it's like this, Pastor; we've gotten paid off down there now—with all thanks to you, ma'am—and now we've finished everything up. And so I was thinking how nice and fitting it'd be if all us honest craftsmen who've been working together all this time—I was thinking, we ought to round things off with a little prayer meeting this evening.

MANDERS. A prayer meeting? Down at the orphanage?

ENGSTRAND. Yes. But of course if the pastor's not agreeable, then—

MANDERS. Oh, it's a splendid thought, but—hm—

ENGSTRAND. I've been holding a few evening prayers down there myself now and then—

MRS. ALVING. You have?

ENGSTRAND. Yes, now and then. Just a little meditation, so to speak. But then I'm a common, ordinary man, with no special gifts, God help me—and so I was thinking, since the pastor was out here—

MANDERS. Now look, Engstrand, first I have to ask you a question. Are you in a proper frame of mind for this kind of meeting? Do you feel your conscience is free and clear?

ENGSTRAND. Oh, Lord help us, Pastor, there's no point going on talking about my conscience.

MANDERS. Ah, but it's exactly what we *are* going to talk about. Well, what's your answer?

ENGSTRAND. My conscience? Yes, that can be pretty nasty at times, it can.

MANDERS. Well, at least you're owning up to it. Now will you tell me, without any subterfuge—just what is your relationship to Regina?

MRS. ALVING (*quickly*). Mr. Manders!

MANDERS (*calming her*). If you'll leave it to me—

ENGSTRAND. To Regina! Jeez, you gave me a turn there! (*Looking at* MRS. ALVING.) There's nothing wrong with Regina, is there?

MANDERS. We hope not. What I mean is, just exactly how are you related to her? You pass for her father, don't you? Well?

ENGSTRAND (*vaguely*). Why—hm—you know, Pastor, this business with me and poor Joanna.

MANDERS. Stop bending the truth. Your late wife told Mrs. Alving everything before she left her service.

ENGSTRAND. But it's supposed to—! She did that, really?

MANDERS. So your secret's out, Engstrand.

ENGSTRAND. And after she swore on a stack of Bibles—!

MANDERS. She swore—!

ENGSTRAND. I mean, she gave me her word. But with such sincerity.

MANDERS. And all these years you've hidden the truth from me. From *me*, who put my absolute trust in you.

ENGSTRAND. Yes, I'm afraid that's just what I've done.

MANDERS. Have I deserved this from you, Engstrand? Haven't I always been ready to help you out in every way, so far as I possibly could? Answer! Haven't I?

ENGSTRAND. There's plenty of times things would've looked pretty bad for me, if it wasn't for Pastor Manders.

MANDERS. And this is the way you pay me back. Get me to make false entries in the parish register, and for years after withhold information you owed as a matter of respect both to me and the plain truth. Your conduct has been unpardonable, Engstrand: and from now on we're through with each other.

ENGSTRAND (*with a sigh*). Well, that's it, I guess.

MANDERS. Yes. Because how can you ever justify yourself?

ENGSTRAND. But how could she go around shaming herself the more by talking about it? If you could just imagine, Pastor, yourself in the same trouble as poor Joanna—

MANDERS. I!

ENGSTRAND. Jeez now, I don't mean the very same. But I mean, supposing you had something to be ashamed of in the eyes of the world, as they say. We menfolk oughtn't to judge a poor woman too hard, Pastor.

MANDERS. But that's not what I'm doing. It's you that I blame.

ENGSTRAND. If I might ask your Reverence one tiny little question—?

MANDERS. Yes, go ahead.

ENGSTRAND. Isn't it right and proper of a man that he raises up the fallen?

MANDERS. Why, of course.

ENGSTRAND. And isn't a man obliged to keep his word of honor?

MANDERS. Certainly he is, but—

ENGSTRAND. At the time Joanna had her downfall at the hands of that Englishman—or maybe it was an American, or a Russian, or whatever—well, it was then she came back to town. Poor thing, she'd turned me down once or twice already; she only had eyes for the handsome ones, see—and I had this crook in my leg. Yes, you remember, Pastor, how I once took it on myself to go into a dance hall where common seamen were rioting in drink and dissipation, like they say. And when I tried to arouse them to seek out a better life—

MRS. ALVING (*over by the window*). Hm—

MANDERS. Yes, I know, Engstrand; those ruffians threw you downstairs. You've told me that before. Your disability does you great credit.

ENGSTRAND. I'm not priding myself on it, Pastor. But what I wanted to say was that then she came and confessed the whole thing to me, streaming down tears and gnashing her teeth. And I have to say, Pastor, it just about ripped the heart out of me to listen.

MANDERS. All of *that*, Engstrand. Well! Then what?

ENGSTRAND. Yes, so I said to her: that American, he's beating over the seas of the world, he is. And you, Joanna, I said—you've had your downfall, and you're a sinful, fallen creature. But Jacob Engstrand, I said, he stands on two stout legs—yes, I meant it like a manner of speaking, Pastor.

MANDERS. Yes, I quite understand. Go on.

ENGSTRAND. Well, so that's how I raised her up and gave her an honorable marriage, so no one'd ever find out about her wild carrying-on with foreigners.

MANDERS. That was all quite commendable of you. What I cannot approve is that you could bring yourself to accept money—

ENGSTRAND. Money? I? Not a penny.

MANDERS (*with an inquiring glance at* MRS. ALVING). But—?

ENGSTRAND. Oh, yes—just a minute; now I remember. Joanna did have a little odd change, all right—but I wanted nothing of *that*. Faugh! I said: Mammon, that's the wages of sin, it is. We'll take that greasy gold—or banknotes, whatever it was—and heave it back into the American's face, I said. But he was off and gone over the rolling sea, Pastor.

MANDERS. Was that it, my dear Engstrand?

ENGSTRAND. That's right. So I and Joanna agreed that the money ought to be put toward the child's bringing up, and that's where it went; and I can give a true reckoning of every penny.

MANDERS. But that changes things substantially.

ENGSTRAND. That's the way it worked out, Pastor. And I'll be bold enough to say I've been a real father to Regina, as far as it lay in my power—for I have to admit, I'm only a poor, frail mortal.

MANDERS. There, there, Engstrand—

ENGSTRAND. But I will say that I brought up the child and looked after my poor, dear Joanna and made them a home, like the gospel says. But it never would have occurred to me to go up to Pastor Manders, priding myself and making much out of a good deed done in this world. No, when that sort of thing happens to Jacob Engstrand, he keeps it to himself, he does. Though it happens none too often, sorry to say. No, when I come to see Pastor Manders, then it's all I can do just to talk out my sins and errors. Because to say what I said before—my conscience does turn pretty nasty at times.

MANDERS. Give me your hand, Jacob Engstrand.

ENGSTRAND. Oh, Jeez, Pastor—

MANDERS. No fuss now. (*Grasping his hand.*) There!

ENGSTRAND. And if I can dare to beg your pardon, Pastor, most humbly—

MANDERS. You? Quite the contrary, I'm the one who should beg your pardon—

ENGSTRAND. Oh, no, no!

MANDERS. Yes, definitely. And I do, with all my heart. Forgive me that I could so misjudge you. If only I could give you some sign of my sincere regret, and the goodwill I have toward you—

ENGSTRAND. You'd like that, Pastor?

MANDERS. It would please me no end.

ENGSTRAND. Because there's a real good opportunity for that right now. With the bit of honest coin I've put aside from my work out here, I was thinking of founding a kind of seaman's home back in town.

MRS. ALVING. *You?*

ENGSTRAND. Yes, it'd be sort of a refuge for the orphans of the sea, so to speak. Temptations are so manifold for a sailor when he comes wandering ashore. But in this house of mine he could live like under a father's protection, that was my thought.

MANDERS. What do you say to that, Mrs. Alving?

ENGSTRAND. It's not much I have to begin with, Lord knows; but if I could just take hold of a helping hand—

MANDERS. Yes, yes, we have to consider this further. Your project interests me enormously. But now, go on down and get things ready—and light some candles, to give it a ceremonial touch. And then we'll have our devotional hour together, my dear Engstrand, for now I'm sure you're in the right frame of mind.

ENGSTRAND. I really do think so, yes. So good-bye, Mrs. Alving, and thanks for everything. And take good care of Regina for me. (*Brushes a tear from his eye.*) Poor Joanna's child—um, isn't it amazing—but it's just as if that girl had grown a part of my very heart. Yes, sir, and that's a fact. (*He bows and goes out.*)

MANDERS. Well, what do you think of the man now, Mrs. Alving? That's quite a different picture of things we got from him.

MRS. ALVING. Yes, quite so, indeed.

MANDERS. There you see how scrupulously careful one has to be about judging one's fellowman. But it's also a wonderful joy to discover one's made a mistake. Well, what do you say?

MRS. ALVING. I say you are and you always will be a big baby, Manders.

MANDERS. I?

MRS. ALVING (placing both hands on his shoulders). And I say I could easily wrap you up in a great, big hug.

MANDERS (pulling back quickly). Oh, bless you, no! What an impulse!

MRS. ALVING (with a smile). Oh, don't be afraid of me.

MANDERS (by the table). You sometimes have the most outrageous way of expressing yourself. Now I first want to collect these documents together and put them in my bag. (Doing so.) There now. And so good-bye for the moment. Keep your eye on Osvald when he comes back. I'll be looking in on you later.

(He takes his hat and goes out by the hall door. MRS. ALVING sighs, gazes a moment out of the window, straightens the room up a bit and starts into the dining room, then stops with a stifled cry in the doorway.)

MRS. ALVING. Osvald! Are you still at the table?

OSVALD (from the dining room). I'm just finishing my cigar.

MRS. ALVING. I thought you'd gone for a walk.

OSVALD. In such weather?

(The chink of a glass and decanter. MRS. ALVING leaves the door open and settles down with her knitting on the sofa by the window.)

OSVALD. Wasn't that Pastor Manders who left just now?

MRS. ALVING. Yes, he went down to the orphanage.

OSVALD. Hm.

(*Again, the chink of glass and decanter.*)

MRS. ALVING (*with an anxious glance*). Osvald dear, you ought to go easy with the liqueur. It's strong.

OSVALD. It keeps the dampness out.

MRS. ALVING. Wouldn't you rather come in here with me?

OSVALD. But I can't smoke in there.

MRS. ALVING. Now you know a cigar is all right.

OSVALD. Oh, well, then I'll come in. Just a tiny drop more—ah, there. (*He enters, smoking his cigar, and shuts the door after him. Short silence.*) Where'd the pastor go?

MRS. ALVING. I told you, he went down to the orphanage.

OSVALD. Oh yes, that's right.

MRS. ALVING. You shouldn't go on sitting at the table so long, Osvald.

OSVALD (*holding his cigar behind his back*). But I think it's so cozy, Mother. (*Patting and fondling her.*) Imagine—what it is for me, coming home, to sit at my mother's own table, in my mother's room, and enjoy her delectable meals.

MRS. ALVING. My dear, dear boy!

OSVALD (*somewhat impatiently, walking about and smoking*). And what else am I going to do here? I can't accomplish anything—

MRS. ALVING. Can't you?

OSVALD. In all this murk? Not a glimmer of sunlight the whole day long? (*Pacing about.*) Oh, this—! This not being able to work—!

MRS. ALVING. Perhaps it wasn't such a good idea for you to come home.

OSVALD. No, Mother, that was essential.

MRS. ALVING. Because I'd ten times rather give up the joy of having you home with me, if it meant that you—

OSVALD (*stops by the table*). Now tell me, Mother—is it really such a great joy for you to have me home?

MRS. ALVING. What a question to ask!

OSVALD (*crumpling a newspaper*). I should have thought it hardly mattered to you whether I was here or not.

MRS. ALVING. You have the heart to say that to your mother, Osvald?

OSVALD. But you lived without me very well before.

MRS. ALVING. Yes, I've lived without you—that's true.

(*Silence. The twilight gradually deepens.* OSVALD *paces the floor, back and forth. He has set his cigar down.*)

OSVALD (*stops by* MRS. ALVING). Do you mind if I sit beside you on the sofa?

MRS. ALVING (*making room for him*). Please sit down, dear.

OSVALD (*sitting*). There's something I have to tell you, Mother.

MRS. ALVING (*nervously*). What?

OSVALD (*staring ahead into space*). Because I can't go on bearing it any longer.

MRS. ALVING. Bearing what? What is it?

OSVALD (*as before*). I couldn't bring myself to write you about it; and ever since I came home—

MRS. ALVING (*gripping his arm*). But, Osvald, what *is* it?

OSVALD. All yesterday and today I've been trying to drive these thoughts away—and free myself. But it doesn't work.

MRS. ALVING (*rising*). You've got to speak out, Osvald!

OSVALD (*drawing her down on the sofa again*). Sit still, and I'll try to tell you—I've been complaining so about my tiredness after the trip here—

MRS. ALVING. Yes? Well?

OSVALD. But that isn't what's wrong with me, not any ordinary tiredness—

MRS. ALVING (*starts to rise*). Osvald, you're not ill!

OSVALD (*draws her down again*). Sit still, Mother. Just

be calm about it. I'm not exactly ill—at least not ill in the ordinary sense. (*Puts his hands to his head.*) Mother, it's my mind that's broken down—out of control—I'll never be able to work again! (*Hands over his face, he throws himself down in her lap and bursts into deep sobs.*)

MRS. ALVING (*pale and trembling*). Osvald! Look at me! No, no, it isn't true.

OSVALD (*looks up despairingly*). Never able to work again! Never—never! It's like a living death! Mother, can you imagine anything as horrible?

MRS. ALVING. My poor boy! How did this awful thing happen to you?

OSVALD (*sitting up again*). That's just what I don't understand. I can't figure it out. I've never lived a wild life—not in any respect. You have to believe me, Mother— that's something I've never done!

MRS. ALVING. I believe you, Osvald.

OSVALD. And yet it's come on me—this horrible thing!

MRS. ALVING. Oh, but dearest, it's going to be all right. It's no more than nervous exhaustion, believe me.

OSVALD (*heavily*). That's what I thought at first—but it's not so.

MRS. ALVING. Tell me everything, right from the start.

OSVALD. Yes, I want to.

MRS. ALVING. When did you first notice anything?

OSVALD. It was just after my last visit home, and I'd returned to Paris. I began having such tremendous pains in my head—mostly toward the back, it seemed. It felt like a tight iron band squeezing me from my neck up—

MRS. ALVING. Go on.

OSVALD. At first I thought they were nothing more than the old, familiar headaches I've been bothered by ever since I was little.

MRS. ALVING. Yes, yes—

OSVALD. But I soon found out: that wasn't it. I couldn't work any longer. I wanted to start a new large painting, but it was as if all my talents had flown, and all my strength was paralyzed; I couldn't focus any of my thoughts; everything swam—around and around. Oh, it was a terrifying state to be in! Finally I sent for a doctor—and through him I discovered the truth.

MRS. ALVING. What do you mean?

OSVALD. He was one of the foremost doctors down there. He had me describe exactly what I was feeling; and then he began asking me a whole lot of questions that didn't seem to bear at all. I couldn't grasp what he was after—

MRS. ALVING. So—?

OSVALD. At last he said: Right from your birth, your whole system has been more or less worm-eaten. The actual expression he used was *vermoulu*.

MRS. ALVING (*anxiously*). What did he mean by that?

OSVALD. I didn't understand either, so I asked him to be more specific. And then that old cynic said— (*Clenching his fist.*) Oh—!

MRS. ALVING. What—?

OSVALD. He said: The sins of the fathers are visited upon the children.

MRS. ALVING (*slowly stands up*). The sins of the fathers—!

OSVALD. I almost hit him in the face.

MRS. ALVING (*moving across the room*). The sins of the fathers—

OSVALD (*smiles sadly*). Yes, can you imagine? Of course I assured him that was absolutely out of the question. But do you think he gave way? No, he had his mind made up; and it was only when I brought out your letters and translated all the parts to him that dealt with Father—

MRS. ALVING. What then—?

OSVALD. Well, then naturally he had to admit he'd been on the wrong track; and that's when I learned the truth—

the incredible truth: that this beautiful, soul-stirring life with my young artist friends was something I should never have entered. It was too much for my strength. So— everything's my own fault.

MRS. ALVING. Osvald, no! You mustn't believe that!

OSVALD. There was no other way to explain it, he said. *That's* the worst of it. The whole of my life ruined beyond repair—all because of my own carelessness. So much that I wanted to do in this world—I don't dare think of it anymore—I'm not *able* to think of it. Oh, if I only could live my life over—and wipe out what I've done!

(*He throws himself face down on the sofa.* MRS. ALVING *wrings her hands and walks silently back and forth, locked in inner struggle. After a moment,* OSVALD *looks up, propping himself on his elbows.*)

OSVALD. If it had only *been* something inherited— something that wasn't my fault. But this! In a shameful, mindless, trivial way, to have thrown away health, happiness, a world of possibility—my future, my life—!

MRS. ALVING. No, no, my own dearest—it can't be! (*Bending over him.*) Things aren't as desperate as you think.

OSVALD. Oh, you don't know— (*Leaps to his feet.*) And then all the pain that I'm causing you, Mother! How often I could almost hope and wish you wouldn't care for me so much.

MRS. ALVING. Oh, Osvald, my only boy! You're all I have in this world, and all I care to have.

OSVALD (*grasps both her hands and kisses them*). Yes, yes, now I see. When I'm home I see it so well. And it's part of what weighs on me— Anyway, now you know the whole story. And let's not talk about it anymore today. I can't bear thinking about it very long. (*Walking about the room.*) Give me something to drink, Mother!

MRS. ALVING. To drink? What do you want to drink now?

OSVALD. Oh, anything. You must have some cold punch in the house.

MRS. ALVING. Oh, but Osvald dear—!

OSVALD. Don't refuse me that, Mother. Be good now! I've got to have something to drown all these gnawing thoughts. (*Goes into the greenhouse.*) And how—how dark it is here!

(MRS. ALVING *goes over to the bell-pull, right, and rings.*)

And this interminable rain. Week after week it can go on; whole months at a time. In all my visits home, I never once remember seeing the sun shine.

MRS. ALVING. Osvald—you're thinking of leaving me!

OSVALD. Hm— (*Sighs deeply.*) I'm not thinking of anything. I can't think of anything! (*In a low tone.*) I've given that up.

REGINA (*entering from the dining room*). You rang, ma'am?

MRS. ALVING. Yes, bring the lamp in.

REGINA. Right away, ma'am. It's already lit. (*Goes out.*)

MRS. ALVING (*going over to* OSVALD). Osvald, don't keep anything from me.

OSVALD. I won't, Mother. (*Moves to the table.*) I've told you a lot, I think.

(REGINA *comes in with the lamp and sets it on the table.*)

MRS. ALVING. Yes, and Regina, you might bring us a half bottle of champagne.

REGINA. Yes, ma'am. (*Goes out again.*)

OSVALD (*clasping* MRS. ALVING *about the neck*). That's the way it should be. I knew you wouldn't let your boy go thirsty.

MRS. ALVING. Ah, my poor dear Osvald—how could I refuse you anything now?

OSVALD (*buoyantly*). Is that true, Mother? You mean it?

MRS. ALVING. Mean what—?

OSVALD. That you won't refuse me *anything*?

MRS. ALVING. But Osvald dear—

OSVALD. Shh!

(REGINA *returns with a half bottle of champagne and two glasses on a tray, which she sets down on the table.*)

REGINA. Should I open it—?

OSVALD. No, thanks, I'll do it.

(REGINA *goes out again.*)

MRS. ALVING (*seating herself at the table*). What did you mean—that I shouldn't refuse you?

OSVALD (*busy opening the bottle*). First a glass—maybe two.

(*The cork pops; he fills one glass and is about to pour the second.*)

MRS. ALVING (*holds her hand over it*). Thanks—not for me.

OSVALD. Well, for me then. (*He drains the glass, refills it, drains it again, then sits down at the table.*)

MRS. ALVING (*expectantly*). Well?

OSVALD (*not looking at her*). Say, tell me—I thought you and Mr. Manders looked so strange—hm, so quiet during lunch.

MRS. ALVING. You noticed that?

OSVALD. Yes. Hm—(*A short silence.*) Tell me, what do you think of Regina?

MRS. ALVING. What do I think?

OSVALD. Yes, isn't she splendid?

MRS. ALVING. Osvald dear, you don't know her as well as I do—

OSVALD. So—?

MRS. ALVING. It's too bad Regina lived at home for so long. I should have taken her in earlier.

OSVALD. Yes, but she's magnificent to look at, isn't she, Mother?

MRS. ALVING. Regina has a good many serious flaws—

OSVALD. Oh, but what does that matter? (*He drinks again.*)

MRS. ALVING. Even so, I'm fond of her; and I'm responsible for her. I wouldn't for the world want anything to hurt her.

OSVALD (*springing to his feet*). Mother, Regina's my only hope!

MRS. ALVING (*rising*). What do you mean by that?

OSVALD. I can't bear this anguish all by myself.

MRS. ALVING. But you have your mother to help you bear it, don't you?

OSVALD. Yes, I thought so—and that's why I came home to you. But it won't work that way. I can see; it won't work. I can't make a life out here.

MRS. ALVING. Osvald!

OSVALD. I have to live differently, Mother. So I will have to leave you. I don't want you to see all this.

MRS. ALVING. Oh, my miserable child! But, Osvald, when you're sick as you are—

OSVALD. If it were only the illness, I'd stay with you, Mother—I would. For you're my best friend in this world.

MRS. ALVING. Yes, it's true; I am, aren't I?

OSVALD (*striding restlessly about*). But it's all the torment, agony, remorse—and the great deathly fear. Oh—this hideous fear!

MRS. ALVING (*following him*). Fear? What fear? What do you mean?

OSVALD. Oh, don't ask me anymore about it. I don't know. I can't describe it to you.

(MRS. ALVING *crosses to the bell-pull, right, and rings.*)

OSVALD. What do you want?

MRS. ALVING. I want my boy to be happy, that's what. He mustn't go around brooding. (*To* REGINA, *who has appeared at the door.*) More champagne. A whole bottle.

(REGINA *goes.*)

OSVALD. Mother!

MRS. ALVING. Don't you think, in the country too, we know how to live?

OSVALD. Isn't she magnificent-looking? The figure she has! And the glow of her health!

MRS. ALVING. Sit down, Osvald, and let's have a quiet talk.

OSVALD (*sits*). You wouldn't know this, Mother, but I have a wrong to make right with Regina.

MRS. ALVING. You!

OSVALD. Or a little indiscretion—you might call it. Quite innocent, actually. When I was home last—

MRS. ALVING. Yes?

OSVALD. She asked me so many times about Paris, and I told her bits and pieces about the life down there. And I remember that one day I chanced to say, "Wouldn't you like to go there yourself?"

MRS. ALVING. Well?

OSVALD. I could see her blushing all shades of red, and then she said, "Yes, I'd very much like to." "All right," I said, "I expect that can be arranged"—or something like that.

MRS. ALVING. Oh?

OSVALD. Of course I forgot the whole thing completely; but then the day before yesterday I happened to ask her if she was glad I'd be staying so long at home this time—

MRS. ALVING. Yes?

OSVALD. And she gave me such a peculiar look and said, "But what about my trip to Paris?"

MRS. ALVING. Her trip!

OSVALD. And then I got it out of her that she'd taken the whole thing seriously, that she'd been thinking of me all this while, and that she'd even started to learn some French—

MRS. ALVING. So that's why—

OSVALD. Mother—when I saw her there in front of me, that splendid girl, so alive with health and beauty—it was as if I'd never noticed her before—but now she was standing there as if her arms were simply waiting to take me in—

MRS. ALVING. Osvald!

OSVALD. Then it struck me that in her was my salvation, because I saw how the joy of life was in her.

MRS. ALVING (*with a start*). The joy of life—? Is there salvation in that?

REGINA (*entering from the dining room with a bottle of champagne*). I'm sorry for taking so long, but I had to go down in the cellar— (*Sets the bottle down on the table.*)

OSVALD. And get one more glass.

REGINA (*looks at him in surprise*). But Mrs. Alving has her glass.

OSVALD. Yes, but bring one for yourself, Regina.

(REGINA *looks startled and flashes a quick, shy glance at* MRS. ALVING.)

OSVALD. Well?

REGINA (*her voice low and hesitant*). Is that your wish, Mrs. Alving—?

MRS. ALVING. Get the glass, Regina.

(REGINA *goes out into the dining room.*)

OSVALD (*his eyes following her*). Can you see the way she walks? So firm and fearless.

MRS. ALVING. Osvald, this can't happen—!

OSVALD. The thing is settled. You must see that. There's no use denying it.

(REGINA *returns with an empty glass in her hands.*)

OSVALD. Sit down, Regina.

(REGINA *looks uncertainly at* MRS. ALVING.)

MRS. ALVING. Sit down.

(REGINA *sits on a chair by the dining-room door, still holding the empty glass in her hand.*)

MRS. ALVING. What were you saying, Osvald, about the joy of life?

OSVALD. Yes, the joy of life, Mother—you don't know much about that here at home. I never feel it here.

MRS. ALVING. Not even with me?

OSVALD. Not when I'm home. But how could you understand that?

MRS. ALVING. Oh, yes, yes. I think I'm beginning to understand—now.

OSVALD. That—and the joy of work. Yes, they're really the same thing, basically. But no one understands that here, either.

MRS. ALVING. Maybe you're right. Go on, I want to hear more of this.

OSVALD. I mean, here everyone's brought up to believe that work is a curse and a punishment, and that life is a miserable thing that we're best off to be out of as soon as possible.

MRS. ALVING. A vale of tears, yes. And we ingeniously manage to make it that.

OSVALD. But they won't hear of such things down there. Nobody abroad believes in that sort of outlook anymore. Down there, simply to be alive in the world is held for a kind of miraculous bliss. Mother, have you noticed how everything I've painted is involved with this joy of life? Always and invariably, the joy of life. With light and sun and holiday scenes—and faces radiant with human content. That's why I'm afraid to stay on at home with you.

MRS. ALVING. Afraid? What are you afraid of here with me?

OSVALD. I'm afraid that everything that's most alive in me will degenerate into ugliness here.

MRS. ALVING (looking fixedly at him). Would that happen, do you think?

OSVALD. I'm sure it would. Live here the same as down there—and it still wouldn't be the same life.

MRS. ALVING (who has been listening intently, rises, her eyes large and thoughtful). Now I see how it all fits together.

OSVALD. What do you see?

MRS. ALVING. I see it now, for the first time. And now I can speak.

OSVALD (*getting up*). I don't understand you, Mother.

REGINA (*who has also gotten up*). Shouldn't I go?

MRS. ALVING. No, stay here. Now I can speak. Now, my son, you have to know everything—and then you can choose. Osvald! Regina!

OSVALD. Quiet! The pastor—

MANDERS (*entering by the hall door*). Well, we've really had a heart-warming session together.

OSVALD. We also.

MANDERS. Engstrand needs help with his seaman's home. Regina will have to move back and accommodate him—

REGINA. No, thank you, Pastor.

MANDERS (*just noticing her*). What—? Here—with a glass in your hand!

REGINA (*hurriedly putting the glass down*). Pardon—!

OSVALD. Regina's leaving with me, Pastor.

MANDERS. Leaving—with you!

OSVALD. Yes, as my wife—if she wants that.

MANDERS. Merciful heavens—!

REGINA. It wasn't my doing, Mr. Manders.

OSVALD. Or she'll stay here if I stay.

REGINA (*involuntarily*). Here!

MANDERS. You petrify me, Mrs. Alving.

MRS. ALVING. Neither one nor the other will happen— because now I can speak out freely.

MANDERS. But you can't do that! No, no, no!

MRS. ALVING. I both can and will. And without demolishing any ideals.

OSVALD. Mother, what is it you're hiding from me?

REGINA (*listening*). Mrs. Alving! Listen! People are

shouting out there. (*She goes into the greenhouse and looks out.*)

OSVALD (*moving toward the window, left*). What's going on? What's that light in the sky?

REGINA (*cries out*). The orphanage—it's burning!

MRS. ALVING (*hurrying to the window*). Burning!

MANDERS. Burning? Impossible. I was just down there.

OSVALD. Where's my hat? Oh, never mind—! Father's orphanage—! (*He runs out through the garden door.*)

MRS. ALVING. My shawl, Regina! It's all ablaze!

MANDERS. How awful! Mrs. Alving, this is God's fiery judgment on a wayward house!

MRS. ALVING. Yes, no doubt. Come along, Regina.

(*She and* REGINA *hurry out the hall door.*)

MANDERS (*clasping his hands together*). And then—no insurance! (*He follows them out.*)

⤙ ACT THREE ⤚

The room as before. All the doors stand open. The lamp is still burning on the table. It is dark outside, with only a faint red glow in the background to the left. MRS. ALVING, *with a large shawl over her head, is standing in the green-house, gazing out.* REGINA, *also with a shawl about her, stands slightly behind her.*

MRS. ALVING. Completely burned out—right to the ground.

REGINA. It's burning still in the basement.

MRS. ALVING. Why Osvald doesn't come up—? There's nothing to save.

REGINA. Should I go down to him with his hat?

MRS. ALVING. He hasn't even got his hat?

REGINA (*pointing into the hall*). No, it's hanging in there.

MRS. ALVING. Oh, leave it be. He has to come up soon. I'll look for him myself. (*She goes into the garden.*)

MANDERS (*entering from the hall*). Isn't Mrs. Alving here?

REGINA. She just went into the garden.

MANDERS. This is the most frightful night I've ever experienced.

REGINA. Yes, it's a terrible catastrophe, isn't it, Pastor?

MANDERS. Oh, don't speak of it! I can hardly think of it even.

REGINA. But how could it have happened—?

MANDERS. Don't ask me, Miss Engstrand. How should I know? You're not also going to—? Isn't it enough that your father—?

REGINA. What about him?

MANDERS. He's got me completely confused.

ENGSTRAND (*entering from the hall*). Pastor—!

MANDERS (*turning away, appalled*). Are you after me even here!

ENGSTRAND. Yes, God strike me dead, but I have to—! Good grief, what a mess this is, Pastor!

MANDERS (*pacing back and forth*). Dreadful, dreadful!

REGINA. What's going on?

ENGSTRAND. Oh, it was on account of this here meeting, see? (*In an undertone.*) Now we've got the old bird snared, my girl. (*Aloud.*) And to think it's all my fault that it's Pastor Manders' fault for something like this!

MANDERS. But I assure you, Engstrand—

ENGSTRAND. But there was nobody besides the pastor who messed around with the candles down there.

MANDERS (*stopping*). Yes, that's what you say. But I absolutely cannot remember ever having a candle in my hand.

ENGSTRAND. And I saw so plainly how the pastor took that candle and pinched it out with his fingers and flicked the tip of the wick down into those shavings.

MANDERS. You saw me do that?

ENGSTRAND. Plain as day, I saw it.

MANDERS. I just don't understand it. It's never been a habit of mine to snuff a candle in my fingers.

ENGSTRAND. Yes, it did look pretty sloppy to me, all right. But could it really do that much damage, Pastor?

MANDERS (*walking restlessly back and forth*). Oh, don't ask me.

ENGSTRAND (*walking along with him*). And then your Reverence hadn't insured it either, had you?

MANDERS (*keeps walking*). No, no, no—you heard me.

ENGSTRAND (*keeps following him*). Not insured. And then to go straight over and set the whole works afire. Lord love us—what awful luck!

MANDERS (*wiping the sweat from his brow*). Yes, you can say that again, Engstrand.

ENGSTRAND. And to think it would happen to a charitable institution that was meant to serve the whole community, so to speak. The papers'll handle you none too gently, Pastor, I can bet.

MANDERS. No, that's just what I've been thinking about. That's almost the worst part of the whole business— all these vicious attacks and innuendoes—! Oh, it's too upsetting to think about!

MRS. ALVING (*coming from the garden*). I can't pull him away from the embers.

MANDERS. Ah, you're back, Mrs. Alving.

MRS. ALVING. So you got out of making your speech, Mr. Manders.

MANDERS. Oh, I would have been only too glad—

MRS. ALVING (*her voice subdued*). It's best that it went like this. This orphanage was never made for anyone's benefit.

MANDERS. You think it wasn't?

MRS. ALVING. You think it was?

MANDERS. It was a frightful misfortune, in any case.

MRS. ALVING. Let's discuss it purely as a business arrangement—Are you waiting for the pastor, Engstrand?

ENGSTRAND (*by the hall door*). Well, actually I was.

MRS. ALVING. Then sit down and rest a moment.

ENGSTRAND. Thanks. I can stand all right.

MRS. ALVING (*to* MANDERS.) I suppose you'll be leaving by the steamer?

MANDERS. Yes. It goes an hour from now.

MRS. ALVING. Would you be so good as to take all the

papers back with you. I don't want to hear another word about this thing. I've got other matters to think about—

MANDERS. Mrs. Alving—

MRS. ALVING. I'll shortly be sending you power of attorney to settle everything however you choose.

MANDERS. I'll be only too glad to take care of it. Of course the original terms of the bequest will have to be changed completely now, I'm afraid.

MRS. ALVING. That's understood.

MANDERS. Just offhand, it strikes me that I might arrange it so the Solvik property is made over to the parish. The land itself can hardly be written off as worthless; it can always be put to some use or other. And the interest on the balance of capital in the bank—I could probably apply that best to support some project or other that might be considered of benefit to the town.

MRS. ALVING. Whatever you wish. The whole thing's utterly indifferent to me now.

ENGSTRAND. Think of my seaman's home, Pastor!

MANDERS. Yes, definitely, that's a possibility. Well, it will bear some investigation.

ENGSTRAND. The hell with investigating—oh, Jeez!

MANDERS (with a sigh). And then too, unfortunately I have no idea how long I'll be able to handle these affairs— or if public opinion won't force me to drop them. That depends entirely on the results of the inquest into the fire.

MRS. ALVING. What are you saying?

MANDERS. And those results aren't predictable in advance.

ENGSTRAND (approaching him). Oh yes, they are! Because here's old Jacob Engstrand, right beside you.

MANDERS. Yes, but—?

ENGSTRAND (lowering his voice). And Jacob Engstrand's not the man to go back on a worthy benefactor in his hour of need, as the expression goes.

MANDERS. Yes, but my dear fellow—how can you—?

ENGSTRAND. Jacob Engstrand's sort of like your guardian angel, Pastor, see?

MANDERS. No, no, that I absolutely cannot accept.

ENGSTRAND. Oh, it's how it's going to be, anyway. It's not like somebody here hasn't taken the blame for somebody else before, you know.

MANDERS. Jacob! (*Grasps his hand.*) You're a rare individual. Well, you're going to have every bit of help you need for your seaman's home, you can count on that.

(ENGSTRAND *tries to thank him, but is overcome by emotion.*)

MANDERS (*slipping the strap of his traveling bag over his shoulder*). Well, time to be off. We can travel together.

ENGSTRAND (*by the dining-room door*). Come along with me, wench! You'll live soft as a yoke in an egg.

REGINA (*tossing her head*). *Merci!* (*She goes out in the hall and fetches* MANDERS' *overcoat and umbrella.*)

MANDERS. Good-bye, Mrs. Alving. And may the spirit of law and order soon dwell again in this house.

MRS. ALVING. Good-bye, Manders. (*She goes into the greenhouse as she notices* OSVALD *coming in through the garden door.*)

ENGSTRAND (*as he and* REGINA *help* MANDERS *on with his coat*). Good-bye, my girl. And if you're ever in any trouble, well, you know where to find Jacob Engstrand. (*Quietly.*) Little Harbor Street, hm—! (*To* MRS. ALVING *and* OSVALD.) And my house for wayfaring seamen—that's going to be known as "Captain Alving's Home." yes. And if I get to run that house after my own devices, I think I can promise you it'll be truly worthy of that great man's memory, bless him.

MANDERS (*in the doorway*). Hm—hm! Come along, my dear Engstrand. Good-bye, good-bye!

(*He and* ENGSTRAND *go out the hall door.*)

OSVALD (*going toward the table*). What is this house he was speaking of?

MRS. ALVING. It's some sort of home that he and the pastor want to establish.

OSVALD. It'll burn up like all this here.

MRS. ALVING. Why do you say that?

OSVALD. Everything will burn. There'll be nothing left in memory of Father. And here I'm burning up, too.

(REGINA *stares perplexed at him.*)

MRS. ALVING. Osvald! Poor boy, you shouldn't have stayed down there so long.

OSVALD (*sitting at the table*). I guess you're right.

MRS. ALVING. Let me dry your face, dear; you're dripping wet.

OSVALD (*gazing indifferently into space*). Thank you, Mother.

MRS. ALVING. Aren't you tired, Osvald? Perhaps you could sleep?

OSVALD (*anxiously*). No, no—not sleep! I never sleep; I only pretend to. (*Dully.*) That comes soon enough.

MRS. ALVING (*looking worriedly at him*). You know, dearest, you really are ill.

REGINA (*tensely*). Is Mr. Alving ill?

OSVALD (*impulsively*). And shut all the doors! This racking fear—!

MRS. ALVING. Shut them, Regina.

(REGINA *shuts the doors and remains standing by the hall door.* MRS. ALVING *removes her shawl;* REGINA *does the same.*)

MRS. ALVING (*draws a chair over beside* OSVALD *and sits by him*). There, now I'll sit with you—

OSVALD. Yes, do that. And Regina must stay here too. I always want her close to me. You'll give me your help, Regina—won't you?

REGINA. I don't understand—

MRS. ALVING. Help?

OSVALD. Yes—when it's needed.

MRS. ALVING. Osvald, don't you have your mother to give you help?

OSVALD. You? (*Smiles.*) No, Mother, that kind of help you'd never give me. (*With a mournful laugh.*) You! Ha, ha! (*Looks soberly at her.*) Although you're the obvious choice. (*Vehemently.*) Regina, why are you so reserved toward me? Why can't you call me Osvald?

REGINA (*softly*). I don't think Mrs. Alving would like it.

MRS. ALVING. You'll have every right to soon—so won't you sit down with us here?

(*After a moment,* REGINA *sits down with shy dignity at the other side of the table.*)

And now, my poor, troubled boy, I'm going to take all this weight off your mind—

OSVALD. You, Mother?

MRS. ALVING. Everything you call the agony of remorse and self-reproach.

OSVALD. Do you think you can?

MRS. ALVING. Yes, Osvald, now I can. You were speaking earlier about the joy of life; and as you said those words, it was as if a new light had been shed over the whole of my life.

OSVALD (*shaking his head*). I don't understand this.

MRS. ALVING. You should have known your father when he was just a young lieutenant. *He* had the joy of life, he did!

OSVALD. Yes, I know.

MRS. ALVING. It was like a holiday just to look at him. And all the energy, the unquenchable power that was in him!

OSVALD. Well—?

MRS. ALVING. And then, so full of that very joy, this child—because he *was* like a child then, really—had to make a life here in a mediocre town that had no joys to offer—only distractions. He had to get along here with no real goal in life—only a routine job to hold down. He never found any activity he could throw himself in heart and soul—only business affairs. He never had one single friend with the slightest sense of what the joy of life can mean—no one but drifters and drunkards—

OSVALD. Mother—!

MRS. ALVING. And finally the inevitable happened.

OSVALD. The inevitable?

MRS. ALVING. You said yourself, earlier this evening, what would happen to you if you stayed at home.

OSVALD. You're saying that Father—?

MRS. ALVING. Your poor father never found any outlet for the overpowering joy of life that he had. And I'm afraid I couldn't make his home very festive, either.

OSVALD. You, too?

MRS. ALVING. They'd drilled me so much in duty and things of that kind that I went on here all too long putting my faith in them. Everything resolved into duties—*my* duties, and *his* duties, and—I'm afraid I made this home unbearable for your poor father.

OSVALD. Why didn't you ever write me any of this?

MRS. ALVING. I've never seen it before as anything I could mention to you—his son.

OSVALD. And how, then, did you see it?

MRS. ALVING (*slowly*). I only saw the one thing: that your father was a ravaged man before you were born.

OSVALD (*with a strangled cry*). Ah—! (*He stands up and goes to the window.*)

MRS. ALVING. And then day after day I had only one thought on my mind: that Regina in reality belonged here in this house—just as much as my own son.

OSVALD (*wheeling about*). Regina—!

REGINA (*brought shaken to her feet, in a choked voice*). I—!

MRS. ALVING. Yes, now you both know.

OSVALD. Regina!

REGINA (*to herself*). So that's what she was.

MRS. ALVING. Your mother was decent in many ways, Regina.

REGINA. Yes, but she was that kind, all the same. Well, I sometimes thought so, but—then, Mrs. Alving, if you don't mind, may I leave right away, at once?

MRS. ALVING. Do you really want to, Regina?

REGINA. Yes, of course I want to.

MRS. ALVING. Naturally you can do as you wish, but—

OSVALD (*going over to* REGINA). Leave now? But you belong here.

REGINA. *Merci*, Mr. Alving—yes, I guess I can call you Osvald now. But it's certainly not the way I wanted to.

MRS. ALVING. Regina, I haven't been straightforward with you—

REGINA. That's putting it mild! If I'd known that Osvald was sick, why— And now that there isn't a chance of anything serious between us— No, I really can't stay out in the country and run myself ragged for invalids.

OSVALD. Not even for someone this close to you?

REGINA. Not on your life, I can't! A poor girl's only got her youth; she'd better use it—or else she'll find herself barefoot at Christmas before she knows it. And I've got this joy of life too, Mrs. Alving—in *me!*

MRS. ALVING. Yes, I'm afraid so. Only don't throw yourself away, Regina.

REGINA. Oh, things go as they go. If Osvald takes after his father, then I take after my mother, I guess. May I ask, Mrs. Alving, if Pastor Manders knows all this about me?

MRS. ALVING. Pastor Manders knows everything.

REGINA (*busy putting on her shawl*). Then I really better see if I can catch the boat out of here as quick as I can. The pastor's so nice to deal with, and I definitely think I've got just as much right to some of that money as he does—that rotten carpenter.

MRS. ALVING. You're quite welcome to it, Regina.

REGINA (*looking sharply at her*). You know, Mrs. Alving, you could have raised me as a gentleman's daughter—

and I would've been a lot better off. (*Tossing her head.*)
But, hell—what's the difference! (*With a bitter glance at
the unopened bottle.*) I'll get my champagne in society
yet, just see if I don't.

MRS. ALVING. If you ever need a home, Regina, you
can come to me.

REGINA. No, thank you, ma'am. Pastor Manders'll look
out for me, all right. And if things really go wrong, I still
know a house where I'll do just fine.

MRS. ALVING. Where?

REGINA. In "Captain Alving's Home."

MRS. ALVING. Regina—I can see now—you'll go to
your ruin!

REGINA. Ahh, ffft! *Adieu.* (*She curtsies and goes out the
hall door.*)

OSVALD (*standing at the window, looking out*). Has she
gone?

MRS. ALVING. Yes.

OSVALD (*murmuring to himself*). I think it's insane, all
this.

MRS. ALVING (*goes over behind him, placing her hands
on his shoulders*). Osvald, dear—has this disturbed you
terribly?

OSVALD (*turning his face toward her*). All that about
Father, you mean?

MRS. ALVING. Yes, about your poor father. I'm afraid
it's been too much of a shock for you.

OSVALD. Why do you think so? It came as quite a
surprise, of course; but basically it can hardly make any
difference to me.

MRS. ALVING (*withdrawing her hands*). No difference!
That your father was so enormously unhappy!

OSVALD. Naturally I can feel sympathy for him as for
any human being, but—

MRS. ALVING. Nothing more—for your own father—!

OSVALD (*impatiently*). Yes, Father—Father! I never

knew a father. My only memory of him is that he once got me to vomit.

MRS. ALVING. That's a dreadful thought! Surely a child ought to feel some love for his father, no matter what.

OSVALD. When that child has nothing to thank him for? Hasn't even known him? Do you really hang on to that old superstition—you, so enlightened in everything else?

MRS. ALVING. And is that just a superstition—!

OSVALD. Yes, you must realize that, Mother. It's one of these ideas that materialize in the world for a while, and then—

MRS. ALVING (*with a shudder*). Ghosts!

OSVALD (*pacing the floor*). Yes, you could very well call them ghosts.

MRS. ALVING (*in an outcry*). Osvald—you don't love me either!

OSVALD. I know you, at least—

MRS. ALVING. Yes, I know—but is that all?

OSVALD. And I know how much you care for me, and I have to be grateful to you for that. And you can be especially useful to me, now that I'm ill.

MRS. ALVING. Yes, I can, Osvald, can't I? Oh, I could almost bless this illness that forced you home to me, because it's made me see you're really not mine; you still have to be won.

OSVALD (*impatiently*). Yes, yes, yes, that's all just a manner of speaking. You have to remember I'm a sick man, Mother. I can't be concerned very much with others; I have enough just thinking about myself.

MRS. ALVING (*softly*). I'll be patient and forebearing.

OSVALD. And cheerful, Mother!

MRS. ALVING. Yes, dearest, you're right. (*Going over to him.*) Now have I taken away all your remorse and self-reproach?

OSVALD. Yes, you have. But who'll take away the fear?

MRS. ALVING. The fear?

OSVALD (*pacing about the room*). Regina would have done it for the asking.

MRS. ALVING. I don't understand. What is all this about fear—and Regina?

OSVALD. Is it very late, Mother?

MRS. ALVING. It's nearly morning. (*Looking out through the greenhouse.*) There's the first light of dawn already on the mountains. It's going to be clear, Osvald! In a little while you'll see the sun.

OSVALD. I look forward to that. Oh, there can be so much still to look forward to, and live for—!

MRS. ALVING. I'm sure there will be!

OSVALD. And even though I can't work, I'll—

MRS. ALVING. Oh, my dearest, you'll find yourself working again so soon. Because now you won't have these worrisome, depressing thoughts to brood on any longer.

OSVALD. Yes, it was good that you could rid me of all those fantasies of mine. And now, if I can only face this one thing more— (*Sits down on the sofa.*) Mother, we have to talk together—

MRS. ALVING. Yes, let's. (*She pushes an armchair over by the sofa and sits beside him.*)

OSVALD. And meanwhile the sun will rise. And by then, you'll know—and I won't have this fear any longer.

MRS. ALVING. Tell me, what will I know?

OSVALD (*not listening*). Mother, didn't you say earlier this evening that there wasn't anything in the world you wouldn't do for me if I asked you?

MRS. ALVING. Why, yes, of course!

OSVALD. And you meant it, Mother?

MRS. ALVING. That you can depend on. You're my one and only boy; I have nothing else to live for but you.

OSVALD. All right, then listen. You have a strong, resilient mind, I know that. I want you to sit very quiet as I tell this.

MRS. ALVING. But what is it that's so terrible—?

OSVALD. You mustn't scream. Do you hear? Promise

me that? We're going to sit and speak of it quietly. Mother, promise me?

MRS. ALVING. Yes, yes, I promise—just tell me!

OSVALD. Well, then you've got to realize that all this about tiredness—and my incapacity for thinking in terms of my work—isn't the real illness—

MRS. ALVING. What is the real illness?

OSVALD. The one that I inherited, the illness—(*Points to his forehead and speaks very softly.*)—that's seated here.

MRS. ALVING (*nearly speechless*). Osvald! No—no!

OSVALD. Don't scream; I can't bear it. Yes, it sits in here and waits. And any day, at any time, it can strike.

MRS. ALVING. Oh, how horrible—!

OSVALD. Just stay calm. So, that's how things are with me.

MRS. ALVING (*springing to her feet*). It's not true, Osvald! It's impossible! It can't be!

OSVALD. I had one attack down there. It soon passed off—but when I found out how things stood with me, then this anxiety took hold, racking me like a cold fever; and with that, I started home here to you as fast as I could.

MRS. ALVING. So that's the fear—!

OSVALD. Yes, I can't tell you how excruciating it is. Oh, if it only had been some ordinary disease that would kill me— I'm not so afraid of dying, though I want to live as long as I can.

MRS. ALVING. Yes, yes, Osvald, you must!

OSVALD. But the thought of it *is* excruciating. To revert back to a helpless child again. To have to be fed, to have to be—oh, it's unspeakable.

MRS. ALVING. My child has his mother to nurse him.

OSVALD (*leaps up*). No, never! That's just what I won't have! I can't abide the thought of lying here like that for years—turning old and gray. And in the meantime you might die before me. (*Sits in* MRS. ALVING's *chair.*) Because the doctor said it needn't be fatal at once. He called it a kind of "softening of the brain"—some phrase like that. (*Smiles sadly.*) I think that expression sounds so nice. It always makes me think of cherry-red velvet draperies—something soft to stroke.

MRS. ALVING (*screams*). Osvald!

OSVALD (*leaps up again and paces the floor*). And now you've taken Regina away from me! If I'd only had her. She would have helped me out, I'm sure.

MRS. ALVING (*going over to him*). My dear boy, what do you mean? Is there any help in this world that I wouldn't willingly give you?

OSVALD. After I'd recovered from the attack down there, the doctor told me that, when it struck again—and it *would* strike—there'd be no more hope.

MRS. ALVING. That he could be so heartless—

OSVALD. I demanded it of him. I told him I had certain arrangements to make. (*With a shy smile.*) And so I had. (*Brings out a small box from his inner breast pocket.*) Mother, you see this?

MRS. ALVING. What's that?

OSVALD. Morphine pills.

MRS. ALVING (*looks at him in horror*). Osvald—my child!

OSVALD. I've saved up twelve of them—

MRS. ALVING (*snatching at it*). Give me the box, Osvald!

OSVALD. Not yet, Mother. (*He returns the box to his pocket.*)

MRS. ALVING. I can't live through this!

OSVALD. You'll have to. If I'd had Regina here now, I'd have told her what state I was in—and asked for her help with this one last thing. She'd have helped me, I'm positive of that.

MRS. ALVING. Never!

OSVALD. If this horrible thing struck me down, and she saw me lying there like an infant child, helpless, and beyond help, lost, hopeless—incurable—

MRS. ALVING. Regina never would have done that!

OSVALD. Yes, she would have. Regina was so wonderfully lighthearted. She soon would have gotten tired of tending an invalid like me.

MRS. ALVING. Then thank God Regina's not here!

OSVALD. So now, Mother, you've got to give me that help.

MRS. ALVING (*in a loud outcry*). I!

OSVALD. What more obvious choice than you?

MRS. ALVING. I! Your mother!

OSVALD. Exactly the reason.

MRS. ALVING. I, who gave you life!

OSVALD. I never asked you for life. And what is this life you gave me? I don't want it! You can take it back!

MRS. ALVING. Help! Help! (*She runs out into the hall.*)

OSVALD (*right behind her*). Don't leave me! Where are you going?

MRS. ALVING (*in the hall*). To get the doctor, Osvald! Let me out!

OSVALD (*also in the hall*). You don't leave. And no one comes in.

(*The sound of a key turning in a lock.*)

MRS. ALVING (*coming in again*). Osvald—Osvald—my child!

OSVALD (*following her*). Have you no mother-love for me at all—to see me suffer this unbearable fear!

MRS. ALVING (*after a moment's silence, controlling her voice*). Here's my hand on it.

OSVALD. Then you will—?

MRS. ALVING. If it becomes necessary. But it won't be necessary. No, no, that's simply impossible!

OSVALD. Well, that we can hope. And now let's live together as long as we can. Thank you, Mother.

(*He settles down in the armchair that* MRS. ALVING *had moved over to the sofa. The day is breaking; the lamp still burns on the table.*)

MRS. ALVING. Now do you feel all right?

OSVALD. Yes.

MRS. ALVING (*bending over him*). What a fearful nightmare this has been for you, Osvald—but it was all a dream. Too much excitement—it hasn't been good for you. But now you can have your rest, at home with your mother near, my own, my dearest boy. Anything you want you can have, just like when you were a little child. There now, the pain is over. You see how quickly it went. Oh, I knew it would— And look, Osvald, what a lovely day we'll have. Bright sunlight. Now you really can see your home.

(*She goes to the table and puts out the lamp. Sunrise. The glaciers and peaks in the background shine in the brilliant light of morning. With his back toward the distant view,* OSVALD *sits motionless in the armchair.*)

OSVALD (*abruptly*). Mother, give me the sun.

MRS. ALVING (*by the table, looks at him, startled*). What did you say?

OSVALD (*repeats in a dull monotone*). The sun. The sun.

MRS. ALVING (*moves over to him*). Osvald, what's the matter?

(OSVALD *appears to crumple inwardly in the chair; all his muscles loosen; the expression leaves his face; and his eyes stare blankly.*)

MRS. ALVING (*shaking with fear*). What is it? (*In a shriek.*) Osvald! What's wrong! (*Drops to her knees beside him and shakes him.*) Osvald! Osvald! Look at me! Don't you know me?

OSVALD (*in the same monotone*). The sun—the sun.

MRS. ALVING (*springs to her feet in anguish, tears at her hair with both hands and screams*). I can't bear this! (*Whispers as if paralyzed by fright.*) I can't bear it!

Never! (*Suddenly.*) Where did he put them? (*Her hand skims across his chest.*) Here! (*She shrinks back several steps and shrieks.*) No, no, no!—Yes!—No, no! (*She stands a few steps away from him, her fingers thrust into her hair, staring at him in speechless horror.*)

OSVALD (*sitting motionless, as before*). The sun—the sun.

AN ENEMY OF THE PEOPLE

THE CHARACTERS

DR. THOMAS STOCKMANN, staff physician at the municipal baths

MRS. STOCKMANN, his wife

PETRA, their daughter, a teacher

EILIF
MORTEN } their sons, aged 12 and 10

PETER STOCKMANN, the doctor's older brother, mayor, police chief, chairman of the board of the municipal baths, etc.

MORTEN KIIL, master tanner; Mrs. Stockmann's foster-father

HOVSTAD, editor of the *People's Courier*

BILLING, his assistant on the paper

CAPTAIN HORSTER

ASLAKSEN, a printer

PARTICIPANTS IN A PUBLIC MEETING: men of all social ranks, several women, and a gang of schoolboys

The action takes place in a coastal town in southern Norway.

⤙ ACT ONE ⤚

Evening. DR. STOCKMANN's *living room, simply but attractively furnished and decorated. In the side wall to the right are two doors, the farther one leading out to the hall, and the nearer into the* DOCTOR's *study. In the facing wall, directly opposite the hall door, is a door to the family's living quarters. At the middle of this wall stands the stove; closer in the foreground, a sofa with a mirror above it, and in front of these, an oval table covered by a cloth. On the table a lamp, shaded and lit. In the back wall, an open door to the dining room. The table is set for dinner within, with a lit lamp on it.*

BILLING, *napkin under his chin, sits at the table inside.* MRS. STOCKMANN *is standing by the table, passing him a plate with a large slice of roast beef. The other places at the table are empty; the settings are in disorder, as after a meal.*

MRS. STOCKMANN. Well, if you come an hour late, Mr. Billing, then you have to accept cold food.

BILLING (*eating*). It tastes simply marvelous—just perfect.

MRS. STOCKMANN. Because you know how precise my husband is about keeping his regular mealtime—

BILLING. Doesn't bother me in the least. In fact, I really think food tastes best to me when I can eat like this, alone and undisturbed.

MRS. STOCKMANN. Yes, well—just so you enjoy it

—(*Turns, listening, toward the hall door.*) Now that must be Hovstad coming.

BILLING. Probably.

(PETER STOCKMANN *enters, wearing an overcoat and the official hat of his mayor's office. He carries a walking stick.*)

MAYOR STOCKMANN. A most pleasant good evening, my dear Katherine.

MRS. STOCKMANN (*comes into the living room*). Why, good evening! So it's you? How nice that you stopped up to see us.

MAYOR STOCKMANN. I was just passing by, so— (*With a glance toward the dining room.*) Ah, but it seems you have company already.

MRS. STOCKMANN (*somewhat embarrassed*). No, no— he was quite unexpected. (*Hurriedly.*) Won't you step in and join him for a bite?

MAYOR STOCKMANN. I? No, thank you. Good heavens, hot food at night! Not with *my* digestion.

MRS. STOCKMANN. Oh, but just this once—

MAYOR STOCKMANN. No, really, that's kind of you; but I'll stick to my bread and butter and tea. It's healthier in the long run—and a bit more economical, too.

MRS. STOCKMANN (*smiling*). Now you mustn't think that Thomas and I live so lavishly, either.

MAYOR STOCKMANN. Not *you*, Katherine. *That* never crossed my mind. (*Points toward the* DOCTOR's *study.*) I suppose he isn't home?

MRS. STOCKMANN. No, he went for a little walk after dinner—he and the boys.

MAYOR STOCKMANN. How healthy is that, I wonder? (*Listening.*) That ought to be him.

MRS. STOCKMANN. No, I don't think it is. (*A knock at the door.*) Come in!

(HOVSTAD *enters from the hall.*)

MRS. STOCKMANN. Ah, so it's Mr. Hovstad—

HOVSTAD. Yes, you'll have to excuse me, but I got held up at the printer's. Good evening, Mr. Mayor.

MAYOR STOCKMANN (*bowing rather stiffly*). Mr. Hovstad. Here on business, I suppose?

HOVSTAD. Partly. It's about something going in the paper.

MAYOR STOCKMANN. I'm not surprised. I hear my brother's become a very active contributor to the *People's Courier*.

HOVSTAD. Yes, he deigns to write for the *Courier* whenever he has a little plain speaking to do about this and that.

MRS. STOCKMANN (*to* HOVSTAD). But won't you—? (*Points toward the dining room.*)

MAYOR STOCKMANN. Oh, well now, I can hardly blame him for writing for the sort of readers who'd give him the best reception. And of course, personally, you know, I haven't the least cause for any ill will toward your paper, Mr. Hovstad.

HOVSTAD. No, I wouldn't think so.

MAYOR. On the whole, there's a fine spirit of tolerance in this town of ours—a remarkable public spirit. And that stems, of course, from our having a great common concern that binds us all together—a concern that involves to the same high degree every right-minded citizen—

HOVSTAD. The spa, yes.

MAYOR STOCKMANN. Exactly. We have our great, new, magnificent installation, the spa. Mark my words, Mr. Hovstad—these baths will become the very life-principle of our town. Unquestionably!

MRS. STOCKMANN. That's what Thomas says, too.

MAYOR STOCKMANN. Why, it's simply extraordinary the way this place has revived in the past two years! People here have some money again. There's life, excitement! Land and property values are rising every day.

HOVSTAD. And unemployment's down.

MAYOR STOCKMANN. Yes, that too. The taxes for public welfare have been cut by a comfortable margin for the propertied classes, and will be still more if we can only have a really good summer this year—hordes of visitors—masses of invalids who can give the baths a reputation.

HOVSTAD. And that's the prospect, I hear.

MAYOR STOCKMANN. The outlook is very auspicious. Every day, inquiries coming in about accommodations and the like.

HOVSTAD. Well, then the doctor's article ought to be quite timely.

MAYOR STOCKMANN. Has he been writing something again?

HOVSTAD. This is something he wrote last winter: a recommendation of the baths, and a report on the health-promoting character of the life here. But I held the article back at the time.

MAYOR STOCKMANN. There was a flaw in it somewhere, I suppose?

HOVSTAD. No, that's not it. I thought it was better to wait till now, in the spring, when people start planning their summer vacations—

MAYOR STOCKMANN. Quite right. Absolutely right, Mr. Hovstad.

MRS. STOCKMANN. Yes, Thomas spares nothing when the baths are involved.

MAYOR STOCKMANN. Well, he *is* on the staff, after all.

HOVSTAD. Yes, and then he's the one, too, who really originated the idea.

MAYOR STOCKMANN. He *did*? Really? Yes, I do occasionally hear that certain people hold that opinion. But I still had an impression that *I* also played some modest part in this enterprise.

MRS. STOCKMANN. Yes, Thomas says that always.

HOVSTAD. No one denies that, Mr. Mayor. You got the thing moving and put it into practical reality—we all know that. I only meant that the idea came from the doctor first.

MAYOR STOCKMANN. Yes, my brother's had more than enough ideas in his time, I'm afraid. But when there's something to be done, it's another sort of man that's called for, Mr. Hovstad. And I really had thought that, at least here, in this house—

MRS. STOCKMANN. But, my dear Peter—

HOVSTAD. Sir, how can you possibly think—?

MRS. STOCKMANN. Mr. Hovstad, do go in and take some refreshment. My husband's sure to be back any moment.

HOVSTAD. Thank you; just a bite, maybe. (*He goes into the dining room.*)

MAYOR STOCKMANN (*dropping his voice*). It's curious with these people of peasant stock: they never can learn any tact.

MRS. STOCKMANN. But why let that bother you? It's not worth it. Can't you and Thomas share the honor, like brothers?

MAYOR STOCKMANN. Yes, it would seem so; but it isn't everyone who can be satisfied with his share, apparently.

MRS. STOCKMANN. Oh, nonsense! You and Thomas get along splendidly together. (*Listening.*) There, now I think we have him. (*Goes over and opens the hall door.*)

DR. STOCKMANN (*laughing and raising commotion outside*). Look, Katherine—you've got another guest here. Isn't this a treat, eh? There we are, Captain Horster; hang your coat up on the peg. Oh, that's right—you don't wear a coat. Imagine, Katherine, I met him on the street, and he almost didn't want to come up.

(CAPTAIN HORSTER *enters and greets* MRS. STOCKMANN. DR. STOCKMANN *appears in the doorway.*)

In you go, boys. They're ravenous all over again! Come on, Captain Horster; now you're going to have some roast beef—

(*He propels* HORSTER *into the dining room;* EILIF *and* MORTEN *follow after.*)

MRS. STOCKMANN. But, Thomas, don't you see—?

DR. STOCKMANN (*turning by the door*). Oh, it's you, Peter! (*Goes over to shake hands.*) Well, this *is* a pleasure.

MAYOR STOCKMANN. I'm afraid I have to be going in just a moment—

DR. STOCKMANN. Rubbish! There's hot toddy on the table now, any minute. You haven't forgotten the toddy, Katherine?

MRS. STOCKMANN. Of course not. The water's boiling. (*She goes into the dining room.*)

MAYOR STOCKMANN. Toddy, too—!

DR. STOCKMANN. Yes, have a seat, so we can get comfortable.

MAYOR STOCKMANN. Thank you, I never take part in toddy parties.

DR. STOCKMANN. But this isn't a party.

MAYOR STOCKMANN. Well, it looks to me— (*Glancing toward the dining room.*) It's astonishing how they put all that food away.

DR. STOCKMANN (*rubbing his hands*). Yes, isn't it wonderful to watch young people eat? Endless appetites—just as it ought to be! They've got to have food—for strength! They're the ones who'll put a kick in the future, Peter.

MAYOR STOCKMANN. May I ask what, here, needs a "kick put in it," in your manner of speaking?

DR. STOCKMANN. Well, you better ask the young ones that—when the time comes. We don't see it, of course. Naturally. A pair of old fogies like you and me—

MAYOR STOCKMANN. Now really! That's a very peculiar term—

DR. STOCKMANN. Oh, you mustn't take things so literally with me, Peter. Because you know, I've been feeling so buoyant and happy. I can't tell you how lucky I feel to be part of this life that's budding and bursting out everywhere. What an amazing age we live in! It's as if a whole new world were rising around us.

MAYOR STOCKMANN. You really believe that?

DR. STOCKMANN. Of course you can't see it as well as I can. You've lived in the midst of it all your life, and that dulls the impression. But I, who've been stuck all these many years in my little limbo up north, hardly ever seeing a stranger with a fresh idea to share—to me, it's as if I'd been plunked down in the middle of a swarming metropolis.

MAYOR STOCKMANN. Hm—metropolis—

DR. STOCKMANN. Oh, I'm well aware this is small scale compared with a lot of other places. But there's life here— a promise, an immensity of things to work and fight for; and *that's* what's important. (*Calls.*) Katherine, didn't the mailman come?

MRS. STOCKMANN (*from the dining room*). No, not today.

DR. STOCKMANN. And then to make a good living, Peter! That's something you learn to appreciate when you've been getting along, as we have, on starvation wages—

MAYOR STOCKMANN. Oh, come—

DR. STOCKMANN. You can just imagine how tight things were for us up there, yes, many times. And now we can live like kings! Today, for instance, we had roast beef for dinner, and we had some more for supper. Don't you want a piece? Or, anyway, let me show it to you. Come here—

MAYOR STOCKMANN. No, definitely not—

DR. STOCKMANN. Well, then come over here. Look, we bought a new tablecloth.

MAYOR STOCKMANN. Yes, so I noticed.

DR. STOCKMANN. And we got a lampshade. See? It's all out of Katherine's savings. And it makes the room so cozy, don't you think? Just stand right here—no, no, no, not there. Just—so! Look, how the light concentrates there where it falls. Really, I find that quite elegant. Don't you?

MAYOR STOCKMANN. Yes, if you can allow yourself luxuries like that—

DR. STOCKMANN. Oh yes. I can allow myself that. Katherine says I'm now earning almost as much as we spend.

MAYOR STOCKMANN. Almost—!

DR. STOCKMANN. But a man of science ought to live with a little style. I'm sure the average district judge spends more in a year than I do.

MAYOR STOCKMANN. Yes, I expect so! A district judge, a superior magistrate—

DR. STOCKMANN. Well, an ordinary businessman then. That kind of man spends a lot more—

MAYOR STOCKMANN. It's a matter of circumstances.

DR. STOCKMANN. In any case, I honestly don't waste anything on luxuries, Peter. But I don't feel I can deny myself the gratification of having people in. You see, I need that. Having been shut out for so long—for me it's a necessity of life to spend time with high-spirited, bold young people, with adventurous minds and a wealth of energy—and that's what they are, all of them sitting and savoring their food in there. I wish you knew Hovstad a bit better—

MAYOR STOCKMANN. Yes, come to think of it, Hovstad told me he'll be printing another of your articles.

DR. STOCKMANN. Of *my* articles?

MAYOR STOCKMANN. Yes, about the baths. Something you wrote last winter.

DR. STOCKMANN. Oh yes, that! No, I don't want that in right now.

MAYOR STOCKMANN. No? It strikes me this is just the opportune time.

DR. STOCKMANN. Yes, you might be right—under ordinary circumstances— (*He paces about the room.*)

MAYOR STOCKMANN (*following him with his eyes*). What's extraordinary about the circumstances now?

DR. STOCKMANN (*stops*). Peter, I swear, at this moment I can't tell you—anyway, not this evening. There could be something quite extraordinary about the circumstances— or it might be nothing at all. It could well be that it's just imagination.

MAYOR STOCKMANN. I have to confess, it sounds very mysterious. Is anything wrong? Something I'm excluded from? I would assume that I, as chairman of the board of the municipal baths—

DR. STOCKMANN. And I would assume that—oh, come on, Peter, let's not fly at each other like this.

MAYOR STOCKMANN. Heaven forbid! I'm not in the habit of flying at people, as you put it. But I most definitely must insist that all necessary steps be taken and carried out in a businesslike manner by the legally constituted authorities. I can't condone any sly or underhanded activities.

DR. STOCKMANN. When have I ever been sly or underhanded?

MAYOR STOCKMANN. You have an inveterate tendency to go your own way, in any case. And in a well-ordered society, that's nearly as inexcusable. The individual has to learn to subordinate himself to the whole—or, I should say, to those authorities charged with the common good.

DR. STOCKMANN. Possibly. But what in thunder does that have to do with me?

MAYOR STOCKMANN. Because, my dear Thomas, it's this you seem never to want to learn. But watch out; someday you're going to pay for it—sooner or later. Now I've told you. Good-bye.

DR. STOCKMANN. Are you stark, raving mad? You're completely on the wrong track—

MAYOR STOCKMANN. That's not my custom. And now, if I may excuse myself— (*With a bow toward the dining room.*) Good night, Katherine. Good night, gentlemen. (*Goes out.*)

MRS. STOCKMANN (*coming into the living room*). He's gone?

DR. STOCKMANN. Yes, and in a foul humor.

MRS. STOCKMANN. Oh, Thomas dear, what did you do to him this time?

DR. STOCKMANN. Nothing at all. He can't demand that I settle accounts with him before the time comes.

MRS. STOCKMANN. What accounts do you have to settle with him?

DR. STOCKMANN. Hm, don't ask me, Katherine. It's odd that the mailman hasn't come.

(HOVSTAD, BILLING, *and* HORSTER *have risen from the*

table and come into the living room. EILIF *and* MORTEN *follow after a moment.*)

BILLING (*stretching his arms*). Ah, a meal like that and, ye gods, you feel like a new man!

HOVSTAD. The mayor wasn't in his best spirits tonight.

DR. STOCKMANN. It's his stomach; he has bad digestion.

HOVSTAD. I'm sure it was mainly us from the *Courier* he couldn't digest.

MRS. STOCKMANN. You were getting on rather well with him, I thought.

HOVSTAD. Oh yes, but it's nothing more than an armistice.

BILLING. That's it! That's the word for it.

DR. STOCKMANN. We have to remember, Peter's a lonely man. Poor fellow, he has no home to give him comfort—just business, business. And all that damn weak tea he's always sloshing down. Well, now, pull up your chairs to the table, boys! Katherine, don't we get any toddy?

MRS. STOCKMANN (*going toward the dining room*). I'm just bringing it.

DR. STOCKMANN. And you sit here on the sofa by me, Captain Horster. A rare guest like you—please, sit down, everyone.

(*The men seat themselves at the table.* MRS. STOCKMANN *comes back with a tray, holding a hotplate, glasses, decanters, and the like.*)

MRS. STOCKMANN. There now. This is arrack, and here's rum, and cognac. So just help yourselves.

DR. STOCKMANN (*taking a glass*). Oh, I think we'll manage! (*While the toddy is mixed.*) And let's have the cigars. Eilif, I'm sure you know where the box is. And, Morten, you can fetch my pipe. (*The boys go into the room on the right.*) I have a suspicion that Eilif sneaks a cigar now and then—but I play innocent. (*Calls.*) And my smoking cap too, Morten! Katherine, can't you tell him where I left it? Ah, he's got it! (*The boys bring in the various items.*) Help yourselves, everybody. I'll stick to my pipe. This one's taken me through a lot of dirty weather on my rounds up north. (*Clinking glasses.*) Skoal! Ah, it's a lot better sitting here, snug and warm.

MRS. STOCKMANN (*sits and starts knitting*). Are you sailing soon, Captain Horster?

HORSTER. I think we'll be ready by next week.

MRS. STOCKMANN. And you'll be going to America then?

HORSTER. That's the intention, yes.

BILLING. But then you can't vote in the new town election.

HORSTER. There's an election coming up?

BILLING. Didn't you know?

HORSTER. No, I don't bother with such things.

BILLING. But you *are* concerned about public affairs, aren't you?

HORSTER. No. I don't understand them.

BILLING. Even so, a person at least ought to vote.

HORSTER. People who don't understand, too?

BILLING. Understand? What do you mean by that? Society's like a ship: all hands have to stand to the wheel.

HORSTER. Maybe on land; but at sea it wouldn't work too well.

HOVSTAD. It's remarkable how most sailors are so little concerned with what happens on land.

BILLING. Very strange.

DR. STOCKMANN. Sailors are like birds of passage: north, south, wherever they are is home. But it's why the rest of us have to be all the more effective, Mr. Hovstad. Anything of general interest in tomorrow's *Courier*?

HOVSTAD. No local items. But I was thinking of running your article the day after tomorrow—

DR. STOCKMANN. Hell's bells, that article! No, listen, you'll have to wait on that.

HOVSTAD. Oh? We have so much space right now, and it seems like the opportune moment—

DR. STOCKMANN. Yes, yes, you're probably right; but you'll have to wait all the same—

(PETRA, *wearing a hat and coat, comes in from the hall, with a stack of exercise books under her arm.*)

PETRA. Good evening.

DR. STOCKMANN. That's you, Petra? Good evening.

(*Greetings all around.* PETRA *takes off her hat and coat and leaves them, with the books, on a chair by the door.*)

PETRA. And here you all sit partying while I'm out slaving away.

DR. STOCKMANN. Well, now it's your party, too.

BILLING. Can I fix you a little drink?

PETRA (*coming to the table*). Thanks, I'll do it myself. You always make it too strong. Oh, Father, by the way, I have a letter for you. (*Goes over to the chair where her things are.*)

DR. STOCKMANN. A letter! Who from?

PETRA (*searching in her coat pocket*). I got it from the mailman as I was just going out—

DR. STOCKMANN (*gets up and goes toward her*). And you don't bring it till now!

PETRA. I really hadn't the time to run up again. Here it is.

DR. STOCKMANN (*seizing the letter*). Let me see, let me see, child. (*Looks at the envelope.*) Yes, that's it—!

MRS. STOCKMANN. Is *this* the one you've been so impatient for?

DR. STOCKMANN. Exactly. I must take it straight in and —where can I find a light, Katherine? Is there no lamp in my room again?

MRS. STOCKMANN. The lamp is lit and standing on your desk.

DR. STOCKMANN. Good, good. Excuse me a minute— (*Goes into his study to the right.*)

PETRA. Mother, what do you suppose that is?

MRS. STOCKMANN. I don't know. These last days he's been asking constantly about the mailman.

BILLING. Most likely some patient out of town—

PETRA. Poor Father, he's taking on too much work. (*Mixing a drink.*) Ooh, this'll be good!

HOVSTAD. Were you teaching night school again today?

PETRA (*sipping her glass*). Two hours.

BILLING. And four hours mornings at the Institute—

PETRA (*sitting by the door*). Five hours.

MRS. STOCKMANN. And papers to correct in the evening, I see.

PETRA. A whole batch, yes.

HORSTER. It looks like you take on your own full share.

PETRA. Yes, but that's fine. You feel so delectably tired afterward.

BILLING. You like that?

PETRA. Yes. Then you sleep so well.

MORTEN. You must be horribly wicked, Petra.

PETRA. Wicked?

MORTEN. Yes, when you work so hard. Mr. Rørland says that work is a punishment for our sins.

EILIF (*snorts*). Pah, how stupid you are, to believe that stuff.

MRS. STOCKMANN. Now, now, Eilif!

BILLING (*laughing*). Oh, marvelous!

HOVSTAD. You'd rather not work so hard, Morten?

MORTEN. No, I wouldn't.

HOVSTAD. Yes, but what do you want to be in life?

MORTEN. Best of all, I want to be a Viking.

EILIF. But then you'd have to be a pagan.

MORTEN. Well, so then I'll be a pagan!

BILLING. I'm with you, Morten! Exactly what I say!

MRS. STOCKMANN (*making signals*). No, you don't really, Mr. Billing.

BILLING. Ye gods, yes—! I *am* a pagan, and proud of it. Just wait, we'll all be pagans soon.

MORTEN. And can we then do anything we want?

BILLING. Well, you see, Morten—

MRS. STOCKMANN. Now, in you go, boys, both of you. I'm sure you've got homework for tomorrow.

EILIF. *I* could stay a little longer—

MRS. STOCKMANN. Oh no, you can't. The two of you, out!

(*The boys say good night and go into the room to the left.*)

HOVSTAD. Do you really think it could hurt the boys to hear these things?

MRS. STOCKMANN. Well, I don't know. But I don't like it.

PETRA. Oh, Mother, I think you're just being silly.

MRS. STOCKMANN. Yes, that's possible; but I don't like it—not here at home.

PETRA. Oh, there's so much hypocrisy, both at home and in school. At home we have to keep quiet, and in school we have to stand there and lie to the children.

HORSTER. You have to lie?

PETRA. Yes, don't you know, we have to teach them all kinds of things we don't believe in ourselves?

BILLING. Yes, that's for certain.

PETRA. If I only had the means, then I'd start a school myself, and things would be different there.

BILLING. Pah, the means—!

HORSTER. Well, if that's your idea, Miss Stockmann, I'll gladly provide you the facilities. My father's old place has been standing nearly empty; there's a huge dining room on the ground floor—

PETRA (*laughing*). Oh, thank you! But nothing'll come of it, I'm sure.

HOVSTAD. No, I think Miss Petra's more apt to go in for journalism. Incidentally, have you had time to look over that English story you promised to translate for us?

PETRA. No, not yet. But I'll get it to you in time.

(DR. STOCKMANN *comes in from his study, the open letter in his hand.*)

DR. STOCKMANN (*waving the letter*). Well, let me tell you, here's news for the town!

BILLING. News?

MRS. STOCKMANN. What sort of news?

DR. STOCKMANN. A great discovery, Katherine!

HOVSTAD. Really?

MRS. STOCKMANN. That you've made?

DR. STOCKMANN. My own, yes. (*Pacing back and forth.*) Now let them come around the way they do, saying it's just whims and wild fantasies. But they better watch out! (*With a laugh.*) They're going to watch out, I think!

PETRA. But, Father, tell what it is!

DR. STOCKMANN. Yes, all right, just give me time, and you'll learn everything. If I only had Peter here now! There you see how we human beings can go around, passing judgments as blind as moles——

HOVSTAD. What do you mean by that, Doctor?

DR. STOCKMANN (*stops by the table*). It's the general opinion, isn't it, that our town is a healthy place?

HOVSTAD. Why, of course.

DR. STOCKMANN. A most outstandingly healthy place, as a matter of fact—a place to be glowingly recommended to sick and well alike——

MRS. STOCKMANN. But, Thomas, dear——

DR. STOCKMANN. And recommend it we have, and praised it to the skies. I've written endlessly in the *Courier* and in pamphlets——

HOVSTAD. All right, so?

DR. STOCKMANN. This establishment, the baths, that's

been called the "main artery" of the town, and its "nerve center," and—who the hell knows what else—

BILLING. "The pulsating heart of our town" I once, in a moment of exuberance, went so far as to—

DR. STOCKMANN. Oh yes, that too. But do you know what they are in reality, these great, splendid, celebrated baths that have cost such a lot of money—you know what they are?

HOVSTAD. No, what are they?

MRS. STOCKMANN. What?

DR. STOCKMANN. The whole setup's a pesthole.

PETRA. The baths, Father!

MRS. STOCKMANN (*simultaneously*). Our baths!

HOVSTAD (*likewise*). But, Doctor—

BILLING. Simply incredible!

DR. STOCKMANN. It's a whited sepulcher, the whole establishment—poisoned, you hear me! A health hazard in the worst way. All that pollution up at Mølledal—all that reeking waste from the mill—it's seeped into the pipes feeding the pump-room; and the same damn poisonous slop's been draining out on the beach as well.

HORSTER. You mean in the bathing area?

DR. STOCKMANN. Exactly.

HOVSTAD. How can you be so certain of all this, Doctor?

DR. STOCKMANN. I've investigated the facts as scrupulously as possible. Oh, I've had suspicions for quite a while. Last year there were a number of unusual cases among the visitors here—typhoid and gastritis—

MRS. STOCKMANN. That's right, there were.

DR. STOCKMANN. At the time we assumed the visitors had brought their maladies with them. But later, over the past winter, I began having second thoughts; so I set out to analyze the water with the best means available.

MRS. STOCKMANN. So *that's* what you've been so involved in!

DR. STOCKMANN. Yes, involved—you can well say that, Katherine. But here, of course, I lacked the necessary scientific equipment, so I sent samples of both the drinking water and the seawater to the university for a strict laboratory analysis.

HOVSTAD. And this you've just gotten?

DR. STOCKMANN (*showing the letter*). This is it! There's irrefutable proof of the presence of decayed organic matter in the water—millions of bacteria. It's positively injurious to health, for either internal or external use.

MRS. STOCKMANN. What a godsend that you found out in time!

DR. STOCKMANN. You can say that again.

HOVSTAD. And what do you plan to do now, Doctor?

DR. STOCKMANN. To see things set to rights, of course.

HOVSTAD. Can that be done?

DR. STOCKMANN. It's got to be. Otherwise, the baths are totally useless—ruined. But there's no need for that. I'm quite clear about what actions have to be taken.

MRS. STOCKMANN. But, Thomas dear, why have you made such a secret of all this?

DR. STOCKMANN. Maybe I should have run out in the streets, blabbering about it before I had sure proof. No thanks, I'm not that crazy.

PETRA. But to us at home—

DR. STOCKMANN. Not to one living soul! But tomorrow you can run over to the Badger—

MRS. STOCKMANN. Really, Thomas—!

DR. STOCKMANN. All right then, your grandfather. Yes, this'll stand the old boy on his ear. He's always thought I'm a bit unhinged—oh yes, and a lot more think the same, I'm aware. But now these good people are going to find out—! (*Walks about, rubbing his hands.*) What a stir this'll make in town, Katherine! You can't imagine. The whole water system has to be relaid.

HOVSTAD (*rising*). The whole water system—?

DR. STOCKMANN. Well, obviously. The intake's too low; it's got to be placed much higher up.

PETRA. So you were right, after all.

DR. STOCKMANN. Ah, you remember that, Petra? I wrote a protest when they were just starting construction. But nobody would listen to me then. Well. now you can bet I'll pour on the heat—yes, because naturally I've written a report for the board of directors. It's been lying in my drawer a whole week; I've just been waiting for this. (*Waving the letter.*) But now it'll be sent right off. (*Goes into his study and returns with a sheaf of papers.*) See here! Four closely written pages! And a covering letter. A newspaper, Katherine—something to wrap this in! Good. that's it. Give it to—to— (*Stamps his foot.*) —what the hell's her name? The maid! Well, give it to her and tell her to take it straight to the mayor.

(MRS. STOCKMANN *takes the packet and goes out through the dining room.*)

PETRA. What do you think Uncle Peter will say, Father?

DR. STOCKMANN. What should he say? Undoubtedly he has to be glad that a fact of such importance is brought to light.

HOVSTAD. May I have permission to run a little item on your discovery in the *Courier*?

DR. STOCKMANN. I'd be most gratified if you would.

HOVSTAD. The public should hear about this, and the sooner the better.

DR. STOCKMANN. Absolutely.

MRS. STOCKMANN (*returning*). She's gone with it.

BILLING. So help me, Doctor, you're the foremost citizen of this town!

DR. STOCKMANN (*walks about, looking pleased*). Oh, come on—really, I haven't done anything more than my duty. I've been a lucky treasure-hunter, and that's it. All the same—

BILLING. Hovstad, don't you think this town owes Doctor Stockmann a parade?

HOVSTAD. I'll come out for it, in any case.

BILLING. And I'll put it up to Aslaksen.

DR. STOCKMANN. No, my dear friends, please—forget all this nonsense. I don't want any ceremonies. And if the board tries to vote me a raise in salary, I won't take it. Katherine, I'm telling you this—I won't take it.

MRS. STOCKMANN. That's only right, Thomas.

PETRA (raising her glass). Skoal, Father!

HOVSTAD and BILLING. Skoal, skoal, Doctor!

HORSTER (clinking glasses with him). May this bring you nothing but joy.

DR. STOCKMANN. Thank you. Dear friends, thank you! My heart is so full of happiness—! Ah, what a blessing it is to feel that you've done some service for your own home town and your fellow citizens. Hurrah, Katherine!

(He wraps both hands around her neck and whirls about the room with her; she screams and struggles against him. Laughter, applause, and cheers for the DOCTOR. The BOYS poke their heads in at the door.)

⤳ ACT TWO ⤲

The DOCTOR'S *living room. The dining-room door is closed. It is morning.* MRS. STOCKMANN, *with a sealed letter in her hand, enters from the dining room, goes across to the door of the* DOCTOR'S *study, and peers inside.*

MRS. STOCKMANN. Are you in, Thomas?

DR. STOCKMANN (*from within*). Yes, I just got back. (*Entering.*) Is there something?

MRS. STOCKMANN. Letter from your brother. (*Hands it to him.*)

DR. STOCKMANN. Ah, let's see. (*Opens the envelope and reads.*) "The enclosed manuscript is returned herewith—" (*Reads on in an undertone.*) Hm—

MRS. STOCKMANN. What does he say?

DR. STOCKMANN (*slips the papers in his pocket*). Only that he'll be stopping up around noon sometime.

MRS. STOCKMANN. You *must* remember not to go out, then.

DR. STOCKMANN. Oh, that's no problem. I've finished my calls for the morning.

MRS. STOCKMANN. I'm terribly curious to know how he takes it.

DR. STOCKMANN. You'll see, he's not going to like it that I made the discovery, and he didn't.

MRS. STOCKMANN. Yes, doesn't that worry you?

138

DR. STOCKMANN. Oh, basically he'll be pleased, you can imagine. All the same—Peter's so damned nervous that somebody besides himself might do this town a little good.

MRS. STOCKMANN. But, you know what, Thomas—that's why you ought to be nice and share the honors with him. Couldn't it get around that he was the one who put you on the track—?

DR. STOCKMANN. Fine, as far as I'm concerned. If I can just get this thing cleared up—

(*Old* MORTEN KIIL *sticks in his head at the hall door, looks about inquisitively, and shakes with silent laughter.*)

MORTEN KIIL (*slyly*). Is is—is it true?

MRS. STOCKMANN (*moving toward him*). Father—it's you!

DR. STOCKMANN. Why, Father-in-law, good morning, good morning!

MRS. STOCKMANN. Oh, but aren't you coming in?

MORTEN KIIL. Yes, if it's true—if not, I'm leaving—

DR. STOCKMANN. If what's true?

MORTEN KIIL. This wild story about the waterworks. Is that true?

DR. STOCKMANN. Of course it's true. But how did *you* hear about it?

MORTEN KIIL (*entering*). Petra flew in on her way to school—

DR. STOCKMANN. Oh, did she?

MORTEN KIIL. Oh yes, and she told me. I thought she was just making a fool of me; but that isn't like Petra, either.

DR. STOCKMANN. You don't mean that!

MORTEN KIIL. Oh, you can't trust anybody. You can be made a fool of before you know it. It really is true, though?

DR. STOCKMANN. Yes, irrefutably. Now, please, have a seat, Father. (*Pressing him down onto the sofa.*) Isn't this a real piece of luck for the town?

MORTEN KIIL (*stifling his laughter*). Luck for the town?

DR. STOCKMANN. Yes, that I made this discovery in the nick of time—

MORTEN KIIL (*as before*). Yes, yes, yes! But I'd never have dreamed that you'd play your monkeyshines on your own brother.

DR. STOCKMANN. Monkeyshines!

MRS. STOCKMANN. But, Father—

MORTEN KIIL (*rests his hands and chin on the handle of his cane and winks slyly at the* DOCTOR). How was it now? You're saying that some animals got loose in the water-pipes?

DR. STOCKMANN. Yes, bacteria.

MORTEN KIIL. And there are lots of those animals in there, Petra said. A huge crowd of them.

DR. STOCKMANN. Up in the millions, most likely.

MORTEN KIIL. But no one can see them—wasn't that it?

DR. STOCKMANN. You can't *see* them, of course not.

MORTEN KIIL (*chuckling to himself*). Damned if this isn't the best one you've pulled off yet.

DR. STOCKMANN. What do you mean?

MORTEN KIIL. But you'll never get the mayor believing anything like that.

DR. STOCKMANN. Well, we'll see.

MORTEN KIIL. You think he's that crazy?

DR. STOCKMANN. I hope the whole town will be that crazy.

MORTEN KIIL. The whole town! Yes, that's not impossible. It'd serve them right—and show them up. They think they're so much smarter than us old boys. They hounded me out of the town council. That's right, I'm telling you, like a dog they hounded me out, they did. But now they're going to get it. You just go on and lay your monkeyshines on them, Stockmann.

DR. STOCKMANN. Yes, but—

MORTEN KIIL. Make monkeys out of them, I say. (*Getting up.*) If you can work it so the mayor and his cronies get their ears pinned back, right then and there I'll donate a hundred crowns to the poor.

DR. STOCKMANN. You're very generous.

MORTEN KIIL. Yes, of course I've got little enough to spare, you understand. But if you can do that, I'll remember the poor next Christmas with a good fifty crowns.

(HOVSTAD *comes in from the hall.*)

HOVSTAD. Good morning! (*Stopping.*) Oh, excuse me—

DR. STOCKMANN. No, come in, come in.

MORTEN KIIL (*chuckling again*). Him! Is he in on this too?

HOVSTAD. What do you mean?

DR. STOCKMANN. Why, of course he is.

MORTEN KIIL. I might have guessed it. It's going into the paper. You're really the limit, Stockmann. Well, now you two get together; I'm leaving.

DR. STOCKMANN. No, stay a while, Father.

MORTEN KIIL. No, I'm leaving. And scheme up all the monkeyshines you can. You damn well aren't going to lose by it!

(*He goes, accompanied by* MRS. STOCKMANN.)

DR. STOCKMANN (*laughing*). What do you think—the old man doesn't believe a word of this about the water system.

HOVSTAD. Oh, was it *that*—?

DR. STOCKMANN. Yes, that's what we were talking about. And I suppose you're here for the same.

HOVSTAD. That's right. Do you have just a moment, Doctor?

DR. STOCKMANN. As long as you like.

HOVSTAD. Have you heard anything from the mayor?

DR. STOCKMANN. Not yet. He's stopping by later.

HOVSTAD. I've been thinking a good deal about this business since last evening.

DR. STOCKMANN. Oh?

HOVSTAD. For you, as a doctor and a scientist, this

condition in the water system is something all to itself. I mean, it hasn't occurred to you that it's interrelated with a lot of other things.

DR. STOCKMANN. How so? Here, let's sit down. No, on the sofa there.

(HOVSTAD *sits on the sofa, and* STOCKMANN *in an armchair on the other side of the table.*)

DR. STOCKMANN. Well? You were thinking—?

HOVSTAD. You said yesterday that the polluted water came from impurities in the soil.

DR. STOCKMANN. Yes, beyond any doubt it comes from that poisoned swamp up at Mølledal.

HOVSTAD. If you'll pardon me, Doctor, I think it comes from another swamp altogether.

DR. STOCKMANN. What sort?

HOVSTAD. The swamp where our whole community lies rotting.

DR. STOCKMANN. What the deuce is that supposed to mean, Mr. Hovstad?

HOVSTAD. Little by little every activity in this town has passed into the hands of a little clique of politicians—

DR. STOCKMANN. Come on now, they're not all of them politicians.

HOVSTAD. No, but those who aren't politicians are their friends and camp followers. All the rich in town, and the old established names—they're the powers that rule our lives.

DR. STOCKMANN. Yes, but then those people have a great deal of competence and vision.

HOVSTAD. Did they show competence and vision when they laid the water mains where they are now?

DR. STOCKMANN. No, of course that was an enormous piece of stupidity. But that'll be straightened out now.

HOVSTAD. You think it'll go so smoothly?

DR. STOCKMANN. Smoothly or not—it's going to go through.

HOVSTAD. Yes, if the press steps in.

DR. STOCKMANN. That won't be necessary, really. I'm positive that my brother—

HOVSTAD. Excuse me, Doctor; but I'm telling you that I plan to take this matter up.

DR. STOCKMANN. In the paper?

HOVSTAD. Yes. When I took over the *Courier*, it was my intention to break up that ring of pig-headed reactionaries who hold all the power.

DR. STOCKMANN. But you've told me yourself what the outcome was: you nearly wrecked the paper over them.

HOVSTAD. Yes, that time we had to back down, it's true. There was some risk that the baths might never have been constructed if those men had fallen. But now we have the baths, and the high and mighty are expendable now.

DR. STOCKMANN. Expendable, yes; but we still owe them a great debt.

HOVSTAD. And we'll acknowledge that, in all fairness. But a journalist of my radical leanings can't let an opportunity like this go by. The myth of the infallibility of the ruling class has to be shattered. It has to be rooted out, like any other superstition.

DR. STOCKMANN. I fully agree with you there, Mr. Hovstad. If it's a superstition, then out with it!

HOVSTAD. Of course I'm rather loath to involve the mayor, since he *is* your brother. But certainly you believe as I do, that the truth comes before anything else.

DR. STOCKMANN. No question of that. (*In an outburst.*) Yes, but—but—!

HOVSTAD. You mustn't think badly of me. I'm no more self-seeking or power-hungry than most people.

DR. STOCKMANN. But—whoever said you were?

HOVSTAD. I come from a poor family, as you know; and I've had ample opportunity to observe what the most pressing need is among the lower classes. Doctor, it's to play some part in directing our public life. That's the thing that develops skills and knowledge and self-respect—

DR. STOCKMANN. I understand absolutely—

HOVSTAD. Yes—and so I think a journalist is terribly remiss if he neglects the least opportunity for the liberation of the powerless, oppressed masses. Oh, I know—those on top are going to label this agitation, among other things; but they can say what they please. So long as my conscience is clear, then—

DR. STOCKMANN. That's it, yes! That's it, Mr. Hovstad. But all the same—damn it—! (*A knock at the door.*) Come in!

(ASLAKSEN, *the printer, appears at the hall door. He is plainly but respectably dressed in black, with a white, somewhat wrinkled cravat; he holds gloves and a high silk hat in his hand.*)

ASLAKSEN (*bowing*). Pardon me, Doctor, for intruding like this—

DR. STOCKMANN (*rises*). Well, now—it's Mr. Aslaksen!

ASLAKSEN. That's right, Doctor.

HOVSTAD (*getting up*). Were you looking for me, Aslaksen?

ASLAKSEN. No, I didn't think to meet you here. No, it was the doctor himself—

DR. STOCKMANN. Well, what can I do for you?

ASLAKSEN. Is it true, what I heard from Mr. Billing, that you're of a mind to get us a better water system?

DR. STOCKMANN. Yes, for the baths.

ASLAKSEN. Of course; I understand. Well, then I'm here to say, I'm throwing my full support behind you in this.

HOVSTAD (*to the* DOCTOR). You see!

ASLAKSEN. Because it might just come in handy to have us small businessmen in back of you. We make up pretty much of a solid majority in this town—that is, when we *choose* to. And it's always good to have the majority with you, Doctor.

DR. STOCKMANN. That's undoubtedly true. But I can hardly believe that any special measures are going to be needed here. With something as clear-cut as this, it would seem to me—

ASLAKSEN. Oh, it could be a good thing all the same. Because I know these local authorities. The ones that run things don't take too kindly to propositions coming from the outside. And so I was thinking it wouldn't be out of the way if we staged a little demonstration.

HOVSTAD. That's the idea.

DR. STOCKMANN. You say, a demonstration? Just how would you plan to demonstrate?

ASLAKSEN. Naturally with great moderation, Doctor. I always make every effort for moderation. Because moderation is a citizen's chief virtue—in *my* opinion, anyway.

DR. STOCKMANN. You're certainly well known for it, Mr. Aslaksen.

ASLAKSEN. Yes, I think that's not too much to say. And this question of the water system, it's immensely important to us little businessmen. The baths show every sign of becoming like a miniature gold mine for this town. It's the baths that'll give us all a living, and especially us home owners. That's why we want to support this operation in every possible way. And since I'm now chairman of the Home Owners Council—

DR. STOCKMANN. Yes—?

ASLAKSEN. And since, moreover, I'm a representative of the Temperance Union—you knew, Doctor, did you not, that I am a temperance worker?

DR. STOCKMANN. Yes, that follows.

ASLAKSEN. Well—so it's quite obvious that I come in contact with a wide variety of people. And since I'm known for being a sober, law-abiding citizen, as you yourself said, Doctor, I've acquired a certain influence in this town—just a little position of power—if I may say so myself.

DR. STOCKMANN. I'm well aware of that, Mr. Aslaksen.

ASLAKSEN. So you see—it would be a small matter for me to work up a tribute, in a pinch.

DR. STOCKMANN. A tribute?

ASLAKSEN. Yes, a kind of tribute of thanks from the townspeople to you, for having advanced such a vital interest for the community. It goes without saying that it's got to be phrased with all due moderation, so it doesn't offend the authorities, or anyone else in power. And if we just watch ourselves *there,* then I don't think anyone will object, do you?

HOVSTAD. So, even if they didn't like it too well—

ASLAKSEN. No, no, no! No affronts to the authorities, Mr. Hovstad. No collisions with people so much involved in our lives. I've had enough of that in my time; and no good ever comes of it, either. But a citizen's sober and honest opinions are not to be scorned by any man.

DR. STOCKMANN (*shaking his hand*). My dear Mr. Aslaksen, I can't tell you how deeply it pleases me to find so much sympathy among my fellow citizens. It makes me so happy—so happy! Listen, why not a little glass of sherry, what?

ASLAKSEN. Many thanks, but no. I never indulge in spirits.

DR. STOCKMANN. Well, then a glass of beer—what do you say to that?

ASLAKSEN. Thanks again, Doctor, but I never partake so early in the day. Just now I want to get around town and talk to some of the home owners and prepare their reactions.

DR. STOCKMANN. That's exceptionally kind of you, Mr. Aslaksen. But I simply can't get it through my head that all these measures are going to be necessary. I think the matter could very well take care of itself.

ASLAKSEN. Authorities tend to need goading, Doctor Stockmann—though, on my soul, I don't mean to be critical of them—!

HOVSTAD. We'll go after them in the paper tomorrow, Aslaksen.

ASLAKSEN. But without violence, Mr. Hovstad. Proceed in moderation, or you'll never get anywhere. You can trust my word on that, because I've gleaned my experience in the school of life. Well, then—I'll say good-bye to you, Doctor. Now you know that, in any event, we small businessmen stand behind you, like a wall. You've got the solid majority on your side, Doctor.

DR. STOCKMANN. Thank you for that, Mr. Aslaksen. (*Shaking his hand.*) Good-bye, good-bye!

ASLAKSEN. Will you be coming along to the pressroom, Mr. Hovstad?

HOVSTAD. I'll be in later. I still have a bit more to do.

ASLAKSEN. Very good.

(*He bows and leaves.* DR. STOCKMANN *accompanies him into the hall.*)

HOVSTAD (*as the* DOCTOR *re-enters*). Well, what do you say now, Doctor? Don't you think it's about time to stir up and air out all the stale, spineless inertia in this town?

DR. STOCKMANN. You're referring to Aslaksen?

HOVSTAD. Yes, I am. He's one of them who's sunk in the swamp—good a man as he is in some other ways. He's what most of them are around here: they go along tacking and trimming from this side to that. With all their scruples and second thoughts, they never dare strike out for anything.

DR. STOCKMANN. But to me Aslaksen seemed so thoroughly well-intentioned.

HOVSTAD. There's something I value more—and that's standing your ground as a strong, self-reliant man.

DR. STOCKMANN. I agree with you there entirely.

HOVSTAD. That's why I want to take this opportunity now and see if I can't force some of these models of intention to make men of themselves for once. The worship of authority in this town has to be uprooted. This inexcusable lapse of judgment about the water system has to be driven home to every eligible voter.

DR. STOCKMANN. All right. If you think it's best for the community, then go ahead. But not before I've talked with my brother.

HOVSTAD. Meanwhile, I'm writing an editorial to have on hand. And if the mayor doesn't get after this thing—

DR. STOCKMANN. Oh, but how can you think he wouldn't?

HOVSTAD. It's quite thinkable. And, if so—?

DR. STOCKMANN. Well, then I promise you—listen—then you can print my report—complete and uncut.

HOVSTAD. May I? Your word on that?

DR. STOCKMANN (*hands him the manuscript*). Here it is. Take it along. It can't hurt if you read it through; and you can give it back to me later.

HOVSTAD. Very good; I'll do that. Good-bye then, Doctor.

DR. STOCKMANN. Good-bye, good-bye. Yes, you'll see now, it'll all go smoothly, Mr. Hovstad. Very smoothly.

HOVSTAD. Hm—we'll see. (*He bows and goes out by the hall door.*)

DR. STOCKMANN (*goes over to the dining room and looks in*). Katherine—! Oh, are you back, Petra?

PETRA (*entering*). Yes, I just came from school.

MRS. STOCKMANN (*entering*). He's still not been in?

DR. STOCKMANN. Peter? No. But I had a long talk with Hovstad. He's very much excited by the discovery I've made. Its repercussions go a lot farther, apparently, than I thought at first. So he's put his paper at my disposal, if it comes to that.

MRS. STOCKMANN. Do you think it will come to that?

DR. STOCKMANN. Oh, of course not. But all the same, it's a heady feeling to know you've got the independent liberal press on your side. Yes, and guess what? I also had a visit from the chairman of the Home Owners Council.

MRS. STOCKMANN. Oh? And what did he want?

DR. STOCKMANN. To support me, as well. They'll all support me, if things get rough. Katherine—do you know what I have backing me up?

MRS. STOCKMANN. Backing you up? No, what do you have?

DR. STOCKMANN. The solid majority.

MRS. STOCKMANN. Really. And that's a good thing, is it, Thomas?

DR. STOCKMANN. Well, I should hope it's a good thing! (*Paces up and down, rubbing his hands together.*) My Lord, how gratifying it is to stand like this, joined together in brotherhood with your fellow citizens.

PETRA. And then to accomplish so much that's fine and useful, Father!

DR. STOCKMANN. And for one's own birthplace in the bargain.

MRS. STOCKMANN. There's the bell.

DR. STOCKMANN. That's got to be him. (*A knock at the door.*) Come in!

MAYOR STOCKMANN (*entering from the hall*). Good morning.

DR. STOCKMANN. Good to see you, Peter!

MRS. STOCKMANN. Morning, Peter. How's everything with you?

MAYOR STOCKMANN. Just so-so, thank you. (*To the* DOCTOR.) Yesterday, after office hours, I received a report from you, discussing the condition of the water at the baths.

DR. STOCKMANN. Yes. Have you read it?

MAYOR STOCKMANN. I have.

DR. STOCKMANN. What have you got to say about it?

MAYOR STOCKMANN (*glancing at the others*). Hm—

MRS. STOCKMANN. Come along, Petra.

(*She and* PETRA *go into the room on the left.*)

MAYOR STOCKMANN (*after a moment*). Was it necessary to press all these investigations behind my back?

DR. STOCKMANN. Well, as long as I didn't have absolute proof, then—

MAYOR STOCKMANN. And now you think you do?

DR. STOCKMANN. You must be convinced of that yourself.

MAYOR STOCKMANN. Is it your object to put this document before the board of directors by way of an official recommendation?

DR. STOCKMANN. Of course. Something has to be done about this. And fast.

MAYOR STOCKMANN. As usual, in your report you let your language get out of hand. You say, among other things, that what we're offering our summer visitors is guaranteed poison.

DR. STOCKMANN. But, Peter, how else can you describe it? You've got to realize—this water *is* poison for internal *or* external use! And it's foisted on poor, suffering creatures who turn to us in good faith and pay us exorbitant fees to gain their health back again!

MAYOR STOCKMANN. And then you arrive at the conclusion, by your line of reasoning, that we have to build a sewer to drain off these so-called impurities from Mølledal, and that all the water mains have to be relaid.

DR. STOCKMANN. Well, do you see any other way out? I don't.

MAYOR STOCKMANN. I invented a little business this morning down at the town engineer's office. And in a half-joking way, I brought up these proposals as something we perhaps ought to take under advisement at some time in the future.

DR. STOCKMANN. Some time in the future!

MAYOR STOCKMANN. He smiled at my whimsical extravagance—naturally. Have you gone to the trouble of estimating just what these proposed changes would cost? From the information I received, the expenditure would probably run up into several hundred thousand crowns.

DR. STOCKMANN. As high as that?

MAYOR STOCKMANN. Yes. But that's not the worst. The work would extend over at least two years.

DR. STOCKMANN. Two years? Two full years?

MAYOR STOCKMANN. At the least. And meanwhile what do we do with the baths? Shut them down? Yes, we'll have to. Do you really think anyone would make the effort to come all the distance here if the rumor got out that the water was contaminated?

DR. STOCKMANN. Yes, but Peter, that's what it is.

MAYOR STOCKMANN. And then all this happens now—just now, when the baths were being recognized. Other towns in this area have the same resources for development as health resorts. Don't you think they'll leap at the chance to attract the whole flow of tourists to them? No question of it. And there we are, left stranded. We'll most likely have to abandon the whole costly enterprise; and then you'll have ruined the town you were born in.

DR. STOCKMANN. I—ruined—!

MAYOR STOCKMANN. It's through the baths alone that this town has any future to speak of. You can see that just as plain as I can.

DR. STOCKMANN. But then what do you think ought to be done?

MAYOR STOCKMANN. From your report I'm unable to persuade myself that the condition of the baths is as critical as you claim.

DR. STOCKMANN. Look, if anything, it's worse! Or it'll be that by summer, when the warm weather comes.

MAYOR STOCKMANN. Once again. I think you're exaggerating considerably. A capable doctor must know the right steps to take—he should be able to control toxic elements, and to treat them if they make their presence too obvious.

DR. STOCKMANN. And then—? What else—?

MAYOR STOCKMANN. The water system for the baths as it now stands is simply a fact and clearly has to be accepted as such. But in time the directors will more than likely agree to take under consideration to what extent—depending on the funds available—they can institute certain improvements.

DR. STOCKMANN. And you can think I'd play along with that kind of trickery!

MAYOR STOCKMANN. Trickery?

DR. STOCKMANN. Yes, it's a trick—a deception, a lie, an out-and-out crime against the public and society at large!

MAYOR STOCKMANN. As I've already observed, I've not yet persuaded myself that there's any real impending danger here.

DR. STOCKMANN. Yes, you have! There's no alternative. My report is perfectly accurate, I know that! And you're very much aware of it, Peter, but you won't admit it. You're the one who got the baths and the water system laid out where they are today; and it's *this*—it's this hellish miscalculation that you won't concede. Pah! You don't think I can see right through you?

MAYOR STOCKMANN. And even if it were true? Even if I seem a bit overanxious about my reputation it's all for the good of the town. Without moral authority I could hardly guide and direct affairs in the way I believe serves the general welfare. For this reason—among many others—it strikes me as imperative that your report not be submitted to the board of directors. It has to be withheld for the common good. Then later I'll bring the matter up for discussion, and we'll do the very best we can, as quietly as possible. But nothing—not the slightest word of this catastrophe must leak out to the public.

DR. STOCKMANN. My dear Peter, there's no stopping it now.

MAYOR STOCKMANN. It must and it will be stopped.

DR. STOCKMANN. I'm telling you, it's no use. Too many people know already.

MAYOR STOCKMANN. Know already! Who? Not those fellows from the *Courier*—?

DR. STOCKMANN. Why, of course they know. The independent liberal press is going to see that you do your duty.

MAYOR STOCKMANN (*after a short pause*). You're an exceptionally thoughtless man, Thomas. Haven't you considered the consequences that can follow for you?

DR. STOCKMANN. Consequences? For me?

MAYOR STOCKMANN. For you and your family as well.

DR. STOCKMANN. What the devil does *that* mean?

MAYOR STOCKMANN. I think, over the years, I've proved a helpful and accommodating brother to you.

DR. STOCKMANN. Yes, you have, and I'm thankful to you for that.

MAYOR STOCKMANN. I'm not after thanks. Because, in part, I was forced into it—for my own sake. I always hoped I could keep you in check somewhat if I helped better your economic status.

DR. STOCKMANN. What? Just for your own sake—!

MAYOR STOCKMANN. In part, I said. It's embarrassing for a public servant when his closest relative goes and compromises himself again and again.

DR. STOCKMANN. And that's what you think I do?

MAYOR STOCKMANN. Yes, unfortunately you do, without your knowing it. You have a restless, unruly, combative nature. And then this unhappy knack of bursting into print on all kinds of likely and unlikely subjects. You're no sooner struck by an idea than right away you have to scribble a newspaper article on it, or a whole pamphlet even.

DR. STOCKMANN. Well, but isn't it a citizen's duty to inform the public if he comes on a new idea?

MAYOR STOCKMANN. Oh, the public doesn't need new ideas. The public is served best by the good, old, timetested ideas it's always had.

DR. STOCKMANN. That's putting it plainly!

MAYOR STOCKMANN. I have to talk to you plainly for once. Up till now I've always tried to avoid that because I know how irritable you are; but now I'm telling you the truth, Thomas. You have no conception how much you injure yourself with your impetuosity. You complain about the authorities and, yes, the government; you rail against them—and insist you're being passed over and persecuted. But what can you expect—someone as troublesome as you.

DR. STOCKMANN. Ah—so I'm troublesome, too?

MAYOR STOCKMANN. Yes, Thomas, you're a very troublesome man to work with. I know from experience. You show no consideration at all. You seem to forget completely that I'm the one you can thank for your post here as staff physician at the baths—

DR. STOCKMANN. I was the inevitable choice—I and nobody else! I was the first to see that this town could become a flourishing spa; and I was the *only* one who could see it then. I stood alone fighting for that idea for years; and I wrote and wrote—

MAYOR STOCKMANN. Unquestionably. But the right moment hadn't arrived yet. Of course you couldn't judge that from up there in the wilds. But when the opportune time came, then I—and a few others—took the matter in hand—

DR. STOCKMANN. Yes, and bungled the whole magnificent plan. Oh yes, it's really coming out now what a brilliant crew you've been!

MAYOR STOCKMANN. All that's coming out, to my mind, is your usual hunger for a good fight. You want to attack your superiors—it's your old pattern. You can't stand any authority over you; you resent anyone in a higher position and regard him as a personal enemy—and then one weapon's as good as another to use. But now I've acquainted you with the vital interests at stake here for this whole town—and, naturally, for me as well. And so I'm warning you, Thomas, I'll be adamant about the demand I'm going to make of you.

DR. STOCKMANN. What demand?

MAYOR STOCKMANN. Since you've been so indiscreet as to discuss this delicate issue with outsiders, even though it should have been kept secret among the directors, it of course can't be hushed up now. All kinds of rumors will go flying around, and the maliciously inclined will dress them up with trimmings of their own. It'll therefore be necessary that you publicly deny these rumors.

DR. STOCKMANN. I! How? I don't understand.

MAYOR STOCKMANN. We can expect that, after further investigation, you'll arrive at the conclusion that things are far from being as critical or dangerous as you'd first imagined.

DR. STOCKMANN. Ah—you expect that!

MAYOR STOCKMANN. Moreover, we expect that you'll support and publicly affirm your confidence in the present directors to take thorough and conscientious measures, as necessary, to rectify any possible defects.

DR. STOCKMANN. But that's utterly out of the question for me, as long as they try to get by with patchwork. I'm telling you that, Peter; and it's my unqualified opinion—!

MAYOR STOCKMANN. As a member of the staff, you're not entitled to any personal opinions.

DR. STOCKMANN (*stunned*). Not entitled—?

MAYOR STOCKMANN. As a staff member, I said. As a private person—why, that's another matter. But as a subordinate official at the baths, you're not entitled to express any opinions that contradict your superiors.

DR. STOCKMANN. That's going too far! I, as a doctor, a man of science, aren't entitled to—!

MAYOR STOCKMANN. What's involved here isn't a purely scientific problem. It's a mixture of both technical and economic considerations.

DR. STOCKMANN. I don't care what the hell it is! I want the freedom to express myself on any problem under the sun!

MAYOR STOCKMANN. Anything you like—except for the baths. We forbid you that.

DR. STOCKMANN (*shouting*). You forbid—! You! A crowd of—!

MAYOR STOCKMANN. *I* forbid it—*I*, your supervisor. And when I forbid you, then you obey.

DR. STOCKMANN (*controls himself*). Peter—if you weren't my brother—

PETRA (*flinging the door open*). You don't have to take this, Father!

MRS. STOCKMANN (*following her*). Petra, Petra!

MAYOR STOCKMANN. Ah, an ear to the keyhole.

MRS. STOCKMANN. You were so loud, we couldn't avoid—

PETRA. Oh, but I was there, listening.

MAYOR STOCKMANN. Well, I'm just as glad, really—

DR. STOCKMANN (*approaching him*). You were talking to me about forbidding and obeying—?

MAYOR STOCKMANN. You forced me to adopt that tone.

DR. STOCKMANN. So you want me to stand up in public and confess I'm a liar?

MAYOR STOCKMANN. We find it absolutely essential that you make a public statement along the lines I've indicated.

DR. STOCKMANN. And what if I don't—obey?

MAYOR STOCKMANN. Then we ourselves will issue a statement to soothe the public.

DR. STOCKMANN. Very well. But then I'll attack you in print. I'll stand my ground. I'll prove that I'm right, and you're wrong. And then what will you do?

MAYOR STOCKMANN. Then I won't be able to prevent your dismissal.

DR. STOCKMANN. What—!

PETRA. Father—dismissal!

MRS. STOCKMANN. Dismissal!

MAYOR STOCKMANN. You'll be dismissed from the staff. I'll find myself obliged to see you put on immediate notice and suspended from all activities involving the baths.

DR. STOCKMANN. And you'll dare that!

MAYOR STOCKMANN. You're the one playing the daredevil.

PETRA. Uncle, this is a shameful way to treat a man like Father!

MRS. STOCKMANN. Will you please be quiet, Petra!

MAYOR STOCKMANN (*regarding* PETRA). Ah, so we've already learned to voice opinions. Yes, naturally. (*To* MRS. STOCKMANN.) Katherine, I expect you're the most sensible member of this household. Use whatever influence you have over your husband, and make him understand what effect this will have on both his family—

DR. STOCKMANN. My family concerns no one else but me.

MAYOR STOCKMANN. As I was saying, on both his family and the town he lives in.

DR. STOCKMANN. I'm the one who really wants the best for the town! I want to expose failings that'll come to light sooner or later anyway. That ought to show that I love this town.

MAYOR STOCKMANN. Yes, by setting out in blind spite to cut off our major source of revenue.

DR. STOCKMANN. That source is poisoned, man! Are you crazy! We live by marketing filth and corruption. The whole affluence of this community has its roots in a lie!

MAYOR STOCKMANN. Sheer fantasy—or something worse. Any man who could hurl such nauseating charges at his own home town must be an enemy of society.

DR. STOCKMANN (*going for him*). You dare—!

MRS. STOCKMANN (*throws herself between them*). Thomas!

PETRA (*seizing her father by the arm*). Easy, Father!

MAYOR STOCKMANN. I don't have to subject myself to violence. Now you've been warned. Just consider what you owe yourself and your family. Good-bye. (*He leaves.*)

DR. STOCKMANN (*pacing up and down*). And I have to take this treatment! In my own house, Katherine! What do you say to that!

MRS. STOCKMANN. Of course it's humiliating, Thomas—

PETRA. Oh, what I could do to Uncle—!

DR. STOCKMANN. It's my own fault. I should have faced them down long ago—shown my teeth—and bit back! Call *me* an enemy of society! So help me God, I'm not going to swallow that!

MRS. STOCKMANN. But, Thomas dear, your brother does have the power—

DR. STOCKMANN. Yes, but I'm in the right!

MRS. STOCKMANN. The right? Ah, what does it help to be in the right if you don't have any power?

PETRA. Mother, no—why do you talk like that?

DR. STOCKMANN. You mean it doesn't help in a free society to be on the side of right? Don't be absurd, Katherine. And besides—don't I have the independent liberal press to lead the way—and the solid majority behind me? There's power enough in them, I'd say!

MRS. STOCKMANN. But Thomas, for heaven's sake—surely you're not thinking of—

DR. STOCKMANN. Thinking of what?

MRS. STOCKMANN. Of setting yourself up against your brother.

DR. STOCKMANN. What in hell do you want me to do? Abandon everything that's true and right?

PETRA. Yes, I'd ask the same.

MRS. STOCKMANN. But it won't do you the least bit of good. If they won't, they won't.

DR. STOCKMANN. Oh ho, Katherine, just give me time! You'll see, I'll push this fight through to the end.

MRS. STOCKMANN. Yes, maybe you'll just push yourself out of your job—that's what you'll do.

DR. STOCKMANN. Then anyway I'll have done my duty to the people—to society. Though they call me its enemy!

MRS. STOCKMANN. And to your family, Thomas? To us at home? You think that's doing your duty to those who depend on you?

PETRA. Oh, stop always thinking of us first of all, Mother.

MRS. STOCKMANN. Yes, it's easy for *you* to talk. If need be, you can stand on your own feet. But remember the boys, Thomas. And think of yourself a little, and of me—

DR. STOCKMANN. You must be utterly mad, Katherine! If I had to crawl like an abject coward to Peter and his damned cohorts—do you think I'd ever know one moment's happiness for the rest of my life?

MRS. STOCKMANN. I don't know about that. But God preserve us from the kind of happiness we'll share if you press your defiance. You'll be back again where you started—no position, no assured income. I thought we'd had enough of that in the old days. Remember that, Thomas; and think of what lies ahead.

DR. STOCKMANN (*clenching his fists and writhing in inner conflict*). And this is how these bureaucrats can clamp down on a plain, honest man! It's despicable, Katherine, isn't it?

MRS. STOCKMANN. Yes, they've acted shamefully toward you, of course. But, my Lord, there's so much injustice that people have to bear with in this world— There are the boys, Thomas! Look at them! What'll become of them? No, no, you wouldn't have the heart—

(*As she speaks,* EILIF *and* MORTEN *come in, carrying their schoolbooks.*)

DR. STOCKMANN. The boys—! (*Suddenly resolved.*) I don't care if all the world caves in, I'm not going to lick the dust. (*He heads for his study.*)

MRS. STOCKMANN (*following him*). Thomas—what are you doing?

DR. STOCKMANN (*at the door*). I want the chance to look my boys straight in the eyes when they've grown up to be free men. (*He goes within.*)

MRS. STOCKMANN (*bursting into tears*). Oh, God help us all!

PETRA. Father—he's wonderful! He's not giving in.

(*The boys, in bewilderment, ask what has happened;* PETRA *signals them to be quiet.*)

ACT THREE

The editorial office of the **People's Courier.** *At the back, left, is the entrance door; to the right in the same wall is another door, through which one can see the pressroom. In the wall to the right, a third door. At the center of the room is a large table covered with papers, newspapers, and books. In the foreground at the left a window and, next to it, a writing desk with a high stool. A couple of armchairs are drawn up by the table; several other chairs along the walls. The room is barren and cheerless, the furnishings old, the armchairs grimy and torn. In the pressroom two typesetters can be seen at work, and, beyond them, a handpress in operation.*

HOVSTAD *is seated at the desk, writing. After a moment* BILLING *enters from the right, the* DOCTOR'S *manuscript in his hand.*

BILLING. Well, that's really something—!

HOVSTAD (*writing*). Did you read it all?

BILLING (*lays the manuscript on the desk*). I'll say I did.

HOVSTAD. He makes a pretty sharp statement, doesn't he?

BILLING. Sharp? Ye gods, it's pulverizing! Every word hits home like a sledgehammer.

HOVSTAD. Yes, but that crowd isn't going to come down at one blow.

160

BILLING. That's true. But then we'll keep on hitting them—blow upon blow, till their whole leadership crumbles. When I sat in there reading this, it was exactly as if I could see the revolution breaking like the dawn.

HOVSTAD (*turning*). Shh! Don't say that so Aslaksen hears.

BILLING (*dropping his voice*). Aslaksen's a chicken-livered coward; there's no spine in the man. But this time you'll carry your own will through, uh? Right? You'll run the doctor's article?

HOVSTAD. Yes, if only the mayor doesn't give in—

BILLING. That'd be boring as hell.

HOVSTAD. Well, fortunately, no matter what happens, we can make something out of the situation. If the mayor won't buy the doctor's proposal, then he gets the small businessmen down on his neck—the Home Owners Council and that sort. And if he does buy it, he'll fall out with a whole host of the big stockholders in the baths, the ones who've been his best supporters up to now—

BILLING. Yes, that's right; they'll have to kick in a lot of new capital—

HOVSTAD. You bet they will! And then the ring is broken, see. And day after day in the paper we'll keep drumming it into the public that the mayor's incompetent on one score after another, and that all the elective offices in town—the whole administration—ought to be placed in the hands of the liberals.

BILLING. Ye gods, that's the living truth! I see it—I can see it! We're right on the verge of a revolution!

(*A knock at the door.*)

HOVSTAD. Shh! (*Calls out.*) Come in!

(DR. STOCKMANN *enters by the door at the back, left.*)

HOVSTAD (*goes to meet him*). Ah, here's the doctor. Well?

DR. STOCKMANN. Roll your presses, Mr. Hovstad!

HOVSTAD. Then it's come to that?

BILLING. Hurray!

DR. STOCKMANN. I said, roll your presses. Yes, it's come to that. But now they'll get what they're asking for. Now it's war in this town, Mr. Billing!

BILLING. War to the knife, I hope! Lay into them, Doctor!

DR. STOCKMANN. This article's only the beginning. My head's already brimming with ideas for four or five more pieces. Where do I find Aslaksen?

BILLING (*shouting into the pressroom*). Aslaksen, come here a minute!

HOVSTAD. Four or five more pieces, you say? On the same subject?

DR. STOCKMANN. No, not by a long shot. No, they're on totally different topics. But they all originate from the water system and the sewers. One thing leads to another, you know. It's the way it is when you start patching up an old building. Precisely like that.

BILLING. Ye gods, but that's the truth. You find out you'll never be done with it till you've torn down the whole rotten structure.

ASLAKSEN (*comes in from the pressroom*). Torn down! You don't plan to tear down the baths, Doctor?

HOVSTAD. Not at all. Don't get frightened.

DR. STOCKMANN. No, that was something else entirely. Well, what do you say about my article, Mr. Hovstad?

HOVSTAD. I think it's a pure masterpiece—

DR. STOCKMANN. Yes, isn't it—? Well, I'm most gratified, most gratified.

HOVSTAD. It's so clear and readable; you don't have to be a specialist at all to follow the argument. I daresay you'll have every reasonable man on your side.

ASLAKSEN. And all the moderates, too?

BILLING. Moderates and immoderates both—well, I mean, practically the entire town.

ASLAKSEN. Then we might take a chance on running it.

DR. STOCKMANN. Yes, I should think so!

HOVSTAD. It'll go in tomorrow morning.

DR. STOCKMANN. Good grief, it better; we can't waste a single day. Look, Mr. Aslaksen, I know what I wanted to ask you: would you give the manuscript your personal attention?

ASLAKSEN. I certainly will.

DR. STOCKMANN. Handle it like gold. No misprints; every word is vital. I'll stop back in again later; maybe I could glance over the proofs. Oh, I can't tell you how I'm dying to see this thing in print—delivered—

BILLING. Delivered—like a lightning-bolt!

DR. STOCKMANN. —addressed to the judgment of every thinking man. Ah, you can't imagine what I've been subjected to today. They've threatened me from all sides; they've tried to deprive me of my most fundamental human rights—

HOVSTAD. Of your rights!

DR. STOCKMANN. They've tried to humiliate me, and turn me into a jellyfish, and make me deny my deepest and holiest convictions for private profit.

BILLING. Ye gods, that's unforgivable.

HOVSTAD. Oh well, you have to expect anything from that crowd.

DR. STOCKMANN. But with me it's not going to work: they're going to get it, spelled out in black and white. I'm going to drop anchor right here at the *Courier* and rake them with broadsides: a fresh article every day—

ASLAKSEN. Yes, but now listen—

BILLING. Hurray! It's war—war!

DR. STOCKMANN. I'll smash them into the ground and shatter them! I'll wreck their defenses in the eyes of every fair-minded man! That's what I'll do!

ASLAKSEN. But do it temperately, Doctor. War, yes—in moderation.

BILLING. No, no! Don't spare the dynamite!

DR. STOCKMANN (*continues, unruffled*). Because now, you see, this isn't simply a matter of sewers and water mains anymore. No, it's the whole society that has to be purged and disinfected—

BILLING. That's the remedy!

DR. STOCKMANN. All these lunkheads in the old generation have to be dumped. And that means: no matter *who* they are! I've had such endless vistas opening up for me today. I haven't quite clarified it yet, but I'm working it out. My friends. we have to go forth and search out fresh, young standard-bearers; we have to have new commanders for all our outposts.

BILLING. Hear, hear!

DR. STOCKMANN. And if we only can stick together, everything will go off smoothly. The entire revolution will be launched as trim as a ship down the ways. Don't you think so?

HOVSTAD. For my part, I think we now have every prospect of seeing community control put right where it belongs.

ASLAKSEN. And if we just move ahead in moderation, I can't believe there's likely to be any danger.

DR. STOCKMANN. Who the hell cares about danger! Whatever I do will be done in the name of truth, for the sake of my conscience.

HOVSTAD. You're a man who deserves support, Doctor.

ASLAKSEN. Yes, that's a fact: the doctor's a true friend to the town, and a real friend to society.

BILLING. Ye gods, Aslaksen; Doctor Stockmann is the people's friend!

ASLAKSEN. I can imagine the Home Owners Council may pick that up as a slogan.

DR. STOCKMANN (*moved, pressing their hands*). Thank you, thank you, my dear, unfailing friends—it's so heartening to hear you say these things—my esteemed brother called me something quite different. Well, I swear he's going to get it back, with interest! But now I've got to look in on a patient, poor devil. I'll stop by again, as I said. Don't forget to look out for my manuscript, Mr. Aslaksen—and, whatever you do, don't cut any exclamation points. If anything, put a few more in! Fine, fine! Good-bye till later, good-bye, good-bye!

(*Amid mutual farewells, he is escorted to the door and departs.*)

HOVSTAD. He can be an exceptionally useful man for us.

ASLAKSEN. As long as he limits himself to the baths. But if he goes further, then it wouldn't be politic to join forces with him.

HOVSTAD. Hm, that all depends—

BILLING. You're always so damn fearful, Aslaksen.

ASLAKSEN. Fearful? Yes, as far as the local authorities go, I'm fearful, Mr. Billing. Let me tell you, it's something I've learned in the school of experience. But put me in the arena of national politics, opposed to the government itself, and then you'll see if I'm fearful.

BILLING. No, you're certainly not. But that's exactly where you're so inconsistent.

ASLAKSEN. I'm a man of conscience, that's the thing. As long as you attack the government, you can't do any real damage to society. You see, the men on that level, they aren't affected—they just ride it out. But the *local* authorities, *they* can be ousted; and then you might wind up with a lot of bunglers in power, who could do enormous damage to the property owners, among others.

HOVSTAD. But how about self-government as part of a citizen's education—don't you care about that?

ASLAKSEN. When a man has material assets at stake, he can't go thinking of everything.

HOVSTAD. Then I hope I'm never burdened with material assets.

BILLING. Hear, hear!

ASLAKSEN (*smiles*). Hm. (*Pointing at the desk.*) In that editor's chair, right there, your predecessor, Councilman Stengaard, used to sit.

BILLING (*spits*). Pah! That renegade.

HOVSTAD. I'm no double-dealer—and I never will be.

ASLAKSEN. A politician has to keep all possibilities open, Mr. Hovstad. And you, Mr. Billing—I think you better take a reef or two in your sails, now that you've put in for a job in the town clerk's office.

BILLING. I—!

HOVSTAD. *You* have, Billing?

BILLING. Yes, uh—you can damn well imagine I only did it to needle the establishment.

ASLAKSEN. Well, it's no business of mine, of course. But when I get labeled fearful and inconsistent in my stand, there's one thing I want to emphasize: my political record is available to all comers. I've never changed my position, except that I've become more moderate. My heart belongs to the people, always; but I can't deny that my reason disposes me toward the authorities—I mean, only the local ones, that is.

(*He goes into the pressroom.*)

BILLING. Shouldn't we call it quits with him, Hovstad?

HOVSTAD. You know any other printer who'll extend us credit for paper and labor costs?

BILLING. It's damnable that we don't have any capital.

HOVSTAD (*sitting at the desk*). Yes, if we only had that—

BILLING. How about approaching Stockmann?

HOVSTAD (*leafing through some papers*). What use would there be in that? He has nothing.

BILLING. No, but he's got a good man backing him: old Morten Kiil—the one they call the Badger.

HOVSTAD (*writing*). How can you know for sure *he* has anything?

BILLING. Ye gods, of course he does! And some part of it has to come to the Stockmanns. He's got to make provision—at least for the children.

HOVSTAD (*half turning*). Are you figuring on *that?*

BILLING. Figuring? I never figure on anything.

HOVSTAD. That's wise. And you'd better not figure on that job with the town, because I can promise you—you won't get it.

BILLING. Don't you think I've known that all along? There's nothing I'd welcome more than not getting it. A rejection like that really kindles your fighting spirit—it's almost like an infusion of fresh gall, and that's exactly what you need in an anthill like this, where hardly anything ever happens to really stir you up.

HOVSTAD (*continues writing*). How true, how true.

BILLING. Well—they'll soon be hearing from *me!* Now I'll go in and write that appeal to the Home Owners Council. (*He goes into the room to the right.*)

HOVSTAD (*sits at the desk, chews the end of his pen and says slowly*). Hm—so that's how it is. (*A knock at the door.*) Come in!

(PETRA *enters by the door at the back, left.*)

HOVSTAD (*getting up*). Oh, it's you? What are you doing here?

PETRA. You'll have to excuse me—

HOVSTAD (*pulls an armchair forward*). Won't you sit?

PETRA. No, thanks—I can't stay.

HOVSTAD. Is it something from your father that—?

PETRA. No, it's something from me. (*Takes a book out of her coat pocket.*) Here's that English story.

HOVSTAD. Why are you giving it back?

PETRA. Because I don't want to translate it.

HOVSTAD. But you promised me, definitely—

PETRA. Well, I hadn't read it then. And of course you haven't read it either.

HOVSTAD. No. You know I don't understand English; but—

PETRA. All right, that's why I wanted to tell you that you'll have to find somebody else. (*Lays the book on the table.*) This could never be used in the *Courier.*

HOVSTAD. Why not?

PETRA. It's totally opposed to everything you stand for.

HOVSTAD. Well, actually—

PETRA. You still don't understand me. It shows how a supernatural power, watching over the so-called good people of this world, arranges everything for the best in their lives—and how all the so-called wicked get their punishment.

HOVSTAD. But that's fair enough. It's exactly what the public wants.

PETRA. And do you want to be the one who feeds the public that sort of thing? You don't believe a word of it yourself. You know perfectly well things don't happen like that in reality.

HOVSTAD. You're perfectly right; but then an editor can't always do what he might prefer. You often have to bow to public opinions in lesser matters. After all, politics is the main thing in life—for a newspaper, in any event. And if I want to lead people toward greater liberation and progress, then I mustn't scare them away. When they find a moral story like this in the back pages, they're more willing to accept what we print up front—they feel more secure.

PETRA. Oh, come! You wouldn't be so tricky and lay snares for your readers. You're not a spider.

HOVSTAD (*smiles*). Thank you for thinking so well of me. No, it really was Billing's scheme, and not mine.

PETRA. Billing's!

HOVSTAD. Yes. At any rate, he was speaking of it just the other day. It's Billing who's been so hot about getting that story in; I don't know the book.

PETRA. But how could Billing, with his liberal attitude—?

HOVSTAD. Oh, Billing is a many-sided man. Now I hear he's out for a job in the town clerk's office.

PETRA. I don't believe it, Hovstad. How could he ever conform himself to that?

HOVSTAD. That's something you'll have to ask him.

PETRA. I never would have thought it of Billing.

HOVSTAD (*looks more sharply at her*). You wouldn't? Does it surprise you so?

PETRA. Yes. Or maybe not, really. Oh, honestly, I don't know—

HOVSTAD. We journalists don't amount to much, Miss Stockmann.

PETRA. You actually mean that?

HOVSTAD. It's what I think sometimes.

PETRA. Yes, in your normal day-to-day existence—I can understand that well enough. But now that you're lending a hand in a great cause—

HOVSTAD. This matter of your father, you mean?

PETRA. Exactly. Now I think you must feel like a man who's more valuable than most.

HOVSTAD. Yes, I feel something of that today.

PETRA. Yes, you do, don't you? Oh, it's a glorious calling you've chosen! To pioneer the way for embattled truths and daring new insights- -or simply to stand up fearlessly for a man who's been wronged—

HOVSTAD. Especially when that man who's been wronged is—hm—I don't quite know how to put it—

PETRA. When he's so direct and honest, you mean?

HOVSTAD (*in a softer voice*). No, I meant—especially when he's your father.

PETRA (*startled*). It's *that!*

HOVSTAD. Yes, Petra—Miss Petra.

PETRA. Is *that* the main thing for you? Not the issue itself? Not the truth? Not my father's compassion for life?

HOVSTAD. Why, yes—of course, that too.

PETRA. No, thanks, Mr. Hovstad; you betrayed yourself. And now I'll never trust you again, in anything.

HOVSTAD. How can you be so hard on me, when it's mostly for your own sake—?

PETRA. What I'm mad at you about is you haven't played fair with Father. You've talked to him as if the truth and the good of the community lay closest to your heart. You've made fools of both him and me. You're not the man you pretend to be. And for that I'll never forgive you—never!

HOVSTAD. You shouldn't be so bitter, Miss Petra—paticularly right now.

PETRA. Why not now?

HOVSTAD. Because your father can't dispense with my help.

PETRA (*scanning him*). And you're that kind, too? So!

HOVSTAD. No, no, I'm not. I don't know what brought that on. You have to believe me.

PETRA. I know what I have to believe. Good-bye.

ASLAKSEN (*entering from the pressroom, brusquely and cryptically*). God Almighty, Hovstad— (*Sees* PETRA.) Oh, what a mess—

PETRA. There's the book; you can give it to somebody else. (*Goes toward the entrance door.*)

HOVSTAD (*following her*). But, Miss Petra—

PETRA. Good-bye. (*She leaves.*)

ASLAKSEN. Mr. Hovstad, listen!

HOVSTAD. Yes, all right, what is it?

ASLAKSEN. The mayor's out there in the pressroom.

HOVSTAD. You say, the mayor?

ASLAKSEN. Yes, he wants to talk to you. He came in the back entrance—didn't want to be seen, I guess.

HOVSTAD. What's this all about? No, wait, I'll go—

(*He crosses to the door of the pressroom, opens it, and beckons the* MAYOR *in.*)

HOVSTAD. Keep an eye out, Aslaksen, so nobody—

ASLAKSEN. I understand— (*Goes into the pressroom.*)

MAYOR STOCKMANN. I imagine you hardly expected to see me here, Mr. Hovstad.

HOVSTAD. No, I really hadn't.

MAYOR STOCKMANN (*looking about*). You've certainly made yourself quite comfortable here. Very nice.

HOVSTAD. Oh—

MAYOR STOCKMANN. And now I come along unceremoniously and monopolize your time.

HOVSTAD. By all means, Mr. Mayor; I'm at your service. But please, let me take your things— (*Sets the* MAYOR'S *hat and stick on a chair.*) Won't you have a seat?

MAYOR STOCKMANN (*sitting at the table*). Thank you. (HOVSTAD *likewise sits at the table.*)

MAYOR STOCKMANN. I've gone through—really a most troublesome episode today, Mr. Hovstad.

HOVSTAD. Yes? Oh well, with all the cares that the mayor has—

MAYOR STOCKMANN. It involves the staff physician at the baths.

HOVSTAD. You mean, the doctor?

MAYOR STOCKMANN. He's penned a kind of report to the board of directors, alleging that the baths have certain deficiencies.

HOVSTAD. He has?

MAYOR STOCKMANN. Yes, didn't he tell you—? I thought he said—

HOVSTAD. Oh yes, that's true. He made some mention of it—

ASLAKSEN (*entering from the pressroom*). I need to have that manuscript—

HOVSTAD (*vexed*). Hm, it's there on the desk.

ASLAKSEN (*locating it*). Good.

MAYOR STOCKMANN. But look—that's *it*, exactly—

ASLAKSEN. Yes, that's the doctor's article, Mr. Mayor.

HOVSTAD. Oh, is *that* what you were talking about?

MAYOR STOCKMANN. None other. What do you think of it?

HOVSTAD. I'm really no expert, and I've barely skimmed through it.

MAYOR STOCKMANN. Still, you're going to print it.

HOVSTAD. A man of his reputation I can hardly refuse—

ASLAKSEN. I have no say at all in this paper, Mr. Mayor.

MAYOR STOCKMANN. Naturally.

ASLAKSEN. I only print what's put in my hands.

MAYOR STOCKMANN. Quite properly.

ASLAKSEN. So, if you'll pardon me— (*Goes toward the pressroom.*)

MAYOR STOCKMANN. No, just a minute, Mr. Aslaksen. With your permission, Mr. Hovstad—

HOVSTAD. My pleasure.

MAYOR STOCKMANN. You're a sober-minded and thoughtful man, Mr. Aslaksen.

ASLAKSEN. I'm glad Your Honor holds that opinion.

MAYOR STOCKMANN. And a man of influence in many circles.

ASLAKSEN. That's mostly among the little people.

MAYOR STOCKMANN. The small taxpayers are the great majority—here, as elsewhere.

ASLAKSEN. That's the truth.

MAYOR STOCKMANN. And I don't doubt that you know the general sentiment among most of them. Am I right?

ASLAKSEN. Yes, I daresay I do, Mr. Mayor.

MAYOR STOCKMANN. Well—if there's such a worthy spirit of self-sacrifice prevailing among the town's less affluent citizens, then—

ASLAKSEN. How's that?

HOVSTAD. Self-sacrifice?

MAYOR STOCKMANN. It's a beautiful token of community spirit, an exceptionally beautiful token. I was close to saying that I wouldn't have expected it. But you know the feelings of these people far better than I.

ASLAKSEN. Yes, but, Your Honor—

MAYOR STOCKMANN. And as a matter of fact, it's no small sacrifice this town will be asked to bear.

HOVSTAD. The town?

ASLAKSEN. But I don't follow— It's the baths—!

MAYOR STOCKMANN. At a tentative estimate, the changes that our staff physician finds desirable run up to a couple of hundred thousand crowns.

ASLAKSEN. That's a lot of money, but—

MAYOR STOCKMANN. Of course it'll be necessary for us to take out a municipal loan.

HOVSTAD (*rises*). It can't be your intention for the town to—

ASLAKSEN. Not out of property taxes! Out of the empty pockets of the home owners!

MAYOR STOCKMANN. Well, my dear Mr. Aslaksen, where else would the capital come from?

ASLAKSEN. The men who own the baths can raise it.

MAYOR STOCKMANN. The owners find themselves in no position to extend themselves further than they are already.

ASLAKSEN. Is that quite definite, Mr. Mayor?

MAYOR STOCKMANN. I've ascertained it for a fact. So if one wants all these elaborate changes, the town itself will have to pay for them.

ASLAKSEN. But hell and damnation—excuse me, sir!— but this is a totally different picture, Mr. Hovstad.

HOVSTAD. It certainly is.

MAYOR STOCKMANN. The worst part of it is that we'll be forced to shut down the baths for a two-year period.

HOVSTAD. Shut down? Completely?

ASLAKSEN. For two years!

MAYOR STOCKMANN. Yes, the work has to take that long—at the least.

ASLAKSEN. But, God Almighty, we'll never last that out, Mr. Mayor! What'll we home owners live on in the meantime?

MAYOR STOCKMANN. Unhappily, it's extremely difficult to answer that, Mr. Aslaksen. But what do you want us to do? You think we'll get a single summer visitor here if anyone goes around posing suppositions that the water is polluted, that we're living in a pesthole, that the whole town—

ASLAKSEN. And it's all just supposition?

MAYOR STOCKMANN. With the best will in the world, I haven't been able to persuade myself otherwise.

ASLAKSEN. Yes, but then it's absolutely indefensible of Dr. Stockmann—begging your pardon, Mr. Mayor, but—

MAYOR STOCKMANN. It's distressingly true, what you imply, Mr. Aslaksen. I'm afraid my brother's always been a reckless man.

ASLAKSEN. And in spite of this, you want to go on supporting him, Mr. Hovstad!

HOVSTAD. But how could anyone have suspected—?

MAYOR STOCKMANN. I've drawn up a brief statement of the relevant facts, as they might appear to a disinterested observer; and I've suggested therein how any possible deficiencies might well be covered without exceeding the current budget for the baths.

HOVSTAD. Do you have this statement with you, Mr. Mayor?

MAYOR STOCKMANN (*groping in his pocket*). Yes, I took it along just in case—

ASLAKSEN (*abruptly*). Oh, my God, there he is!

MAYOR STOCKMANN. Who? My brother?

HOVSTAD. Where—where!

ASLAKSEN. Coming through the pressroom.

MAYOR STOCKMANN. How embarrassing! I don't want to run up against him here, and I still have things to talk to you about.

HOVSTAD (*pointing toward the door at the right*). Step in there for a moment.

MAYOR STOCKMANN. But—?

HOVSTAD. It's just Billing in there.

ASLAKSEN. Quick, Your Honor! He's coming!

MAYOR STOCKMANN. Yes, all right, but try to get rid of him fast.

(*He goes out the door, right, as* ASLAKSEN *opens and closes it for him.*)

HOVSTAD. Look like you're doing something, Aslaksen.

(*He sits and starts to write.* ASLAKSEN *rummages in a pile of papers on a chair to the right.*)

DR. STOCKMANN (*entering from the pressroom*). Here I am again. (*Puts down his hat and stick.*)

HOVSTAD (*writing*). Already, Doctor? Get going on what we were talking about, Aslaksen. We can't waste time today.

DR. STOCKMANN (*to* ASLAKSEN). I gather, no proofs as yet.

ASLAKSEN (*without turning*). How could you expect that, Doctor?

DR. STOCKMANN. No, no, I'm just impatient—you have to understand. I won't have a moment's peace till I see it in print.

HOVSTAD. Hm—it's bound to be a good hour still. Don't you think so, Aslaksen?

ASLAKSEN. Yes, I'm afraid so.

DR. STOCKMANN. My dear friends, that's quite all right; I'll come back. I'll gladly come back twice, if necessary. With anything so important—the welfare of this whole town—it's no time to take it easy. (*Starts to go, then pauses and returns.*) Oh, listen—there's still something I want to mention to you.

HOVSTAD. Sorry, but couldn't we some other time—?

DR. STOCKMANN. I can say it in two seconds. It's simply this—when people read my article in the paper tomorrow and find out as well that I've spent the whole winter in seclusion, working for the good of the town—

HOVSTAD. Yes, but Doctor—

DR. STOCKMANN. I know what you'll say. You don't think it was any more than my blasted duty—ordinary civic responsibility. Well, of course; I know that just as well as you do. But my fellow townspeople, you see— bless their souls, they hold such a high regard for me—

ASLAKSEN. Yes, the people have held you in the highest regard—up till now, Doctor.

DR. STOCKMANN. Yes, and it's just the reason I'm afraid that— What I'm trying to say is this: my article, if it affects the people—especially the deprived classes—as an incitement to take the future affairs of the town into their own hands—

HOVSTAD (*getting up*). Hm, Doctor, I don't want to mislead you—

DR. STOCKMANN. Aha—I thought there was something brewing! But I won't hear of it. So if they go preparing anything—

HOVSTAD. Such as?

DR. STOCKMANN. Oh, anything of the kind—a parade or a banquet or a testimonial award or whatever, then you promise me by all that's holy to get it quashed. And you too, Mr. Aslaksen; you hear me!

HOVSTAD. Pardon me, Doctor, but we'd better tell you the unvarnished truth right now—

(MRS. STOCKMANN, *in hat and coat, comes in by the entrance door, back left.*)

MRS. STOCKMANN (*seeing the* DOCTOR). I thought so!

HOVSTAD (*going toward her*). Mrs. Stockmann, you too?

DR. STOCKMANN. Katherine, what the deuce are you doing here?

MRS. STOCKMANN. You know very well what I want.

HOVSTAD. Won't you have a seat? Or perhaps—

MRS. STOCKMANN. Thanks, but don't bother. And please, don't be offended that I'm here to fetch Stockmann; because I'm the mother of three children, I want you to know.

DR. STOCKMANN. Oh, bosh! We know all that.

MRS. STOCKMANN. Well, it really doesn't seem as if you're thinking much of your wife and children these days, or else you wouldn't have gone on this way, hurling us all into perdition.

DR. STOCKMANN. Are you utterly insane. Katherine? Does a man with a wife and children have no right to proclaim the truth—no right to be an effective citizen—or to serve the town he lives in?

MRS. STOCKMANN. All those things—in moderation, Thomas!

ASLAKSEN. I agree. Moderation in all things.

MRS. STOCKMANN. That's why you wrong us terribly, Mr. Hovstad, when you inveigle my husband out of house and home and down here to make a fool of himself in this.

HOVSTAD. I don't make fools of people—

DR. STOCKMANN. Fools! Nobody fools *me!*

MRS. STOCKMANN. Oh yes, they do. I know you're the smartest man in town, but you're so very easy to fool, Thomas. (*To* HOVSTAD.) And just consider that he'll lose his job at the baths if you print what he's written—

ASLAKSEN. What!

HOVSTAD. Yes, but you know, Doctor—

DR. STOCKMANN (*laughing*). Just let them try! Oh, no—they won't dare. Because, you see, I've got the solid majority behind me.

MRS. STOCKMANN. Yes, that's the trouble, exactly. An ugly lot like that behind you.

DR. STOCKMANN. Balderdash, Katherine! Go home and take care of your house and let me take care of society. How can you be so scared, when I'm so secure and happy? (*Walks up and down, rubbing his hands.*) Truth and the people will win the battle, you can count on that. Oh, I can see all the liberal-minded citizens everywhere gathering into a victorious army—! (*Stops by a chair.*) What—what the hell is *this?*

ASLAKSEN (*looking over*). Ow-ah!

HOVSTAD (*likewise*). Hm—!

DR. STOCKMANN. Here we see the summit of authority. (*He takes the* MAYOR'S *hat delicately between his fingertips and holds it high.*)

MRS. STOCKMANN. The mayor's hat!

DR. STOCKMANN. And here's the scepter of command, too. How in blazes—?

HOVSTAD. Well, uh—

DR. STOCKMANN. Ah, I get it! He's been here to coax you over. Ho ho, he knew right where to come. And then he caught sight of me in the pressroom. (*Explodes with laughter.*) Did he run, Mr. Aslaksen?

ASLAKSEN (*hurriedly*). Oh yes, Doctor, he ran off.

DR. STOCKMANN. Ran away from his stick and his— My eye! Peter never runs from anything. But where the devil have you put him? Ah—inside, of course. Now you watch this, Katherine!

MRS. STOCKMANN. Thomas—please—!

ASLAKSEN. Watch yourself, Doctor!

(DR. STOCKMANN *sets the* MAYOR's *hat on his head and takes his stick; he then goes over, throws open the door, and raises his hand in salute. The* MAYOR *comes in, red with anger.* BILLING *enters behind him.*)

MAYOR STOCKMANN. What's the meaning of this rowdyism?

DR. STOCKMANN. Some respect, if you will, Peter. I'm the authority in town now. (*He parades up and down.*)

MRS. STOCKMANN (*nearly in tears*). Thomas, no!

MAYOR STOCKMANN (*following him*). Give me my hat and my stick!

DR. STOCKMANN. If you're the police chief, then I'm the mayor. I'm in charge of the whole town, see!

MAYOR STOCKMANN. I'm telling you, take off that hat. Remember, that's an insignia of office!

DR. STOCKMANN. Pah! Do you think the waking lion of the people's strength is going to be scared of a hat? Yes, because you better know: tomorrow we're making a revolution in town. You threatened me with my dismissal, but now I'm dismissing you—from all your public offices. You don't think I can? Oh yes, you'll see. I've got the ascendant forces of society on my side. Hovstad and Billing will thunder in the *People's Courier;* and Aslaksen will take the field, leading the whole Home Owners Council—

ASLAKSEN. I won't do it, Doctor.

DR. STOCKMANN. Why, of course you will—

MAYOR STOCKMANN. Ah, but perhaps, even so, Mr. Hovstad will be joining this rebellion?

HOVSTAD. No, Mr. Mayor.

ASLAKSEN. No, Mr. Hovstad isn't so crazy that he'd go and wreck both himself and the paper for the sake of a mere surmise.

DR. STOCKMANN (*looking about*). What's going on here?

HOVSTAD. You've presented your case in a false light, Doctor; and that's why I can't support it.

BILLING. No, after what the mayor was good enough to tell me in there—

DR. STOCKMANN. False! You can leave that to me. Just print my article. I can take care of defending it.

HOVSTAD. I'm not printing it. I cannot and will not and dare not print it.

DR. STOCKMANN. You dare not? What kind of rot is that? You're the editor, aren't you? And it's the editors who run the press, I hope!

ASLAKSEN. No, it's the readers, Doctor.

MAYOR STOCKMANN. Thankfully, yes.

ASLAKSEN. It's public opinion, the informed citizens, the home owners, and all the rest—they're the ones that run the press.

DR. STOCKMANN (*comprehending*). And all these powers I have against me?

ASLAKSEN. That's right. If your article is printed, it'll mean absolute ruin for this town.

DR. STOCKMANN. I see.

MAYOR STOCKMANN. My hat and my stick!

(DR. STOCKMANN *removes the hat and sets it, along with the stick, on the table.*)

MAYOR STOCKMANN (*reclaiming them both*). That was a sudden end to your first term in office.

DR. STOCKMANN. It's not the end yet. (*To* HOVSTAD.)

Then there's no possibility of getting my article in the *Courier?*

HOVSTAD. None whatever. Partly out of regard for your family.

MRS. STOCKMANN. Oh, never mind about this family, Mr. Hovstad.

MAYOR STOCKMANN (*takes a sheet of paper from his pocket*). For the protection of the public, it will be sufficient if this goes in. It's an authorized statement. If you will.

HOVSTAD (*taking the sheet*). Good. We'll insert it right away.

DR. STOCKMANN. But not mine! People think they can stifle me and choke off the truth! But it won't go as smooth as you think. Mr. Aslaksen, would you take my manuscript and issue it at once as a pamphlet—at my expense—under my own imprint. I'll want four hundred copies; no, five—six hundred I'll need.

ASLAKSEN. Even if you gave me its weight in gold, I couldn't put my plant to that use, Doctor. I wouldn't dare, in view of public opinion. You won't get that printed anywhere in this town.

DR. STOCKMANN. Then give it back.

HOVSTAD (*hands him the manuscript*). There.

DR. STOCKMANN (*picks up his hat and stick*). It's coming out, no matter what. I'll hold a mass meeting and read it aloud. All my fellow townspeople are going to hear the voice of truth.

MAYOR STOCKMANN. There's not an organization in town that'll rent you a hall for such a purpose.

ASLAKSEN. Not one. I'm positive of that.

BILLING. Ye gods, no!

MRS. STOCKMANN. But this is shameful. Why do they all turn against you, these men?

DR. STOCKMANN (*furiously*). I'll tell you why! It's because all the so-called men in this town are old women—like you. They all just think of their families and never the common good.

MRS. STOCKMANN (*taking his arm*). Then I'll show them a—an old woman who can be a man for once. I'm standing with you, Thomas!

DR. STOCKMANN. That was well said, Katherine. And, by God, I'll get this out! If I can't rent a hall, then I'll hire a drummer to walk the town with me, and I'll cry out the truth on every street corner.

MAYOR STOCKMANN. You're not going to act like a raving maniac!

DR. STOCKMANN. Yes, I am!

ASLAKSEN. In this whole town, you won't get one solitary man to go with you.

BILLING. Ye gods, I'll say you won't!

MRS. STOCKMANN. Don't give in, Thomas. I'll ask the boys to go with you.

DR. STOCKMANN. That's a marvelous idea!

MRS. STOCKMANN. Morten would love to do it; and Eilif—he'll go along

DR. STOCKMANN. Yes, and Petra too! And you yourself, Katherine!

MRS. STOCKMANN. No, no, that's not for me. But I'll stand at the window and watch you; that I'll do.

DR. STOCKMANN (*throws his arms about her and kisses her*). Thanks for that! And now, gentlemen, let's try our steel. I'd just like to see if conniving hypocrisy can gag the mouth of a patriot who's out to clean up society!

(*He and* MRS. STOCKMANN *leave by the entrance door, back left.*)

MAYOR STOCKMANN (*gravely shaking his head*). Now he's driven her crazy, too.

⤙ ACT FOUR ⤚

A large, old-fashioned room in CAPTAIN HORSTER'S *house. Double doors, standing open at the back, lead to an anteroom. Spaced along the wall, left, are three windows. At the middle of the opposite wall a platform has been prepared, with a small table; on it are two candles, a water carafe, a glass, and a bell. The room is mainly illuminated by wall lamps between the windows. In the left foreground stands a table with candles on it, and a chair. Farther forward at the right is a door, with several chairs beside it.*

There is a large assemblage of TOWNSPEOPLE *from all levels of society. Scattered among them are a few* WOMEN *and some* SCHOOLBOYS. *More and more people gradually crowd in from the rear, until the room is full.*

A CITIZEN (*to another, as he jostles against him*). Are you here too, Lamstad?

SECOND CITIZEN. I never miss a public meeting.

THIRD CITIZEN. I hope you brought along your whistle?

SECOND CITIZEN. You bet I did. And you?

THIRD CITIZEN. Of course. Skipper Evensen has a whopping big horn he said he'd bring.

SECOND CITIZEN. He's a character, that Evensen.

(*Laughter among the group.*)

FOURTH CITIZEN (*joining them*). Say, tell me, what's going on here tonight?

SECOND CITIZEN. It's Dr. Stockmann; he's giving a speech against the mayor.

FOURTH CITIZEN. But the mayor's his brother.

FIRST CITIZEN. What of it? The doctor isn't afraid.

THIRD CITIZEN. Yes, but he's all wrong. The *Courier* said so.

SECOND CITIZEN. Yes, he really must be this time, because nobody'll rent him a hall—neither the Home Owners Council nor the civic club.

FIRST CITIZEN. Even the hall at the baths wouldn't have him.

SECOND CITIZEN. Well, that you can imagine.

A MAN (*in another group*). Who are we backing in this?

ANOTHER MAN (*next to him*). Just watch Aslaksen and do what he does.

BILLING (*with a portfolio under his arm, forcing his way through the crowd*). Excuse me, gentlemen! If you'll let me by, please? I'm covering this for the *Courier.* Thank you so much! (*He sits at the table on the left.*)

A WORKMAN. Who's he?

ANOTHER WORKMAN. You don't know *him?* That's Billing—writes for Aslaksen's paper.

(CAPTAIN HORSTER *conducts* MRS. STOCKMANN *and* PETRA *in through the door to the right.* EILIF *and* MORTEN *follow.*)

HORSTER. I was thinking the family could sit here. If anything should happen, you could slip out quietly.

MRS. STOCKMANN. Do you think there'll be a disturbance?

HORSTER. You never can tell—with so many people. But sit down and rest easy.

MRS. STOCKMANN. How kind of you to offer Thomas this room.

HORSTER. When nobody else would, then—

PETRA (*who also has seated herself*). And it was brave of you, too, Captain Horster.

HORSTER. Oh, I don't think it took much courage for that.

(HOVSTAD *and* ASLAKSEN *make their way forward at the same time, but separately, through the crowd.*)

ASLAKSEN (moves across to HORSTER). Hasn't the doctor come yet?

HORSTER. He's waiting inside.

(*A flurry of activity by the doorway in back.*)

HOVSTAD (*to* BILLING). Here's the mayor. Look!

BILLING. Ye gods, he showed up after all!

(*The* MAYOR *proceeds quietly through the crowd, exchanging polite greetings, and then stations himself by the wall, left. After a moment* DR. STOCKMANN *enters through the door to the right. He is dressed in a black frock coat with a white tie. There is scattered, hesitant applause, which is met by subdued hissing. The room grows silent.*)

DR. STOCKMANN (*in an undertone*). How do you feel, Katherine?

MRS. STOCKMANN. Oh, I'm all right. (*Lowering her voice.*) Now, Thomas, don't fly off the handle.

DR. STOCKMANN. I can manage myself, you know that. (*Looks at his watch, then ascends the platform and bows.*) It's already a quarter past—so I'd like to begin— (*Taking his manuscript out.*)

ASLAKSEN. First, we really ought to elect a chairman.

DR. STOCKMANN. No, that's quite unnecessary.

SEVERAL VOICES (*shouting*). Yes, yes!

MAYOR STOCKMANN. I also submit that we ought to elect a moderator.

DR. STOCKMANN. But I've called this meeting to present a lecture, Peter!

MAYOR STOCKMANN. The doctor's lecture is likely to arouse some contrary opinions.

MORE VOICES FROM THE CROWD. A chairman! A moderator!

HOVSTAD. The will of the people seems to demand a chairman.

DR. STOCKMANN (*restraining himself*). All right, then, let the will of the people rule.

ASLAKSEN. Would the mayor agree to accept the chair?

THREE GENTLEMEN (*applauding*). Bravo! Bravo!

MAYOR STOCKMANN. For certain self-evident reasons, I must decline. But luckily we have in our midst a man whom I think we can all accept. I'm referring to the chairman of the Home Owners Council, Mr. Aslaksen.

MANY VOICES. Yes, yes! Aslaksen! Hurray for Aslaksen!

(DR. STOCKMANN *puts away his manuscript and leaves the platform.*)

ASLAKSEN. If my fellow townspeople express their confidence in me, I cannot refuse—

(*Applause and shouts of approval.* ASLAKSEN *mounts the platform.*)

BILLING (*writing*). So—"Mr. Aslaksen chosen by acclamation—"

ASLAKSEN. And since I'm standing here now in this role, permit me to say a few brief words. I am a man of peace and quiet who's dedicated himself to prudent moderation and to—and to moderate prudence; everyone who knows me can attest to that.

MANY VOICES. Right! You said it, Aslaksen!

ASLAKSEN. I've learned in life's school of experience that moderation is the most rewarding of all virtues for the citizen—

MAYOR STOCKMANN. Hear, hear!

ASLAKSEN. And, moreover, that prudence and temperance are what serve society best. Therefore, I would urge the estimable gentleman who convened this meeting that he make every effort to stay within the bounds of moderation.

A DRUNK (*near the door*). To the Temperance Union, skoal!

A VOICE. Shut the hell up!

MANY VOICES. Sh, sh!

ASLAKSEN. No interruptions, gentlemen! Does anyone have something to say?

MAYOR STOCKMANN. Mr. Chairman!

ASLAKSEN. The chair recognizes the mayor.

MAYOR STOCKMANN. Considering my close relationship, which you all know, to the present staff physician of the baths, I would very much have wished not to express myself here this evening. But my official connection with the baths, and a due regard for the crucial interests of this town, compel me to present a proposal. I think it safe to assume that not a single citizen here tonight would find it desirable that exaggerated and unreliable charges about the sanitary conditions of the baths should gain currency abroad.

MANY VOICES. No, no, no! Of course not! We protest!

MAYOR STOCKMANN. I therefore move that this gathering refuse to permit the staff physician to read or otherwise report on his version of the matter.

DR. STOCKMANN (*infuriated*). Refuse permission— What's that?

MRS. STOCKMANN (*coughing*). Hm, hm!

DR. STOCKMANN (*controls himself*). Permission refused —all right.

MAYOR STOCKMANN. In my statement to the *People's Courier*, I've acquainted the public with the pertinent facts, so that every right-minded citizen can easily form his own judgment. You'll see there that the doctor's proposal—besides being a vote of no confidence in the leadership of this town—would actually mean afflicting our local taxpayers with a needless expenditure of at least a hundred thousand crowns.

(*Cries of outrage and the sound of whistles.*)

ASLAKSEN (*ringing the bell*). Quiet, gentlemen! Allow me to second the mayor's proposal. It's *my* opinion, also, that the doctor's agitation has an ulterior motive. He talks about the baths, but it's a revolution he's after. He wants to put the government into different hands. No one doubts the doctor's honest intentions; Lord knows there's no divided opinion on that. I'm also a friend of self-determination by the people—as long as it doesn't hit the taxpayer too hard. But that exactly would be the case here; and it's why I'll be damned—excuse me—if I can go along with Dr. Stockmann in this. You can pay too much, even for gold; that's *my* opinion.

(*Lively approval from all sides.*)

HOVSTAD. Likewise I feel obligated to clarify my own position. Dr. Stockmann's agitation seemed at first to be winning a good deal of acceptance, and I supported it as impartially as I could. But then we began to sense that we'd let ourselves be misled by a false interpretation—

DR. STOCKMANN. False—!

HOVSTAD. A less reliable interpretation, then. The mayor's statement has proved that. I hope no one here tonight would challenge my liberal sentiments; the *Courier*'s policy on our great political issues is well known to all of you. Still, I've learned from men of wisdom and experience that in purely local matters a paper ought to move with a certain caution.

ASLAKSEN. I agree perfectly.

HOVSTAD. And, in the matter in question, it's now indisputable that Dr. Stockmann has the will of the majority against him. But an editor's first and foremost responsibility—what is that, gentlemen? Isn't it to work in collaboration with his readers? Hasn't he received something on the order of an unspoken mandate to strive actively and unceasingly on behalf of those who share his beliefs? Or maybe I'm wrong in this?

MANY VOICES. No, no, no! He's right.

HOVSTAD. It's been a bitter struggle for me to break with a man in whose home I've lately been a frequent guest—a man who, until today, could bask in the undivided esteem of the community—a man whose only fault, or whose greatest fault at least, is that he follows his heart more than his head.

SOME SCATTERED VOICES. That's true! Hurray for Dr. Stockmann!

HOVSTAD. But my duty to society compelled me to break with him. And then there's another consideration that prompts me to oppose him and, if possible, to deter him from the ominous course he's chosen: namely, consideration for his family—

DR. STOCKMANN. Stick to the sewers and water mains!

HOVSTAD. —consideration for his wife and his distressed children.

MORTEN. Is that us, Mother?

MRS. STOCKMANN. Hush!

ASLAKSEN. I hereby put the mayor's proposal to a vote.

DR. STOCKMANN. Never mind that! It's not my intention to speak tonight of all that squalor in the baths. No, you're going to hear something quite different.

MAYOR STOCKMANN (*muttering*). Now what?

THE DRUNK (*from the main doorway*). I'm a taxpayer! And, therefore, so I got rights to an opinion! And I have the sotted—solid and incomprehensible opinion that—

SEVERAL VOICES. Quiet over there!

OTHERS. He's drunk! Throw him out!

(*The* DRUNK *is ejected.*)

DR. STOCKMANN. Do I have the floor?

ASLAKSEN (*ringing the bell*). Dr. Stockmann has the floor!

DR. STOCKMANN. If it had been only a few days ago that anyone had tried to gag me like this tonight—I'd have fought for my sacred human rights like a lion! But it doesn't matter to me now. Because now I have greater things to discuss.

(*The* CROWD *presses in closer around him;* MORTEN KIIL *becomes visible among them.*)

DR. STOCKMANN (*continuing*). I've been thinking a lot these past few days—pondering so many things that finally my thoughts began running wild—

MAYOR STOCKMANN (*coughs*). Hm—!

DR. STOCKMANN. But then I got everything in place again, and I saw the whole structure so distinctly. It's why I'm here this evening. I have great disclosures to make, my friends! I'm going to unveil a discovery to you of vastly different dimension than this trifle that our water system is polluted and that our health spa is built on a muckheap.

MANY VOICES (*shouting*). Don't talk of the baths! We won't listen! Enough of that!

DR. STOCKMANN. I've said I'd talk about the great discovery I've made these last few days: the discovery that all the sources of our spiritual life are polluted, and that our entire community rests on a muckheap of lies.

STARTLED VOICES (*in undertones*). What's he saying?

MAYOR STOCKMANN. Of all the insinuations—

ASLAKSEN (*his hand on the bell*). The speaker is urged to be moderate.

DR. STOCKMANN. I've loved my birthplace as much as any man can. I was barely grown when I left here; and distance and deprivation and memory threw a kind of enchantment over the town, and the people, too.

(*Scattered applause and cheers.*)

For many years, then, I practiced in the far north, at the dead end of nowhere. When I came in contact with some of the people who lived scattered in that waste of rocks, I many times thought it would have done those poor starved creatures more good if they'd gotten a veterinary instead of someone like me.

(*Murmuring among the crowd.*)

BILLING (*setting down his pen*). Ye gods, why I never heard such—!

HOVSTAD. That's an insult to the common man!

DR. STOCKMANN. Just a minute—! I don't think anyone could ever say that I'd forgotten my home town up there. I brooded on my egg like an eider duck; and what I hatched—was the plan for the baths.

(*Applause and objections.*)

And finally, at long last, when fate relented and allowed me to come back home—my friends, then it seemed as though I had nothing left to wish for in this world. No, I did have one wish: a fierce, insistent, burning desire to contribute to the best of my town and my people.

MAYOR STOCKMANN (*gazing into space*). It's a funny way to—hm.

DR. STOCKMANN. And so I went around, exulting in my blind happiness. But yesterday morning—no, actually it was the night before last—the eyes of my spirit were opened wide, and the first thing I saw was the consummate stupidity of the authorities—

(*Confusion, outcries, and laughter.* MRS. STOCKMANN *coughs vigorously.*)

MAYOR STOCKMANN. Mr. Chairman!

ASLAKSEN (*ringing his bell*). By the powers vested in me—!

DR. STOCKMANN. It's petty to get hung up on a word, Mr. Aslaksen! I only mean that it came to me then what a consummate mess our local leaders had made out of the baths. Our leaders are one group that, for the life of me, I can't stand. I've had enough of that breed in my days. They're like a pack of goats in a stand of new trees—they strip off everything. They get in a free man's way wherever he turns—and I really don't see why we shouldn't exterminate them like any other predator—

(*Tumult in the room.*)

MAYOR STOCKMANN. Mr. Chairman, can you let such a statement pass?

ASLAKSEN (*his hand on the bell*). Doctor—!

DR. STOCKMANN. I can't imagine why I've only now taken a really sharp look at these gentlemen, because right before my eyes almost daily I've had a superb example—my brother Peter—slow of wit and thick of head—

(*Laughter, commotion, and whistles.* MRS. STOCKMANN *coughs repeatedly.* ASLAKSEN *vehemently rings his bell.*)

THE DRUNK (*who has gotten in again*). Are you referring to me? Yes, my name's Pettersen all right—but I'll fry in hell, before—

ANGRY VOICES. Out with that drunk! Throw him out!

(*Again the* DRUNK *is ejected.*)

MAYOR STOCKMANN. Who was that person?

A BYSTANDER. I don't know him, Your Honor.

ANOTHER. He's not from this town.

A THIRD. It must be that lumber dealer from over in— (*The rest is inaudible.*)

ASLAKSEN. The man was obviously muddled on Munich beer. Go on, Dr. Stockmann, but try to be more temperate.

DR. STOCKMANN. So then, my friends and neighbors, I'll say nothing further about our leading citizens. If, from what I've just said, anyone imagines that I'm out to get those gentlemen here this evening, then he's wrong—most emphatically wrong. Because I nourish a benign hope that all those mossbacks, those relics of a dying world of thought, are splendidly engaged in digging their own graves—they don't need a doctor's aid to speed them off the scene. And besides, *they're* not the overwhelming menace to society; *they're* not the ones most active in poisoning our spiritual life and polluting the very ground we stand on; *they're* not the most insidious enemies of truth and freedom in our society.

SHOUTS FROM ALL SIDES. Who, then! Who are they? Name them!

DR. STOCKMANN. Yes, you can bet I'll name them! Because *that's* exactly my great discovery yesterday. (*Raising his voice.*) The most insidious enemy of truth and freedom among us is the solid majority. Yes, the damned, solid, liberal majority—that's it! Now you know.

(*Wild turmoil in the room. Almost all those present are shouting, stamping, and whistling. Several elderly gentlemen exchange sly glances and appear to be amused.* EILIF *and* MORTEN *move threateningly toward the* SCHOOLBOYS, *who are making a disturbance.* ASLAKSEN *rings his bell and calls for order. Both* HOVSTAD *and* BILLING *are talking, without being heard. Finally quiet is restored.*)

ASLAKSEN. As chairman, I urge the speaker to withdraw his irresponsible comments.

DR. STOCKMANN. Not a chance, Mr. Aslaksen. It's that same majority in our community that's stripping away my freedom and trying to keep me from speaking the truth.

HOVSTAD. The majority is always right.

BILLING. And it acts for truth. Ye gods!

DR. STOCKMANN. The majority is never right. I say, never! That's one of those social lies that any free man who thinks for himself has to rebel against. Who makes up the majority in any country—the intelligent, or the stupid? I think we've got to agree that, all over this whole wide earth, the stupid are in a fearsomely overpowering majority. But I'll be damned to perdition if it's part of the eternal plan that the stupid are meant to rule the intelligent!

(*Commotion and outcries.*)

Oh yes, you can shout me down well enough, but you can't refute me. The majority has the might—unhappily —but it lacks the *right*. The right is with me, and the other few, the solitary individuals. The minority is always right.

(*Renewed turmoil.*)

HOVSTAD (*laughs*). So, in a couple of days, the doctor's turned aristocrat.

DR. STOCKMANN. I've told you I'm not going to waste any words on that wheezing, little, narrow-chested pack of reactionaries. The tide of life has already passed them by. But I'm thinking of the few, the individuals among us, who've mastered all the new truths that have been germinating. Those men are out there holding their positions like outposts, so far in the vanguard that the solid majority hasn't even begun to catch up—and *there's* where they're fighting for truths too newly born in the world's consciousness to have won any support from the majority.

HOVSTAD. Well, and now he's a revolutionist!

DR. STOCKMANN. Yes, you're damn right I am, Mr. Hovstad! I'm fomenting a revolution against the lie that only the majority owns the truth. What are these truths the majority flocks around? They're the ones so ripe in age they're nearly senile. But, gentlemen, when a truth's grown that old, it's gone a long way toward becoming a lie.

(*Laughter and jeers.*)

Oh yes, you can believe me as you please; but truths aren't at all the stubborn old Methuselahs people imagine. An ordinary, established truth lives, as a rule—let's say—some seventeen, eighteen, at the most twenty years; rarely more.

But those venerable truths are always terribly thin. Even so, it's only *then* that the majority takes them up and urges them on society as wholesome spiritual food. But there isn't much nutriment in that kind of diet, I promise you; and as a doctor, I know. All these majority-truths are like last year's salt meat—like rancid, tainted pork. And there's the cause of all the moral scurvy that's raging around us.

ASLAKSEN. It strikes me that the distinguished speaker has strayed rather far from his text.

MAYOR STOCKMANN. I must agree with the chairman's opinion.

DR. STOCKMANN. You're out of your mind, Peter! I'm sticking as close to the text as I can. Because this is exactly what I'm talking about: that the masses, the crowd, this damn solid majority—that *this* is what I say is poisoning our sources of spiritual life and defiling the earth under our feet.

HOVSTAD. And the great liberal-minded majority does this because they're reasonable enough to honor only basic, well-accepted truths?

DR. STOCKMANN. Ah, my dear Mr. Hovstad, don't talk about basic truths! The truths accepted by the masses now are the ones proclaimed basic by the advance guard in our grandfathers' time. We fighters on the frontiers today, we no longer recognize them. There's only one truth that's basic in my belief: that no society can live a healthy life on the bleached bones of that kind of truth.

HOVSTAD. Instead of standing there rambling on in the blue, it might be interesting to describe some of those bleached bones we're living on.

(*Agreement from various quarters.*)

DR. STOCKMANN. Oh, I could itemize a whole slew of abominations; but to start with, I'll mention just one recognized truth that's actually a vicious lie, though Mr. Hovstad and the *Courier* and all the *Courier's* devotees live on it.

HOVSTAD. That being—?

DR. STOCKMANN. That being the doctrine inherited from your ancestors, which you mindlessly disseminate far and

wide—the doctrine that the public, the mob, the masses
are the vital core of the people—in fact, that they *are* the
people—and that the common man, the inert, unformed
component of society, has the same right to admonish and
approve, to prescribe and to govern as the few spiritually
accomplished personalities.

BILLING. Well, I'll be—

HOVSTAD (*simultaneously, shouting*). Citizens, did you
hear that!

ANGRY VOICES. Oh, we're not the people, uh? So, only
the accomplished rule!

A WORKMAN. Out with a man who talks like that!

OTHERS. Out the door! Heave him out!

A MAN (*yells*). Evensen, blow the horn!

(*Deep blasts on a horn are heard; whistles and furious
commotion in the room.*)

DR. STOCKMANN (*when the noise has subsided a bit*).
Now just be reasonable! Can't you stand hearing the truth
for a change? I never expected you all to agree with me
on the spot. But I really did expect that Mr. Hovstad
would admit I'm right, after he'd simmered down a little.
Mr. Hovstad claims to be a freethinker—

STARTLED VOICES (*in undertones*). What was that? A
freethinker? Hovstad a freethinker?

HOVSTAD (*loudly*). Prove it, Dr. Stockmann! When
have I said that in print?

DR. STOCKMANN (*reflecting*). No, by God, you're right
—you've never had the courage. Well, I don't want to put
you in hot water. Let's say I'm the freethinker then.
Because I'm going to demonstrate scientifically that the
Courier's leading you shamelessly by the nose when they
say that you—the public, the masses—are the vital core of
the people. You see, that's just a journalistic lie! The
masses are no more than the raw material out of which a
people is shaped.

(*Mutterings, laughter, and disquiet in the room.*)

Well, isn't that a fact throughout all the rest of life? What
about the difference between a thoroughbred and a hybrid

animal? Look at your ordinary barnyard fowl. What meat can you get off such scrawny bones? Not much! And what kind of eggs does it lay? Any competent crow or raven could furnish about the same. But now take a purebred Spanish or Japanese hen, or a fine pheasant or turkey—there's where you'll see the difference! Or again with dogs, a family we humans so closely resemble. First, think of an ordinary stray dog—I mean, one of those nasty, ragged, common mongrels that run around the streets, and spatter the walls of houses. Then set that stray alongside a poodle whose pedigree runs back through a distinguished line to a house where fine food and harmonious voices and music have been the rule. Don't you think the mentality of that poodle will have developed quite differently from the stray's? Of course it will! A young pedigreed poodle can be raised by its trainer to perform the most incredible feats. Your common mongrel couldn't learn such things if you stood him on his head.

(*Tumult and derision generally.*)

A CITIZEN (*shouting*). Now you're making us into dogs, uh?

ANOTHER MAN. We're not animals, Doctor!

DR. STOCKMANN. Oh yes, brother, we *are* animals! We're the best animals, all in all, that any man could wish for. But there aren't many animals of quality among us. There's a terrible gap between the thoroughbreds and the mongrels in humanity. And what's amusing is that Mr. Hovstad totally agrees with me as long as we're talking of four-legged beasts—

HOVSTAD. Well, but they're a class by themselves.

DR. STOCKMANN. All right. But as soon as I extend the law to the two-legged animals, Mr. Hovstad stops cold. He doesn't dare think his own thoughts any longer, or follow his ideas to a logical conclusion. So he turns the whole doctrine upside down and declares in the *Courier* that the barnyard fowl and the mongrel dog—that *these* are the real paragons of the menagerie. But that's how it always goes as long as conformity is in your system, and you haven't worked through to a distinction of mind and spirit.

HOVSTAD. I make no claim of any kind of distinction. I was born of simple peasants, and I'm proud that my roots run deep in those masses that he despises.

NUMEROUS WOMEN. Hurray for Hovstad! Hurray, hurray!

DR. STOCKMANN. The kind of commonness I'm talking of isn't only found in the depths: it teems and swarms all around us in society—right up to the top. Just look at your own neat and tidy mayor. My brother Peter's as good a common man as any that walks on two feet—

(*Laughter and hisses.*)

MAYOR STOCKMANN. I protest against these personal allusions.

DR. STOCKMANN (*unruffled*). —and that's not because he's descended, just as I am, from a barbarous old pirate from Pomerania or thereabouts—because so we are—

MAYOR STOCKMANN. A ridiculous fiction. I deny it!

DR. STOCKMANN. —no, he's that because he thinks what the higher-ups think and believes what they believe. The people who do that are the spiritually common men. And that's why my stately brother Peter, you see, is in fact so fearfully lacking in distinction—and consequently so narrowminded.

MAYOR STOCKMANN. Mr. Chairman—!

HOVSTAD. So you have to be distinguished to be liberalminded in this country. That's a completely new insight.

(*General laughter.*)

DR. STOCKMANN. Yes, that's also part of my new discovery. And along with it goes the idea that broadmindedness is almost exactly the same as morality. That's why I say it's simply inexcusable of the *Courier*, day in and day out, to promote the fallacy that it's the masses, the solid majority, who stand as the guardian of tolerance and morality—and that degeneracy and corruption of all kinds are a sort of by-product of culture, filtering down to us like all the pollution filtering down to the baths from the tanneries up at Mølledal.

(*Turmoil and interruptions.*)

DR. STOCKMANN (*unfazed, laughing in his enthusiasm*).

And yet this same *Courier* can preach that the deprived masses must be raised to greater cultural opportunities. But, hell's bells—if the *Courier's* assumption holds true, then raising the masses like that would be precisely the same as plunging them smack into depravity! But luckily it's only an old wives' tale—this inherited lie that culture demoralizes. No, it's ignorance and poverty and ugliness in life that do the devil's work! In a house that isn't aired and swept every day—my wife Katherine maintains that the floors ought to be scrubbed as well, but that's debatable—anyway—I say in a house like that, within two or three years, people lose all power for moral thought and action. Lack of oxygen dulls the conscience. And there must be a woeful dearth of oxygen in the houses of this town, it seems, if the entire solid majority can numb their consciences enough to want to build this town's prosperity on a quagmire of duplicity and lies.

ASLAKSEN. It's intolerable—such a gross attack on a whole community.

A GENTLEMAN. I move the chairman rule the speaker out of order.

FURIOUS VOICES. Yes, yes! That's right! Out of order!

DR. STOCKMANN (*vehemently*). Then I'll cry out the truth from every street corner. I'll write to newspapers in other towns! The entire country'll learn what's happened here!

HOVSTAD. It almost looks like the doctor's determined to destroy this town.

DR. STOCKMANN. Yes, I love my home town so much I'd rather destroy it than see it flourishing on a lie.

ASLAKSEN. That's putting it plain.

(*Tumult and whistling.* MRS. STOCKMANN *coughs in vain; the* DOCTOR *no longer hears her.*)

HOVSTAD (*shouting above the noise*). Any man who'd destroy a whole community must be a public enemy!

DR. STOCKMANN (*with mounting indignation*). What's the difference if a lying community gets destroyed! It ought to be razed to the ground, I say! Stamp them out like vermin, everyone who lives by lies! You'll contaminate this entire nation in the end, till the land itself deserves to be destroyed. And if it comes to that even, then I say with all my heart: let this whole land be destroyed, let its people all be stamped out!

A MAN. That's talking like a real enemy of the people!

BILLING. Ye gods, but *there's* the people's voice!

THE WHOLE CROWD (*shrieking*). Yes, yes, yes! He's an enemy of the people! He hates his country! He hates all his people!

ASLAKSEN. Both as a citizen and as a human being, I'm profoundly shaken by what I've had to listen to here. Dr. Stockmann has revealed himself in a manner beyond anything I could have dreamed. I'm afraid that I have to endorse the judgment just rendered by my worthy fellow citizens; and I propose that we ought to express this judgment in a resolution, as follows: "This meeting declares that it regards Dr. Thomas Stockmann, staff physician at the baths, to be an enemy of the people."

(*Tumultuous cheers and applause. Many onlookers close in around the* DOCTOR, *whistling at him.* MRS. STOCK-MANN *and* PETRA *have risen.* MORTEN *and* EILIF *are fighting with the other* SCHOOLBOYS, *who have also been whistling. Several grown-ups separate them.*)

DR. STOCKMANN (*to the hecklers*). Ah, you fools—I'm telling you—

ASLAKSEN (*ringing his bell*). The doctor is out of order! A formal vote is called for; but to spare personal feelings, it ought to be a secret ballot. Do you have any blank paper, Mr. Billing?

BILLING. Here's some blue and white both—

ASLAKSEN (*leaving the platform*). Fine. It'll go faster that way. Cut it in slips—yes, that's it. (*To the gathering.*) Blue means no, white means yes. I'll go around myself and collect the votes.

(*The* MAYOR *leaves the room.* ASLAKSEN *and a couple of other citizens circulate through the crowd with paper slips in their hats.*)

A GENTLEMAN (*to* HOVSTAD). What's gotten into the doctor? How should we take this?

HOVSTAD. Well, you know how hot-headed he is.

ANOTHER GENTLEMAN (*to* BILLING). Say, you've visited there off and on. Have you noticed if the man drinks?

BILLING. Ye gods, I don't know what to say. When anybody stops in, there's always toddy on the table.

A THIRD GENTLEMAN. No, I think at times he's just out of his mind.

FIRST GENTLEMAN. I wonder if there isn't a strain of insanity in the family?

BILLING. It's quite possible.

A FOURTH GENTLEMAN. No, it's pure spite, that's all. Revenge for something or other.

BILLING. He was carrying on about a raise at one time—but he never got it.

ALL THE GENTLEMEN (*as one voice*). Ah, there's the answer!

THE DRUNK (*within the crowd*). Let's have a blue one! And—let's have a white one, too!

CRIES. There's that drunk again! Throw him out!

MORTEN KIIL (*approaching the* DOCTOR). Well, Stockmann, now you see what your monkeyshines come to?

DR. STOCKMANN. I've done my duty.

MORTEN KIIL. What was that you said about the tanneries at Mølledal?

DR. STOCKMANN. You heard it. I said all the pollution came from them.

MORTEN KIIL. From *my* tannery, too?

DR. STOCKMANN. I'm afraid your tannery's the worst of them.

MORTEN KIIL. You're going to print *that* in the papers?

DR. STOCKMANN. I'm sweeping nothing under the carpet.

MORTEN KIIL. That could cost you plenty, Stockmann. (*He leaves.*)

A FAT GENTLEMAN (*going up to* HORSTER, *without greeting the ladies*). Well, Captain, so you lend out your house to enemies of the people?

HORSTER. I think I can dispose of my property, sir, as I see fit.

THE MAN. So you'll certainly have no objection if I do the same with mine.

HORSTER. What do you mean?

THE MAN. You'll hear from me in the morning. (*He turns and leaves.*)

PETRA (*to* HORSTER). Doesn't he own your ship?

HORSTER. Yes, that was Mr. Vik.

ASLAKSEN (*ascends the platform with ballots in hand and rings for order*). Gentlemen, let me make you acquainted with the outcome. All of the votes with one exception—

A YOUNG MAN. That's the drunk!

ASLAKSEN. All of the votes, with the exception of an intoxicated man, are in favor of this assembly of citizens declaring the staff physician of the baths, Dr. Thomas Stockmann, an enemy of the people. (*Shouts and gestures of approval.*) Long live our ancient and glorious community! (*More cheers.*) Long live our capable and effective mayor, who so loyally has suppressed the ties of family! (*Cheers.*) This meeting is adjourned. (*He descends from the platform.*)

BILLING. Long live the chairman!

THE ENTIRE CROWD. Hurray for Aslaksen!

DR. STOCKMANN. My hat and coat, Petra. Captain, have you room for several passengers to the New World?

HORSTER. For you and your family, Doctor, we'll make room.

DR. STOCKMANN (*as* PETRA *helps him on with his coat*). Good. Come, Katherine! Come on, boys!

(*He takes his wife by the arm.*)

MRS. STOCKMANN (*dropping her voice*). Thomas, dear, let's leave by the back way.

DR. STOCKMANN. No back ways out, Katherine. (*Raising his voice.*) You'll be hearing from the enemy of the people before he shakes this dust off his feet! I'm not as meek as one certain person; I'm not saying, "I forgive them, because they know not what they do."

ASLAKSEN (*in an outcry*). That's a blasphemous comparison, Dr. Stockmann!

BILLING. That it is, so help me— It's a bit much for a pious man to take.

A COARSE VOICE. And then he threatened us, too!

HEATED VOICES. Let's smash his windows for him! Dunk him in the fjord!

A MAN (*in the crowd*). Blast your horn, Evensen! Honk, honk!

(*The sound of the horn; whistles and wild shrieks. The* DOCTOR *and his family move toward the exit,* HORSTER *clearing the way for them.*)

THE WHOLE CROWD (*howling after them*). Enemy! Enemy! Enemy of the people!

BILLING (*organizing his notes*). Ye gods, I wouldn't drink toddy at the Stockmanns' tonight!

(*The crowd surges toward the exit; the noise diffuses outside; from the street the cry continues: "Enemy! Enemy of the people!"*)

Act Five • ENEMY OF THE PEOPLE   203

and comes back immediately.) Here's a letter for you,
course—

◁ ACT FIVE ▷

DR. STOCKMANN's *study. Bookcases and cabinets filled with
various medicines line the walls. In the back wall is a door
to the hall; in the foreground, left, the door to the living
room. At the right, opposite, are two windows, with all
their panes shattered. In the middle of the room is the*
DOCTOR's *desk, covered with books and papers. The room is
in disorder. It is morning.* DR. STOCKMANN, *in a dressing
gown, slippers, and a smoking cap, is bent down, raking
under one of the cabinets with an umbrella; after some
effort, he sweeps out a stone.*

DR. STOCKMANN (*calling through the open living-room
door*). Katherine, I found another one.

MRS. STOCKMANN (*from the living room*). Oh, I'm sure
you'll find a lot more yet.

DR. STOCKMANN (*adding the stone to a pile of others on
the table*). I'm going to preserve these stones as holy
relics. Eilif and Morten have got to see them every day;
and when they're grown, they'll inherit them from me.
(*Raking under a bookcase.*) Hasn't—what the hell's her
name—the maid—hasn't she gone for the glazier yet?

MRS. STOCKMANN (*enters*). Of course, but he said he
didn't know if he could come today.

DR. STOCKMANN. More likely he doesn't dare.

MRS. STOCKMANN. Yes, Randina thought he was afraid
of what the neighbors might say. (*Speaking into the living
room.*) What do you want, Randina? Oh yes. (*Goes out*

and comes back immediately.) Here's a letter for you, Thomas.

DR. STOCKMANN. Let me see. (*Opens it and reads.*) Of course.

MRS. STOCKMANN. Who's it from?

DR. STOCKMANN. The landlord. He's giving us notice.

MRS. STOCKMANN. Is that true! He's such a decent man—

DR. STOCKMANN (*reading on in the letter*). He doesn't dare not to, he says. It pains him to do it, but he doesn't dare not to—in fairness to his fellow townspeople—a matter of public opinion—not independent—can't affront certain powerful men—

MRS. STOCKMANN. You see, Thomas.

DR. STOCKMANN. Yes, yes, I see very well. They're cowards, all of them here in town. Nobody dares do anything, in fairness to all the others. (*Hurls the letter on the table.*) But that's nothing to us, Katherine. We're off for the New World now—

MRS. STOCKMANN. But, Thomas, is that really the right solution, to emigrate?

DR. STOCKMANN. Maybe I ought to stay here, where they've pilloried me as an enemy of the people, branded me, smashed in my windows! And look at this, Katherine; they even tore my black trousers.

MRS. STOCKMANN. Oh, no—and they're the best you have!

DR. STOCKMANN. One should never wear his best trousers when he goes out fighting for truth and freedom. It's not that I'm so concerned about the trousers, you understand; you can always mend them for me. But what grates is that mob setting on me bodily as if they were my equals—by God, that's the thing I can't bear!

MRS. STOCKMANN. Yes, they've abused you dreadfully in this town, Thomas. But do we have to leave the country entirely because of *that?*

DR. STOCKMANN. Don't you think the common herd is just as arrogant in other towns as well? Why, of course—

it's all one and the same. Ahh, shoot! Let the mongrels yap; they're not the worst. The worst of it is that everyone the country over is a slave to party. But *that's* not the reason—it's probably no better in the free United States; I'm sure they have a plague of solid majorities and liberal public opinions and all the other bedevilments. But the scale there is so immense, you see. They might kill you, but they don't go in for slow torture; they don't lock a free soul in the jaws of a vise, the way they do here at home. And, if need be, there's space to get away. (*Pacing the floor.*) If I only knew of some primeval forest, or a little South Sea island at a bargain price—

MRS. STOCKMANN. But, Thomas, think of the boys.

DR. STOCKMANN (*stopping in his tracks*). You are remarkable, Katherine! Would you rather they grew up in a society like ours? You saw yourself last night that half the population are raging maniacs; and if the other half haven't lost their reason, it's because they're such muttonheads they haven't any reason to lose.

MRS. STOCKMANN. Yes, but dear, you're so intemperate in your speech.

DR. STOCKMANN. Look! Isn't it true, what I'm saying? Don't they turn every idea upside down? Don't they scramble right and wrong up completely? Don't they call everything a lie that I know for the truth? But the height of insanity is that here you've got all these full-grown liberals going round in a bloc and deluding themselves and the others that they're independent thinkers! Did you ever hear the like of it, Katherine?

MRS. STOCKMANN. Yes, yes, it's all wrong of course, but—

(PETRA *enters from the living room.*)

MRS. STOCKMANN. You're back from school already?

PETRA. Yes. I got my notice.

MRS. STOCKMANN. Your notice.

DR. STOCKMANN. You, too!

PETRA. Mrs. Busk gave me my notice, so I thought it better to leave at once.

DR. STOCKMANN. You did the right thing!

MRS. STOCKMANN. Who would have thought Mrs. Busk would prove such a poor human being!

PETRA. Oh, Mother, she really isn't so bad. It was plain to see how miserable she felt. But she said she didn't dare not to. So I got fired.

DR. STOCKMANN (*laughs and rubs his hands*). She didn't dare not to, either. Oh, that's charming.

MRS. STOCKMANN. Well, after that awful row last night—

PETRA. It was more than just that. Father, listen now!

DR. STOCKMANN. What?

PETRA. Mrs. Busk showed me no less than three letters she'd gotten this morning.

DR. STOCKMANN. Anonymous, of course?

PETRA. Yes.

DR. STOCKMANN. Because they don't *dare* sign their names, Katherine.

PETRA. And two of them stated that a gentleman who's often visited this household had declared in the club last night that I had extremely free ideas on various matters—

DR. STOCKMANN. And that you didn't deny, I hope.

PETRA. No, you know that. Mrs. Busk has some pretty liberal ideas herself, when it's just the two of us talking. But with this all coming out about me, she didn't dare keep me on.

MRS. STOCKMANN. And to think—It was one of our regular visitors! You see, Thomas, there's what you get for your hospitality.

DR. STOCKMANN. We won't go on living in a pigsty like this. Katherine, get packed as soon as you can. Let's get out of here, the quicker the better.

MRS. STOCKMANN. Be quiet—I think there's someone in the hall. Have a look, Petra.

PETRA (*opening the door*). Oh, is it you, Captain Horster? Please, come in.

HORSTER (*from the hall*). Good morning. I thought I ought to stop by and see how things stand.

DR. STOCKMANN (*shaking his hand*). Thanks. That certainly is kind of you.

MRS. STOCKMANN. And thank you, Captain Horster, for helping us through last night.

PETRA. But how did you ever make it home again?

HORSTER. Oh, no problem. I can handle myself pretty well; and they're mostly a lot of hot air, those people.

DR. STOCKMANN. Yes, isn't it astounding, this bestial cowardice? Come here, and I'll show you something. See, here are all the stones they rained in on us. Just look at them! I swear, there aren't more than two respectable paving blocks in the whole pile; the rest are nothing but gravel—only pebbles. And yet they stood out there, bellowing, and swore they'd hammer me to a pulp. But action—action—no, you don't see much of that in this town!

HORSTER. I'd say this time that was lucky for you, Doctor.

DR. STOCKMANN. Definitely. But it's irritating, all the same; because if it ever comes to a serious fight to save this country, you'll see how public opinion is all for ducking the issue, and how the solid majority runs for cover like a flock of sheep. That's what's so pathetic when you think of it; it makes me heartsick— Damn it all, no—this is sheer stupidity; they've labeled me an enemy of the people, so I better act like one.

MRS. STOCKMANN. You never could be that, Thomas.

DR. STOCKMANN. Don't count on it, Katherine. To be called some ugly name hurts like a stabbing pain in the lung. And that damnable label—I can't shake it off; it's fixed itself here in the pit of my stomach, where it sits and rankles and corrodes like acid. And there's no magnesia to work against that.

PETRA. Oh, Father, you should just laugh at them.

HORSTER. People will come around in their thinking Doctor.

MRS. STOCKMANN. As sure as you're standing here they will.

DR. STOCKMANN. Yes, maybe after it's too late. Well, they've got it coming! Let them stew in their own mess and rue the day they drove a patriot into exile. When are you sailing, Captain Horster?

HORSTER. Hm—as a matter of fact, that's why I stopped by to talk to you—

DR. STOCKMANN. Oh, has something gone wrong with the ship?

HORSTER. No. But it looks like I won't sail with her.

PETRA. You haven't been fired, have you?

HORSTER (smiles). Yes, exactly.

PETRA. You, too.

MRS. STOCKMANN. See there, Thomas.

DR. STOCKMANN. And all this for the truth! Oh, if only I could have foreseen—

HORSTER. Now, don't go worrying about me; I'll find a post with some shipping firm out of town.

DR. STOCKMANN. And there we have Mr. Vik—a merchant, a man of wealth, independent in every way—! What a disgrace!

HORSTER. He's quite fair-minded otherwise. He said himself he'd gladly have retained me if he dared to—

DR. STOCKMANN. But he didn't dare? No, naturally!

HORSTER. It's not so easy, he was telling me, when you belong to a party—

DR. STOCKMANN. There's a true word from the merchant prince. A political party—it's like a sausage grinder; it grinds all the heads up together into one mash, and then it turns them out, link by link, into fatheads and meatheads!

MRS. STOCKMANN. Thomas, really!

PETRA (to HORSTER). If you just hadn't seen us home, things might not have gone like this.

HORSTER. I don't regret it.

PETRA (extending her hand to him). Thank you!

HORSTER (to the DOCTOR). So, what I wanted to say was, if you're still serious about leaving, then I've thought of another plan—

DR. STOCKMANN. Excellent. If we can only clear out of here fast—

MRS. STOCKMANN. Shh! Didn't someone knock?

PETRA. It's Uncle, I'll bet.

DR. STOCKMANN. Aha! (*Calls.*) Come in!

MRS. STOCKMANN. Thomas dear, you must promise me—

(*The* MAYOR *enters from the hall.*)

MAYOR STOCKMANN (*in the doorway*). Oh, you're occupied. Well, then I'd better—

DR. STOCKMANN. No, no, come right in.

MAYOR STOCKMANN. But I wanted to speak to you alone.

MRS. STOCKMANN. We'll go into the living room for a time.

HORSTER. And I'll come by again later.

DR. STOCKMANN. No, you go in with them, Captain Horster. I need to hear something more about—

HORSTER. Oh yes, I'll wait then.

(*He accompanies* MRS. STOCKMANN *and* PETRA *into the living room. The* MAYOR *says nothing, but glances at the windows.*)

DR. STOCKMANN. Maybe you find it a bit drafty here today? Put your hat on.

MAYOR STOCKMANN. Thank you, if I may. (*Does so.*) I think I caught cold last night. I was freezing out there—

DR. STOCKMANN. Really? It seemed more on the warm side to me.

MAYOR STOCKMANN. I regret that it wasn't within my power to curb those excesses last evening.

DR. STOCKMANN. Do you have anything else in particular to say to me?

MAYOR STOCKMANN (*taking out a large envelope*). I have this document for you from the board of directors.

DR. STOCKMANN. It's my notice?

MAYOR STOCKMANN. Yes, effective today. (*Places the envelope on the table.*) This pains us deeply, but—to be quite candid—we didn't dare not to, in view of public opinion.

DR. STOCKMANN (*smiles*). Didn't dare? Seems as though I've already heard those words today.

MAYOR STOCKMANN. I suggest that you face your position clearly. After this, you mustn't count on any practice whatsoever here in town.

DR. STOCKMANN. To hell with the practice! But how can you be so sure?

MAYOR STOCKMANN. The Home Owners Council is circulating a resolution, soliciting all responsible citizens to dispense with your services. And I venture to say that not one single householder will risk refusing to sign. Quite simply, they wouldn't dare.

DR. STOCKMANN. I don't doubt it. But what of it?

MAYOR STOCKMANN. If I could give you some advice, it would be that you leave this area for a while—

DR. STOCKMANN. Yes, I've been half thinking of just that.

MAYOR STOCKMANN. Good. Then, after you've had some six months, more or less, to reconsider things, if on mature reflection you find yourself capable of a few words of apology, acknowledging your mistakes—

DR. STOCKMANN. Then maybe I could get my job back, you mean?

MAYOR STOCKMANN. Perhaps. It's not at all unlikely.

DR. STOCKMANN. Yes, but public opinion? You could hardly dare, in that regard.

MAYOR STOCKMANN. Opinion tends to go from one extreme to another. And to be quite honest, it's especially important to us to get a signed statement to that effect from you.

DR. STOCKMANN. Yes, wouldn't you lick your chin-choppers for that! But, damnation, don't you remember what I already said about that kind of foxy game?

MAYOR STOCKMANN. Your position was much more favorable then. You could imagine then that you had the whole town in back of you—

DR. STOCKMANN. Yes, and I feel now as if the whole town's on my back— (*Flaring up.*) But even if the devil and his grandmother were riding me—never! Never, you hear me!

MAYOR STOCKMANN. A family provider can't go around risking everything the way you do. You can't risk it, Thomas!

DR. STOCKMANN. Can't risk! There's just one single thing in this world a free man can't risk; and do you know what that is?

MAYOR STOCKMANN. No.

DR. STOCKMANN. Of course not. But I'll tell you. A free man can't risk befouling himself like a savage. He doesn't dare sink to the point that he'd like to spit in his own face.

MAYOR STOCKMANN. This all sounds highly plausible; and if there weren't another prior explanation for your stubborn arrogance—but then of course, there is—

DR. STOCKMANN. What do you mean by *that?*

MAYOR STOCKMANN. You understand perfectly well. But as your brother and as a man of some discernment, let me advise you not to build too smugly on prospects that might very well never materialize.

DR. STOCKMANN. What in the world are you driving at?

MAYOR STOCKMANN. Are you actually trying to make me believe you're ignorant of the terms of Morten Kiil's will?

DR. STOCKMANN. I know that the little he has is going to a home for destitute craftsmen. But how does that apply to me?

MAYOR STOCKMANN. First of all, the amount under discussion is far from little. Morten Kiil is a rather wealthy man.

DR. STOCKMANN. I hadn't the slightest idea—!

MAYOR STOCKMANN. Hm—really? And you hadn't any idea, either, that a considerable part of his fortune will pass to your children, with you and your wife enjoying the interest for life. He hasn't told you that?

DR. STOCKMANN. Not one blessed word of it! Quite the contrary, he goes on fuming endlessly about the outrageously high taxes he pays. But how do you know this for sure, Peter?

MAYOR STOCKMANN. I have it from a totally reliable source.

DR. STOCKMANN. But, my Lord, then Katherine's provided for—and the children too! I really must tell her—(*Shouts.*) Katherine, Katherine!

MAYOR STOCKMANN (*restraining him*). Shh, don't say anything yet!

MRS. STOCKMANN (*opening the door*). What is it?

DR. STOCKMANN. Nothing, dear. Go back inside.

(MRS. STOCKMANN *shuts the door.*)

DR. STOCKMANN (*pacing the floor*). Provided for! Just imagine—every one of them, provided for. And for life! What a blissful feeling, to know you're secure!

MAYOR STOCKMANN. Yes, but that's precisely what you aren't. Morten Kiil can revise his will any time he pleases.

DR. STOCKMANN. But my dear Peter, he won't do that. The Badger's enraptured by the way I've gone after you and your smart friends.

MAYOR STOCKMANN (*starts and looks penetratingly at him*). Aha, that puts a new light on things.

DR. STOCKMANN. What things?

MAYOR STOCKMANN. So this whole business has been a collusion. These reckless, violent assaults you've aimed, in the name of truth, at our leading citizens were—

DR. STOCKMANN. Yes—were what?

MAYOR STOCKMANN. They were nothing more than a calculated payment for a piece of that vindictive old man's estate.

DR. STOCKMANN (*nearly speechless*). Peter—you're the cheapest trash I've known in all my days.

MAYOR STOCKMANN. Between us, everything is through.

Your dismissal is irrevocable—for now we've got a weapon against you. (*He goes.*)

DR. STOCKMANN. Why, that scum—aaah! (*Shouts.*) Katherine! Scour the floors where he's been! Have her come in with a pail—that girl—whozzis, damn it—the one with the smudgy nose—

MRS. STOCKMANN (*in the living-room doorway*). Shh, Thomas. Shh!

PETRA (*also in the doorway*). Father, Grandpa's here and wonders if he can speak to you alone.

DR. STOCKMANN. Yes, of course he can. (*By the door.*) Come in.

(MORTEN KIIL *enters. The* DOCTOR *closes the door after him.*)

DR. STOCKMANN. Well, what is it? Have a seat.

MORTEN KIIL. Won't sit. (*Looking about.*) You've made it very attractive here today, Stockmann.

DR. STOCKMANN. Yes, don't you think so?

MORTEN KIIL. Really attractive. And fresh air, too. Today you've got enough of that oxygen you talked about yesterday. You must have a marvelous conscience today, I imagine.

DR. STOCKMANN. Yes, I have.

MORTEN KIIL. I can imagine. (*Tapping his chest.*) But do you know what *I* have here?

DR. STOCKMANN. Well, I'm hoping a marvelous conscience, too.

MORTEN KIIL. Pah! No, it's something better than that. (*He takes out a thick wallet, opens it, and displays a sheaf of papers.*)

DR. STOCKMANN (*stares at him, amazed*). Shares in the baths.

MORTEN KIIL. They weren't hard to get today.

DR. STOCKMANN. And you were out buying—?

MORTEN KIIL. As many as I could afford.

DR. STOCKMANN. But, my dear Father-in-law—with everything at the baths in jeopardy!

MORTEN KIIL. If you go back to acting like a reasonable man, you'll soon get the baths on their feet again.

DR. STOCKMANN. You can see yourself, I'm doing all I can; but the people are crazy in this town.

MORTEN KIIL. You said yesterday that the worst pollution came from my tannery. But now if that *is* true, then my grandfather and my father before me and I myself over numbers of years have been poisoning this town right along, like three angels of death. You think I can rest with that disgrace on my head?

DR. STOCKMANN. I'm afraid you'll have to learn how.

MORTEN KIIL. No thanks. I want my good name and reputation. People call me the Badger, I've heard. A badger's a kind of pig, isn't it? They're not going to be right about that. Never. I want to live and die a clean human being.

DR. STOCKMANN. And how are you going to do that?

MORTEN KIIL. You'll make me clean, Stockmann.

DR. STOCKMANN. I!

MORTEN KIIL. Do you know where I got the money to buy these shares? No, you couldn't know that, but now I'll tell you. It's the money Katherine and Petra and the boys will be inheriting from me someday. Yes, because, despite everything, I've laid a little aside, you see.

DR. STOCKMANN (*flaring up*). So you went out and spent Katherine's money for *those!*

MORTEN KIIL. Yes, now the money's completely bound up in the baths. And now I'll see if you're really so ranting, raging mad after all, Stockmann. Any more about bugs and such coming down from my tannery, it'll be exactly the same as cutting great strips out of Katherine's skin, and Petra's, and the boys'. But no normal man would do that—he'd *have* to be mad.

DR. STOCKMANN (*pacing back and forth*). Yes, but I *am* a madman; I *am* a madman!

MORTEN KIIL. But you're not so utterly out of your senses as to flay your wife and children.

DR. STOCKMANN (*stopping in front of him*). Why

couldn't you talk with me before you went out and bought all that worthless paper?

MORTEN KIIL. When a thing's been done, it's best to hang on.

DR. STOCKMANN (*paces the room restlessly*). If only I weren't so certain in this—! But I'm perfectly sure I'm right.

MORTEN KIIL (*weighing the wallet in his hand*). If you keep on with this foolishness, then these aren't going to be worth much, will they? (*He replaces the wallet in his pocket.*)

DR. STOCKMANN. Damn it, science should be able to provide some counter-agent, some kind of germicide—

MORTEN KIIL. You mean something to kill those little animals?

DR. STOCKMANN. Yes, or else make them harmless.

MORTEN KIIL. Couldn't you try rat poison?

DR. STOCKMANN. Oh, that's nonsense! But—everyone says this is all just imagination. Well, why not? Let them have what they want! Stupid, mean little mongrels—didn't they brand me enemy of the people? And weren't they spoiling to tear the clothes off my back?

MORTEN KIIL. And all the windows they broke for you.

DR. STOCKMANN. And I do have family obligations! I must talk this over with Katherine; she's very shrewd in these things.

MORTEN KIIL. Good. You pay attention to a sensible woman's advice.

DR. STOCKMANN (*turning on him*). And you, too—how could you make such a mess of it! Gambling with Katherine's money; tormenting me with this horrible dilemma! When I look at you, I could be seeing the devil himself—!

MORTEN KIIL. I think I'd better be going. But by two o'clock I want your answer: yes—or no. If it's no, the stock gets willed to charity—and right this very day.

DR. STOCKMANN. And what does Katherine get then?

MORTEN KIIL. Not a crumb.

(*The hall door is opened.* HOVSTAD *and* ASLAKSEN *come into view, standing outside.*)

MORTEN KIIL. Well, will you look at *them?*

DR. STOCKMANN (*staring at them*). *What—!* You still dare to come around here?

HOVSTAD. Of course we do.

ASLAKSEN. You see, we've something to talk with you about.

MORTEN KIIL (*in a whisper*). Yes or no—by two o'clock.

ASLAKSEN (*glancing at* HOVSTAD). Aha!

(MORTEN KIIL *leaves.*)

DR. STOCKMANN. Well now, what do you want? Cut it short.

HOVSTAD. I can easily realize your bitterness toward us for the posture we took at last night's meeting—

DR. STOCKMANN. You call that a posture! Yes, that was a lovely posture! I call it spinelessness, like a bent old woman—holy God!

HOVSTAD. Call it what you will, we couldn't do otherwise.

DR. STOCKMANN. You didn't *dare*, you mean. Isn't that right?

HOVSTAD. Yes, if you like.

ASLAKSEN. But why didn't you pass us the word beforehand? Just the least little hint to Hovstad or me.

DR. STOCKMANN. A hint? What about?

ASLAKSEN. The reason why.

DR. STOCKMANN. I simply don't understand you.

ASLAKSEN (*nods confidentially*). Oh, yes, you do, Dr. Stockmann.

HOVSTAD. Let's not make a mystery out of it any longer.

DR. STOCKMANN (*looking from one to the other*). What in sweet blazes *is* this—!

ASLAKSEN. May I ask—hasn't your father-in-law been combing the town to buy up stock in the baths?

DR. STOCKMANN. Yes, he's bought a few shares today; but—?

ASLAKSEN. It would have been more clever if you'd gotten someone else to do it—someone less closely related.

HOVSTAD. And you shouldn't have moved under your own name. No one had to know the attack on the baths came from you. You should have brought me in on it, Doctor.

DR. STOCKMANN (*stares blankly in front of him; a light seems to dawn on him, and he says as if thunderstruck*). It's unbelievable! Do these things happen?

ASLAKSEN (*smiles*). Why, of course they do. But they only happen when you use finesse, if you follow me.

HOVSTAD. And they go better when a few others are involved. The risk is less for the individual when the responsibility is shared.

DR. STOCKMANN (*regaining his composure*). In short, gentlemen, what is it you want?

ASLAKSEN. Mr. Hovstad can best—

HOVSTAD. No, Aslaksen, you explain.

ASLAKSEN. Well, it's this—that now that we know how it all fits together, we thought we might venture to put the *People's Courier* at your disposal.

DR. STOCKMANN. Ah, so now you'll venture? But public opinion? Aren't you afraid there'll be a storm raised against us?

HOVSTAD. We're prepared to ride out the storm.

ASLAKSEN. And you should be prepared for a quick reversal in position, Doctor. As soon as your attack has served its purpose—

DR. STOCKMANN. You mean as soon as my father-in-law and I have cornered all the stock at a dirt-cheap price—?

HOVSTAD. I suppose it's mostly for scientific purposes that you want control of the baths.

DR. STOCKMANN. Naturally. It was for scientific purposes that I got the old Badger in with me on this. So
we'll tinker a bit with the water pipes and dig around a
little on the beach, and it won't cost the town half a
crown. That ought to do it, don't you think? Hm?

HOVSTAD. I think so—as long as you've got the *Courier*
with you.

ASLAKSEN. The press is a power in a free society, Doctor.

DR. STOCKMANN. How true. And so's public opinion. Mr.
Aslaksen, I assume you'll take care of the Home Owners
Council?

ASLAKSEN. The Home Owners Council and the Temperance Union both. You can count on that.

DR. STOCKMANN. But, gentlemen—it embarrasses me to
mention it, but—*your* compensation—?

HOVSTAD. Preferably, of course, we'd like to help you
for nothing, as you can imagine. But the *Courier*'s on
shaky legs these days; it's not doing too well; and to shut
the paper down now when there's so much to work for in
the larger political scene strikes me as insupportable.

DR. STOCKMANN. Clearly. That would be a hard blow for
a friend of the people like you. (*In an outburst.*) But *I'm*
an enemy of the people! (*Lunges about the room.*) Where
do I have my stick? Where in hell is that stick?

HOVSTAD. What's this?

ASLAKSEN. You're not going to—?

DR. STOCKMANN (*stops*). And what if I didn't give you
one iota of my shares? We tycoons aren't so free with our
money, don't forget.

HOVSTAD. And don't *you* forget that this matter of
shares can be posed in two different lights.

DR. STOCKMANN. Yes, you're just the man for that. If I
don't bail out the *Courier*, you'll put a vile construction on
it all. You'll hound me down—set upon me—try to choke
me off like a dog chokes a hare!

HOVSTAD. That's the law of nature. Every animal has to
struggle for survival.

ASLAKSEN. We take our food where we can find it, you know.

DR. STOCKMANN. Then see if you can find yours in the gutter! (*Striding about the room.*) Because now we're going to learn, by God, who's the strongest animal among the three of us! (*Finds his umbrella and flourishes it.*) Hi, look out—!

HOVSTAD. Don't hit us!

ASLAKSEN. Watch out with that umbrella!

DR. STOCKMANN. Out of the window with you, Hovstad.

HOVSTAD (*by the hall door*). Have you lost your mind?

DR. STOCKMANN. Out of the window, Aslaksen! I said, jump! Don't be the last to go.

ASLAKSEN (*running around the desk*). Moderation, Doctor! I'm out of condition—I'm not up to this— (*Shrieks.*) Help! Help!

(MRS. STOCKMANN, PETRA, and HORSTER *enter from the living room.*)

MRS. STOCKMANN. My heavens, Thomas, what's going on in here?

DR. STOCKMANN (*swinging his umbrella*). Jump, I'm telling you! Into the gutter!

HOVSTAD. This is unprovoked assault! Captain Horster, I'm calling you for a witness. (*He scurries out down the hall.*)

ASLAKSEN (*confused*). If I just knew the layout here— (*Sneaks out through the living-room door.*)

MRS. STOCKMANN (*holding onto the* DOCTOR). Now you control yourself, Thomas!

DR. STOCKMANN (*flings the umbrella away*). Damn, they got out of it after all!

MRS. STOCKMANN. But what did they want you for?

DR. STOCKMANN. You can hear about it later. I have other things to think about now. (*Goes to the desk and writes on a visiting card.*) See, Katherine. What's written here?

MRS. STOCKMANN. "No," repeated three times. Why is that?

DR. STOCKMANN. You can hear about that later, too. (*Holding the card out.*) Here, Petra, tell Smudgy-face to run over to the Badger's with this, quick as she can. Hurry!

(PETRA *leaves with the card by the hall door.*)

Well, if I haven't had visits today from all the devil's envoys, I don't know what. But now I'll sharpen my pen into a stiletto and skewer them; I'll dip it in venom and gall; I'll sling my inkstand right at their skulls!

MRS. STOCKMANN. Yes, but we're leaving here, Thomas.

(PETRA *returns.*)

DR. STOCKMANN. Well?

PETRA. It's on its way.

DR. STOCKMANN. Good. Leaving, you say? The hell we are! We're staying here where we are, Katherine!

PETRA. We're staying?

MRS. STOCKMANN. In this town?

DR. STOCKMANN. Exactly. This is the battleground; here's where the fighting will be; and here's where I'm going to win! As soon as I've got my trousers patched, I'm setting out to look for a house. We'll need a roof over our heads by winter.

HORSTER. You can share mine.

DR. STOCKMANN. I can?

HORSTER. Yes, perfectly well. There's room enough, and I'm scarcely ever home.

MRS. STOCKMANN. Oh, how kind of you, Horster.

PETRA. Thank you!

DR. STOCKMANN (*shaking his hand*). Many, many thanks! So that worry is over. Now I can make a serious start right today. Oh, Katherine, it's endless, the number of things that need looking into here! And it's lucky I have so much time now to spend—yes, because, I meant to tell you, I got my notice from the baths—

MRS. STOCKMANN (*sighing*). Ah me, I've been expecting it.

DR. STOCKMANN. And then they want to take my practice away, too. Well, let them! I'll keep the poor people at least—the ones who can't pay at all; and, Lord knows, they're the ones that need me the most. But, by thunder, they'll have to hear me out. I'll preach to them in season and out of season, as someone once said.

MRS. STOCKMANN. But, dear, I think you've seen how much good preaching does.

DR. STOCKMANN. You really are preposterous, Katherine. Should I let myself be whipped from the field by public opinion and the solid majority and other such barbarities? No, thank you! Besides, what I want is so simple and clear and basic. I just want to hammer into the heads of these mongrels that the so-called liberals are the most insidious enemies of free men—that party programs have a way of smothering every new, germinal truth—that acting out of expediency turns morality and justice into a hollow mockery, until it finally becomes monstrous to go on living. Captain Horster, don't you think I could get people to recognize that?

HORSTER. Most likely. I don't understand much about such things.

DR. STOCKMANN. Don't you see—let me explain! The party leaders have to be eradicated—because a party leader's just like a wolf, an insatiable wolf that needs so and so many smaller animals to feed off per annum, if he's going to survive. Look at Hovstad and Aslaksen! How many lesser creatures haven't they swallowed up—or they maul and mutilate them till they can't be more than home owners and subscribers to the *Courier!* (*Sitting on the edge of the desk.*) Ah, come here, Katherine—look at that sunlight, how glorious, the way it streams in today. And how wonderful and fresh the spring air is.

MRS. STOCKMANN. Yes, if we only could live on sunlight and spring air, Thomas.

DR. STOCKMANN. Well, you'll have to skimp and save a

bit here and there—it'll turn out. That's my least concern. No, what's worse is that I don't know any man who's free-spirited enough to carry my work on after me.

PETRA. Oh, don't think of that, Father; you've lots of time. Why, look—the boys, already.

(EILIF and MORTEN *come in from the living room.*)

MRS. STOCKMANN. Did you get let out early?

MORTEN. No. We had a fight with some others at recess—

EILIF. That isn't true; it was the others that fought us.

MORTEN. Yes, and so Mr. Rørland said we'd better stay home for a few days.

DR. STOCKMANN (*snapping his fingers and jumping down off the desk*). I've got it! So help me, I've got it! You'll never set foot in school again.

THE BOYS. No more school?

MRS. STOCKMANN. But, Thomas—

DR. STOCKMANN. I said, never! I'll teach you myself—by that, I mean, you won't learn a blessed fact—

THE BOYS. Hurray!

DR. STOCKMANN. But I'll make you into free-spirited and accomplished men. Listen, you have to help me, Petra.

PETRA. Yes, of course I will.

DR. STOCKMANN. And the school—that'll be held in the room where they assailed me as an enemy of the people. But we have to be more. I need at least twelve boys to begin with.

MRS. STOCKMANN. You'll never get them from this town.

DR. STOCKMANN. Let's see about that. (*To the* BOYS.) Don't you know any boys off the street—regular little punks—

MORTEN. Sure, I know lots of them!

DR. STOCKMANN. So, that's fine. Bring around a few samples. I want to experiment with mongrels for a change. There might be some fantastic minds out there.

MORTEN. But what'll we do when we've become free-spirited and accomplished men?

DR. STOCKMANN. You'll drive all the wolves into the Far West, boys!

(EILIF *looks somewhat dubious;* MORTEN *jumps about and cheers.*)

MRS. STOCKMANN. Ah, just so those wolves aren't hunting you anymore, Thomas.

DR. STOCKMANN. Are you utterly mad, Katherine! Hunt *me* down! Now, when I'm the strongest man in town!

MRS. STOCKMANN. The strongest—now?

DR. STOCKMANN. Yes, I might go farther and say that now I'm one of the strongest men in the whole world.

MORTEN. You mean it?

DR. STOCKMANN (*lowering his voice*). Shh, don't talk about it yet—but I've made a great discovery.

MRS. STOCKMANN. What, again?

DR. STOCKMANN. Yes, why not! (*Gathers them around him and speaks confidentially.*) And the essence of it, you see, is that the strongest man in the world is the one who stands most alone.

MRS. STOCKMANN (*smiling and shaking her head*). Oh, Thomas, Thomas—!

PETRA (*buoyantly, gripping his hands*). Father!

THE LADY FROM THE SEA

THE CHARACTERS

DR. WANGEL, district physician
ELLIDA WANGEL, his second wife
BOLETTE } daughters by
HILDA } his first marriage
ARNHOLM, headmaster of a school
LYNGSTRAND
BALLESTED
A STRANGER
YOUNG PEOPLE OF THE TOWN
TOURISTS AND SUMMER VISITORS

The action takes place during the summer in a small town on a fjord in northern Norway.

⫍ ACT ONE ⫎

DR. WANGEL's *house. A spacious veranda to the left, with a garden to the front and side of the house. Below the veranda, a flagpole. In the garden to the right, an arbor, containing a table and chairs. A hedge with a small gate in the background. Beyond the hedge, a path along the shore, lined by trees. Through the trees the fjord can be seen, with high peaks and mountain ranges in the distance. It is a warm, brilliantly clear summer morning.*

BALLESTED, *middle-aged, wearing an old velvet jacket and a broad-brimmed artist's hat, stands under the flagpole, adjusting the ropes. The flag lies on the ground. Not far from him is an easel with canvas in place. Beside it on a campstool are brushes, a palette, and a paint-box.*

BOLETTE WANGEL *comes out through the open door to the veranda. She is carrying a large vase of flowers, which she sets down on the table.*

BOLETTE. Well, Ballested—can you get it to work?

BALLESTED. Why, certainly, miss. It's nothing, really. If you'll pardon the question—are you expecting visitors today?

BOLETTE. Yes, we expect Mr. Arnholm here this morning. He arrived in town last night.

BALLESTED. Arnholm? But wait—wasn't his name Arnholm, the man who was tutor here some years ago?

BOLETTE. Yes, that's the man.

227

BALLESTED. I see. So he's back in these parts again.

BOLETTE. That's why we want the flag up.

BALLESTED. Well, that makes sense, I guess.

(BOLETTE *goes back into the house. After a moment* LYNGSTRAND *comes down the road from the right and stops, interested, as he catches sight of the easel and painting materials. He is a slender young man, poorly but neatly dressed, and has a rather frail appearance.*)

LYNGSTRAND (*from the other side of the hedge*). Good morning.

BALLESTED (*turning*). What—! Good morning. (*Runs up the flag.*) There—she's off. (*Fastens the rope and begins busying himself at the easel.*) Good morning, sir. I really don't believe I've had the pleasure—

LYNGSTRAND. You must be a painter.

BALLESTED. Naturally. And why shouldn't I be a painter?

LYNGSTRAND. Yes, I can see you are. Would it be all right if I just stopped in a moment?

BALLESTED. Maybe you'd like to look at it?

LYNGSTRAND. Yes, I really would, very much.

BALLESTED. Oh, there's nothing remarkable to see yet. But please, if you want to, come in.

LYNGSTRAND. Thank you. (*He enters through the gate.*)

BALLESTED (*painting*). It's the fjord there between those islands that I'm trying to get.

LYNGSTRAND. Yes, I see.

BALLESTED. But the figure's still lacking. In this town there's not a model to be found.

LYNGSTRAND. Is there going to be a figure as well?

BALLESTED. Yes. In here by this rock in the foreground, there'll be a mermaid lying, half dead.

LYNGSTRAND. Why half dead?

BALLESTED. She's wandered in from the sea and can't find her way out again. And so, you see, she lies here, expiring in the tide pools.

LYNGSTRAND. Yes, of course.

BALLESTED. It was the lady of this house who gave me the idea.

LYNGSTRAND. What will you call the painting when it's finished?

BALLESTED. I've thought of calling it "The Dying Mermaid."

LYNGSTRAND. Very effective. You certainly can make something fine out of this.

BALLESTED (*looking at him*). A fellow craftsman, perhaps?

LYNGSTRAND. A painter, you mean?

BALLESTED. Yes.

LYNGSTRAND. No, I'm not that. But I'm going to be a sculptor. My name is Hans Lyngstrand.

BALLESTED. So you're going to be a sculptor? Yes, yes, sculpture's one of the better arts, too—quite elegant. I think I've seen you a couple of times on the street. Have you been in town very long?

LYNGSTRAND. No, I've been here only two weeks. But if I can manage it, I'd like to stay the whole summer.

BALLESTED. And savor the ocean bathing, hm?

LYNGSTRAND. Yes, I need to build up my strength a little.

BALLESTED. Not in delicate health, I hope.

LYNGSTRAND. Yes, my health's been a bit uncertain. But it's nothing really serious. It's my chest—just some trouble getting my breath.

BALLESTED. Pah—that's nothing! All the same, you still ought to see a good doctor.

LYNGSTRAND. I was thinking of Dr. Wangel, if I have the chance.

BALLESTED. Yes, do that. (*Looks off to the left.*) There's another steamer, jammed full of people. It's incredible how many more tourists have been coming here these last few years.

LYNGSTRAND. Yes, it seems like pretty heavy traffic to me.

BALLESTED. And with all the summer visitors, too. I'm often afraid our town's going to lose its character with all these strangers around.

LYNGSTRAND. Were you born here?

BALLESTED. No, I wasn't. But I've accli—acclimatized myself. I've grown attached to the place—time and habit, I guess.

LYNGSTRAND. Then you've lived here quite a while?

BALLESTED. Oh, some seventeen, eighteen years. I came with Skive's Theater Company. But then we ran into financial problems, and the company broke up and scattered to the winds.

LYNGSTRAND. But you stayed on.

BALLESTED. I stayed. And I did rather well for myself. Actually, in those days I was mainly a scene painter, if you want to know.

(BOLETTE *comes out with a rocking chair, which she sets down on the veranda.*)

BOLETTE (*speaking toward the room within*). Hilda— see if you can find the embroidered footstool for Father.·

LYNGSTRAND (*going over to the veranda to greet her*). Good morning, Miss Wangel!

BOLETTE (*by the railing*). Oh my, is it you, Mr. Lyngstrand? Good morning. Excuse me a moment—I just have to— (*Goes within.*)

BALLESTED. Do you know the family?

LYNGSTRAND. Not really. I've only met the girls here and there in company. And then I talked a while with Mrs. Wangel at the last concert in the park. She said I was welcome to come and call on them.

BALLESTED. Ah, you know what—you ought to cultivate that connection.

LYNGSTRAND. Yes, I was thinking of making a visit. Sort of a courtesy call, you might say. Now if I could only find some excuse—

BALLESTED. Some—what? Excuse! (*Glances off to the left.*) Damnation! (*Gathering his things together.*) The steamer's already docked. I'm due at the hotel. It might be some of the new arrivals will need me. Actually, if you want to know, I'm working as a barber and a hairdresser, too.

LYNGSTRAND. You're really very versatile.

BALLESTED. In small towns you have to know how to ac—acclimatize yourself in various fields. If you ever need anything in the way of hair preparations—a little pomade or something, then ask for Ballested, the dance instructor.

LYNGSTRAND. Dance instructor—?

BALLESTED. Director of the Wind Ensemble, if you like. We're giving a concert in the park this evening. Good-bye—good-bye!

(*He carries his painting materials through the garden gate and goes off to the left.* HILDA *comes out with the footstool.* BOLETTE *brings more flowers.* LYNGSTRAND *nods to* HILDA *from below in the garden.*)

HILDA (*by the railing, without returning his greeting*). Bolette said that you'd ventured inside today.

LYNGSTRAND. Yes, I took the liberty of coming inside just a little.

HILDA. Have you had your morning walk already?

LYNGSTRAND. Oh, no—I didn't get very far today.

HILDA. Did you have a swim then?

LYNGSTRAND. Yes, I was in for a short while. I saw your mother down there. She went into her bathhouse.

HILDA. Who did?

LYNGSTRAND. Your mother.

HILDA. You don't say. (*She places the footstool in front of the rocking chair.*)

BOLETTE (*breaking in*). Did you see anything of Father's boat out on the fjord?

LYNGSTRAND. Yes, I thought I saw a sailboat heading inshore.

BOLETTE. That must be Father. He's been on a sick call out in the islands. (*She straightens up the table.*)

LYNGSTRAND (*taking one step up the stairs to the veranda*). How marvelous, with all these flowers—!

BOLETTE. Yes, doesn't it look nice?

LYNGSTRAND. Oh, it looks lovely. It looks as if there were a holiday in the house.

HILDA. That's just what it is.

LYNGSTRAND. I thought as much. It has to be your father's birthday today.

BOLETTE (*warningly to* HILDA). Uh-uh!

HILDA (*paying no attention*). No, Mother's.

LYNGSTRAND. Oh, it's your mother's?

BOLETTE (*in a low, angry voice*). Really, Hilda—!

HILDA (*likewise*). Leave me alone! (*To* LYNGSTRAND.) I suppose you'll be going home for lunch now?

LYNGSTRAND (*stepping down off the stairs*). Yes, I guess I better get something to eat.

HILDA. You must find it a pretty good life at the hotel.

LYNGSTRAND. I'm not living at the hotel any longer. It was too expensive.

HILDA. Where are you living now?

LYNGSTRAND. I'm boarding up at Mrs. Jensen's.

HILDA. Which Mrs. Jensen?

LYNGSTRAND. The midwife.

HILDA. Pardon me, Mr. Lyngstrand—but I'm really much too busy to—

LYNGSTRAND. Oh, I know I shouldn't have said that.

HILDA. Said what?

LYNGSTRAND. What I said.

HILDA (*measuring him with a cool look*). I absolutely don't understand you.

LYNGSTRAND. No, no. Well, then I'll be saying good-bye to you both for now.

BOLETTE (*coming forward to the stairs*). Good-bye, good-bye, Mr. Lyngstrand. You really must excuse us today. But some other time—when you really can stay a while—and if you'd like to—then you must stop by again and see Father and—and the rest of us.

LYNGSTRAND. Oh, thank you. I'd like that very much. (*He bows and goes out by the gate. As he passes along the road to the left, he nods and smiles again up to the veranda.*)

HILDA (*in an undertone*). *Adieu, monsieur!* Do give my best to Mother Jensen.

BOLETTE (*softly, shaking her by the arm*). Hilda—! You naughty child! Are you crazy! He could have heard you!

HILDA. Ffft! Who cares!

BOLETTE (*looking off to the right*). There's Father.

(DR. WANGEL, *dressed for travel and carrying a small bag, comes up the footpath from the left.*)

WANGEL. So, my little girls, you have me back! (*He comes in through the gate.*)

BOLETTE (*going toward him across the garden*). Oh, how lovely that you're here.

HILDA (*also going down to him*). Are you taking the rest of the day off, Father?

WANGEL. Oh, no, I'll still have to go down to the office for a spell. Say, do you know if Arnholm's come?

BOLETTE. Yes, he arrived last night. We had word from the hotel.

WANGEL. Then you haven't seen him yet?

BOLETTE. No. But he's sure to be out here this morning.

WANGEL. Yes, he undoubtedly will.

HILDA (*tugging at him*). Father, now you must look around.

WANGEL (*glancing over at the veranda*). Yes, child, I can see. It's really quite festive.

BOLETTE. Yes, don't you think we've made it attractive?

WANGEL. Well, I should say so! Are—are we alone here, just the three of us?

HILDA. Yes, she went in—

BOLETTE (*hurriedly*). Mother's in swimming.

WANGEL (*looks fondly at* BOLETTE *and pats her head, then says somewhat hesitantly*). But listen, you girls—do you want to leave all these things here, like this, all day long? And the flag up, too, all day?

HILDA. Oh, but Father, of course! What else do you think!

WANGEL. Hm—all right, but you see—

BOLETTE (*nodding and winking at him*). Can't you imagine how we went and did all this for Mr. Arnholm's sake. When such a good old friend comes back to visit you the very first time—

HILDA (*smiling and shaking him*). Just think—he used to be Bolette's tutor, Father!

WANGEL (*with a half smile*). What a pair of sly ones you are! Well, after all—it's only natural that we go on remembering her, although she's no longer with us. But even so—Hilda, see here. (*Handing over his bag.*) This goes down to the office. No, children—I don't like this. It just isn't right, you understand. Every year we shouldn't have to— Well, what can one say! I don't know that it'll ever be different.

HILDA (*starts through the garden, left, with the bag, then stops and turns, pointing*). See that man there, walking this way? That must be your tutor.

BOLETTE (*following her gaze*). Him? (*Laughs.*) Oh, you are the limit! You think that decrepit specimen is Arnholm!

WANGEL. Not so fast, there. So help me if it isn't him—! Yes, it most certainly is!

BOLETTE (*staring, hushed in astonishment*). My Lord, yes, I think you're right—!

(ARNHOLM, *in elegant morning dress, with gold-rimmed glasses and a thin cane, appears on the path from the right. He looks rather tired, as if overworked. Approaching the garden he waves a friendly greeting and enters through the gate.*)

WANGEL (*going toward him*). Welcome, my dear old friend! Welcome back to the old grounds!

ARNHOLM. Thank you, Dr. Wangel! Many, many thanks. (*They shake hands and walk up through the garden together.*) And these are the children! (*Taking their hands and looking at them.*) Why, I can hardly recognize them.

WANGEL. No, I'm not surprised.

ARNHOLM. Oh, well—perhaps Bolette. Yes, Bolette I would have known.

WANGEL. Just barely, I imagine. It's been nine, ten years now since you saw her last. Ah, yes, a great deal has changed here since then.

ARNHOLM (*looking around*). As a matter of fact, I was thinking just the opposite. Except that the trees have grown considerably—and an arbor has been built over there—

WANGEL. Oh, no, if you mean outwardly—

ARNHOLM (*with a smile*). And then not to mention that now you have two grown-up, marriageable daughters in the house.

WANGEL. Oh, there's only one who's marriageable yet.

HILDA (*in an undertone*). Father, honestly!

WANGEL. But now I think we'll set ourselves up on the veranda. It's cooler than here. If you will.

ARNHOLM. Thank you, Doctor.

(*They mount the stairs,* WANGEL *motioning* ARNHOLM *into the rocking chair.*)

WANGEL. There now. You just sit perfectly quiet and relax. Because, really, you look quite done in from the trip.

ARNHOLM. Oh, that's nothing. In these surroundings here—

BOLETTE (*to* WANGEL). Shouldn't we bring you some

soda water and lemonade? And perhaps you'd like it inside? It's going to be very hot out.

WANGEL. Yes, do that, girls. Some soda water and lemonade. And then maybe a little cognac.

BOLETTE. Cognac, too?

WANGEL. Just a little. In case somebody wants it.

BOLETTE. All right, then. Hilda, you go down to the office with the bag.

(BOLETTE *goes into the house, closing the door after her.* HILDA *takes the bag and goes through the garden around the house to the left.*)

ARNHOLM (*who has followed* BOLETTE *with his eyes*). What an attractive— How attractively your two daughters have turned out!

WANGEL (*sitting*). Yes, don't you think?

ARNHOLM. Why, Bolette is simply astonishing. And Hilda, too. But—about yourself, now, Doctor. Have you decided to stay here permanently?

WANGEL. Yes, so it seems. After all, I was born and raised in these parts, as they say. And then I had those years of marvelous happiness here with her—who was taken from us so soon. And who you remember from your time here, Arnholm.

ARNHOLM. Yes—yes.

WANGEL. And now I've been made happy again by my second wife. I must say, in the sum of things, fate's been kind to me.

ARNHOLM. But no children in your second marriage?

WANGEL. We had a little boy about two, two and a half years ago. But we didn't keep him long. He died when he was some four, five months old.

ARNHOLM. Is your wife not home today?

WANGEL. Oh, yes, she'll be along any time. She went down for a swim. It's her regular practice now, every day—and in all sorts of weather.

ARNHOLM. Not for reasons of health, I hope.

WANGEL. No, not exactly. Although she's definitely

shown signs of nervousness in the past two years. Off and on, I mean. I really can't make out just what the trouble is. But this bathing in the sea—it's become almost the one ruling passion of her life.

ARNHOLM. I remember something of the kind from before.

WANGEL (*with an almost imperceptible smile*). That's right, you know Ellida from the time you were teaching out at Skjoldvik.

ARNHOLM. Of course. She often visited the rectory where I boarded. And then I nearly always saw her whenever I was out at the lighthouse visiting her father.

WANGEL. I can tell you, the life out there has left its mark on her. The people in town here can't understand her. They call her "the lady from the sea."

ARNHOLM. They do?

WANGEL. Yes. So, if you would—talk to her now about the old days, Arnholm. It would do her a world of good.

ARNHOLM (*looking skeptically at him*). Have you really any reason to think so?

WANGEL. I'm sure of it.

ELLIDA'S VOICE (*from the garden, off to the right*). Are you there, Wangel?

WANGEL (*rising*). Yes, dear.

(ELLIDA WANGEL, *wearing a large, light robe, her hair wet and falling loose over her shoulders, comes through the trees near the arbor.* ARNHOLM *gets up.*)

WANGEL (*smiling and reaching his hands out toward her*). Well, there's our mermaid!

ELLIDA (*moving quickly to the veranda and taking his hands*). Thank goodness you're here! When did you come?

WANGEL. Just now. Only a moment ago. (*Gesturing toward* ARNHOLM.) But aren't you going to greet an old acquaintance—?

ELLIDA (*holding her hand out to* ARNHOLM). So, we finally got you here. Welcome! And forgive me that I wasn't home—

ARNHOLM. Don't mention it. No standing on ceremony—

WANGEL. Was the water nice and fresh today?

ELLIDA. Fresh! Good Lord, this water's never fresh. So stale and tepid. Ugh! The water's sick here in the fjord.

ARNHOLM. Sick?

ELLIDA. Yes, it's sick. And I think it makes people sick, too.

WANGEL (*smiling*). Well, you're a fine testimonial for a summer resort.

ARNHOLM. It seems more likely to me, Mrs. Wangel, that you have a peculiar tie to the sea and everything connected with it.

ELLIDA. Oh, yes, it's possible. At times I almost think so— But just look, how festive the girls have made things in your honor!

WANGEL (*embarrassed*). Hm— (*Looks at his watch.*) Now I will have to run—

ARNHOLM. Is this really in my honor—?

ELLIDA. Obviously. We don't have displays like this every day. Phew! It's stifling under this roof! (*Going down into the garden.*) Come on over here. At least there's the semblance of a breeze. (*She settles herself in the arbor.*)

ARNHOLM (*following after*). The air here seems quite refreshing to me.

ELLIDA. Yes, you're used to that foul city air. I've heard it's just dreadful there in the summer.

WANGEL (*who also has gone down into the garden*). Ellida dear—now it's up to you to entertain our friend for a while.

ELLIDA. You have work to do?

WANGEL. Yes, I have to go down to my office. And then I want to change my clothes. But I won't be long—

ARNHOLM (*sitting down in the arbor*). Don't rush yourself, Doctor. I'm sure your wife and I will find much to talk about.

WANGEL (*nods*). I'm counting on that. Well—till later, then. (*He goes out through the garden to the left.*)

ELLIDA (*after a short pause*). Isn't it lovely to sit here?

ARNHOLM. I think it's lovely now.

ELLIDA. We call this place the summerhouse. *My* summerhouse, because I had it built. Or rather Wangel did— for my sake.

ARNHOLM. Do you often sit here?

ELLIDA. Yes, most of the day.

ARNHOLM. I suppose, with the children?

ELLIDA. No, the children—they keep to the veranda.

ARNHOLM. And Wangel?

ELLIDA. Oh, Wangel goes back and forth. First he's here with me, and then he's over with them.

ARNHOLM. Is it you who want it like that?

ELLIDA. I think all parties concerned prefer it that way. We can talk across to each other—whenever we have something to say.

ARNHOLM (*after a moment's thought*). The last time we saw each other—out at Skjoldvik, I mean—hm—it seems so long ago now—

ELLIDA. It's all of ten years since you came out to see us.

ARNHOLM. Yes, about that. But when I remember you out there at the lighthouse—! "The pagan"—as the old priest used to call you, because your father gave you the name of a ship instead of a proper Christian name—

ELLIDA. Well—?

ARNHOLM. The last thing I'd ever have believed was that I would see you again down here, as Mrs. Wangel.

ELLIDA. No, at that time Wangel wasn't yet— The girls' mother was still alive then. Their real mother, I mean.

ARNHOLM. Yes, I understand. But even if that hadn't been— Even if he'd been quite unattached—I never would have imagined that this could happen.

ELLIDA. Nor I, either. Not for anything—then.

ARNHOLM. Wangel is such a good man. So honest. So genuinely kind toward everyone—

ELLIDA (*with warm affection*). Yes, he is!

ARNHOLM. But to me, the two of you seem different as night and day.

ELLIDA. You're right. We are.

ARNHOLM. Well, but how did this happen then? How did it happen!

ELLIDA. Oh, Arnholm, don't ask me that. I'd never be able to explain it. And even if I could, you'd never understand one particle of it.

ARNHOLM. Hm. (*His voice dropping slightly.*) Have you ever told your husband anything about me? I mean, about that futile gesture I once let myself be charmed into?

ELLIDA. Certainly not! I've said nothing at all to him about—what you mean.

ARNHOLM. I'm glad. Because I've been feeling a bit oppressed by the idea that—

ELLIDA. You needn't be. I've only told him what's perfectly true, that I was very fond of you, and that you were the best and truest friend I had up there.

ARNHOLM. Thank you. But tell me then—why did you never write me after I left?

ELLIDA. I thought it might be painful for you to hear from someone who—who couldn't respond as you wanted. It seemed to me rather like reopening a wound.

ARNHOLM. Hm—yes, yes, you may be right.

ELLIDA. But why did you never write yourself?

ARNHOLM (*regarding her with a half-reproachful smile*). I make the overtures? Maybe arouse suspicion of trying to start things up again? After the kind of rejection I got?

ELLIDA. Yes, I can understand. But has there never been any other involvement since?

ARNHOLM. Never. I've stayed faithful to my memories.

ELLIDA (*half joking*). Oh, nonsense! Let the old memories go. You should be thinking instead of becoming a happily married man.

ARNHOLM. That'll have to be soon then. You realize I've already passed thirty-seven?

ELLIDA. Well, all the more reason to hurry up. (*She is silent a moment, then speaks in a low, serious voice.*) But listen, Arnholm—I want to tell you something now that I couldn't have mentioned then to save my life.

ARNHOLM. What's that?

ELLIDA. When you made what you just called your futile gesture—there was no other answer I *could* have given you.

ARNHOLM. I know you only had friendship to offer. I know that.

ELLIDA. But you didn't know that my whole being and all my thoughts were directed elsewhere at the time.

ARNHOLM. At the time!

ELLIDA. Yes.

ARNHOLM. But that's impossible! You're mistaken about the time! You hardly knew Wangel then.

ELLIDA. I don't mean Wangel.

ARNHOLM. You don't—? But up in Skjoldvik—I can't recall one single, solitary person you could possibly have been interested in.

ELLIDA. No, I can imagine. Because it was all so utterly insane.

ARNHOLM. But then you must tell me more about this!

ELLIDA. Oh, it's enough for you to know I wasn't free then. And you know that now.

ARNHOLM. But if you *had* been free—?

ELLIDA. Yes?

ARNHOLM. Would you have answered my letter differently?

ELLIDA. How do I know? When Wangel came, I answered differently.

ARNHOLM. Then what's the good of telling me you weren't free?

ELLIDA (*rising with a troubled, anxious air*). Because I've got to confide in someone. No, no, don't get up.

ARNHOLM. Your husband knows nothing of this?

ELLIDA. I let him know from the first that I'd once set my heart on somebody else. He never asked to know more, and we've never discussed it since. After all, it was nothing but madness. And it was over before it started. That is—more or less.

ARNHOLM (*rises*). More or less? Not definitely!

ELLIDA. Yes, yes, definitely! Good Lord, Arnholm, it's not what you're thinking at all. It's something so incomprehensible, I don't know how to begin telling you. You'd only believe I was ill—or out of my mind.

ARNHOLM. My dear Ellida—there's no other way: you've got to tell me everything.

ELLIDA. All right! At least I can try. How would you, as a reasonable man, presume to account for— (*Looks away and breaks off.*) Wait a while. Someone's coming.

(LYNGSTRAND *appears on the road to the left and enters the garden. He is wearing a flower in his lapel and carries a large, colorful bouquet wrapped in paper and silk ribbons. He stops, with a hesitant, uncertain look, by the veranda.*)

ELLIDA (*coming forward in the arbor*). Are you looking for the girls, Mr. Lyngstrand?

LYNGSTRAND (*turning*). Oh, are you there, Mrs. Wangel? (*Bows and approaches.*) No, actually not. Not for the girls. For you, Mrs. Wangel. You suggested that I might come and call on you—

ELLIDA. I certainly did. You're always welcome here.

LYNGSTRAND. Thank you. And since it just so happens that you're having a celebration here today—

ELLIDA. Ah, you know about that?

LYNGSTRAND. Oh, yes. That's why I'd like to take the liberty of presenting you, Mrs. Wangel, with this— (*He bows and offers the bouquet.*)

ELLIDA (*smiling*). But my dear Mr. Lyngstrand, wouldn't it be better if you gave those beautiful flowers to

Mr. Arnholm directly? Because, you see, it's really for his sake that—

LYNGSTRAND (*looking indecisively at them both*). Pardon me—but I don't know this gentleman. This is—I brought it for a birthday present.

ELLIDA. Birthday? Then you're mistaken, Mr. Lyngstrand. It's no one's birthday here today.

LYNGSTRAND (*smiling broadly*). Oh, I know it is. But I never thought it was such a secret.

ELLIDA. Just what do you know?

LYNGSTRAND. That it's your birthday, Mrs. Wangel.

ELLIDA. Mine?

ARNHOLM (*looks inquiringly at her*). Today? No, it can't be.

ELLIDA (*to* LYNGSTRAND). Whatever gave you that idea?

LYNGSTRAND. It was Hilda who let it slip. I stopped by here a moment earlier today, and I happened to ask the girls why all the decorations, the flowers, the flag—

ELLIDA. Yes, and—?

LYNGSTRAND. And so Hilda answered: "Because today it's Mother's birthday."

ELLIDA. Mother's—! I see.

ARNHOLM. Aha! (*Exchanges an understanding look with* ELLIDA.) Well, Mrs. Wangel, since the young man already knows—

ELLIDA. Yes, now that you know, of course—

LYNGSTRAND (*presenting the bouquet again*). If you'll permit me to offer my very best wishes—

ELLIDA (*taking the flowers*). Thank you very much. Please, come and sit for a moment, Mr. Lyngstrand.

(ELLIDA, ARNHOLM, *and* LYNGSTRAND *sit down in the arbor.*)

ELLIDA. This business—about my birthday—it was supposed to have been a secret, Mr. Arnholm.

ARNHOLM. Yes, I'm sure of that. It wasn't for us outsiders.

ELLIDA (*laying the bouquet aside*). Yes, quite so. Not for outsiders.

LYNGSTRAND. I promise I won't tell a living soul.

ELLIDA. Oh, it's really not that important. But how are things going for you? I think you're looking better now than you did.

LYNGSTRAND. Yes, I believe I'm doing quite well. And then next year, if maybe I can get to the south of Europe—

ELLIDA. And you will, the girls tell me.

LYNGSTRAND. Yes, because I have a patron in Bergen who'll back me. And he's agreed to help me next year.

ELLIDA. How did you get to know him?

LYNGSTRAND. Ah, that was a rare piece of luck. I went to sea once on one of his ships.

ELLIDA. Really? So you had the sea in your blood?

LYNGSTRAND. No, not at all. But when my mother died, my father didn't want me lolling around the house any longer, so he packed me off to sea. Then on the home trip we went down in the English Channel. Yes, and that was lucky for me.

ARNHOLM. How so?

LYNGSTRAND. Well, because it was through the shipwreck that I got the condition here in my chest. I stayed so long in the icy waters before they pulled me out that I had to quit the sea. Yes, it was really my good fortune.

ARNHOLM. You believe that?

LYNGSTRAND. Yes. Because this condition is hardly dangerous. And now I can be a sculptor, which I want more than anything else. Imagine—a chance to work in that beautiful clay, to feel it so supple under your fingers, and to model it into form.

ELLIDA. What kind of form? Mermen and mermaids? Or the old Vikings—?

LYNGSTRAND. No, nothing like that. As soon as I'm able, I want to try for a large work—a group, as they call it.

ELLIDA. Oh, yes. But what will this group portray?

LYNGSTRAND. It'll be based on something out of my own experience.

ARNHOLM. Good—stay close to that.

ELLIDA. But what will it be?

LYNGSTRAND. Well, my idea was to have the figure of a young woman, a sailor's wife, stretched out, lying in a strangely troubled sleep. And she would be dreaming, too. I really believe I can develop it so you can actually see that she's dreaming.

ARNHOLM. But isn't there more to the idea?

LYNGSTRAND. Oh, yes, there'll be one other figure. A kind of specter, you might say. It would be her husband, that she'd been unfaithful to while he was away. And he's been drowned at sea.

ARNHOLM. What—?

ELLIDA. He's been drowned?

LYNGSTRAND. Yes. He was drowned on a voyage. But then the strange thing is that he comes home all the same. It's night, and now he stands there over her bed, looking down at her. He'll stand there, dripping wet, like a man dragged out of the sea.

ELLIDA (*leaning back in her chair*). What an astonishing conception! (*Shuts her eyes.*) Yes, I can see it as clear as crystal.

ARNHOLM. But how on earth, Mr.—Mr.—! You said it was something you'd experienced yourself.

LYNGSTRAND. That's right. I did experience all this—at least up to a point.

ARNHOLM. You witnessed a dead man that—

LYNGSTRAND. Well now, I didn't mean experience, strictly speaking. Not actuality. But something very much like it—

ELLIDA (*with lively anticipation*). Tell me more—all you can—about this! I want to know everything.

ARNHOLM (*smiling*). Yes, this is just the thing for you. It has the spell of the sea.

ELLIDA. What was it, Mr. Lyngstrand?

LYNGSTRAND. We were to sail for home from a town called Halifax when, as it happened, the boatswain took sick, and we had to leave him behind in the hospital there. So we signed on an American as a replacement. This new boatswain—

ELLIDA. The American?

LYNGSTRAND. Yes. One day he borrowed a stack of old newspapers from the captain, and he used to read them by the hour. He said he wanted to learn Norwegian.

ELLIDA. Yes? And then!

LYNGSTRAND. Then one evening we were running in a tremendous gale. All the crew were on deck—except the boatswain and me. He'd turned his ankle so he couldn't walk on it, and I was on the sick list, laid up in my bunk. Well, so he was sitting there in the forecastle, reading in one of those old papers again—

ELLIDA. Yes! Go on!

LYNGSTRAND. Then all of a sudden I heard him give out almost a kind of howl. And when I looked at him, I could see that his face had gone chalk-white. Then he twisted and tore the paper in his hands and ripped it to a thousand little pieces. But he did it all so quietly, so quietly.

ELLIDA. Did he say anything? Did he speak?

LYNGSTRAND. Not at first. But after a time he said, as if to himself: "Married. To another man. While I was away."

ELLIDA (closing her eyes, in a near whisper). He said that?

LYNGSTRAND. Yes. And, you know—he said it in perfect Norwegian. He must have a rare gift for learning languages, that man.

ELLIDA. And then what? What happened after?

LYNGSTRAND. Well, then came this incredible thing that I'll never forget as long as I live. For he went on, again very quietly, and said: "But she's mine, and mine she'll always be. And if I go home and fetch her, she'll have to go off with me, even if I came as a drowned man up out of the dark sea."

ELLIDA (*pouring herself a glass of water, her hand trembling*). Phew—how humid it is today—!

LYNGSTRAND. And he said that with such a power of will, I thought he'd be the man to do it, too.

ELLIDA. Do you have any idea—what became of this man?

LYNGSTRAND. Oh, I'm sure he's no longer alive.

ELLIDA (*quickly*). Why do you think so?

LYNGSTRAND. Well, because we went down in the Channel right after. I got away in the longboat with the captain and five others. The mate went with the dinghy, along with the American and another man.

ELLIDA. And nothing's been heard of them since?

LYNGSTRAND. No, not a word. My patron mentioned it again just recently in a letter. But that's exactly why I feel such an urge to turn all this into a work of art. I can see the unfaithful wife so vividly in my mind. And then the avenger, drowned, and yet coming back from the sea. I can picture them both so clearly.

ELLIDA. And I, too. (*Rising.*) Come, let's go in. Or better, down to Wangel. I think it's stifling here. (*She goes out of the arbor.*)

LYNGSTRAND (*who likewise has risen*). For my part, I'll have to be saying good-bye. This was only meant for a short visit on account of your birthday.

ELLIDA. As you wish. (*Giving him her hand.*) Good-bye, and thank you for the flowers.

(LYNGSTRAND *bows and leaves through the gate and off to the left.*)

ARNHOLM (*rises and goes over to* ELLIDA). It's plain to see this has struck you to the heart, Ellida.

ELLIDA. Yes, that's a good way of putting it—although—

ARNHOLM. But, after all, is it really any more than you should have expected?

ELLIDA (*staring at him*). Expected!

ARNHOLM. Yes, I'd say so.

ELLIDA. Expect someone to return again—! Return like that!

ARNHOLM. What in the world—! Is it that crazy sculptor's story—?

ELLIDA. Perhaps he's not so crazy, Arnholm.

ARNHOLM. Is it this nonsense about a dead man that's shaken you so? And I was thinking—

ELLIDA. What?

ARNHOLM. I was thinking, of course, that you were simply putting on an act. That actually you were sitting here suffering because you'd discovered that a family ritual was being kept secret from you. That your husband and his children had a private life that you weren't part of.

ELLIDA. Oh, no. That's as it has to be. I have no right to demand that my husband be mine and mine alone.

ARNHOLM. I'd say you have that right.

ELLIDA. Yes. But, even so, I don't. That's the point. I also have a life—that the others aren't part of.

ARNHOLM. You! (*Lowering his voice.*) Does that mean—? Do you—not really love your husband?

ELLIDA. Yes, yes! With all my heart, I've learned to love him! And that's just what makes it so terrible—so baffling—so utterly inconceivable—!

ARNHOLM. Now you *must* tell me your troubles, freely and openly, Ellida! Will you do that?

ELLIDA. Oh, my dear friend, I can't. Not now, in any case. Perhaps later.

(BOLETTE *comes out on the veranda and down into the garden.*)

BOLETTE. Father's back from the office. Couldn't we all sit inside?

ELLIDA. Yes, let's do that.

(WANGEL, *in fresh clothes, comes with* HILDA *around the house from the left.*)

WANGEL. There! Now I'm totally at your service! How about a nice glass of something cool to drink?

ELLIDA. Just a moment. (*She goes into the arbor and gets the bouquet.*)

HILDA. Oh, look! What lovely flowers! Where did you get them?

ELLIDA. From Mr. Lyngstrand, dear.

HILDA (*startled*). From Lyngstrand?

BOLETTE (*uneasily*). Was Lyngstrand here—again?

ELLIDA (*with a half smile*). Yes. He stopped by with these. For a birthday present, you know.

BOLETTE (*glancing at* HILDA). Oh—!

HILDA (*under her breath*). The beast!

WANGEL (*painfully embarrassed, to* ELLIDA). Uh—yes, you see—I should explain, Ellida, my dear—dearest—

ELLIDA (*interrupting*). Come along, girls! We can put my flowers in water with the others. (*She goes up onto the veranda.*)

BOLETTE (*softly to* HILDA). She really *is* kind at heart.

HILDA (*in an angry whisper*). Flimflam! She's just bewitching Father.

WANGEL (*on the veranda, presses* ELLIDA'*s hand*). Thank you! Thank you for that, Ellida!

ELLIDA (*arranging the flowers*). Nonsense. Shouldn't I play my part too in celebrating—Mother's birthday?

ARNHOLM. Hm!

(*He goes up and joins* WANGEL *and* ELLIDA. BOLETTE *and* HILDA *remain below in the garden.*)

~⟨ ACT TWO ⟩~

*In a local park, high on a wooded hill behind the town. A
cairn of stones and a weather vane stand in the near
background. Large stones, serving as seats, are grouped
about the cairn and in the foreground. Far below, the
outer fjord can be seen in the distance, with islands and
jutting headlands. The open sea is not visible. It is one of
the light summer nights of the north. There is a red-gold
tinge to the twilight sky and over the mountain peaks far
off on the horizon. The sound of four-part singing drifts
faintly up the hill from the right. Young men and women
from the town come in couples up from the right and,
conversing casually, pass the cairn and go out, left. A
moment later* BALLESTED *appears, guiding a party of foreign tourists with their ladies. He is loaded down with
shawls and traveling bags.*

BALLESTED (*pointing upward with his stick*). *Sehen Sie,
meine Herrschaften—dort* over there *liegt eine andere* hill.
Das willen wir also *besteigen, und so herunter*— (*He continues in French and leads the group out to the left.*)

(HILDA *comes briskly up the slope on the right, stops and
looks back. After a moment* BOLETTE *comes up after her.*)

BOLETTE. But, Hilda, why should we run away from
Lyngstrand?

HILDA. Because I can't stand climbing hills like that. So
slow! Look! Look at him, creeping along!

250

BOLETTE. Oh, you know how sickly he is.

HILDA. Do you think it's very serious?

BOLETTE. Yes, I think so, definitely.

HILDA. He was in to see Father this afternoon. I'd give anything to know what Father thinks.

BOLETTE. He told me it was a hardening of the lungs—or something like that. And Father said he hasn't too long to live.

HILDA. No! He said that? Imagine—I guessed the same, exactly.

BOLETTE. But, for heaven's sake now, don't show anything.

HILDA. Oh, what an idea! (*Lowering her voice.*) There, now Hans has finally made it. Hans—doesn't he just look like his name should be Hans?

BOLETTE (*whispers*). Will you behave yourself! You're going to get it!

(LYNGSTRAND *comes in from the right, carrying a parasol*).

LYNGSTRAND. You girls will have to forgive me that I can't go as fast as you can.

HILDA. Did you get yourself a parasol too, now?

LYNGSTRAND. It's your mother's. She said I should use it for a stick. I forgot to bring one.

BOLETTE. Are they down there still? Father and the others?

LYNGSTRAND. Yes. Your father stopped in at the restaurant a moment, and the others are sitting outside, listening to the music. But your mother said they'll be up later.

HILDA (*stands staring at him*). You really look tired now.

LYNGSTRAND. Yes, I almost think I'm a bit tired out. I really do believe I'll have to sit down a while. (*He sits on a stone in the foreground, right.*)

HILDA (*standing in front of him*). Did you know there's going to be a dance later, down by the bandstand?

LYNGSTRAND. Yes, I heard some talk about that.

HILDA. Don't you think it's fun, going dancing?

BOLETTE (*who has begun picking wild flowers in the heather*). Now, Hilda—let Mr. Lyngstrand get his breath.

LYNGSTRAND (*to* HILDA). Yes, I'm sure I'd love dancing— if I only could.

HILDA. You've never learned?

LYNGSTRAND. No, I haven't, actually—but that's not what I meant. I meant, I can't because of my chest.

HILDA. Because of what you call your "condition"?

LYNGSTRAND. Yes, that's it.

HILDA. Does having your "condition" make you very unhappy?

LYNGSTRAND. Oh, no, I can't really say that. (*Smiles.*) Because I think it's why people are always being so kind and considerate—and so charitable to me.

HILDA. Yes, and then it's not at all serious, either.

LYNGSTRAND. No, not in the least. Your father was quite reassuring on that.

HILDA. Then as soon as you're able to travel, it'll pass off.

LYNGSTRAND. Oh, yes. It'll pass off.

BOLETTE (*with flowers*). Here you are, Mr. Lyngstrand —these go in your buttonhole.

LYNGSTRAND. Ah, thank you so much! This is really too kind of you.

HILDA (*looking downward to the right*). They're coming up the path.

BOLETTE (*also looking down*). If they only know where to turn off. No, they're missing it.

LYNGSTRAND (*gets up*). I'll run down to the bend and call them.

HILDA. You'll really have to shout.

BOLETTE. No, it's not worth it. You'll only tire yourself out again.

LYNGSTRAND. Oh, it's easy going downhill. (*He hurries off to the right.*)

HILDA. Yes—downhill. (*Looking after him.*) He's even jumping! And it never occurs to him that he's got to climb back up again.

BOLETTE. Poor thing—

HILDA. If Lyngstrand proposed to you, would you accept him?

BOLETTE. Are you out of your mind?

HILDA. I mean, naturally, if he didn't have this condition in his chest. And if he weren't going to die so soon. Would you have him then?

BOLETTE. I think you better have him.

HILDA. Not on your life! He doesn't have a pin to his name. He hasn't even got enough to live on himself.

BOLETTE. Then why are you so taken up with him?

HILDA. Oh, I'm interested in his disease, that's all.

BOLETTE. I've never noticed you pitying him for that.

HILDA. I don't, either. But I think it's fascinating.

BOLETTE. What?

HILDA. To watch him and to get him to say it isn't serious and that he's going to travel abroad and be an artist. He really believes every bit of it, and it fills him with such a joy. And yet it's all going to come to nothing, absolutely nothing. Because he won't live long enough. When I think of it, it seems so thrilling.

BOLETTE. Thrilling!

HILDA. Yes, I do think it's thrilling. That's my privilege.

BOLETTE. Hilda, you really are a nasty brat!

HILDA. That's what I want to be. Just for spite! (*Looking down.*) Well, at last! Arnholm doesn't like all this climbing. (*Turns.*) That's for sure. You know what I saw about Arnholm at lunch?

BOLETTE. What?

HILDA. He's beginning to lose his hair—right up here, in the middle of his head.

BOLETTE. What nonsense! It's not true.

HILDA. Oh, yes. And then he has wrinkles here around

his eyes. Oh, Bolette, how could you have had such a crush on him when he was your tutor!

BOLETTE (*smiling*). Yes, would you believe it? I remember crying my heart out once because he said he thought Bolette was an ugly name.

HILDA. Imagine! (*Looking down again.*) Well, will you look at that! There goes our "lady from the sea," babbling away to Arnholm. Father's all by himself. Hm—I wonder if those two don't have eyes for each other.

BOLETTE. You should be ashamed of yourself, really! How can you stand there and talk about her like that? Just when we were getting along so well—

HILDA. That's right—dream on, my little goose! Oh, no, we'll never get along with her, never. She's not our kind. And we're not hers, either. God knows why Father ever dragged her into the house—! I wouldn't be surprised if, one fine day, she was to go quite mad.

BOLETTE. Mad! How'd you get that idea?

HILDA. Oh, it's not so inconceivable. After all, her mother went crazy. She died insane, I know that.

BOLETTE. Good grief, what you don't have your nose in! But just don't go around talking about it. Try to be good now—for Father's sake. Do you hear me, Hilda?

(WANGEL, ELLIDA, ARNHOLM, *and* LYNGSTRAND *come up from the right.*)

ELLIDA (*pointing off into the distance*). It lies out there.

ARNHOLM. That's right. It must be in that direction.

ELLIDA. Out there, the sea.

BOLETTE (*to* ARNHOLM). Don't you think it's pretty up here?

ARNHOLM. I think it's magnificent. The view's superb.

WANGEL. Yes, I expect you've never been up here before.

ARNHOLM. No, never. I think in my time it was nearly inaccessible. Not even a footpath then.

WANGEL. And no park, either. This has all come about in the last few years.

BOLETTE. The view is even more marvelous over there from Lodskoll.

WANGEL. Perhaps we should go there, Ellida?

ELLIDA (*sitting down on a stone to the right*). Thanks, but not for me. You others can go. I don't mind sitting here for a while.

WANGEL. Well, then I'll stay with you. The girls can show Arnholm around.

BOLETTE. Would you like to go with us, Mr. Arnholm?

ARNHOLM. Yes, very much. Is there a path over there too?

BOLETTE. Oh, yes. A fine, wide path.

HILDA. The path's so wide, two people can easily go arm in arm.

ARNHOLM (*lightly*). Can I believe that, my little Hilda? (*To* BOLETTE.) Shall the two of us see if she's right?

BOLETTE (*suppressing a smile*). All right. Let's. (*They go out, left, arm in arm.*)

HILDA (*to* LYNGSTRAND). Shall we go too—?

LYNGSTRAND. Arm in arm—?

HILDA. Well, why not? Suits me.

LYNGSTRAND (*takes her arm and laughs delightedly*). This really is droll!

HILDA. Droll—?

LYNGSTRAND. I mean, it looks exactly as if we were engaged.

HILDA. You've never gone strolling before with a girl on your arm, Mr. Lyngstrand? (*They go out to the left.*)

WANGEL (*standing by the cairn*). So, Ellida dear, now we have time to ourselves—

ELLIDA. Yes, come and sit here by me.

WANGEL (*sitting*). How free and calm it is. Now we can talk a little.

ELLIDA. What about?

WANGEL. About you. And about our life together. I see all too well that it can't go on like this.

ELLIDA. What would you have instead?

WANGEL. Full confidence between us. A closeness of man and wife—like the old days.

ELLIDA. Oh, I wish it could be! But it's impossible.

WANGEL. I think I understand. From certain remarks you've dropped now and then, I think I know.

ELLIDA (*passionately*). But you don't! Don't say you understand—!

WANGEL. And yet, I do. Ellida, you're such an honest person. So loyal.

ELLIDA. Yes—loyal.

WANGEL. Any relationship in which you could feel secure and happy would have to be complete and unreserved.

ELLIDA (*looking tensely at him*). And so?

WANGEL. You were never made to be a man's second wife.

ELLIDA. Why do you say that—now?

WANGEL. I've often had my misgivings. Today made it clear. The children celebrating the birthday anniversary—you saw me as a kind of accomplice. And—well, a man's memories can't be erased. Not mine, anyway. I'm not like that.

ELLIDA. I know that. Oh, I know it so well.

WANGEL. But you're mistaken, all the same. For you it's almost as if the children's mother were still alive. As if she were there, invisible, among us. You think my feelings are divided equally between you and her. It's that thought that unsettles you. You find something almost immoral in our relationship. And that's why you no longer can—or no longer want to live with me as a wife.

ELLIDA (*rising*). Is this how you see it, Wangel? Like this?

WANGEL. Yes, today I finally saw the whole thing, down to the bottom.

ELLIDA. Down to the bottom, you say. Oh, don't be too sure.

WANGEL (*rising*). I know quite well there's still more to it.

ELLIDA (*anxiously*). More?

WANGEL. Yes. The fact is, you can't bear these surroundings. The mountains oppress and weigh down your spirit. There's not enough light for you here. Not enough space. Not enough strength and sweep to the wind.

ELLIDA. You're right. Night and day, winter and summer, I feel it—this overpowering homesickness for the sea.

WANGEL. Ellida dear, I know that. (*Putting his hand on her head.*) It's why the poor sick child will be going back home again.

ELLIDA. What do you mean?

WANGEL. Just what I said. We're moving away.

ELLIDA. Away!

WANGEL. Yes. Away somewhere by the open sea. Someplace where you can find a true home after your own heart.

ELLIDA. Oh, don't even think of it! It's impossible. You'd never be happy anywhere on earth but here.

WANGEL. Let that take care of itself. Besides—do you think I could live here happily—without you?

ELLIDA. But I'm here. And I'll stay here. I'm yours.

WANGEL. Are you mine, Ellida?

ELLIDA. Oh, don't talk about this other. Here's where you have everything you live for. Your whole lifework is right here.

WANGEL. I said, let that take care of itself. We're moving. Going somewhere out there. It's all settled now, Ellida.

ELLIDA. But what do you think we'll gain by that?

WANGEL. You'll regain your health and your peace of mind.

ELLIDA. By some remote chance. But what of you? Think of yourself. What would you gain?

WANGEL. You, back again.

ELLIDA. But you can't! No, no, you can't do that, Wangel! That's just what's so terrible—and so desolating to think about.

WANGEL. It's worth the risk. If you're going around thinking like this, then there's really no other solution for you than—a move. And the sooner, the better. It's all settled, you hear.

ELLIDA. No! In heaven's name then, I'd better tell you everything straight out—just as it is.

WANGEL. Yes, if you only would!

ELLIDA. I don't want you unhappy for my sake. Especially when it won't get us anywhere.

WANGEL. You gave me your word now that you'll tell me everything—just as it is.

ELLIDA. I will, as best I can. And as much as I understand it. Come here and sit by me.

(*They sit on the stones.*)

WANGEL. Well, Ellida? So—?

ELLIDA. That day when you came out to the lighthouse and asked if I'd be yours—you spoke to me so openly and so honestly about your first marriage. It had been so very happy, you said.

WANGEL. And it was.

ELLIDA. Yes, dear, I believe you. That's not why I bring it up now. I only want to remind you that, on my side also, I was straightforward with you. I told you quite frankly that once in my life I had loved someone else. That it had developed into—into a kind of engagement between us.

WANGEL. A kind of—?

ELLIDA. Yes, something of the sort. Well, it lasted no time at all, hardly. He went away. And so I took it as over and done with. I told you all that.

WANGEL. But, Ellida dear, why drag this up? Really, it has nothing to do with me. And I've never so much as asked you once who he was.

ELLIDA. No, you haven't. You're always so considerate of me.

WANGEL (*smiling*). Oh, in any case—I think I could more or less guess the name.

ELLIDA. The name!

WANGEL. Up there around Skjoldvik there weren't so many to choose from. As a matter of fact, there was actually only one choice—

ELLIDA. You're thinking it was—Arnholm.

WANGEL. Well, wasn't it?

ELLIDA. No.

WANGEL. It wasn't? Well, then I'm really at a loss.

ELLIDA. Do you remember once in late autumn a large American ship that put in to Skjoldvik for repairs?

WANGEL. Yes, I remember very well. They found the captain in his cabin one morning, murdered. I went out myself and did the postmortem.

ELLIDA. That's right, you did.

WANGEL. It was the mate, supposedly, who killed him.

ELLIDA. Who can tell! It was never proved.

WANGEL. There's not much doubt about it, all the same. Why else should he go off and drown himself?

ELLIDA. He didn't drown himself. He shipped out, to the north.

WANGEL (*surprised*). How do you know?

ELLIDA (*with an effort*). You see—it was the mate that I was—engaged to.

WANGEL (*springing up*). What are you saying! Impossible!

ELLIDA. Yes—but true. He was the one.

WANGEL. But, Ellida, how on earth—! How could you do such a thing! Get engaged to someone like him! A total stranger—! What was his name?

ELLIDA. At that time he called himself Freeman. Later, in his letters, he signed himself Alfred Johnston.

WANGEL. And where was he from?

ELLIDA. From Finmark, he said. But actually he was

born in Finland and came to Norway as a child—with his father, I think.

WANGEL. A Quain, then.

ELLIDA. Yes, I guess that's what they're called.

WANGEL. What else do you know about him?

ELLIDA. Only that he went to sea quite young. And that he'd made some long voyages.

WANGEL. Nothing else?

ELLIDA. No. We never talked of his past.

WANGEL. What did you talk of?

ELLIDA. Mainly about the sea.

WANGEL. Ah—! About the sea.

ELLIDA. About the storms and the calms. The dark nights at sea. And the sea in the sparkling sunlight, that too. But mostly we talked of whales and dolphins, and of the seals that would lie out on the skerries in the warm noon sun. And then we spoke of the gulls and the eagles and every kind of seabird you can imagine. You know— it's strange, but when we talked in such a way, then it seemed to me that all these creatures belonged to him.

WANGEL. And you yourself—?

ELLIDA. Yes, I almost felt that I belonged among them, too.

WANGEL. I see. So that's how you got engaged.

ELLIDA. Yes. He said I must.

WANGEL. Must? Had you no will of your own?

ELLIDA. Not when he was near. Oh—afterward I thought it was utterly incomprehensible.

WANGEL. Were you often together with him?

ELLIDA. No, not very often. One day he came out for a look around the lighthouse. That's how we met. And later we saw each other occasionally. But then came this thing with the captain, and he had to leave.

WANGEL. Yes, tell me a bit more about that.

ELLIDA. It was early one morning, just getting light— when I had a message from him. In it he said that I should meet him out at Bratthammer—you know, that headland between the lighthouse and Skjoldvik.

WANGEL. Of course—I remember it well.

ELLIDA. I was to go there right away, he wrote, because he had to speak to me.

WANGEL. And you went?

ELLIDA. Yes, I had to. Well, he told me then that he'd stabbed the captain that night.

WANGEL. He said it himself! Confessed!

ELLIDA. Yes. But he'd only done what was necessary and right, he said.

WANGEL. Necessary and right? Then why did he kill him?

ELLIDA. He wouldn't discuss it. Only that it was nothing for me to hear.

WANGEL. And you believed him, on his word alone?

ELLIDA. I never thought to doubt him. Well, anyway he had to get away. But just before he was to say good-bye—you'll never guess what he did.

WANGEL. Well, tell me.

ELLIDA. He took a key-ring out of his pocket, and then pulled a ring that he'd always worn from his finger. I also had a little ring, and he took that too. He slipped both of them together onto the key-ring—and then he said that we two would marry ourselves to the sea.

WANGEL. Marry—?

ELLIDA. Yes, that's what he said. And then he threw the rings together, with all his strength, as far as he could out in the ocean.

WANGEL. And you, Ellida? You accepted all this?

ELLIDA. Yes, can you imagine—I felt then as if it were fated to be. But then, thank God—he went away!

WANGEL. And when he'd gone—?

ELLIDA. Oh, I came to my senses soon enough—and saw how mad and meaningless it had all been.

WANGEL. But you mentioned some letters before. So you *have* heard from him since.

ELLIDA. Yes, I've heard from him. First I got a few short lines from Archangel. He wrote only that he was going on to America. And he enclosed an address where I could write him.

WANGEL. And did you?

ELLIDA. At once. I wrote, of course, that everything had to be ended between us. That he was no longer to think of me, just as I would never again think of him.

WANGEL. And he wrote back, even so?

ELLIDA. Yes, he wrote back.

WANGEL. And what did he say to your terms?

ELLIDA. Not a word. It was as if I'd never broken with him at all. His answer was cool and calm, that I should wait for him. When he could provide for me, he would let me know, and then I should come to him at once.

WANGEL. So he wouldn't let you go?

ELLIDA. No. I wrote him again. Almost word for word the same as before—but in even stronger terms.

WANGEL. Did he give up then?

ELLIDA. Oh, no, nothing like that. He wrote as calmly as ever. Not a word that I'd broken it off. Then I realized it was useless, so I never wrote him again.

WANGEL. Or heard from him, either?

ELLIDA. Yes, I had three more letters from him. He wrote me once from California, and another time from China. The last letter I had was from Australia. He said then that he was going to the gold mines. I haven't heard from him since.

WANGEL. That man has had an unearthly power over you, Ellida.

ELLIDA. Yes. Yes, he's horrible!

WANGEL. But you mustn't think of him anymore. Never! My dearest Ellida, promise me that! Now we have to try a better cure for you. Fresher air than here in the fjords. The sting of the salt sea breeze. What do you say?

ELLIDA. Oh, don't talk about it! Or think of it even! There's no help for me there. I can feel it in my bones—I won't get rid of this out there either.

WANGEL. Of what? Just what do you mean?

ELLIDA. I mean the horror. The fantastic hold on my mind—

WANGEL. But you *have* gotten rid of it. Long ago. When you broke with him. It's over and done with now.

ELLIDA (*springing to her feet*). No, that's just the thing, it isn't.

WANGEL. Not over!

ELLIDA. No, Wangel—it's not over. And I'm afraid it never will be.

WANGEL (*in a strangled voice*). Are you saying, then, that in your heart of hearts, you'll never be able to forget this man?

ELLIDA. I *had* forgotten him. But suddenly one day it was as if he returned.

WANGEL. When was that?

ELLIDA. About three years ago now—or a little more. It was while I was carrying the child.

WANGEL. Ah—then! Yes, now I begin to understand.

ELLIDA. No, dear, you're wrong! This thing that's happened to me—oh, I don't think it can ever be understood.

WANGEL (*looking sorrowfully at her*). To think—that here you've gone for three whole years loving another man. Another man. Not me—but somebody else!

ELLIDA. Oh, you're so absolutely wrong. I love no one else but you.

WANGEL (*quietly*). Why, then, in all this time, have you not wanted to live with me as my wife?

ELLIDA. Because of the terror I feel of him, of the stranger.

WANGEL. Terror—?

ELLIDA. Yes, terror. A terror so huge that only the sea could hold it. All right, I'll tell you, Wangel—

(*The young people of the town come back from the left, nod as they pass and go out to the right. Along with them come* ARNHOLM, BOLETTE, HILDA, *and* LYNGSTRAND.)

BOLETTE (*as they go by*). Well, are you still enjoying the view?

ELLIDA. Yes, it's so cool and nice up here.

ARNHOLM. We've decided to go dancing.

WANGEL. Very good. We'll be down right away.

HILDA. See you soon then.

ELLIDA. Mr. Lyngstrand—oh, just a moment.

(LYNGSTRAND *stops.* ARNHOLM, BOLETTE, *and* HILDA *go out to the right.*)

ELLIDA (*to* LYNGSTRAND). Are you going dancing, too?

LYNGSTRAND. No, Mrs. Wangel, I don't think I should.

ELLIDA. Yes, you'd better be careful. That chest trouble—you're not fully over it, you know.

LYNGSTRAND. Not entirely, no.

ELLIDA (*somewhat hesitantly*). How long can it be now since you made that trip—?

LYNGSTRAND. When I got this condition?

ELLIDA. Yes, the voyage you told about this morning.

LYNGSTRAND. Oh, I guess that was around—let me see—yes, it's a good three years ago now.

ELLIDA. Three years.

LYNGSTRAND. Or a shade more. We left America in February, and we went down in March. It was the equinoctial gales that finished us off.

ELLIDA (*looking at* WANGEL). So it was at that time—

WANGEL. But, Ellida dear—?

ELLIDA. Well, don't let us keep you, Mr. Lyngstrand. Go on now. But don't dance.

LYNGSTRAND. No, I'll just look on. (*He goes out, right.*)

WANGEL. Ellida, why did you question him about the voyage?

ELLIDA. Johnston was with him on board, I'm positive of that.

WANGEL. Why do you think so?

ELLIDA (*without answering*). It was then that he learned I'd married someone else while he was away. And then—at that same moment, this thing came over me.

WANGEL. This terror?

ELLIDA. Yes. Sometimes, suddenly, I can see him standing large as life in front of me. Or actually—a little to one side. He never looks at me. He's simply there.

WANGEL. How does he seem to look?

ELLIDA. Exactly as I saw him last.

WANGEL. Ten years ago?

ELLIDA. Yes, out at Bratthammer. And clearest of all I can see the stickpin he wore, with a great blue-white pearl in it. That pearl is like the eye of a dead fish. And it seems to be staring at me.

WANGEL. In God's name—! Ellida, you're ill—much more than I thought. Or than you can possibly know.

ELLIDA. Yes! Yes, help me! I feel it's tightening— tightening around me. More and more.

WANGEL. And you've been going about in this state for three whole years, bearing your suffering in secret, without confiding in me.

ELLIDA. But I couldn't tell you! Not till now, not till I had to—for your sake. If I'd confessed all this to you, I'd also have had to tell you—what's unspeakable.

WANGEL. Unspeakable—?

ELLIDA (*averting her face*). No, no, no! Don't talk! Just one other thing, then I'm through. Wangel—how can we ever fathom this—this—mystery about the child's eyes—?

WANGEL. My dearest Ellida, I promise you, that was nothing but your own imagination. The child had exactly the same eyes as all other normal children.

ELLIDA. He did not! And you can't see it! His eyes changed color with the sea. When the fjord lay still in the sunlight, his eyes were like that. And in the storms, too— oh, I saw it well enough, even if you didn't.

WANGEL (*indulgently*). Well—so be it. But even so—what then?

ELLIDA (*quietly, coming closer*). I've seen eyes like that before.

WANGEL. When? And where?

ELLIDA. Out on Bratthammer—ten years ago.

WANGEL (*stepping back*). What do you—?

ELLIDA (*whispers, with a shudder*). The child had the stranger's eyes.

WANGEL (*with an involuntary cry*). Ellida—!

ELLIDA (*clasping her hands in misery about her head*). Now you can understand why I never again *want*—why I never again *dare* to live with you as your wife! (*She turns quickly and runs off down the hill to the right.*)

WANGEL (*hurrying after her and calling*). Ellida—Ellida! My poor, miserable Ellida!

⤳ ACT THREE ⤳

A remote corner of DR. WANGEL's *garden. It is a damp, marshy place, overshadowed by large old trees. To the right the edge of a stagnant pond is visible. A low picket fence separates the garden from the footpath and the fjord in the background. Beyond the fjord on the horizon, high peaks and mountain ranges. It is late afternoon, near evening.* BOLETTE *sits, sewing, on a stone bench to the left. On the bench lie a couple of books and a sewing basket.* HILDA *and* LYNGSTRAND, *both with fishing rods, walk along the edge of the pond.*

HILDA (*making a sign to* LYNGSTRAND). Don't move! There, I can see a big one.

LYNGSTRAND (*looking*). Where?

HILDA (*pointing*). Can't you see—down there. And there! Holy God, look at that one! (*Peering off through the trees.*) Ahh! Here he comes to scare them away.

BOLETTE (*glancing up*). Who's coming?

HILDA. Your tutor, ma'am.

BOLETTE. My—?

HILDA. Well, I'll bet you he's never been *mine*.

(ARNHOLM *comes through the trees from the right.*)

ARNHOLM. Are there fish in the pond now?

HILDA. Yes, some enormously old carp.

ARNHOLM. Really? So the old carp are still alive?

HILDA. Yes, they're tough, all right. But we're going to pull in a few of them.

ARNHOLM. You'd probably do better out by the fjord.

LYNGSTRAND. No, the pond is—I think it's more mysterious.

HILDA. Yes, it's more thrilling here. Have you been in the water?

ARNHOLM. Moments ago. I'm just now coming from the bathhouse.

HILDA. You stick close to the shore, I guess.

ARNHOLM. Yes, I'm not very much of a swimmer.

HILDA. Can you swim on your back?

ARNHOLM. No.

HILDA. I can. (*To* LYNGSTRAND.) Let's try over there on the other side.

(*They go around the pond off to the right.*)

ARNHOLM (*going closer to* BOLETTE). Sitting all by yourself, Bolette?

BOLETTE. Oh, yes, I do that quite often.

ARNHOLM. Isn't your mother here in the garden?

BOLETTE. No, she's gone for a walk with Father.

ARNHOLM. How is she this afternoon?

BOLETTE. I'm not quite sure. I forgot to ask.

ARNHOLM. What are the books you have there?

BOLETTE. Oh, one of them's something on plant life. And the other's a geography book.

ARNHOLM. Do you like reading that sort of thing?

BOLETTE. Yes, when I can find time for it. But I have to put the housework first.

ARNHOLM. But doesn't your mother—your stepmother—help you with that?

BOLETTE. No, that's up to me. I had to look after it the two years that Father was alone. And it's gone on that way since.

ARNHOLM. But you're as fond of reading as ever.

BOLETTE. Yes, I read every book I can get hold of and that I think I can learn from. One wants so much to know something about the world. Because here we live so completely cut off from everything that's going on. Well, almost completely.

ARNHOLM. Now, Bolette, you mustn't say that.

BOLETTE. It's true. I don't think we live very differently from the carp down there in the pond. They have the fjord so close to them, and there the shoals of great, wild fish go streaking in and out. But these poor, tame pet fish know nothing of that, and they'll never be part of that life.

ARNHOLM. I hardly think they'd do very well out there.

BOLETTE. As well as here, I expect.

ARNHOLM. Besides, you really can't say you're so very removed from life here. Not in the summer, at least. Nowadays it seems like this place is a rendezvous for the whole live world. Almost *the* social capital for tourists.

BOLETTE (*smiling*). Oh, yes, since you're here only as one of the tourists, it's easy enough for you to make fun of us.

ARNHOLM. I make fun—? What gives you that idea?

BOLETTE. Oh, because all that rendezvous and tourist capital talk is something you've heard in town. They always say things like that.

ARNHOLM. Well, as a matter of fact—so I've noticed.

BOLETTE. But actually there's not a word of truth in it. Not for us year-round people. What good is it to us if the great, strange world goes by on its way up to see the midnight sun? We never go along. We never see the midnight sun. Oh, no, we live our snug little lives out here, in our fish pond.

ARNHOLM (*sitting down beside her*). Tell me, Bolette— I'm wondering, as you go about your life here, isn't there something—I mean some definite thing—that you long for?

BOLETTE. Yes—perhaps.

ARNHOLM. And what's that? Tell me.

BOLETTE. Mostly to get away.

ARNHOLM. That most of all?

BOLETTE. Yes. And afterward, a chance to learn. To get to know something about—just everything.

ARNHOLM. In those days when I was tutoring you, your father often said you'd be going on to the university.

BOLETTE. Oh, poor Father—he says so many things. But when it comes right down to it—there's no real willpower in him.

ARNHOLM. Yes. I'm afraid you're right; there isn't. But have you ever spoken to him about it? I mean, quite seriously and unequivocally?

BOLETTE. No, I haven't exactly.

ARNHOLM. But you know, you absolutely should. Before it's too late, Bolette. Why haven't you?

BOLETTE. Oh, I suppose it's because there's no real willpower in me, either. That's one trait I've picked up from him.

ARNHOLM. Hm—don't you think you're being unfair to yourself?

BOLETTE. I wish I were, but—no. Besides, Father has so little time to think of me and my future. And not much interest, either. That kind of thing he'd rather avoid, if he possibly can. Because he's so involved with Ellida—

ARNHOLM. Involved—? How—?

BOLETTE. I mean, he and my stepmother— (*Breaking off*.) Father and Mother have their own world, you can see that.

ARNHOLM. Well, so much the better, then, if you get away from here.

BOLETTE. Yes, but I don't think I have any right to go—to leave Father.

ARNHOLM. But, Bolette dear, you're going to have to someday, anyway. So I'd say, the sooner the better.

BOLETTE. Oh, I guess it's the only thing. I ought to think of myself, too. Try to get some kind of work. When

Father goes, I'll have no one to turn to. But poor Father—
I dread leaving him.

ARNHOLM. Dread—?

BOLETTE. Yes, for his sake.

ARNHOLM. But, good Lord, your stepmother! She'll be
with him.

BOLETTE. That's true. But she simply hasn't any grasp
of all those things that Mother took on so well. There's so
much this one just doesn't see. Or maybe doesn't want to
see —or bother with. I don't know which it is.

ARNHOLM. Hm. I think I know what you mean.

BOLETTE. Poor Father—he's weak in certain respects.
Perhaps you've noticed it yourself. Then too, he hasn't
enough work to fill up his time. And she's so incapable of
giving him any support. But that's partly his own fault.

ARNHOLM. How so?

BOLETTE. Oh, Father only wants to see happy faces
around him. There has to be sunshine and joy in the
house, he says. So I'm afraid that many times he's given
her medicine that in the long run does her no good.

ARNHOLM. Do you really think so?

BOLETTE. I can't think anything else. She acts so strange
at times. (*Heatedly.*) But it does seem so unfair that I
should have to stay on here at home! It's really no earthly
use to Father. And I have obligations to myself, too.

ARNHOLM. You know, Bolette—we have to talk all this
over more fully.

BOLETTE. Oh, that's not going to help any. I'm just
fated to stay in my fish pond, that's all.

ARNHOLM. Nonsense! It depends completely on you.

BOLETTE (*suddenly buoyant*). You really think so?

ARNHOLM. Yes, I know so. The whole thing is there,
right in your own hands.

BOLETTE. Oh, if that could be true—! Would you
maybe put in a good word for me with Father?

ARNHOLM. Of course. But first of all I want to speak
frankly and freely with you, Bolette. (*Glancing off to the*

left.) Shh! Don't give it away. We'll come back to this later.

(ELLIDA *appears from the left, hatless, with a large scarf thrown over her head and shoulders*.)

ELLIDA (*nervously animated*). It's lovely here! Simply beautiful!

ARNHOLM (*getting up*). Have you been out walking?

ELLIDA. Yes, a long, long glorious walk through the hills with Wangel. And now we're going out for a sail.

BOLETTE. Won't you sit down?

ELLIDA. No, thanks. I won't sit.

BOLETTE (*moving along the bench*). There's plenty of room,

ELLIDA. No, no, no—I won't sit. Won't sit.

ARNHOLM. That walk certainly did you good. You look so elated.

ELLIDA. Oh, I feel so marvelously well! So indescribably happy! And safe! So safe— (*Looking off to the left*.) What's that big steamer coming in there?

BOLETTE (*rises and looks out*). It must be the large English one.

ARNHOLM. It's putting in by the buoy. Does it usually stop here?

BOLETTE. Just half an hour. It goes farther on up the fjord.

ELLIDA. And then tomorrow—out again. Out on the great open sea. Straight over the sea. Imagine—just to be on board! If one could! If only one could!

ARNHOLM. Have you never taken a long sea voyage, Mrs. Wangel?

ELLIDA. Never at all. Only these short trips here in the fjord.

BOLETTE (*with a sigh*). Ah, yes, we have to make do with dry land.

ARNHOLM. Well, after all, it's our natural home.

ELLIDA. I don't believe that in the slightest.

ARNHOLM. But—we belong to the land, no?

ELLIDA. No. I don't believe it. I believe that, if only mankind had adapted itself from the start to a life on the sea—or perhaps *in* the sea—then we would have become something much different and more advanced than we are now. Both better—and happier.

ARNHOLM. You really believe that?

ELLIDA. I don't see why not. I've often discussed it with Wangel.

ARNHOLM. Yes, and he—?

ELLIDA. He thinks it's entirely possible.

ARNHOLM (*playfully*). Well—maybe. But what's done is done. So once and for all we took the wrong turn and became land animals, instead of sea creatures. Considering the circumstances, it's a little late now to amend the error.

ELLIDA. Yes, there's the unhappy truth. And I think people have some sense of it, too. They bear it about inside them like a secret sorrow. And I can tell you—there, in that feeling, is the deepest source of all the melancholy in man. Yes—I'm sure of it.

ARNHOLM. But, my dear Mrs. Wangel—I never got the impression humanity was so very melancholy. Quite the contrary, I think the majority take life for the best, as it comes—and with a great, quiet, instinctive joy.

ELLIDA. Oh no, that isn't true. The joy—it's much like our joy in these long, light summer days and nights. It has the hint in it of dark times to come. And that hint is what throws a shadow over our human joy—like the drifting clouds with their shadows over the fjord. Everything lies there so bright and blue—and then all of a sudden—

ARNHOLM. You shouldn't give way to these sad thoughts now. A moment ago you were so gay, so elated—

ELLIDA. Yes. Yes, so I was. Oh, this—I'm so stupid. (*Looking around uneasily.*) If Wangel would only come. He promised me he would, definitely. But he still hasn't come. He must have forgotten. Oh, my dear Arnholm, please, try to find him for me, won't you?

ARNHOLM. Yes, gladly.

ELLIDA. Tell him he has to come right away. Because now I can't see him—

ARNHOLM. Can't see him—?

ELLIDA. Oh, you wouldn't understand. When he's not near me, then often I can't remember how he looks. And then it's as if I'd lost him for good. It's a horrible feeling. Please, go! (*She walks aimlessly about by the pond.*)

BOLETTE (*to* ARNHOLM). I'll go with you. You won't know where—

ARNHOLM. Don't bother. I'll manage—

BOLETTE (*in an undertone*). No, no, I'm worried. I'm afraid he's gone on the ship.

ARNHOLM. Afraid?

BOLETTE. Yes, he likes to see if there are people he knows. And then there's the bar on board—

ARNHOLM. Oh, yes. Well, come on then.

(*He and* BOLETTE *go off, left.* ELLIDA *stands a moment, staring down into the pond. Intermittently she speaks in broken whispers to herself. Outside, on the path behind the fence, a* STRANGER, *dressed for traveling, comes from the left. He has bushy, reddish hair and a beard. He has a Scotch tam on his head and a musette bag on a strap over his shoulder. The* STRANGER *walks slowly along the fence, scanning the garden. When his eyes fall on* ELLIDA, *he stops and stares at her with an intense, probing gaze.*)

STRANGER (*in a low voice*). Good evening, Ellida!

ELLIDA (*turning with a cry*). Oh, my love—you've come at last!

STRANGER. Yes, at last.

ELLIDA (*looks with astonishment and terror at him*). Who are you? What do you want here?

STRANGER. You know well enough.

ELLIDA (*starting*). What's that! Why are you speaking to me. Who are you looking for?

STRANGER. I've been looking for you.

ELLIDA (*with a shudder*). Ah—! (*Stares at him, falters back and breaks out in a half-stifled cry.*) The eyes! The eyes!

STRANGER. Well—you're finally beginning to know me again? I knew you at once, Ellida.

ELLIDA. The eyes! Don't look at me like that! I'll cry for help!

STRANGER. Shh, shh! Don't be afraid. I won't hurt you.

ELLIDA (*her hands over her eyes*). I said, don't look at me that way!

STRANGER (*leaning his arms on the fence*). I came on the English ship.

ELLIDA (*glancing fearfully at him*). What do you want of me?

STRANGER. I promised you I'd return as soon as I could—

ELLIDA. Go! Go away! Don't ever come back—ever! I wrote you that everything was over between us! Completely! You know that!

STRANGER (*unperturbed, not answering her*). I wanted to come before this. But I couldn't. Now, at last, I'm able. And so you have me, Ellida.

ELLIDA. What is it you want of me? What are you thinking of? What have you come here for?

STRANGER. You must know that I've come to take you.

ELLIDA (*wincing in fright*). To take me! Is that your idea!

STRANGER. Why, of course.

ELLIDA. But—you must know that I'm married.

STRANGER. Yes, I know.

ELLIDA. And yet—even so, you've come here to—to take me!

STRANGER. That's what I'm doing.

ELLIDA (*pressing her fists to her head*). Oh, it's monstrous! It's horrible—horrible!

STRANGER. Do you think you won't come?

ELLIDA (*in confusion*). Don't look at me that way!

STRANGER. I'm asking if you don't want to come.

ELLIDA. No, no, no! I don't! Never! I don't want to, I

tell you! I neither can nor will! (*More quietly.*) Nor dare to.

STRANGER (*climbing over the fence and entering the garden*). All right, Ellida—then let me just say one thing to you before I move on.

ELLIDA (*tries to run, but cannot, and stands as if paralyzed by fright, supporting herself against a tree by the pond*). Don't touch me! Stay away from me! Not—nearer! Don't touch me, you hear!

STRANGER (*cautiously coming a few steps closer*). You needn't be afraid of me, Ellida.

ELLIDA (*covering her eyes with her hands*). Don't look at me like that!

STRANGER. Don't be afraid. Don't be afraid.

(DR. WANGEL *comes through the garden from the left.*)

WANGEL (*still half hidden by the trees*). Well, you've been waiting a mighty long while for me.

ELLIDA (*rushes to him and clings tightly to his arm, crying out*). Oh, Wangel—save me. Save me—if you can!

WANGEL. Ellida—what in God's name—!

ELLIDA. Save me, Wangel! Can't you see him? He's standing right over there!

WANGEL. That man? (*Approaching him.*) If I may—who are you? And why are you here in the garden?

STRANGER (*indicating* ELLIDA *with a nod*). I want to talk to her.

WANGEL. I see. So it was you— (*To* ELLIDA.) I heard some stranger had been up at the house, asking for you.

STRANGER. Yes, it was me.

WANGEL. And what do you want with my wife? (*Turning.*) Do you know him, Ellida?

ELLIDA (*quietly, wringing her hands*). Do I know him? Yes, yes!

WANGEL (*brusquely*). Well?

ELLIDA. It's him, Wangel! He's the man! The one I told you about—!

WANGEL. What? What did you say? (*Turning.*) Are you the Johnston who once—

STRANGER. You can call me Johnston—it's all right with me. But that's not my name.

WANGEL. It's not?

STRANGER. Not any longer, no.

WANGEL. And what is it you want with my wife? Because you know, of course, that the lighthouse keeper's daughter has been married for some time now. And I guess you must also know who she's married to.

STRANGER. I've known for more than three years.

ELLIDA (*in suspense*). How did you find out?

STRANGER. I was on my way home to you, when I came on an old newspaper—one from these parts—and it told there about the wedding.

ELLIDA (*staring into space*). The wedding—so that was it—

STRANGER. I found it so strange. Because those rings in the sea—they were a wedding, too, Ellida.

ELLIDA (*hiding her face in her hands*). Ah—!

WANGEL. How dare you!

STRANGER. Had you forgotten?

ELLIDA (*feeling his eyes on her*). Stop looking at me like that!

WANGEL (*moving up to him*). Better deal with me, not her. All right, to the point—since you know the situation, what business do you have around here? Why have you sought out my wife?

STRANGER. I promised Ellida I'd come to her as soon as I could.

WANGEL. Ellida—again!

STRANGER. And Ellida promised faithfully to wait till I came.

WANGEL. I hear you calling my wife by her first name. That kind of familiarity isn't appreciated around here.

STRANGER. I understand. But, after all, she belongs to me first—

WANGEL. To you! Still—!

ELLIDA (*retreating behind* WANGEL). Oh—! He'll never let go!

WANGEL. To you! You say she belongs to you!

STRANGER. Did she tell you anything about the two rings? Mine and Ellida's?

WANGEL. She did. But what of it? She put an end to that long ago. You've had her letters. You should know.

STRANGER. Ellida and I both agreed that joining our rings would have all the binding force of an actual marriage.

ELLIDA. But I don't want it, you hear me! I never want to see you again! Keep your eyes off me! I don't want this!

WANGEL. You must be crazy if you think you can come here and base your rights on such adolescent games.

STRANGER. It's true, I have no rights—in your sense.

WANGEL. Then what do you intend to do? You certainly can't imagine you could take her away from me forcibly— against her will?

STRANGER. No. What good would that be? If Ellida goes off with me, she'll have to come of her own free will.

ELLIDA (*with a start, crying out*). My own free will—!

WANGEL. How can you think—!

ELLIDA (*to herself*). My own free will—!

WANGEL. You must be out of your head! Get on your way. We've nothing more to do with you.

STRANGER (*looking at his watch*). It's almost time for me to be on board again. (*Approaching a step.*) Well, Ellida—I've kept my promise. (*Closer still.*) I've kept the word I gave you.

ELLIDA (*shrinking aside*). Oh, don't—don't touch me!

STRANGER. And now you've got till tomorrow night to think it over.

WANGEL. There's nothing here to think over. Let's see you clear out!

STRANGER (*still to* ELLIDA). I'll be going up the fjord now with the ship. Tomorrow night I'll come by here again—and I'll look for you. You must wait for me here in the garden. Because I'd rather settle this matter with you alone, you understand?

ELLIDA (*in a low, tremulous voice*). Oh, you hear that, Wangel?

WANGEL. Don't worry. I think we can forestall that visit.

STRANGER. Good-bye until then, Ellida. Till tomorrow night.

ELLIDA (*imploringly*). No, no—not tomorrow night! Not ever again!

STRANGER. And if, by that time, you've made up your mind to follow me over the sea—

ELLIDA. Don't look at me that way!

STRANGER. Then be ready to leave right away.

WANGEL. Go up to the house, Ellida!

ELLIDA. I can't. Oh, help me! Save me, Wangel!

STRANGER. Because you have to remember one thing: if you don't go with me tomorrow, it's all over.

ELLIDA (*trembling as she looks at him*). All over? Forever?

STRANGER (*nods*). It can never be altered then, Ellida. I'll never be back in these parts again. You won't see me anymore. Or hear from me, either. Never. Then I'll be dead and gone from you forever.

ELLIDA (*her breathing labored*). Oh—!

STRANGER. So think over carefully what you'll do. Good-bye. (*Goes to the fence, climbs over, stops and says.*) Yes, Ellida—be ready to travel tomorrow night. I'm coming to take you away. (*He goes slowly and calmly off down the path to the right.*)

ELLIDA (*looking after him a moment*). He said, of my

own free will! Imagine—he said I should go with him of my own free will.

WANGEL. Don't get upset. He's gone now—and you won't see him anymore.

ELLIDA. How can you say that? He's coming back tomorrow night.

WANGEL. Let him come. He's not seeing you, at any rate.

ELLIDA (*shaking her head*). Ah, Wangel, don't think you can stop him.

WANGEL. Oh, yes, dear, I can—just leave it to me.

ELLIDA (*deep in thought, not hearing him*). After he's been here tomorrow night—and after he's sailed off to sea with the ship—

WANGEL. Yes?

ELLIDA. I wonder if he'll never—never come back?

WANGEL. Ellida dear, that you can be quite sure of. What would he be doing here afterward? Now that he's heard from your own lips that you've no more interest in him at all. That closes the case.

ELLIDA (*to herself*). Tomorrow, then. Or never.

WANGEL. And even if he did come back—

ELLIDA. Then what?

WANGEL. Then it's within our power to render him harmless.

ELLIDA. Don't you believe it.

WANGEL. I'm telling you, we have that power! If you can't have peace from him any other way, he's going to pay for the murder of the captain.

ELLIDA (*passionately*). No! No, not that! We know nothing about the captain's murder! Nothing at all!

WANGEL. We don't know? He confessed to you himself!

ELLIDA. No, nothing of that! If you say anything, I'll deny it. Don't cage him in! He belongs to the open sea. He belongs out there.

WANGEL (*gazes at her and says slowly*). Ah, Ellida—Ellida!

ELLIDA (*clinging to him passionately*). Oh, my dearest own—save me from that man!

WANGEL (*gently freeing himself*). Come! Come with me!

(LYNGSTRAND *and* HILDA, *both with fishing rods, appear from the right by the pond.*)

LYNGSTRAND (*goes quickly up to* ELLIDA). You know what, Mrs. Wangel—it's the most amazing thing!

WANGEL. What is?

LYNGSTRAND. Just think—we saw the American.

WANGEL. The American?

HILDA. Yes, I saw him, too.

LYNGSTRAND. He passed up behind the garden and then onto that big English steamer.

WANGEL. How do you know this man?

LYNGSTRAND. I once went to sea with him. I was positive he'd been drowned—and there he was, live as could be.

WANGEL. You know anything more about him?

LYNGSTRAND. No. But he must have come back to have revenge on his faithless wife.

WANGEL. What did you say?

HILDA. Lyngstrand's going to make him into a piece of sculpture.

WANGEL. I don't understand one word—

ELLIDA. You can hear it all later.

(ARNHOLM *and* BOLETTE *come along the path from the left outside the fence.*)

BOLETTE (*to those in the garden*). Come and see! It's the English steamer sailing up the fjord.

(*A large steamer glides slowly by in the distance.*)

LYNGSTRAND (*to* HILDA, *near the fence*). Tonight he'll be standing over her.

HILDA (*nods*). Over the faithless wife—yes.

LYNGSTRAND. Imagine—as midnight strikes.

HILDA. I think it's just thrilling.

ELLIDA (*watching the ship*). Tomorrow, then—

WANGEL. And then, never again.

ELLIDA (*in a low, uncertain voice*). Oh, Wangel—save me from myself.

WANGEL (*looking anxiously at her*). Ellida—I feel something behind this.

ELLIDA. Yes. You can feel the undertow.

WANGEL. The undertow—?

ELLIDA. That man is like the sea.

(*She goes slowly and pensively out through the garden to the left.* WANGEL *walks uneasily beside her, observing her searchingly.*)

⤙ ACT FOUR ⤚

DR. WANGEL's *conservatory. Doors right and left. In the rear wall, between the two windows, a glass door, open, leading out to the veranda. Beyond, some of the garden can be seen. A sofa and table in the left foreground. To the right a piano, and farther back a large flower stand. In the center of the room, a round table with chairs grouped about it. On the table a blossoming rose tree, and various potted plants elsewhere around the room. It is morning.*

By the table to the left, BOLETTE *sits on the sofa, occupied with some embroidery.* LYNGSTRAND *is seated on a chair at the upper end of the table. Below in the garden* BALLESTED *sits painting.* HILDA *stands next to him, looking on.*

LYNGSTRAND (*sits for a time in silence, his arms resting on the table, studying the way* BOLETTE *works*). It must really be very hard to sew a border like that, Miss Wangel.

BOLETTE. Oh, no, it's not so difficult—if you just keep your counting straight—

LYNGSTRAND. Counting? You mean you're counting as well?

BOLETTE. Yes, the stitches. See here.

LYNGSTRAND. Why, of course! That's amazing! You know, it's almost a kind of art. Can you also sketch?

BOLETTE. Oh, yes—if I can copy something.

LYNGSTRAND. Otherwise, no?

283

BOLETTE. Otherwise no.

LYNGSTRAND. Then it's not a real art, after all.

BOLETTE. No, I guess it's mostly a kind of—handiwork.

LYNGSTRAND. But I do think that you could maybe learn an art.

BOLETTE. When I haven't any talent?

LYNGSTRAND. In spite of that—if you were to spend your time in the company of a real, authentic artist—

BOLETTE. You think I could learn from him?

LYNGSTRAND. I don't mean learn in the conventional sense. But I think it would dawn on you little by little— almost like a kind of miracle, Miss Wangel.

BOLETTE. That would be something.

LYNGSTRAND (*after a moment*). Have you ever thought imminently—I mean—have you ever thought deeply and seriously about marriage, Miss Wangel?

BOLETTE (*giving him a quick glance*). About—? No.

LYNGSTRAND. I have.

BOLETTE. Oh? Have you really?

LYNGSTRAND. Oh, yes. I think very often about things like that. Most of all, about marriage. And then, of course, I've read about it, too, in quite a few books. I think that marriage has to be accounted almost a kind of miracle. The way a woman little by little makes herself over until she becomes like her husband.

BOLETTE. Takes on his interests, you mean?

LYNGSTRAND. Yes, exactly!

BOLETTE. Well, but his powers too? His skills, and his talents?

LYNGSTRAND. Hm—yes, I wonder if all that couldn't as well—

BOLETTE. Then perhaps you also believe that whatever a man has studied, or thought out for himself—that this, too, can become a part of his wife?

LYNGSTRAND. That too, yes. Little by little, almost miraculously. But I'm quite sure it can only happen in a marriage that's faithful and loving and truly happy.

BOLETTE. Has it ever occurred to you that perhaps a man could also be absorbed that way, over into his wife? Become like her, I mean?

LYNGSTRAND. A man? No, I never thought of that.

BOLETTE. But why couldn't it work as well one way as the other?

LYNGSTRAND. No, because a man has his vocation to live for. And that's the thing that makes a man strong and stable, Miss Wangel. He has a calling in life, you see.

BOLETTE. All men? Every last one?

LYNGSTRAND. Oh, no. I was thinking particularly of artists.

BOLETTE. Do you think it's right for an artist to go and get married?

LYNGSTRAND. Yes, of course I think so. If he can find someone that he cares for deeply—

BOLETTE. All the same, I think he'd do best simply to live for his art alone.

LYNGSTRAND. Well, naturally he will. But he can do that just as well if he's also married.

BOLETTE. Yes, but what about her?

LYNGSTRAND. Her? Who?

BOLETTE. The one that he marries. What's she going to live for?

LYNGSTRAND. She'll live for his art, also. I think that a woman must feel a profound happiness in that.

BOLETTE. Hm—I wonder really—

LYNGSTRAND. Oh, yes, that you can believe. Not only from all the honor and esteem that she'll win through him—because I think that ought to be reckoned about the least of it. But that she can help him to create—that she can ease his work for him by being there and making him comfortable and taking care of him and seeing that his life is really enjoyable. I think that must be thoroughly satisfying for a woman.

BOLETTE. Why, you have no idea how self-centered you are!

LYNGSTRAND. I—self-centered! My Lord in heaven, if you only knew me a little better—! (*Leaning closer to her.*) Miss Wangel, once I'm gone—and I will be soon enough—

BOLETTE (*looking compassionately at him*). Please, don't start thinking sad thoughts.

LYNGSTRAND. There's nothing so sad about that.

BOLETTE. What do you mean then?

LYNGSTRAND. I'll be leaving now in about a month's time. First from here, and then, soon after, I'll be traveling south.

BOLETTE. Oh, I see. Of course.

LYNGSTRAND. Miss Wangel, will you think of me then, every so often?

BOLETTE. Yes, of course I will.

LYNGSTRAND (*happily*). Promise me that!

BOLETTE. Yes, I promise.

LYNGSTRAND. By all that's holy—Bolette?

BOLETTE. By all that's holy. (*In a changed tone.*) But what can it come to, really? It won't lead to anything at all.

LYNGSTRAND. How can you say that! For me it will be so beautiful to know that you're here at home, thinking of me.

BOLETTE. Yes, but what else?

LYNGSTRAND. Well, beyond that I really don't know exactly—

BOLETTE. Nor I either. It has so much working against it. Everything works against it, I think.

LYNGSTRAND. But miracles can happen, you know. A marvelous spell of good fortune—something like that. Because I really believe that luck is with me.

BOLETTE (*vivaciously*). Yes, that's right! You believe it, don't you!

LYNGSTRAND. I believe it unshakably, beyond all doubt. And then—in a few years—when I come home again as a famous sculptor, comfortably fixed, in the fullness of health—

BOLETTE. Yes. Yes, that's what we're hoping for you.

LYNGSTRAND. You can count on it. If only you'll think warm, faithful thoughts of me while I'm away in the south. And now I have your word for that.

BOLETTE. You have my word. (*Shaking her head.*) But it can never lead anywhere, all the same.

LYNGSTRAND. Oh, yes, at the least it's sure to do one thing—make my work as an artist go easier and faster.

BOLETTE. You really think so?

LYNGSTRAND. Yes, I can feel it intuitively. And then I should think it would be quite exhilarating for you, too—out here so remote from everything—to know secretly that you were helping me to create.

BOLETTE (*looks at him*). And you, for your part—?

LYNGSTRAND. I—?

BOLETTE (*glancing out toward the garden*). Shh! Talk about something else. Mr. Arnholm's coming.

(ARNHOLM *comes into view below in the garden from the left. He stops and speaks with* BALLESTED *and* HILDA.)

LYNGSTRAND. Are you fond of your old teacher, Bolette?

BOLETTE. Fond of him?

LYNGSTRAND. Yes, I mean, do you think a lot of him?

BOLETTE. Why, of course. He's been wonderful to have as an adviser and a friend. He never fails to be helpful whenever he can be.

LYNGSTRAND. But isn't it surprising that he's never married?

BOLETTE. You think it's so very surprising?

LYNGSTRAND. Yes. Because they tell me he's quite well off.

BOLETTE. I suppose he is. But then it hasn't been so easy for him to find someone who'll have him.

LYNGSTRAND. Why?

BOLETTE. Well, almost all the young girls he knows have been his students. He says that himself.

LYNGSTRAND. So—what's the difference?

BOLETTE. But, my Lord, you don't go marrying someone who's been your teacher!

LYNGSTRAND. Don't you think that a young girl can fall in love with her teacher?

BOLETTE. Not after she's really grown up.

LYNGSTRAND. What an amazing idea!

BOLETTE (*warning him*). Shh, shh, shh!

(BALLESTED *has, in the meantime, been gathering his things together; he carries them off to the right in the garden,* HILDA *helping him.* ARNHOLM *comes up onto the veranda and enters the room.*)

ARNHOLM. Good morning, my dear Bolette. Good morning, Mr.—Mr.—hm!

(*He looks irritated and nods coolly to* LYNGSTRAND, *who gets up and bows.*)

BOLETTE (*rising and going to* ARNHOLM). Good morning, Mr. Arnholm.

ARNHOLM. How's everything here today?

BOLETTE. Just fine, thank you.

ARNHOLM. I suppose your stepmother's down swimming again today?

BOLETTE. No, she's up in her room.

ARNHOLM. Not feeling well?

BOLETTE. I don't know. She's locked herself in.

ARNHOLM. Hm—has she?

LYNGSTRAND. Mrs. Wangel had a horrible shock from that American yesterday.

ARNHOLM. What do you know about that?

LYNGSTRAND. I told Mrs. Wangel that I'd seen him go walking large as life past the garden.

ARNHOLM. Oh, I see.

BOLETTE (*to* ARNHOLM). You and Father were certainly up late last night.

ARNHOLM. Yes, rather late. We got into a serious discussion.

BOLETTE. Did you get to talk a little about me and my plans?

ARNHOLM. No, Bolette dear. I hadn't a chance—he was completely caught up in something else.

BOLETTE (*sighs*). Ah, yes—he always is.

ARNHOLM (*gives her a meaningful look*). But later today the two of us will have to talk some more about all this. Where's your father now? Gone out, perhaps?

BOLETTE. Oh, no, he must be down at the office. Let me go fetch him.

ARNHOLM. Please don't. I'd just as soon go down there.

BOLETTE (*hearing sounds to the left*). Wait a bit, Mr. Arnholm. I think that's Father on the stairs. Yes. I guess he's been up to see her.

(DR. WANGEL *comes in through the door, left.*)

WANGEL (*shaking hands with* ARNHOLM). Well, my friend—you're here already? It was good of you to come so early. I want to talk some more with you.

BOLETTE (*to* LYNGSTRAND). Maybe we should go out in the garden a while with Hilda?

LYNGSTRAND. Oh, I'd like to, very much.

(*He and* BOLETTE *go down into the garden and out through the trees in the background.*)

ARNHOLM (*having followed them with his eyes, turns to* WANGEL). Do you know that young man fairly well?

WANGEL. No, not at all.

ARNHOLM. But then what do you think of him hanging around the girls so much?

WANGEL. Does he? I really hadn't noticed.

ARNHOLM. Seems to me, you ought to keep an eye on him.

WANGEL. Yes, you're entirely right. But, my Lord, what

can a poor man do? The girls are so used to looking after themselves. They can't be told anything, by me or Ellida.

ARNHOLM. Not by her, either?

WANGEL. No. Besides, I can hardly expect her to get mixed up in these matters. They're beyond her competence. (*Breaking off.*) But we're not here to talk about that. Tell me—have you thought anymore about this business—about everything I told you?

ARNHOLM. I've thought of nothing else since I left you last night.

WANGEL. And what do you think ought to be done?

ARNHOLM. I think that you, as a doctor, must know far better than I.

WANGEL. Oh, if you only knew how hard it is for a doctor to prescribe for someone he loves! And then this is no ordinary illness. No ordinary doctor can help here— and no ordinary medicines.

ARNHOLM. How is she today?

WANGEL. I was up to see her just now, and she seemed quite calm. But behind all her moods there's something mysterious that I just can't fathom. And then she's so erratic—so elusive—so thoroughly unpredictable.

ARNHOLM. That goes with the morbid state of her mind.

WANGEL. Only in part. If you come right down to it, she was born that way. Ellida's one of the sea people. There's the crux of it.

ARNHOLM. What do you really mean by that?

WANGEL. Haven't you ever noticed that the people who live out close by the sea are almost like a race to themselves? It's as though they lived the sea's own life. There's the surge of the waves—the ebb and the flow—in their thoughts and their feelings both. And they never can be transplanted. Oh, I should have remembered that. It was a plain sin against Ellida to take her away from there and bring her inland.

ARNHOLM. You've come to that conclusion?

WANGEL. Yes, more and more I have. But I should have seen it from the start. Oh, basically I knew it, all right.

But I didn't want to look at it. Because I loved her so much, you see. So first and foremost I thought of myself. I was just inexcusably selfish then!

ARNHOLM. Hm—any man would be a bit selfish under those circumstances. As a matter of fact, that's a flaw I don't think I've noticed in you, Doctor.

WANGEL (*pacing about restlessly*). Oh, yes! And I've gone on being selfish, too. I'm so very much older than she is. I should have been something of a father to her—and a guide. I should have done my best toward helping her mind develop and grow. But unhappily nothing came of it. I hadn't the willpower for it. I wanted her just as she was. But then she grew worse and worse. And here I was, not knowing what I should do. (*Quieter.*) That was why, in my perplexity, I wrote you and asked you here for a visit.

ARNHOLM (*staring astounded at him*). What! Is that why you wrote?

WANGEL. Yes. But don't give it away.

ARNHOLM. But of all things—what earthly good did you expect of me? I don't understand.

WANGEL. That's not surprising. You see, I was off on the wrong track. I thought that Ellida had once set her heart on you—and that secretly she still cared for you a little. I thought maybe it would do her good to see you again and talk of home and the old days.

ARNHOLM. It was your wife, then, that you meant when you wrote that there was someone here thinking of me and—and perhaps longing to see me.

WANGEL. Yes, who else?

ARNHOLM (*quickly*). No, no, that's all right. I just hadn't understood.

WANGEL. It's not at all surprising, as I said. I was completely on the wrong track.

ARNHOLM. And you say that you're selfish!

WANGEL. Oh, I have a lot to atone for. I felt I shouldn't neglect anything that could possibly ease her mind a little.

ARNHOLM. How can you explain the power this stranger has over her?

WANGEL. Well—there may be aspects of the problem that just don't admit explanation.

ARNHOLM. You mean something that *can't* be explained, inherently—and permanently.

WANGEL. Something that can't, anyway—by what we know now.

ARNHOLM. Then you believe in such things.

WANGEL. I neither believe nor disbelieve. I simply don't know. So I leave it open.

ARNHOLM. Yes, but tell me one thing: this peculiar, grim insistence of hers about the child's eyes—

WANGEL (*fiercely*). I don't believe one word of it! I won't believe anything like that! It's pure imagination on her part—and nothing else.

ARNHOLM. Did you notice the man's eyes when you saw him yesterday?

WANGEL. Of course I did.

ARNHOLM. And you found no such resemblance?

WANGEL (*evasively*). Well, my Lord—what can I say? There wasn't much light when I saw him. And then I've always heard so much about that resemblance from Ellida—I really don't know if I was able to see him objectively.

ARNHOLM. Well, that's quite possible. But the other thing then. That all this anxiety and unrest came over her at exactly the time the stranger seems to have been on his voyage home?

WANGEL. Yes, you know—that's also something she must have dreamed up overnight. It never came on her as suddenly—all at once—as she's claiming now. Ever since she heard from this young Lyngstrand that Johnston—or Freeman—or whatever he's called—that he was on his way here three years ago in March, she's honestly believed that all her mental turmoil dates from that very month.

ARNHOLM. You mean it doesn't?

WANGEL. Not by any means. There were ample warning signs long before that time. It *is* true that—as it happens—

just in March three years ago, she had a rather violent siege of it—

ARNHOLM. Well, then—!

WANGEL. Yes, but that could easily be a sign of what she was going through, of her condition then. She was expecting at the time.

ARNHOLM. So—signs against signs.

WANGEL (*knitting his hands*). And then not to be able to help her! Not to know what to say! Not to see the way out!

ARNHOLM. If only you could bring yourself to move away and live elsewhere. Someplace where she'd be able to feel more at home.

WANGEL. Oh, don't you think I've suggested that, too? I proposed that we move back to Skjoldvik. But she won't.

ARNHOLM. Not even there?

WANGEL. No. She doesn't see any use to that. And maybe she's right.

ARNHOLM. Hm—you think so?

WANGEL. Yes. What's more—on second thought—I really don't know how I could carry through with it. For the girls' sakes, I scarcely think I could justify a move into such isolation. After all, they have to live where there are at least some prospects for a decent marriage.

ARNHOLM. Marriage? Are you already so concerned about that?

WANGEL. Well, my Lord—I do have to think about it! But then, on the other hand again, there's my poor, sick Ellida—! Ah, my dear Arnholm—in many ways, I really feel caught between fire and water.

ARNHOLM. You hardly need to worry about Bolette— (*Breaking off.*) I wonder where she's—where they've gone? (*He goes to the open door and looks out.*)

WANGEL (*over by the piano*). I'd gladly make any sacrifice for all three of them—if I only knew what.

(ELLIDA *comes through the door on the left.*)

ELLIDA (*hurriedly to* WANGEL). You mustn't go out this morning.

WANGEL. No, of course not. I'll stay home with you. (*Gesturing toward* ARNHOLM, *who approaches them.*) But aren't you going to greet our friend?

ELLIDA (*turning*). Oh, you're here, Mr. Arnholm. (*Gives him her hand.*) Good morning.

ARNHOLM. Good morning, Mrs. Wangel. Not taking your swim today?

ELLIDA. No, no! Don't even mention it. But won't you sit down just a moment?

ARNHOLM. No, thank you—not now. (*Looks at* WANGEL.) I promised the girls I'd meet them in the garden.

ELLIDA. Well, goodness knows if you'll find them. I never know where they've gone.

WANGEL. Oh, now, they're sure to be down by the pond.

ARNHOLM. Well, I guess I can follow their trail. (*He nods and crosses the veranda into the garden and off, right.*)

ELLIDA. What time is it, Wangel?

WANGEL (*looking at his watch*). A little after eleven.

ELLIDA. A little after. And at eleven—or half-past eleven tonight, the steamer will come. Oh, to be done with it!

WANGEL (*going closer to her*). Ellida dear—there's one thing I want to ask you about.

ELLIDA. What is it?

WANGEL. The night before last—up there in the park— you said, in these last three years, you'd seen him so often before you, large as life.

ELLIDA. Yes, that's true. I have.

WANGEL. But how did you see him?

ELLIDA. How did I see him—?

WANGEL. I mean—how did he look when you saw him?

ELLIDA. But you know yourself, Wangel, how he looks.

WANGEL. Did he look just like that in these visions of yours?

ELLIDA. Yes, exactly.

WANGEL. But how did it happen, then, that you didn't recognize him at once?

ELLIDA (*with a start*). I didn't?

WANGEL. No. You said yourself, later, that you didn't have any idea at first who this stranger was.

ELLIDA (*struck with wonder*). Yes, actually—you're right! But isn't that odd, Wangel? Imagine—that I didn't know him at once.

WANGEL. It was only by the eyes, you said—

ELLIDA. Yes—the eyes! The eyes!

WANGEL. But at the park you said he always appeared to you the way he looked when you parted—out there, ten years ago.

ELLIDA. I said that?

WANGEL. Yes.

ELLIDA. Then he must have looked about the same in those days as he does now.

WANGEL. No. Walking back, the night before last, you gave me quite a different picture of him. You said he had no beard ten years ago. He was dressed quite differently, too. And then the stickpin with the pearl—the man yesterday had nothing like that.

ELLIDA. No, that's right.

WANGEL (*looks searchingly at her*). Try to think back now, Ellida. Or—maybe you can't remember any longer how he looked when he stood with you on Bratthammer?

ELLIDA (*concentrating with her eyes closed*). Not very clearly. No—today I can't at all. Isn't that strange?

WANGEL. Not so strange, actually. There's a new image in you now, shaped out of reality—and it's eclipsing the old one so you can't see it anymore.

ELLIDA. Do you think so, Wangel?

WANGEL. Yes. And it's shutting out the sick fantasies, too. It's a good thing the reality came.

ELLIDA. Good? You call it good?

WANGEL. Yes. The fact that it came—may well be the cure you've needed.

ELLIDA (*sitting down on the sofa*). Wangel—come and sit here by me. I have to tell you all that's on my mind.

WANGEL. Yes, my dear, please do. (*He sits on a chair on the other side of the table.*)

ELLIDA. It was really a stroke of misfortune—for both of us—that we two, of all people, had to come together.

WANGEL (*startled*). What are you saying!

ELLIDA. Oh, yes—it was. And that was only natural. It could only end in misfortune—considering the way that we came together.

WANGEL. What was so wrong about the way we—!

ELLIDA. Now listen, Wangel—there's no need for us going around any longer, lying to ourselves—and to each other.

WANGEL. We're doing what! Lying?

ELLIDA. Yes. Or anyway, concealing the truth. Because the truth—the plain, simple truth is that you came out there and—and bought me.

WANGEL. Bought—! You say—bought!

ELLIDA. Oh, I wasn't one particle better than you. I met your offer—and sold myself to you.

WANGEL (*gives her a pained look*). Ellida—how can you be so heartless?

ELLIDA. But what else can I call it? You couldn't bear the emptiness in your house any longer. You were out after a new wife—

WANGEL. And a new mother for the children, Ellida.

ELLIDA. Perhaps that too—on the side. Although you had no idea if I'd fit that role. You'd no more than seen me, and talked a bit with me a couple of times. Then you wanted me, and so—

WANGEL. Yes, you can put it that way, if you choose.

ELLIDA. And I, on my side—I was helpless then, not knowing which way to turn—and so utterly alone. It was such good sense to accept your offer—since you proposed maintaining me for life.

WANGEL. It never struck me in terms of maintainance. I asked you, in all honesty, if you'd be willing to share with me and the children the little I had.

ELLIDA. Yes, so you did. But the point is, I never should have accepted. Never, for any price! I never should have sold myself! The meanest work—the poorest conditions would have been better—if I'd chosen them myself, by my own free will!

WANGEL (*rising*). Then these five, six years we've lived together—have they been such a total waste?

ELLIDA. Oh, you mustn't think that, Wangel! I've lived as well here with you as anyone could hope for. But I didn't come into your house by my own free will. That's the thing.

WANGEL (*studying her*). Not by your own free will!

ELLIDA. No. I didn't go with you freely.

WANGEL (*quietly*). Ah—I remember those words— from yesterday.

ELLIDA. Everything came together in those words—like a beam of light—and I can see things now, as they are.

WANGEL. What do you see?

ELLIDA. I see that this life we're living with each other— is really no marriage at all.

WANGEL (*bitterly*). What you say is true enough. The life we have *now* is no marriage.

ELLIDA. Nor earlier, either. Never. Not from the very start. (*Gazing into space.*) The first—*that* one might have been full and complete.

WANGEL. The first? What first do you mean?

ELLIDA. Mine—with him.

WANGEL (*stares bewildered at her*). I absolutely don't understand you.

ELLIDA. Oh, Wangel—let's not lie to each other. Or to ourselves, either.

WANGEL. All right! Go on.

ELLIDA. You see—we can never get away from one thing: that a promise freely given is just as binding as a marriage license.

WANGEL. But what in God's name—!

ELLIDA (*rising impetuously*). I want to be free to leave you, Wangel.

WANGEL. Ellida—! Ellida—!

ELLIDA. Yes, yes—give me my freedom! You have to believe me—things aren't going to change. Not after the way we met and married.

WANGEL (*mastering his feelings*). Have we really come to this point?

ELLIDA. We had to. There was no other way.

WANGEL (*looking sorrowfully at her*). Then all we've shared hasn't won you to me. You've never belonged to me—never.

ELLIDA. Oh, Wangel—if only I could love you as much as I want to! As completely as you deserve! But now I can tell—it's not going to be.

WANGEL. Divorce, then? That's what you want? An absolute divorce?

ELLIDA. You understand me so little. I'm not concerned about the formalities. This isn't a matter of outward things. What I want is simply that the two of us agree, of our own free will, to release each other.

WANGEL (*bitterly, nodding slowly*). Dissolve the contract—hm?

ELLIDA. Exactly. Dissolve the contract.

WANGEL. And then what, Ellida? Afterward? Have you thought over what lies ahead of us then? How life might turn out both for you and for me?

ELLIDA. That doesn't matter. Life will take care of itself. What I'm begging and pleading for, Wangel, is all that's important. Let me go free! Give me my full freedom back!

WANGEL. Ellida, this is a fearful thing you're asking. At least give me some time to collect my thoughts and come to a decision. Let's talk it over some more. And give yourself time to consider what you're doing.

ELLIDA. There isn't the time for that. I must have my freedom today.

WANGEL. Why so soon?

ELLIDA. Because he'll be here tonight.

WANGEL (*with a start*). He! Coming! What's this stranger got to do with it?

ELLIDA. I want to be free, completely, when I go to him.

WANGEL. And what—what good will that do you?

ELLIDA. I won't hide behind the fact of being another man's wife. I won't claim that I have no choice—because then there'd be no decision made.

WANGEL. You talk of choice! Choice, Ellida! Choice in this thing!

ELLIDA. Yes, I must have freedom of choice. Choice either way. To send him away alone—or, as well, to go with him.

WANGEL. Do you know what you're saying? To go with him! To put your whole fate in his hands!

ELLIDA. But I put my whole fate in your hands—without any question.

WANGEL. That's true. But he! He's a total stranger! You hardly know him.

ELLIDA. But I think I knew you even less—and still I went off with you.

WANGEL. At least at that time you knew something of what kind of life you'd be taking on. But here, with him? Just consider! What do you know about him? Nothing! Not even who he is—or what he is.

ELLIDA (*staring into space*). It's true. But that's exactly the horror of it.

WANGEL. Yes—well, it *is* horrible.

ELLIDA. And it's also why, it seems to me, I've got to face it.

WANGEL (*looking at her*). Because you find it horrible?

ELLIDA. Yes. Precisely.

WANGEL (*comes closer*). Tell me, Ellida—what do you really mean when you speak of the horror?

ELLIDA (*after a moment's thought*). It's something that—that terrifies and attracts.

WANGEL. Attracts, too?

ELLIDA. Attracts most of all—I think.

WANGEL (*deliberately*). Ellida—you belong to the sea.

ELLIDA. That's part of the horror.

WANGEL. And part of the horror in you. You both terrify—and attract.

ELLIDA. You think so, Wangel?

WANGEL. I've really never known you—at least, to any depth. I'm beginning to see that now.

ELLIDA. Then you have to set me free! Completely free from whatever's yours! I'm not the person you took me for. Now you can see it yourself. We can separate now as friends—by our own free choice.

WANGEL (*heavily*). It might be best for us both—if we parted—but even so, I just can't! You have for me this same horrifying spell, Ellida, this attraction—that's so powerful in you.

ELLIDA. You can say that?

WANGEL. Let's try to get through this day resolutely—with calm in our spirits. I don't dare let you go or free you today. I can't take that liberty. Not for your sake, Ellida. I have my right and my duty to defend you.

ELLIDA. Defend me? Against what? There's no threat here from the outside. The horror goes deeper, Wangel. The horror—is the force of attraction in my own mind. And what can you do about that?

WANGEL. I can steady and strengthen you to fight against it.

ELLIDA. Yes—if I want to fight it.

WANGEL. You don't want to?

ELLIDA. That's it—I don't know!

WANGEL. It will all be settled tonight, Ellida—

ELLIDA (*in an outburst*). Yes, to think—! The decision so near! And for the rest of my life!

WANGEL. And tomorrow—

ELLIDA. Yes, tomorrow! By then the future I was meant for may have been ruined!

WANGEL. You were meant for—?

ELLIDA. A whole, full life of freedom ruined, wasted—for me—and maybe for him.

WANGEL (*in a lower tone, gripping her by the wrist*). Ellida—do you love this stranger?

ELLIDA. Do I—? Oh, how do I know! I only know that for me he has a terrifying attraction, and that—

WANGEL. And that—?

ELLIDA (*tearing herself away*). That I think I belong with him.

WANGEL (*bowing his head*). I begin to understand nearly everything.

ELLIDA. And how can you help against this? What do you prescribe for me?

WANGEL (*looks sadly at her*). Tomorrow—he'll be gone. This misfortune will have blown over. And then I'll be willing to let you go free. We'll dissolve the contract then, Ellida.

ELLIDA. Oh, Wangel—! Tomorrow—then it's too late!

WANGEL (*looking out toward the garden*). The children! We ought to spare them at least—while we can.

(ARNHOLM, BOLETTE, HILDA, *and* LYNGSTRAND *appear in the garden.* LYNGSTRAND *excuses himself and goes out left. The others come into the room.*)

ARNHOLM. We've been making some marvelous plans—

HILDA. We'll be going out on the fjord tonight, and—

BOLETTE. No, don't say anything!

WANGEL. We've been making some plans here, too.

ARNHOLM. Oh—really?

WANGEL. Tomorrow Ellida's going away to Skjoldvik—for a while.

BOLETTE. Going away—?

ARNHOLM. Why, that's a fine idea, Mrs. Wangel.

WANGEL. She wants to go home again. Home to the sea.

HILDA (*darting several steps toward* ELLIDA). You're going? You're leaving us!

ELLIDA (*alarmed*). But, Hilda! What's got into you?

HILDA (*controlling herself*). Oh, it's nothing. (*Under her breath, turning away.*) Go! Go on then!

BOLETTE (*anxiously*). Father—I can see it in your face. You're going away, too—to Skjoldvik.

WANGEL. No, certainly not! I may be out there at times—

BOLETTE. But you'll come back to us—?

WANGEL. I'll be here, too.

BOLETTE. Yes, at times!

WANGEL. My dear child, it has to be. (*He crosses the room.*)

ARNHOLM (*in a whisper to* BOLETTE). We'll talk this over later. (*He follows* WANGEL. *They talk quietly together by the door.*)

ELLIDA (*to* BOLETTE, *her voice lowered*). What was that with Hilda? She looked so upset.

BOLETTE. Haven't you ever noticed what it is that Hilda longs for day and night?

ELLIDA. Longs for?

BOLETTE. Ever since you came to this house.

ELLIDA. No. No, what's that?

BOLETTE. One small expression of love from you.

ELLIDA. Ah—! Then—I do have some purpose here?

(*She clasps her hands tight over her head and stares intently off into space, as if riddled by conflicting thoughts and feelings.* WANGEL *and* ARNHOLM *come forward in hushed conversation.* BOLETTE *goes over and glances into the room to the right, then opens the door wide.*)

BOLETTE. Father dear—the food's on the table—if you'd like to—

WANGEL (*with forced composure*). Is it, dear? That's good. Arnholm, please! Now we'll go drink a parting cup to the health of—of our "lady from the sea."

(*They move toward the door on the right.*)

⮌ ACT FIVE ⮑

The far corner of DR. WANGEL's *garden by the carp pond. The deepening twilight of a summer night.* ARNHOLM, BOLETTE, LYNGSTRAND, *and* HILDA, *in a boat, are punting along the bank from the left.*

HILDA. See, we can easily jump ashore from here!

ARNHOLM. No, no, don't!

LYNGSTRAND. I can't jump, Hilda.

HILDA. And you, Arnholm, can't you jump either?

ARNHOLM. I'd rather pass it up.

BOLETTE. Then let's put in by the bathhouse steps.

(*They pole off to the right. At the same time* BALLESTED *appears on the footpath from the right, carrying music scores and a French horn. He waves to those in the boat, turns and talks to them. Their answers are heard farther and farther off in the distance.*)

BALLESTED. What did you say—? Yes, that's right—for the English steamer. It's her last trip of the year. But if you want to relish the music, you better not wait too long. (*Shouts.*) What? (*Shaking his head.*) Can't hear you!

(ELLIDA, *with a shawl over her head, comes in from the left, followed by* DR. WANGEL.)

WANGEL. But, Ellida dear—I tell you, there's still plenty of time.

ELLIDA. No, no—there isn't! He can come any moment.

304

BALLESTED (*outside the garden fence*). Well, good evening, Doctor! Good evening, Mrs. Wangel!

WANGEL (*becoming aware of him*). Oh, is that you? Are we having music tonight?

BALLESTED. Yes. The Wind Ensemble's going to make itself heard. There's no shortage of festivities these days. Tonight we're saluting the English ship.

ELLIDA. The English ship! Has she been sighted?

BALLESTED. Not yet. But she slips her way in, you know—between the islands. There's no sign of her—and then, suddenly, there she is.

ELLIDA. Yes—that's just the way it is.

WANGEL (*half to* ELLIDA). Tonight's the last voyage. And then—no more.

BALLESTED. A doleful thought, Doctor. But all the more reason, as I say, for making a celebration. Ah, me! These delightful summer days will soon be over. The sea-lanes will soon be locked in ice—as the old tragedy has it.

ELLIDA. The sea-lanes locked—yes.

BALLESTED. How sad to think. We've been summer's happy children now for weeks and months. It's hard to reconcile oneself with the dark days coming. Yes, I mean, it is at first. Because, you know, people learn to accli— acclimatize themselves, Mrs. Wangel. Yes, they really do.

(*He bows and goes out left.*)

ELLIDA (*looking out across the fjord*). Oh, this agonizing suspense! This feverish last half hour before the decision.

WANGEL. Then you definitely do want to talk to him yourself?

ELLIDA. I have to talk to him myself. It's the only way I can make a free choice.

WANGEL. You have no choice, Ellida. You haven't the right. I won't permit it.

ELLIDA. You can't keep me from choosing. Neither you nor anyone else. You can forbid me to go with him—if I choose that. You can hold me here by force—against my will. That you can do. But that I choose—choose from the depths of my being—choose him, and not you—if I have to—*that* you can never prevent.

WANGEL. No, you're right. I can't prevent you.

ELLIDA. So I have nothing at all to stop me. Not one earthly tie here at home. I've been so completely without roots in this house, Wangel. I have no place with the children—in their hearts, I mean. I never have. When I go—if I go—either with him tonight, or to Skjoldvik tomorrow—I won't even have a key to give up, or a set of instructions to leave behind about anything at all. That's how rootless—how totally outside of things I've been from the moment I came.

WANGEL. You wanted it that way yourself.

ELLIDA. No, I didn't. I had no wants this way or that. I've simply left everything just as it was on the day I arrived. It was you, and nobody else, who wanted it like that.

WANGEL. I tried to do what was best for you.

ELLIDA. Yes, Wangel—I know you did! But these things retaliate on us; they take revenge. Now I have nothing to hold me here—no foundation—no support—no impulse toward everything that should have been our dearest common bonds.

WANGEL. Yes, that's clear enough. So you'll have your freedom from tomorrow on. You can live your own life then.

ELLIDA. My own life, you call it! Oh, no, the real thread of my life snapped when I came here to live with you. (*Clenching her fists in a tremor of fear.*) And now, tonight—in half an hour, he'll be here, the man I broke faith with, the man whose word I should have kept sacred, as he kept mine. He's coming to ask me—this one last time—to start my life over—to live a life out of my own truth—the life that terrifies and attracts—and that I *can't* give up, not of my own free will!

WANGEL. Exactly why you need me, as your husband—and your doctor—to assume that power, and act in your own behalf.

ELLIDA. Yes, Wangel, I understand very well. Oh, don't think there aren't times when I'm sure there'd be peace and security for me in taking refuge completely in you—and trying to defy all the tempting, treacherous powers. But I can't. No, no—I can't do it!

WANGEL. Come, Ellida—let's walk up and down by the shore for a while.

ELLIDA. I'd like to. But I don't dare. He said I should wait for him here.

WANGEL. Come along. You have plenty of time.

ELLIDA. You think so?

WANGEL. More than enough, yes.

ELLIDA. Let's walk a bit then.

(*They go off in the foreground to the right. As they depart,* ARNHOLM *and* BOLETTE *appear by the upper bank of the pond.*)

BOLETTE (*noticing the others leaving*). Look—!

ARNHOLM (*softly*). Shh—let them go.

BOLETTE. Have you any idea what's been happening between them the last few days?

ARNHOLM. Have you noticed anything?

BOLETTE. I'll say!

ARNHOLM. Something special?

BOLETTE. Oh, this and that. Haven't you?

ARNHOLM. Oh, I really don't know—

BOLETTE. Yes, you know all right. But you won't come out with it.

ARNHOLM. I think it'll be good for your stepmother to take that little trip.

BOLETTE. You think so?

ARNHOLM. Yes, I'm wondering if it wouldn't be a good thing for all parties if she could get away now and then?

BOLETTE. If she goes home to Skjoldvik tomorrow, she'll never come back here again to us.

ARNHOLM. But, Bolette dear, where did you ever get that notion?

BOLETTE. I'm absolutely convinced. You just wait! You'll see—she won't come back again. At least, not while Hilda and I are around the house.

ARNHOLM. Hilda, too?

BOLETTE. Well, with Hilda it might work out. She's still not much more than a child. And then I think, underneath, she really worships Ellida. But with me, it's another story. A stepmother who's hardly much older than oneself—

ARNHOLM. Bolette—for you it might not be so long before you could get away.

BOLETTE (*fervently*). You mean it! Then you've talked it over with Father?

ARNHOLM. Yes, I've done that.

BOLETTE. Well—and what did he say?

ARNHOLM. Hm—of course, right now your father's so absorbed in other things—

BOLETTE. Yes, that's what I told you before.

ARNHOLM. But I did get this much out of him: that you mustn't be counting on any help from him.

BOLETTE. None—!

ARNHOLM. He made his situation quite clear to me. Something of that order, he felt, would be totally out of the realm of possibility for him.

BOLETTE (*reproachfully*). And you can simply stand there and tease me.

ARNHOLM. I'm not teasing at all, Bolette. It's completely up to you whether or not you can break away.

BOLETTE. You say it's up to me?

ARNHOLM. That is, if you really want to enter the world—and learn about everything that interests you most—share in whatever you've longed for here at home—and live a more ample life. What do you say, Bolette?

BOLETTE (*clasping her hands*). My God in heaven—!

But—it's all so impossible. If Father won't or can't, then—
Because there's no one else I can turn to.

ARNHOLM. Couldn't you accept a helping hand from
your old—I mean, your former teacher?

BOLETTE. From you, Mr. Arnholm! You'd be willing
to—?

ARNHOLM. To stand by you? Yes, with all my heart. In
both word and deed. You can rely on that. So—do you
agree? Well? Is it a bargain?

BOLETTE. A bargain! To leave—to see the world—to
learn what life really is! It's like some beautiful, unattainable dream.

ARNHOLM. But it all can come true for you now—if
you'll try for it.

BOLETTE. So much happiness—it's breathtaking! And
you'll help me to it. But—tell me, is it right to take such a
gift from a stranger?

ARNHOLM. From me, Bolette, you certainly can. Whatever you need.

BOLETTE (seizing his hands). Yes, I almost believe I
can! I don't know why it is, but— (In an outburst of
feeling.)—oh, I could both laugh and cry for joy! I feel so
happy. Oh—so I am going to live, after all. I was beginning to feel so afraid that life would pass me by.

ARNHOLM. That's nothing you have to fear. But now
you must tell me very frankly—if there's anything—anything to bind you here.

BOLETTE. Bind me? No, there isn't.

ARNHOLM. No one in particular?

BOLETTE. No one at all. Well, I mean—Father, of
course, in a way. And Hilda, too. But—

ARNHOLM. Well—you'd be leaving your father sooner or
later. And Hilda will be going her own way, too, before
long. It's only a question of time, that's all. But otherwise
you've no other ties? No other kind of relationship?

BOLETTE. No, nothing. So I can just as well leave as I
wish.

ARNHOLM. Well, if that's the case—then you must leave with me.

BOLETTE (*clapping her hands*). Oh, God—I can't believe it!

ARNHOLM. Because I hope you have full confidence in me?

BOLETTE. Why, of course.

ARNHOLM. And you feel quite safe in trusting yourself and your future in my hands? You do, don't you?

BOLETTE. Naturally! Why shouldn't I? How can you ask? You're my old teacher—I mean, my teacher from the old days.

ARNHOLM. Not only that. That aspect of it I'd just as soon forget. But—well—anyway you're free, Bolette. There are no ties binding you. So I'm asking you then—if you'd—you'd be willing to join yourself to me—for life.

BOLETTE (*recoiling, startled*). Oh—what are you saying?

ARNHOLM. For the rest of your life, Bolette. If you'll be my wife.

BOLETTE (*half to herself*). No, no, no! This is impossible. Quite impossible.

ARNHOLM. Does it really seem so utterly impossible to you that—?

BOLETTE. But you don't mean—you can't mean what you're saying, Mr. Arnholm! (*Looking at him.*) Or—anyway— Is that what you meant when you offered to do so much for me?

ARNHOLM. Now listen to me a minute. I've surprised you considerably, I guess.

BOLETTE. How could something like this—from you—how could it not surprise me?

ARNHOLM. Perhaps you're right. Of course you didn't—and couldn't—know that it was for your sake I made the trip here.

BOLETTE. You came here—for my sake!

ARNHOLM. Yes. Last spring I got a letter from your

father. There were some lines in it that gave me the idea—hm—that your memories of me were a little more than—just friendly.

BOLETTE. How could Father write like that!

ARNHOLM. He didn't mean it at all that way. But I persuaded myself into imagining that a young girl was going around the house here, yearning for me to return— No, Bolette, now don't interrupt! And you have to understand—when someone like me, who's past the pride of his youth, has that kind of belief—or illusion—it makes a powerful impression. From then on, there grew in me a warm—and grateful affection for you. I felt I had to come to you—see you again—and tell you that I shared those feelings which I'd dreamed myself into believing you felt for me.

BOLETTE. But now you know it wasn't true! That it was a mistake!

ARNHOLM. It's no help, Bolette. Your image—as I carry it within me—will always be colored now by those mistaken emotions. Maybe you can't understand all this. But it's the way it is.

BOLETTE. Anything like this I never would have believed possible.

ARNHOLM. But now that you know it is—what do you say, Bolette? Won't you promise yourself in—in marriage to me?

BOLETTE. But, Mr. Arnholm, to me it's simply unthinkable. You were my teacher. I can't imagine ever being in any other kind of relationship to you.

ARNHOLM. Well, all right—if you really don't think you can— But, in any case, the old relationship is still unchanged.

BOLETTE. What do you mean?

ARNHOLM. Naturally, I stand by my offer, just the same. I'll make sure that you get out and see something of the world—study what interests you—and have a secure and independent life. And I'll see that your future's taken care of. I want you to know you'll always find me a staunch, reliable friend.

BOLETTE. But—Mr. Arnholm—that's all become quite impossible now.

ARNHOLM. Is that impossible, too?

BOLETTE. Yes, isn't that obvious! After what you've told me here—and the answer I gave you—oh, how could you think me capable of helping myself at your expense! There's absolutely nothing I can take from you—nothing after this!

ARNHOLM. You mean you'd rather stay here at home and watch life slipping away from you?

BOLETTE. Oh, that's too horribly depressing to think about!

ARNHOLM. You want to throw away your chance to see the outside world and be part of everything you've longed for? To know there's so infinitely much to life—and that, after all, you've never really experienced any of it? Think well on what you're doing, Bolette.

BOLETTE. Yes, yes—you're very right, Mr. Arnholm.

ARNHOLM. And then, when your father's no longer here —maybe to stand alone and helpless in the world. Or else to have to give yourself to another man for whom you— quite possibly—might also feel no affection.

BOLETTE. Oh, yes—I can see quite well how true it is—everything you say. But still—! Or—perhaps—

ARNHOLM (*quickly*). Well?

BOLETTE (*looking irresolutely at him*). Perhaps it isn't so utterly impossible, after all—

ARNHOLM. What, Bolette?

BOLETTE. It might do, then—to try what—what you suggested.

ARNHOLM. You mean that perhaps you'd be willing to—? That at least you'd give me the satisfaction of being able to help you as a friend?

BOLETTE. No, no! That's absolutely impossible! No— Mr. Arnholm—if, instead, you'll take me—

ARNHOLM. Bolette! Then you will?

BOLETTE. Yes—I think—I want that.

ARNHOLM. Then you *will* be my wife?

BOLETTE. Yes. If you still think that—that you want me.

ARNHOLM. If I still—! (*Seizes her hand.*) Oh, thank you—thank you, Bolette! All this that you've said—these doubts you've had—they don't frighten me. If I don't have you wholeheartedly now, I'll find the ways to win you. Oh, Bolette, how I'll treasure you!

BOLETTE. Now I can live in the world, in the midst of life. You promised me that.

ARNHOLM. And I'll keep my word.

BOLETTE. And I can study anything I want.

ARNHOLM. I'll teach you, just as I used to. Remember that last school year—?

BOLETTE (*musing quietly*). Imagine—to be free—and to come out—into the unknown. And not to worry about the future, or scrimping to get along—

ARNHOLM. No, you won't have to waste your thoughts like that anymore. Which ought to be quite a relief in itself, don't you think?

BOLETTE. Yes, definitely.

ARNHOLM (*putting his arms around her waist*). Ah, wait till you see how easy and comfortable we'll be with each other. And how competently we'll manage things together, Bolette!

BOLETTE. Yes, I'm beginning to think—I really believe—this is going to work. (*Looks off to the right and hurriedly frees herself.*) Ah! Don't say anything yet!

ARNHOLM. Dear, what is it?

BOLETTE. Oh, it's that poor— (*Pointing.*) See, there.

ARNHOLM. Is it your father—?

BOLETTE. No, it's that young sculptor. He's over there walking with Hilda.

ARNHOLM. Oh, Lyngstrand. What's the matter with him?

BOLETTE. Well, you know how frail and sickly he is.

ARNHOLM. Yes, if it isn't all in his mind.

BOLETTE. No, it's serious enough. He can't live much longer. But maybe it's the best thing for him.

ARNHOLM. How could *that* be the best thing?

BOLETTE. Well, because—because nothing could ever come of his art, anyway. Let's go before they get here.

ARNHOLM. With the greatest pleasure, dearest. Let's.

(HILDA *and* LYNGSTRAND *appear by the pond.*)

HILDA. Hey—hey! Won't your majesties wait for us?

ARNHOLM. We'd rather stay in the lead.

(*He and* BOLETTE *go out to the left.*)

LYNGSTRAND (*laughs quietly*). It's really delightful here around this hour. Humanity comes in couples. Everyone's two by two.

HILDA (*looking after them*). I could almost swear that he's been courting her.

LYNGSTRAND. Really? Have you noticed something?

HILDA. Oh, yes. It's not too difficult—if you've got eyes in your head.

LYNGSTRAND. Bolette wouldn't have him. I'm positive of that.

HILDA. No. She thinks he's beginning to look horribly old. And also that he's going to be bald soon.

LYNGSTRAND. Those aren't the only reasons. She wouldn't have him, anyhow.

HILDA. How do you know that?

LYNGSTRAND. Because there's someone else she's promised to give her thoughts to.

HILDA. Just her thoughts?

LYNGSTRAND. While he's away, yes.

HILDA. Oh, in other words, it's *you* that she's going to go thinking about!

LYNGSTRAND. Well, it might just be.

HILDA. Did she promise you that?

LYNGSTRAND. Yes, just think—she promised me that! But you mustn't ever tell her you know.

HILDA. Oh, so help me God, I'll be quiet as the grave.

LYNGSTRAND. I think it's awfully kind of her.

HILDA. And when you come back here again—will you get engaged to her? And marry her?

LYNGSTRAND. No, that wouldn't be too good a match. I don't dare think about marrying for the first few years. And when I finally do arrive, then I expect she'll probably be too old for me.

HILDA. But all the same, you want to have her going around thinking about you?

LYNGSTRAND. Well, it's very necessary for me. You know, as an artist. And it's easy enough for her to do, when she hasn't any real vocation in life, anyhow. But it's kind of her, all the same.

HILDA. Do you believe you can work better on your art if you know Bolette's up here thinking about you?

LYNGSTRAND. Yes, I'm convinced of it. To know that someplace on this earth there's a young woman of rare breeding, living quietly in her dreams—of me—why, I think that must be so—so— Well, I really don't know what to call it.

HILDA. You mean—thrilling?

LYNGSTRAND. Thrilling? Yes, it's thrilling; you could call it that. Or something like it. (*Looks at her a moment.*) You're so perceptive, Hilda. Amazingly perceptive. When I come home again, you'll be about the same age your sister is now. Maybe then you'll look like her as well. And maybe you'll have gotten her temperament, too. Almost as if you and she had grown together—in one form, so to speak.

HILDA. Would that please you?

LYNGSTRAND. I really don't know. Yes, I guess it would. But now—for this summer—I'd prefer you to be just yourself alone. Exactly what you are.

HILDA. You like me best that way?

LYNGSTRAND. Yes, I like you very well that way.

HILDA. Hm—tell me—as an artist, do you think it's right for me always to wear these light summer dresses?

LYNGSTRAND. Yes, I think they're just the thing for you.

HILDA. Do you find the bright colors becoming on me?

LYNGSTRAND. Very becoming on you, at least to my taste.

HILDA. But tell me—as an artist—how do you think I'd look in black?

LYNGSTRAND. In black, Hilda?

HILDA. Yes, all in black. Do you think it would set me off well?

LYNGSTRAND. Black really isn't quite the thing for summer. Although you certainly would look striking in black. Especially with your complexion.

HILDA (*gazing into the distance*). In black right up to the neck. Black ruffles. Black gloves. And a long black veil hanging down behind.

LYNGSTRAND. If you were to dress up like that, Hilda— I'd wish myself into a painter—and I'd paint you as a young, beautiful, grieving widow.

HILDA. Or a young, grieving bride.

LYNGSTRAND. Yes, that would be even better. But you can't really want to dress like that?

HILDA. It's hard to say. But I think it's thrilling.

LYNGSTRAND. Thrilling?

HILDA. Thrilling to think of, yes. (*Points suddenly out to the left.*) Oh, look there!

LYNGSTRAND (*following her stare*). The English steamer! And she's already docked.

(WANGEL *and* ELLIDA *appear by the pond.*)

WANGEL. No, Ellida, I tell you—you're wrong! (*Notices the others.*) Well, are you two here? What's the word, Mr. Lyngstrand—she's not in sight yet, is she?

LYNGSTRAND. The English ship?

WANGEL. What else!

LYNGSTRAND (*pointing*). She's right there, Doctor.

ELLIDA. Ah—! I knew it.

WANGEL. Already come!

LYNGSTRAND. Like a thief in the night, you could say. Gliding soundlessly in—

WANGEL. You better take Hilda down to the pier. Hurry up! She'll want to hear the music.

LYNGSTRAND. Yes, we were just now leaving, Doctor.

WANGEL. We may come along later. In a little while.

HILDA (*whispering to* LYNGSTRAND). See, still another couple.

(*She and* LYNGSTRAND *go out through the garden to the left. During what follows, the music of a brass band is heard far off out on the fjord.*)

ELLIDA. He's come! He's here! Yes, yes—I can feel that.

WANGEL. You'd best go inside, Ellida. Let me talk to him alone.

ELLIDA. Oh—it's impossible! Impossible, I tell you! (*Crying out.*) Oh—there he is, Wangel!

(*The* STRANGER *appears from the left and stops on the footpath outside the fence.*)

STRANGER (*bowing*). Good evening. So you see I'm back, Ellida.

ELLIDA. Yes. The hour has come.

STRANGER. Are you ready to leave, or not?

WANGEL. You can see yourself that she's not.

STRANGER. I'm not talking about traveling clothes, and that sort of thing—or whether her trunks are packed. Everything she needs on the trip I have with me on board. I've also reserved her a cabin. (*To* ELLIDA.) I'm asking, then, if you're ready to come with me—of your own free will?

ELLIDA. Oh, don't ask me! You mustn't!

(*A ship's bell sounds in the distance.*)

STRANGER. They're ringing the first warning. Now you've got to say yes or no.

ELLIDA (*wringing her hands*). To decide! Decide for the rest of my life! And never the chance to go back!

STRANGER. Never! In half an hour it'll be too late.

ELLIDA (*with a shy, inquiring look*). Why are you so determined not to let me go?

STRANGER. Don't you feel, as I do, that we belong together?

ELLIDA. You mean, because of the promise?

STRANGER. Promises bind no one. Neither man nor woman. I don't let you go—because I can't.

ELLIDA (*in a low, tremulous voice*). Why didn't you come before?

WANGEL. Ellida!

ELLIDA (*in an outburst*). Oh—this power that charms and tempts and allures me—into the unknown! All the force of the sea is in this man!

(*The* STRANGER *climbs over the fence.*)

ELLIDA (*retreating behind* WANGEL). What is it? What do you want?

STRANGER. I can see it and I can hear it in you, Ellida—it will be me that you choose in the end.

WANGEL (*steps toward him*). My wife has no choice in this. I'll both decide—and defend—where she's concerned. Yes, defend! If you don't clear out of here—out of this country—and never come back—then you better know what you're in for!

ELLIDA. No, no, Wangel! Don't!

STRANGER. What will you do to me?

WANGEL. I'll have you arrested—as a criminal! Right now, before you board ship! I know all about the murder up at Skjoldvik.

ELLIDA. Oh, Wangel—how can you—?

STRANGER. I was prepared for that. And so— (*Draws a revolver from his breast pocket.*)—so I provided myself with this.

ELLIDA (*flinging herself in front of* WANGEL). No—don't kill him! Kill me instead!

STRANGER. I'm not killing either of you, so don't get

excited. This is for my own use. I want to live and die a free man.

ELLIDA (*in a rising tumult of feeling*). I have to say this—and say it so he can hear! Yes, you can lock me in here! You've got the power and the means! And that's what you want to do! But my mind—my thoughts—all my longing dreams and desires—those you can never constrain! They'll go raging and hunting out—into the unknown that I was made for—and that you've shut out for me!

WANGEL (*in quiet pain*). I see it so well, Ellida. Inch by inch you're slipping away from me. This hunger for the boundless, the infinite—the unattainable—will finally drive your mind out completely into darkness.

ELLIDA. Oh, yes, yes—I feel it—like black, soundless wings hanging over me!

WANGEL. It's not going to come to that. There's no other way to save you. At least, not that I can see. And so—so I agree that—our contract's dissolved. Right now, this moment. Now you can choose your own path—in full freedom.

ELLIDA (*stares at him briefly as if struck dumb*). Is that true—true—what you're saying? You mean it—with all your heart?

WANGEL. Yes, I mean it—with all my miserable heart.

ELLIDA. Then you *can*—? You can let this *be*?

WANGEL. Yes, I can. Because I love you so much.

ELLIDA (*her voice soft and tremulous*). Have I grown so close—and so dear to you?

WANGEL. With the years and the living together, yes.

ELLIDA (*striking her hands together*). And I—who've been so blind!

WANGEL. Your thoughts have gone other ways. But now—now you're entirely free from me—my life—my world. Now you can pick up the thread of your own true existence again. Because now you can choose in freedom—on your own responsibility.

ELLIDA (*hands to her head, staring blankly at* WANGEL). In freedom—responsible to myself! Responsible? How this—transforms everything!

(*The ship's bell rings again.*)

STRANGER. Ellida, listen! It's ringing for the last time now. Come!

ELLIDA (*turns, looks fixedly at him, and speaks in a firm voice*). I could never go with you after this.

STRANGER. Never!

ELLIDA (*holding tight to* WANGEL). No—I'll never leave you now!

WANGEL. Ellida—Ellida!

STRANGER. Then it's over?

ELLIDA. Yes. Over forever.

STRANGER. I see. There's something stronger here than my will.

ELLIDA. Your will hasn't a shred of power over me now. To me you've become a dead man who came up out of the sea—and who's drifting back down again. There's no terror in you now. And no attraction.

STRANGER. Good-bye, then. (*He vaults over the fence.*) From now on, you're nothing more than—a shipwreck I barely remember. (*Goes out to the left.*)

WANGEL (*looks at her a moment*). Ellida, your mind is like the sea—it ebbs and flows. What brought the change?

ELLIDA. Oh, don't you understand that the change came—that it *had* to come—when I could choose in freedom?

WANGEL. And the unknown—it doesn't attract you anymore?

ELLIDA. It neither terrifies nor attracts. I've been able to see deep into it—and I could have plunged in, if I'd wanted to. I could have chosen it now. And that's why, also, I could reject it.

WANGEL. I begin to understand you—little by little. You think and feel in images—and in visions. Your longing and craving for the sea—your attraction toward him, toward this stranger—these were the signs of an awakened, growing rage for freedom in you. Nothing else.

ELLIDA. Oh, I don't know what to say. Except that

you've been a good doctor for me. You found, and you
dared to use the right treatment—the only one that could
help me.

WANGEL. Yes—when it comes to extreme cases, we
doctors have to risk desperate remedies. But now—will
you be coming back to me, Ellida?

ELLIDA. Yes, my dear, faithful Wangel—I'm coming
back to you now. I can now, because I come to you
freely—and on my own.

WANGEL (*regarding her warmly*). Ellida! Ellida! Ah—to
think that now we can live wholly for one another—

ELLIDA. And with the shared memories of our lives.
Yours—and mine.

WANGEL. Yes, darling, we will.

ELLIDA. And with our two children, Wangel.

WANGEL. You call them *ours!*

ELLIDA. They're not mine—but I'll win them to me.

WANGEL. Ours—! (*Joyfully and quickly kissing her
hands.*) Oh—how can I thank you for that one word!

(HILDA, BALLESTED, LYNGSTRAND, ARNHOLM, *and* BOLETTE
*come from the left into the garden. At the same time a
number of the young people of the town, along with summer visitors, come along the footpath outside.*)

HILDA (*in a whisper to* LYNGSTRAND). Why, she and
Father—they look as if they're just engaged!

BALLESTED (*having overheard*). But it's summertime,
little one.

ARNHOLM (*glancing at* WANGEL *and* ELLIDA). There,
she's casting off now—for England.

BOLETTE (*going to the fence*). Here's the place to see
her best.

LYNGSTRAND. The last sailing of the year.

BALLESTED. The sea-lanes will soon be locked in ice, as
the poet says. It's sad, Mrs. Wangel. And now we'll lose
you, too, for a while. Tomorrow, I hear, you're off for
Skjoldvik.

WANGEL. No, not anymore. We changed our minds this evening.

ARNHOLM (*looking from one to the other*). No—really!

HILDA (*goes to* ELLIDA). You'll stay with us, after all?

ELLIDA. Yes, Hilda dear—if you'll have me.

HILDA (*struggling between joy and tears*). Oh—if I'll have—what an idea!

ARNHOLM (*to* ELLIDA). Well, this is quite a surprise—!

ELLIDA (*smiling gravely*). You see, Mr. Arnholm—you remember, we talked about it yesterday. Once you've really become a land animal, then there's no going back again—into the sea. Or the life that belongs to the sea, either.

BALLESTED. But that's just how it is with my mermaid.

ELLIDA. Yes, much the same.

BALLESTED. Except for the difference—that the mermaid dies of it. But people, human beings—they can acclam—acclimatize themselves. Yes, yes—that's the thing, Mrs. Wangel. They can ac-cli-matize themselves.

ELLIDA. Yes, they can, Mr. Ballested—once they're free.

WANGEL. And responsible, Ellida.

ELLIDA (*quickly takes his hand*). How very true!

(*The great steamer glides silently out over the fjord. The music can be heard closer in toward shore.*)

JOHN GABRIEL BORKMAN

THE CHARACTERS

JOHN GABRIEL BORKMAN, formerly president of a bank
GUNHILD BORKMAN, his wife
ERHART BORKMAN, their son, a student
MISS ELLA RENTHEIM, Mrs. Borkman's twin sister
MRS. FANNY WILTON
VILHELM FOLDAL, part-time clerk in a government office
FRIDA FOLDAL, his daughter
MRS. BORKMAN'S MAID

The action takes place during a winter evening on the Rentheim family estate near the capital city.

ACT ONE

MRS. BORKMAN's *living room, furnished in old-fashioned, faded elegance. In the background is an open sliding door, leading into a garden room with windows and a glass door. Through these, a view into the garden, where a snowstorm swirls in the dusk. In the wall to the right, the entry door from the hall. Further forward, a large old iron stove with a fire burning in it. On the left, set back somewhat, a single, smaller door. In front of this on the same side, a window hung with heavy curtains. Between the window and the door, a sofa covered in horsehair, and in front of it, a table with a cloth on it. On the table, a lighted lamp with a shade. Near the stove, a high-backed armchair.*

MRS. GUNHILD BORKMAN *is seated on the sofa, crocheting. She is an elderly woman, cold and distinguished in appearance, with a stiff bearing and impassive features. Her abundant hair has turned iron-gray; her hands are delicate and translucent. She wears a thick, dark silk dress that once was stylish, but now is somewhat frayed and worn, and a woolen shawl over her shoulders.*

For a short while she sits erect and immobile at her crocheting. Then from outside comes the sound of bells on a passing sleigh. She listens, her eyes lighting up with joy.

MRS. BORKMAN (*in an involuntary whisper*). Erhart! At last!

(*She rises and gazes out through the curtains; then, with a look of disappointment, she settles again on the sofa at her work. Some moments later the* MAID *enters from the hall with a visiting card on a small tray.*)

MRS. BORKMAN (*quickly*). Was it Mr. Erhart after all?

MAID. No, ma'am. But there's a lady here—

MRS. BORKMAN (*setting her crocheting aside*). Oh, Mrs. Wilton, then—

MAID (*approaching*). No, it's a strange lady—

MRS. BORKMAN (*takes the card*). Let me see— (*Reads it, rises abruptly, and fixes her eyes on the* MAID.) Are you quite certain this is for me?

MAID. Yes, I understood it was meant for you.

MRS. BORKMAN. She asked to speak to Mrs. Borkman?

MAID. That's right, ma'am.

MRS. BORKMAN (*brusquely, with resolution*). Good. Then say that I'm at home.

(*The* MAID *opens the door for the stranger and goes out.* MISS ELLA RENTHEIM *enters the room. She resembles her sister in appearance, but her face has more of suffering than of hardness in its expression. Its former great beauty and character is still clearly evident. Her thick hair, now turned silvery white, is swept back in natural waves from her forehead. She is dressed in black velvet, with a hat and fur-lined coat of the same material. The two sisters stand in silence for a moment as they look probingly at each other. Each is apparently waiting for the other to speak first.*)

ELLA (*hesitating by the door*). You look quite surprised to see me, Gunhild.

MRS. BORKMAN (*standing stiffly upright between the sofa and the table, steadying her fingertips against the cloth*). Aren't you mistaken? The manager of the estate lives in the annex, you know.

ELLA. I'm not here to see the manager today.

MRS. BORKMAN. Did you want me for something?

ELLA. Yes. I need a few words with you.

MRS. BORKMAN (*moving toward her*). Well—then have a seat.

ELLA. Thank you; I can just as well stand for the moment.

MRS. BORKMAN. Whatever you like. But at least open your coat a bit.

ELLA (*unbuttoning her coat*). Yes, it's terribly warm in here.

MRS. BORKMAN. I'm always freezing.

ELLA (*stands for a time looking at her, with her arms resting on the back of the armchair*). Well—Gunhild, it's nearly eight years now since we saw each other last.

MRS. BORKMAN (*coldly*). Or since we've spoken, at any rate.

ELLA. Since we've spoken; yes, that's better. Because you must have seen me at times—when I made my yearly visit to the manager.

MRS. BORKMAN. I think, once or twice.

ELLA. I've also had a glimpse of you a few times. There, in the window.

MRS. BORKMAN. That must have been through the curtains. You have sharp eyes, Ella. (*Hard and caustic.*) But the last time we *spoke* together—that was here in this room—

ELLA (*defensively*). Yes, yes, I know, Gunhild!

MRS. BORKMAN. The week before he—before he was released.

ELLA (*walking away toward the back*). Oh, don't start on *that!*

MRS. BORKMAN (*in a firm but muted voice*). It was the week before he—Borkman was set free again.

ELLA (*coming forward*). Oh, yes, yes, yes! I haven't forgotten that time! But it's simply too heartbreaking to think about—even to dwell on for one instant—oh!

MRS. BORKMAN (*dully*). And yet the mind can never stop brooding on it alone. (*In an outburst, striking her hands together.*) No, I can't understand it! I never will! I can't comprehend how anything like this—anything so appalling could overwhelm one family! And, that it's *our* family! A family so distinguished! Why did it have to strike *us!*

ELLA. Oh, Gunhild—there were many, many besides *our* family struck down by that blow.

MRS. BORKMAN. Yes, but all those others don't concern me especially. It was only a little money, or some papers, that they lost. But for *us*—! For me! And for Erhart— no more than a child then! (*With rising passion.*) What shame for us, the innocent! What dishonor! The ugly, stupefying dishonor! And then, everything in ruins!

ELLA (*cautiously*). Tell me, Gunhild—how is he bearing it?

MRS. BORKMAN. Erhart, you mean?

ELLA. No, he himself. How is he bearing it?

MRS. BORKMAN (*with contempt*). Do you think I'd ask?

ELLA. Ask? You shouldn't have to ask—

MRS. BORKMAN (*stares at her, astonished*). You really believe I consort with him? Or cross his path? Or lay eyes on him?

ELLA. Not even that!

MRS. BORKMAN. A man for five years in prison! (*Buries her face in her hands.*) Oh, such a vile disgrace! (*In a surge of fury.*) And to think what the name John Gabriel Borkman once used to mean! No, no, no, I never want to see him again! Never!

ELLA (*regarding her briefly*). You have a hard heart, Gunhild.

MRS. BORKMAN. Toward him, yes.

ELLA. He's still your husband.

MRS. BORKMAN. Didn't he tell the court that *I* was the one who began his ruin? That I needed too much money—?

ELLA (*gently*). But wasn't there some truth in that?

MRS. BORKMAN. But that's just the way he wanted it! Everything had to be so impossibly luxurious—

ELLA. I'm aware of that. It's exactly why you should have held back—which you certainly didn't do.

MRS. BORKMAN. How could I know it wasn't his—the money he gave me to squander? And that he squandered, too—ten times beyond what I spent!

ELLA (*quietly*). Well, I guess his position required it—in good part, anyway.

MRS. BORKMAN (*scornfully*). Yes, I always heard that we had to "set the style." So he set the style all right—to a fault! Drove a four-in-hand—as if he were a king. Let people bow and scrape to him, as if to a king. (*With a laugh*.) And they called him by his forename—all through the country—exactly like the king himself. "John Gabriel. John Gabriel." They all knew "John Gabriel" for a great man then.

ELLA. He *was* a great man then.

MRS. BORKMAN. Yes, outwardly. But never one single word to let me know what his real position was. Never an inkling of where he got his funds.

ELLA. No, no—the others never suspected either.

MRS. BORKMAN. Oh, forget about the others. But he was duty-bound to tell *me* the truth. And he never did! He only lied—lied interminably to me—

ELLA (*interrupting*). Certainly not, Gunhild! He may have concealed things. But he surely didn't lie.

MRS. BORKMAN. Yes, call it what you will; it's one and the same— And then it shattered. Everything. All that splendor overthrown.

ELLA (*to herself*). Everything shattered—for him—and for others.

MRS. BORKMAN (*draws herself up grimly*). But I can tell you this, Ella—I'm not giving in! I'll find my way through to restitution. You can take my word for it!

ELLA (*tensely*). Restitution? What do you mean by that?

MRS. BORKMAN. Restitution for my name and honor and fortune! For the whole of my desolated life, that's what I mean! I have somebody to turn to, you know! Someone who'll cleanse everything that—that Borkman tarnished.

ELLA. Gunhild! Gunhild!

MRS. BORKMAN (*with swelling emotion*). There's an avenger living! One who'll make up for all his father's wrongs against me!

ELLA. Erhart.

MRS. BORKMAN. Yes, Erhart—my own good son! He'll find the way to restore the family, the house, our name. Everything that *can* be restored. And maybe something more.

ELLA. And just how do you expect that to happen?

MRS. BORKMAN. It'll come about in its own way. I don't know exactly *how*. But I know that it *will* and it *must* happen someday. (*Looks inquisitively at her.*) But Ella— isn't this the same, essentially, as what you've been thinking ever since he was a child?

ELLA. No, I really can't say it is.

MRS. BORKMAN. It isn't? Then why did you take him in, when the storm broke over—over our house?

ELLA. You couldn't manage things yourself, Gunhild.

MRS. BORKMAN. No—that's right, I couldn't. And his father—he was legally incompetent—there where he sat— so nicely protected—

ELLA (*infuriated*). Oh, how can you talk like that—! You!

MRS. BORKMAN (*with a venomous expression*). And how could *you* bring yourself to take in a child of—of John Gabriel! Absolutely as if that child were yours. Take him from *me*—to go home with you—and to keep him, year after year, till the boy was nearly grown. (*Regarding her distrustfully.*) What did you really do it for, Ella? Why did you keep him?

ELLA. I came to love him so much—

MRS. BORKMAN. More than I—his mother!

ELLA (*evasively*). That's beyond me to say. And then, of course, Erhart was rather frail as a child—

MRS. BORKMAN. Erhart—frail!

ELLA. Yes, I thought so—at the time, anyhow. And the air out there on the west coast is so much milder than here, you know.

MRS. BORKMAN (*with a wry smile*). Hm. Is it really? (*Breaking off.*) Yes, you truly have done a great deal for Erhart. (*Her tone alters.*) Well, it's understandable; you could well afford it. (*Smiles.*) You've been so lucky, Ella. You got back everything of yours untouched.

ELLA (*hurt*). I had nothing to do with that, believe me. I hadn't any suspicion—not till long, long after—that the securities made over to me at the bank—that they'd been spared—

MRS. BORKMAN. Oh, well, I can't fathom such things! I'm only saying that you were lucky. (*Looks questioningly at her.*) But when you set about, all on your own, to bring up Erhart for me—what was your motive in that?

ELLA (*looking at her*). My motive—?

MRS. BORKMAN. Yes, you must have had a motive. What did you want to make of him? Make out of him, I mean.

ELLA (*slowly*). I wanted to open a path for Erhart to be happy here on earth.

MRS. BORKMAN (*scornfully*). Pah! People of our standing have better things to do than think about happiness.

ELLA. What else—in your opinion?

MRS. BORKMAN (*regards her solemnly*). Erhart has an obligation, before all else, to achieve a brilliance of such height and scope that not one person in this country will still recall the shadow his father cast over me—and over my son.

ELLA (*incisively*). Tell me, Gunhild—is that the aim Erhart himself has for his own life—?

MRS. BORKMAN (*startled*). Well, let's hope so!

ELLA. Or isn't it rather an aim that you've imposed on him?

MRS. BORKMAN (*brusquely*). Erhart and I always share the same goals.

ELLA (*slowly and sadly*). Are you so very sure of your son, then, Gunhild?

MRS. BORKMAN (*secretly exulting*). Yes, thank God, I am. You can be positive of that!

ELLA. Then, I think, at heart you must feel you've been lucky after all. In spite of everything.

MRS. BORKMAN. Oh, I do—in that respect. But, every other moment, you see, the rest of it comes sweeping over me like a tempest.

ELLA (*her tone changing*). Tell me—and you might as well right away, since it's actually why I've come—

MRS. BORKMAN. What?

ELLA. Something I feel I have to talk to you about— Tell me, Erhart doesn't live out here with—with the family?

MRS. BORKMAN (*sharply*). Erhart *can't* live out here with me. He's got to live in town—

ELLA. He wrote me that.

MRS. BORKMAN. He's got to, because of his studies. But every evening he stops out and visits me for a while.

ELLA. Then perhaps I could see him? And speak to him right now?

MRS. BORKMAN. He hasn't come yet. But I expect him any minute.

ELLA. But, Gunhild—I'm sure he's here. I hear him walking upstairs.

MRS. BORKMAN (*with a quick upward glance*). Up in the salon?

ELLA. Yes. I've heard him walking there ever since I came.

MRS. BORKMAN (*averting her eyes*). That's not Erhart, Ella.

ELLA (*puzzled*). Not Erhart? (*Surmising.*) Who is it then?

MRS. BORKMAN. It's him.

ELLA (*quietly, with stifled grief*). Borkman! John Gabriel!

MRS. BORKMAN. That's how he walks, up and down. Back and forth. From morning to night. Day in and day out.

ELLA. Of course I've heard rumors about—things—

MRS. BORKMAN. No doubt. There must be a lot of rumors about us.

ELLA. Erhart has hinted of it. In his letters. That his father kept mainly to himself—up there. And you, alone down here.

MRS. BORKMAN. Yes. We've lived like that, Ella. Ever since they released him, and sent him home to me. All these eight long years.

ELLA. But I've never thought it could really be true. Or possible—!

MRS. BORKMAN (*nods*). It's true. And it can never be different.

ELLA (*looking at her*). It must be a horrible existence, Gunhild.

MRS. BORKMAN. More than horrible. I can't bear it much longer.

ELLA. I understand.

MRS. BORKMAN. Always hearing his footsteps up there. From early morning till far into the night. And so loud, as if they were here in this room!

ELLA. Yes, it's strange how the sound carries.

MRS. BORKMAN. Often I have the feeling that I have a sick wolf pacing his cage up in the salon. Right over my head. (*Listens, then whispers.*) Hear that, Ella! Listen! Back and forth—back and forth, the wolf pacing.

ELLA (*hesitatingly*). Couldn't things be different, Gunhild?

MRS. BORKMAN (*with a disdainful gesture*). He's never made one move in that direction.

ELLA. Couldn't you make the first move, then?

MRS. BORKMAN (*incensed*). I? After all I've suffered from him! No thanks! Let the wolf go on roaming his cage.

ELLA. It's too warm for me in here. If I may, I'll take my coat off after all.

MRS. BORKMAN. Yes, I asked you before—

(ELLA *removes her hat and coat, laying them on a chair by the hall door*.)

ELLA. Don't you ever run into him outside the house?

MRS. BORKMAN (*with a bitter laugh*). Out in society, you mean?

ELLA. I mean, when he's out for some air. On a path in the woods, or—

MRS. BORKMAN. He never goes out.

ELLA. Not even at dusk.

MRS. BORKMAN. Never.

ELLA (*touched*). He can't even face that?

MRS. BORKMAN. Apparently not. He has his great cape and his hat hanging in the closet. In the hall, you know—

ELLA (*to herself*). The one we played in when we were little—

MRS. BORKMAN (*nodding*). And every so often—late in the evening—I hear him coming down—to put on his things and go out. But then he stops, usually halfway down the stairs—and turns back. Back to the salon.

ELLA (*softly*). Don't any of his old friends ever stop up to see him?

MRS. BORKMAN. He has no old friends.

ELLA. He had so many, once.

MRS. BORKMAN. Hm! He found a very nice way to shed them. He became an expensive friend to have, this John Gabriel.

ELLA. Yes, I guess you're right.

MRS. BORKMAN (*heatedly*). Nevertheless, I must say it's mean, cheap, petty, and contemptible to lay so much weight on any minor losses they may have suffered through him. It was only money, after all.

ELLA (*not answering*). So he lives up there quite alone. In isolation.

MRS. BORKMAN. Yes, that's about it. I hear there's an old clerk or copyist who stops up to see him occasionally.

ELLA. Oh yes. That would be Foldal, most likely. I know they were friends in their early years.

MRS. BORKMAN. Yes, I believe so. I know nothing about him, otherwise. He was never part of our set. When we had one—

ELLA. But *now* he comes out to Borkman?

MRS. BORKMAN. Yes, he's not fastidious. But naturally he only comes after dark.

ELLA. This Foldal—he was among the ones who had losses when the bank failed.

MRS. BORKMAN (*indifferently*). I do seem to remember that he lost some money also. But it was quite insignificant.

ELLA (*stressing her words slightly*). It was everything he had.

MRS. BORKMAN (*smiles*). Well, but, my Lord—what he had: that was next to nothing. Hardly worth mentioning.

ELLA. It never was mentioned, was it, at the trial—by Foldal?

MRS. BORKMAN. Furthermore, I can tell you that Erhart has amply compensated for any pittance he may have lost.

ELLA (*surprised*). Erhart? How has he managed that?

MRS. BORKMAN. He's been looking after Foldal's younger daughter. And helping to educate her—so she can make something of herself and be independent someday. That's certainly more than her father ever could have done for her.

ELLA. Yes, her father must be starving along, I can imagine.

MRS. BORKMAN. And then Erhart's arranged music lessons for her. She's already so practiced at it that she can go up—up to him in the salon and play for him.

ELLA. So he still loves music?

MRS. BORKMAN. Oh, I suppose so. He's got the piano you sent out—when he was expected home—

ELLA. And she plays on that?

MRS. BORKMAN. Yes, just now and then. In the evenings. Erhart took care of that, too.

ELLA. The poor girl has to travel all the way out here? And then back to town again?

MRS. BORKMAN. Not at all. Erhart's settled it that she stays with a lady here in the neighborhood. A Mrs. Wilton—

ELLA (*fascinated*). Mrs. Wilton!

MRS. BORKMAN. A very rich woman. Not anyone you know.

ELLA. I've heard the name. Mrs. Fanny Wilton, I believe—

MRS. BORKMAN. Yes, exactly—

ELLA. Erhart's written about her in several of his letters. Is she living out here now?

MRS. BORKMAN. Yes, she rented a house and moved out from town a while ago.

ELLA (*hesitating a bit*). They say that she's divorced.

MRS. BORKMAN. Her husband's been dead for several years.

ELLA. Yes, but they were divorced. He divorced her.

MRS. BORKMAN. He deserted her, actually. The fault certainly wasn't on her side.

ELLA. Do you know her fairly well, Gunhild?

MRS. BORKMAN. Why, yes, of course. She lives quite near and looks in on me every so often.

ELLA. You like her?

MRS. BORKMAN. She's exceptionally understanding. And remarkably clear in her perceptions.

ELLA. Of people, you mean?

MRS. BORKMAN. Particularly of people. She's made a thorough study of Erhart. Really profound—into his very soul. And consequently, she idolizes him—which is only reasonable.

ELLA (*slyly*). So perhaps she knows Erhart even more intimately than she knows you.

MRS. BORKMAN. Yes, they got together quite a bit in town. Before she moved out here.

ELLA (*impulsively*). And still she moved from town—?

MRS. BORKMAN (*starts and looks narrowly at her*). Still!
What do you mean by that?

ELLA (*evasively*). Oh, now really—by that?

MRS. BORKMAN. You said it in such a peculiar way. You
did mean something, Ella!

ELLA (*meeting her eyes directly*). Yes, it's true, Gunhild. I meant something, all right.

MRS. BORKMAN. Well then, out with it!

ELLA. First of all *this:* that I feel I also have a certain
kind of right to Erhart. Or maybe you don't agree?

MRS. BORKMAN (*gazing about the room*). My gracious
—after the amounts you've spent on him—

ELLA. Oh, that's no reason, Gunhild. But because I love
him—

MRS. BORKMAN (*smiles scornfully*). My son? Can you
love him? You? In spite of everything?

ELLA. Yes, I can, in spite of everything. And I do. I
love Erhart—as much as I could ever love anyone—now,
at my age.

MRS. BORKMAN. Yes, yes, all right—

ELLA. So you see, that's why I get upset the instant I see
anything threatening him.

MRS. BORKMAN. Threatening Erhart! Well, but what
threatens him? Or *who* does?

ELLA. You, to start with—in *your* way—

MRS. BORKMAN. I!

ELLA. And then this Mrs. Wilton, too—she frightens
me.

MRS. BORKMAN (*stares at her, momentarily speechless*).
How can you think anything of the kind about Erhart!
About my own son! He, with his great mission to fulfill!

ELLA (*disdainfully*). Oh, come, his mission—!

MRS. BORKMAN (*furiously*). How dare you take that
arrogant tone!

ELLA. Do you suppose that a young person of Erhart's

age—healthy and exuberant—do you suppose that he'll go out and sacrifice himself—for anything like a "mission"?

MRS. BORKMAN (*tenaciously*). Erhart will! I know it for a fact!

ELLA (*shaking her head*). You neither know it nor believe it, Gunhild.

MRS. BORKMAN. Don't I!

ELLA. It's only something you dream about. Because if you didn't have that to cling to, you're afraid you'd give way to total despair.

MRS. BORKMAN. Yes, then I'd really be in despair. (*Fiercely.*) And perhaps that's what you'd like to see most, Ella!

ELLA (*her head held high*). Yes, I would—if you can't liberate yourself except by victimizing Erhart.

MRS. BORKMAN (*threateningly*). You want to come between us! Between mother and son! *You!*

ELLA. I want to free him from your power—your control—your domination.

MRS. BORKMAN (*triumphantly*). You've lost your chance! You had him in your net—right up to his fifteenth year. But now, you see, I've won him back!

ELLA. Then I'll win him again from you! (*In a rasping, near whisper.*) The two of us, we've already fought like savages once for a man!

MRS. BORKMAN (*looks at her, gloatingly*). Yes, and *I* was victorious.

ELLA (*with a mocking smile*). Do you still think that victory won you anything?

MRS. BORKMAN (*somberly*). No—that's God's own truth.

ELLA. You won't win anything this time, either.

MRS. BORKMAN. Won't win, by asserting a mother's power over her boy!

ELLA. No, because it's only *power* over him that you want.

MRS. BORKMAN. And you?

ELLA (*with warmth*). I want his affections—his soul—his whole heart—!

MRS. BORKMAN (*explosively*). You won't get them again, ever in this world!

ELLA (*eyeing her*). You've seen to that?

MRS. BORKMAN (*smiles*). Yes. I've indulged that privilege. Couldn't you read that in his letters?

ELLA (*slowly nods*). Yes. His last letters have been you, completely.

MRS. BORKMAN (*baiting her*). I've made use of these eight years—while I've had him under my eyes, you see.

ELLA (*with restraint*). What have you told him about me? If it's proper to discuss?

MRS. BORKMAN. Oh, it's quite proper to.

ELLA. Then discuss it!

MRS. BORKMAN. I've merely told him the truth.

ELLA. Well?

MRS. BORKMAN. I've everlastingly impressed upon him that he must please be sure to remember that it's you we have to thank for the fact that we can live as decently as we do. Or that we *can* live at all.

ELLA. No more than that?

MRS. BORKMAN. Oh, such knowledge festers. It does in me.

ELLA. But it's hardly different from what Erhart knew before.

MRS. BORKMAN. When he came back home to me, he imagined that you did all this out of a kind heart. (*Looks vindictively at her.*) Now he doesn't think that any longer.

ELLA. What does he think now?

MRS. BORKMAN. He thinks the truth. I asked him how he could explain why Aunt Ella never came to visit us—

ELLA (*interrupting*). He knew why already!

MRS. BORKMAN. Now he knows even better. You'd made him believe that it was to spare me—and him, upstairs.

ELLA. And it was.

MRS. BORKMAN. Erhart doesn't believe a word of it any-more.

ELLA. What have you gotten him to believe about me?

MRS. BORKMAN. He believes the truth: that you're ashamed of us—and you despise us. Or maybe you don't? Didn't you once intend to take him away from me alto-gether? Think, Ella. You're sure to remember.

ELLA (*shrugging it off*). That was at the worst of the scandal—when the case was in court. I no longer cherish that thought.

MRS. BORKMAN. It wouldn't profit you if you did. Then what would become of his mission? No, thank you! It's me Erhart needs—not you. And so he's the same as dead for you! And you for him!

ELLA (*coldly determined*). We'll see. Because now I'm staying here.

MRS. BORKMAN (*staring at her*). At this house?

ELLA. Yes.

MRS. BORKMAN. Here—with us? Overnight?

ELLA. I'm staying here all the rest of my days, if it's so granted.

MRS. BORKMAN (*composing herself*). Yes, yes, Ella—of course, the house is yours.

ELLA. Oh, stop—!

MRS. BORKMAN. Everything in it is yours. The chair I sit on is yours. The bed I lie on, tossing sleeplessly, belongs to you. The food we eat we get thanks to you.

ELLA. There's no other way of doing things. Borkman can't have property in his own name. In no time someone would come and take possession of it.

MRS. BORKMAN. I'm aware of that. We have to bear with living on your mercy and charity.

ELLA (*coldly*). I can't help your seeing it that way, Gunhild.

MRS. BORKMAN. No, you can't. When will you want us to move?

ELLA (*looking at her*). To move?

MRS. BORKMAN (*excitedly*). Yes, you certainly don't imagine that I'll remain living here under the same roof with you! I'd rather go to the poorhouse, or take to the roads!

ELLA. All right. Then let me have Erhart—

MRS. BORKMAN. Erhart! My only son? My child?

ELLA. Yes. Because in that case I'll go right back home.

MRS. BORKMAN (*after a brief deliberation, firmly*). Erhart himself can choose between us.

ELLA (*looking doubtfully at her*). Let *him* choose? But —can you risk that, Gunhild?

MRS. BORKMAN (*with a hard laugh*). Can I risk—my boy choosing between his mother and you! Why, yes, I'll risk that.

ELLA (*listening*). Is someone coming? I think I hear—

MRS. BORKMAN. That's probably Erhart—

(*There is a brisk knock on the hall door, which then is opened right away.* MRS. WILTON, *wearing an evening gown under her winter coat, comes in. The* MAID, *having had no time to announce her, follows her in, looking bewildered.* MRS. WILTON *is a singularly handsome woman, with a ripe figure, somewhere in her thirties. She has full, red, smiling lips, mischievous eyes, and rich, dark hair.*)

MRS. WILTON. Mrs. Borkman, dear, good evening!

MRS. BORKMAN (*somewhat dryly*). Good evening, Mrs. Wilton. (*To the* MAID, *pointing to the garden room.*) Take the lamp in there out and light it.

(*The* MAID *fetches the lamp and goes out with it.*)

MRS. WILTON (*seeing* ELLA). Oh, excuse me—you have guests—

MRS. BORKMAN. Only my sister, Ella Rentheim, who's visiting—

(ERHART BORKMAN *comes storming through the half-opened door, flinging it back. He is a young man, elegantly dressed, with gay, sparkling eyes. He shows early signs of a moustache.*)

ERHART (*radiating delight, as he pauses on the threshold*). What's this! Has Aunt Ella come? (*He rushes up to her, seizing her hands.*) Aunt Ella! No, is it possible! Are *you* here?

ELLA (*throwing her arms about him*). Erhart! My dear, sweet boy. My, how big you've grown! Oh, it does me good to see you again!

MRS. BORKMAN (*sharply*). What does this mean, Erhart? Hiding yourself out in the hall.

MRS. WILTON (*hurriedly*). Erhart—Mr. Borkman arrived with me.

MRS. BORKMAN (*gauging him with her eyes*). So, Erhart. You don't come first to your mother?

ERHART. I only had to stop by Mrs. Wilton's for a second—to pick up Frida.

MRS. BORKMAN. You have Miss Foldal along, too?

MRS. WILTON. Yes, we've left her waiting in the entryway.

ERHART (*calling out through the doorway*). Just go right up, Frida.

(*A pause.* ELLA *studies* ERHART. *He appears self-conscious and rather impatient; his face assumes a tense, colder expression. The* MAID *comes in with the lighted lamp for the garden room, then withdraws, closing the door behind her.*)

MRS. BORKMAN (*with constrained politeness*). Well, Mrs. Wilton—if you'd like to settle down here for the evening, why—

MRS. WILTON. Thank you ever so much, Mrs. Borkman, dear—but I don't see how I can. We've got another invitation. We're expected down at Mr. Hinkel's.

MRS. BORKMAN (*looking at her*). We? Which "we" do you mean?

MRS. WILTON (*laughing*). Well, really I just mean myself. But I was delegated by the ladies of the house to bring along Mr. Borkman—if I happened to set eyes on him.

MRS. BORKMAN. And you happened to, as I can see.

MRS. WILTON. Yes, fortunately. Since he was so accommodating as to look in on me—for little Frida's sake.

MRS. BORKMAN (*dryly*). But, Erhart—I had no idea you were acquainted with this family—the Hinkels.

ERHART (*vexed*). No, I'm really not acquainted with them at all. (*Continues somewhat impatiently.*) You know very well yourself, Mother, the people I do or don't know.

MRS. WILTON. Oh, pish! One soon gets acquainted in *that* house! Gay, amusing, hospitable people. And teeming with young ladies.

MRS. BORKMAN (*emphatically*). If I know my son, Mrs. Wilton, that's scarcely the proper company for him.

MRS. WILTON. But, my gracious, dear, he's young himself, you know!

MRS. BORKMAN. Yes, luckily he's young. With those people he'd have to be.

ERHART (*masking his impatience*). Yes, yes, yes, Mother—it's self-evident that I have no business going down to the Hinkels' this evening. Naturally, I'll be staying here with you and Aunt Ella.

MRS. BORKMAN. I was sure you would, dear.

ELLA. No, Erhart—don't stay away on my behalf—

ERHART. Why, certainly, Aunt Ella; there's nothing more to discuss. (*Looks hesitantly at* MRS. WILTON.) But how can we explain it? Will it be acceptable? After all, you've already told them "yes" for me.

MRS. WILTON (*vivaciously*). What nonsense! Why shouldn't it be acceptable? When I make my way down into that room after room of shimmering festivities— lonely and abandoned—can you picture it?— Why, then I'll have to tell them "no"—for you.

ERHART (*grudgingly*). Well, if you honestly think it'll be acceptable—

MRS. WILTON (*dismissing it lightly*). I've said a great many "yeses" and "noes" in my time—for myself. And how could you leave your aunt, when she's only now just come? For shame, Monsieur Erhart—is that any way for a son to behave?

MRS. BORKMAN (*piqued*). For a son?

MRS. WILTON. Well, for a foster son, then, Mrs. Bork-man.

MRS. BORKMAN. Yes, you ought to add that.

MRS. WILTON. Oh, I think one has more to thank a good foster mother for than one's real mother.

MRS. BORKMAN. Was that your own experience?

MRS. WILTON. Regrettably. I hardly even knew my mother. But if I'd had such a good foster mother, then perhaps I wouldn't have turned out as—as wicked as people say I am. (*To* ERHART.) So you stay snug at home now with mama and your aunt—and drink tea! (*To the ladies.*) Good-bye, good-bye, Mrs. Borkman, dear. Good-bye, Miss Rentheim!

(*The ladies bow silently. She goes toward the door.*)

ERHART (*following her*). Shouldn't I escort you part-way—?

MRS. WILTON (*by the door, motioning him away*). Not one step. I'm very well accustomed to making my way along. (*Standing in the doorway, eyeing him and nodding.*) But now you better watch out, Mr. Borkman—I'm warning you.

ERHART. Why must I watch out?

MRS. WILTON (*roguishly*). Because when I'm going down the road—lonely and abandoned, as I said—then I'll try to cast a spell on you.

ERHART (*laughing*). Oh, I see! You're going to try *that* again.

MRS. WILTON (*half seriously*). Yes, so you be careful. When I'm going along, I'll talk to myself—right out of my innermost secret will, and I'll say: "Erhart Borkman, take your hat this instant!"

MRS. BORKMAN. And do you think he will?

MRS. WILTON (*laughing*). Oh, absolutely; he'll pick up his hat like a shot. And then I'll say: "Put on your overcoat nicely, Erhart Borkman. And the galoshes! Don't you dare forget your galoshes! And then, follow after me! Tenderly. Tenderly. Tenderly."

ERHART (*with forced gaiety*). Yes, you can depend on me.

MRS. WILTON (*her forefinger uplifted*). Tenderly! Tenderly! Good night!

(*She laughs, nods to the ladies, and shuts the door after her.*)

MRS. BORKMAN. Does she really perform such tricks?

ERHART. Oh, of course not. How can you think so? It's only a joke. (*Breaking off.*) But let's not talk now about Mrs. Wilton. (*He presses* ELLA *to sit in the armchair by the stove and stands looking at her briefly.*) Imagine your taking the long trip here, Aunt Ella. And now, in the dead of winter!

ELLA. In the end I just couldn't put it off, Erhart.

ERHART. Oh? Why was that?

ELLA. I had to come in for a consultation with the doctors.

ERHART. Well, that's good.

ELLA (*smiles*). You think that's good?

ERHART. That you finally decided to, I mean.

MRS. BORKMAN (*from the sofa, coldly*). Ella, are you ill?

ELLA. You know very well I'm ill.

MRS. BORKMAN. Well, I know you've been semi-invalid for a good many years.

ERHART. The whole time I stayed with you I kept telling you that you ought to be seeing a doctor.

ELLA. Oh, up where I live, there's nobody I have any confidence in. Besides, it didn't bother me so much then.

ERHART. You're feeling worse now?

ELLA. Oh yes, dear; I've taken something of a turn for the worse.

ERHART. But nothing dangerous, though?

ELLA. Well, that's all in the way one takes it.

ERHART (*warmly*). Yes, but now listen, Aunt Ella—then you mustn't make the trip home again so soon.

ELLA. No, I don't intend to, either.

ERHART. You've got to stay here in town. Because here you have all the best doctors to choose from.

ELLA. Yes, that was my thought when I left home.

ERHART. Then you should try to find some really nice accommodations—in some quiet, cozy pension.

ELLA. I checked in this morning at the old place where I've stayed before.

ERHART. Oh yes, *there* you can be comfortable.

ELLA. All the same, I don't think I'll be staying there.

ERHART. Really? Why not?

ELLA. No, I decided differently when I came out here.

ERHART (*puzzled*). Oh—? You decided—?

MRS. BORKMAN (*crocheting, without looking up*). Your aunt wants to live here on her estate, Erhart.

ERHART (*glancing from one to the other*). Here? With us! With all of us! Is that true, Aunt Ella?

ELLA. Yes, that's my decision now.

MRS. BORKMAN (*as before*). Everything here is your aunt's, you know.

ELLA. So I'll be staying on here, Erhart. At first, anyway. For a time. I'll make my own provisions, over in the annex—

ERHART. That's the right idea. There are always rooms standing empty over there. (*Suddenly animated.*) But actually, Aunt Ella—aren't you pretty tired after your trip?

ELLA. Oh, I'm a bit tired, yes.

ERHART. Well, then I think you ought to go off early to bed.

ELLA (*regards him with a smile*). So I shall.

ERHART (*fervently*). Because then we could talk more freely tomorrow—or another day. About everything possible. You and Mother and I. Wouldn't that be much better, Aunt Ella?

MRS. BORKMAN (*vehemently, rising from the sofa*). Erhart—I can see by your look that you want to leave me!

ERHART (*unsettled*). What do you mean?

MRS. BORKMAN. You want to go on to—to the Hinkels' place!

ERHART (*involuntarily*). Oh, that! (*Composing himself.*) Well, do you think I ought to sit here, keeping Aunt Ella up until way into the night? She *is* ill, Mother. Remember that.

MRS. BORKMAN. You want to go to the Hinkels', Erhart!

ERHART (*impatiently*). Well, but good Lord, Mother—I don't see how I can very well pass it up. What do you say, Aunt Ella?

ELLA. It's best if you'll act in complete freedom, Erhart.

MRS. BORKMAN (*turns on her menacingly*). You want to tear him from me!

ELLA (*rising*). Yes, Gunhild, if I only could!

(*Music is heard overhead.*)

ERHART (*writhing as if in pain*). Oh, I can't take this anymore! (*He peers about him.*) Where'd I leave my hat? (*To* ELLA.) Do you know that music upstairs?

ELLA. No. What is it?

ERHART. It's the *Danse Macabre*. The Dance of Death. Don't you know the Dance of Death, Aunt Ella?

ELLA (*smiles sorrowfully*). Not yet, Erhart.

ERHART (*to* MRS. BORKMAN). Mother—I appeal to you, please—do let me go!

MRS. BORKMAN (*looks sternly at him*). From your mother? You want that?

ERHART. I'll be coming out again—maybe tomorrow.

MRS. BORKMAN (*in passionate agitation*). You want to leave me! To be out with those strangers! With—with— no, I won't even think of it!

ERHART. There are so many shimmering lights down there. And young, happy faces. And there's music there, Mother!

MRS. BORKMAN (*pointing up toward the ceiling*). Up- stairs there's also music, Erhart.

ERHART. Yes, it's that music *there*—that's what's hounding me out of this house.

ELLA. Can't you allow your father a little chance to forget himself?

ERHART. Yes, I can. I can allow it a thousand times over—if I just don't have to hear it myself.

MRS. BORKMAN (*looks reprovingly at him*). Be strong, Erhart! Strong, my son! Don't ever forget you have a great mission!

ERHART. Oh, Mother—don't make those phrases! I wasn't created to be a missionary! Good night, Aunt Ella. Good night, Mother.

(*He hurries out down the hall.*)

MRS. BORKMAN (*after a short silence*). You've retaken him soon enough, at any rate, Ella.

ELLA. I wish I dared believe that.

MRS. BORKMAN. But you're not going to hold him for long, you'll see.

ELLA. Thanks to you?

MRS. BORKMAN. To me, or—to her, that other one.

ELLA. Better her than you.

MRS. BORKMAN (*nodding slowly*). I understand that. I say the same. Better her than you.

ELLA. Whatever the end result for him—

MRS. BORKMAN. That scarcely matters now, I think.

ELLA (*taking her coat over her arm*). For the first time in our lives, we two twin sisters are of one mind. Good night, Gunhild. (*Goes out down the hall.*)

(*The music swells in sound from overhead.*)

MRS. BORKMAN (*stands quietly a moment, gives a start, recoils and whispers involuntarily*). The wolf howling again. The sick wolf. (*She stays standing a moment, then hurls herself down on the floor, writhing and moaning, and whispers in anguish.*) Erhart! Erhart—be true to me! Oh, come home and help your mother! I can't bear this life any longer!

ᖰ ACT TWO ᖳ

The former grand salon upstairs in the Rentheim house.
The walls are covered with old tapestries, depicting hunt-
ing scenes, shepherds and shepherdesses, in faded, mottled
colors. In the wall to the left, a sliding door, and closer in
the foreground, a piano. In the left rear corner, an un-
framed door decorated with tapestry to blend with the
background. At the middle of the right-hand wall, a large
curved oak desk, with many books and papers. Further
forward on the same side, a sofa, along with a table and
chairs. All the furniture is in austere Empire style. On the
desk and table, lighted lamps.

JOHN GABRIEL BORKMAN *is standing by the piano, his*
hands clasped behind his back, listening to FRIDA FOLDAL,
who sits playing the last measures of the Danse Macabre.
BORKMAN *is a man in his sixties, of medium height, strong-*
ly and compactly built. His appearance is distinguished,
with a finely chiseled profile, piercing eyes, and curling,
grayish-white hair and beard. He is dressed in a black,
somewhat old-fashioned suit, with a white necktie. FRIDA
FOLDAL *is a good-looking, pale girl of fifteen, with a rather*
tired, strained expression; she wears a cheap, light-colored
dress. The music comes to an end. Silence.

BORKMAN. Can you guess where I first heard such music
as this?

FRIDA (*looking up at him*). No, Mr. Borkman.

BORKMAN. It was down in the mines.

FRIDA (*not understanding*). You did? In the mines?

351

BORKMAN. I'm a miner's son, as I guess you know. Or maybe you didn't know that?

FRIDA. No, Mr. Borkman.

BORKMAN. A miner's son. And my father took me down with him sometimes, into the mines. Down there the metal sings.

FRIDA. Really? It sings.

BORKMAN (*nods*). When the ore is loosened. The hammer blows that loosen it—they're like the midnight bell that strikes and sets it free. And so the metal sings—for joy—in its way.

FRIDA. Why does it do that, Mr. Borkman?

BORKMAN. It wants to come up into daylight and serve mankind. (*He paces back and forth across the salon, his hands still behind his back.*)

FRIDA (*sits and waits for a moment, then looks at her watch and gets up*). Pardon me, Mr. Borkman—but I'm afraid I have to go now.

BORKMAN (*stopping in front of her*). You're going so soon?

FRIDA (*putting her music away in a folder*). Yes, I really have to. (*Visibly embarrassed.*) I've been engaged for this evening elsewhere.

BORKMAN. Elsewhere, meaning a party?

FRIDA. Yes.

BORKMAN. And you're going to give them a concert?

FRIDA (*biting her lip*). No—I'm going to play for the dancing.

BORKMAN. Only for dancing?

FRIDA. Yes, they want to dance after supper.

BORKMAN (*stands, looking at her*). Do you like to play for dances? Around in different houses?

FRIDA (*putting on her winter coat*). Yes, when I can get an engagement— It always brings in a little something.

BORKMAN. Is *that* what you think about most while you sit playing for the dancers?

FRIDA. No. I mostly think how sad it is that I can't join in the dancing myself.

BORKMAN (*nods*). That's precisely what I wanted to know. (*Walks restlessly about the salon.*) Yes, yes, yes— this thing that one can't join in oneself, that hurts the most. (*Stops.*) But then there *is* something that evens it up for you, Frida.

FRIDA (*looks curiously at him*). What's that, Mr. Borkman?

BORKMAN. The sense that you've got ten times more music in you than in all the dancers put together.

FRIDA (*smiles diffidently*). Oh, that's far from certain.

BORKMAN (*admonishing her with upraised forefinger*). Don't ever be so foolish as to doubt yourself!

FRIDA. But, good heavens, if nobody knows it—?

BORKMAN. As long as *you* know it, then that's enough. Where is it you're playing this evening?

FRIDA. Over at Mr. Hinkel's.

BORKMAN (*gives her an abrupt, penetrating look*). Mr. Hinkel's, you say!

FRIDA. Yes.

BORKMAN (*with a bitter smile*). Do guests come to that man's house? Can he get people to visit him?

FRIDA. Yes, lots of people are coming, from what Mrs. Wilton says.

BORKMAN (*heatedly*). But what kind of people? Can you tell me that?

FRIDA (*a bit apprehensively*). No, I really don't know. Oh, for one—I do know young Mr. Borkman's going.

BORKMAN (*jarred*). Erhart! My son?

FRIDA. Yes, he'll be there.

BORKMAN. How do you know that?

FRIDA. He said so himself. Just an hour ago.

BORKMAN. Is he out here today?

FRIDA. Yes, he's been at Mrs. Wilton's the whole afternoon.

BORKMAN (*probingly*). Do you know if he stopped here, too? If he was in to speak with anyone downstairs, I mean?

FRIDA. Yes, he was in seeing Mrs. Borkman a while.

BORKMAN (*stung*). Aha—I might have known.

FRIDA. But there was also a strange lady with her, I think.

BORKMAN. Oh? Was there? Ah well, I expect people do visit her every so often.

FRIDA. Should I tell your son, if I meet him later, that he ought to come up to see you, too?

BORKMAN (*brusquely*). Don't say anything! I expressly forbid it! People who want to look in on me can find their way by themselves. I beg from no one.

FRIDA. No, no, then I won't say anything. Good night, Mr. Borkman.

BORKMAN (*roams about the room and growls*). Good night.

FRIDA. Do you suppose I could run down the spiral staircase? It's quicker.

BORKMAN. Oh, good grief—run down whatever stairs you like, for all I care. Good night to you!

FRIDA. Good night, Mr. Borkman.

(*She leaves through the little tapestry door in the left background.* BORKMAN, *deep in thought, goes over to the piano, about to close it, then lets it be. He gazes at all the emptiness surrounding him and starts pacing up and down the floor from the corner by the piano to the corner in the right background—disquieted and restless, ceaselessly back and forth. Finally he goes over to the desk, listens in the direction of the sliding door, quickly picks up a hand-mirror, studies himself in it, and adjusts his necktie. There is a knock on the sliding door.* BORKMAN *hears it, glances hastily toward the door, but remains silent. A moment later, the knock sounds again, louder this time.*)

BORKMAN (*standing by the desk, his left hand resting on its top, his right thrust in the breast of his coat*). Come in!

(VILHELM FOLDAL *warily enters the room. He is a bent,*
worn man with mild blue eyes and long, thin gray hair
falling down over his coat collar. He has a portfolio under
his arm, a soft felt hat in one hand and large horn-rimmed
glasses, which he pushes up on his forehead.)

BORKMAN (*changes his stance and regards his visitor*
with a half-disappointed, half-gratified expression). Oh, it's
only you.

FOLDAL. Good evening, John Gabriel. Yes, quite so, it's
me.

BORKMAN (*with a severe look*). By the way, I think
you're rather late.

FOLDAL. Well, the distance isn't exactly short, you
know. Especially for someone on foot.

BORKMAN. But why do you always walk, Vilhelm?
You're right by the streetcar.

FOLDAL. It's healthier to walk. And then there's the
carfare saved. Well, has Frida been up to play for you
lately?

BORKMAN. She left only this minute. You didn't meet
her outside?

FOLDAL. No, I haven't set eyes on her for a long time.
Not since she started living at this Mrs. Wilton's.

BORKMAN (*sits on the sofa and motions with a wave of*
his hand toward a chair). You're welcome to a seat,
Vilhelm.

FOLDAL (*perching on the edge of a chair*). Many thanks.
(*Looks at him in dejection.*) Oh, you can't imagine how
lonely I feel since Frida left home.

BORKMAN. Oh, come—you've got more in reserve.

FOLDAL. God knows I do. Five in the lot. But Frida was
the only one that understood me a little. (*Shakes his head*
dolefully.) The others can't understand me at all.

BORKMAN (*somberly, staring into space and drumming*
his fingers on the table). No, that's a fact. *That's* the curse
that we, the exceptional, the chosen human beings have to
bear. The masses—all the gray average—they don't understand us, Vilhelm.

FOLDAL (*resignedly*). Understanding can take care of itself. With a little patience, one can always wait a bit longer for that. (*His voice chokes with tears.*) But there's something more bitter still.

BORKMAN (*fiercely*). Nothing's more bitter than that!

FOLDAL. Yes, there is, John Gabriel. I've just had a domestic scene—before I came out here.

BORKMAN. Really? Why?

FOLDAL (*in an outburst*). My family—they have contempt for me.

BORKMAN (*incensed*). Contempt—!

FOLDAL (*wiping his eyes*). I've been sensing it for a long time. But today it really came out.

BORKMAN (*after a pause*). You made a decidedly poor choice when you married.

FOLDAL. I scarcely had any choice. And besides—one has an urge to get married when one starts getting on in years. And then being so distressed, so down at the heels as I was then—

BORKMAN (*springing up angrily*). Is that a recrimination against me! A reproof—!

FOLDAL (*anxiously*). No, for God's sake, John Gabriel—!

BORKMAN. Yes, you've been brooding about all the trouble that struck the bank—!

FOLDAL (*reassuringly*). But I don't blame *you* for *that!* I swear—!

BORKMAN (*resumes his seat, grumbling*). Well, that's good.

FOLDAL. Also, you mustn't think it's my wife I'm complaining about. She hasn't much refinement, poor thing, it's true. But, all the same, she does pretty well. No, it's the children—

BORKMAN. I'm not surprised.

FOLDAL. Because the children—you see, they have more culture. And make more demands on life.

BORKMAN (*looks sympathetically at him*). And that's why your young ones have contempt for you, Vilhelm?

FOLDAL (*shrugging his shoulders*). I haven't made much of a career, you see. No getting around that—

BORKMAN (*drawing closer and laying his hand on* FOLDAL'*s arm*). Don't they know that you wrote a tragedy when you were young?

FOLDAL. Yes, they know that, of course. But it doesn't seem to make any particular impression on them.

BORKMAN. Then they're insensitive. Because your tragedy is good. I believe that unshakably.

FOLDAL (*brightening*). Yes, don't you feel there's a lot that's good in it, John Gabriel? Lord love me, if I only could get it staged—! (*He eagerly opens the portfolio and shuffles the papers in it.*) Look here! Now let me show you something I revised—

BORKMAN. You have it with you?

FOLDAL. Yes, I brought it along. It's such a long time now since I read it to you. So I thought it might divert you to hear an act or two—

BORKMAN (*waving him off as he gets up*). No, no, it can better wait till another time.

FOLDAL. Yes, yes, as you like.

(BORKMAN *paces back and forth across the room.* FOLDAL *packs away his manuscript again.*)

BORKMAN (*stopping in front of him*). You were right in what you were just saying—that you hadn't made a career. But I promise you this, Vilhelm, that once the hour of restitution strikes for me—

FOLDAL (*starts to rise*). Ah, thank you—!

BORKMAN (*motioning him down*). If you'll just stay seated, please. (*With mounting fervor.*) When the hour of restitution strikes for me—when they realize that they can't dispense with me—when they come up to me here in this room—and eat crow and beg me to take the reins of the bank again—! The new bank that they've founded— and can't direct— (*He poses by the desk as before and strikes his chest.*) Here's where I'll stand and greet them! And all over this land they'll ask and they'll learn what terms John Gabriel Borkman sets before he'll— (*Stops abruptly and stares at* FOLDAL.) You're giving me such a doubtful look! Maybe you don't think they'll come? That they *must—must—must* come to me one of these days? You don't think so!

FOLDAL. Why, God knows I do, John Gabriel, yes.

BORKMAN (*sitting again on the sofa*). I believe that, unshakably. I *know*—with absolute certainty—that they'll come. If I didn't have that certainty—then I would have put a bullet through my head long ago.

FOLDAL (*in alarm*). Oh, no, don't ever say—!

BORKMAN (*exultantly*). But they'll come! They're coming! You wait! Any day, any hour, I can expect them here. And, as you can see, I hold myself in readiness to welcome them.

FOLDAL (*with a sigh*). If only they'd get here soon.

BORKMAN (*restlessly*). Yes, old friend, time passes; the years pass; life—oh, no—I mustn't think about that! (*Looking at him.*) You know what I feel like sometimes?

FOLDAL. What?

BORKMAN. I feel like a Napoleon, maimed in his first battle.

FOLDAL (*touching his portfolio*). I know that feeling.

BORKMAN. Oh yes, well, that's on a smaller scale.

FOLDAL (*quietly*). My little world of poetry has tremendous worth to *me*, John Gabriel.

BORKMAN (*heatedly*). Yes, but I, who could have made millions! All the mines I could have controlled! Drilling new shafts, endlessly! Waterfalls! Stone quarries! Trade routes and shipping lines, girdling the globe. And all of these, I alone should have managed!

FOLDAL. Yes, I know that. There wasn't a thing you wouldn't take on.

BORKMAN (*kneading his hands*). And now I have to sit here like a wounded eagle and watch the others pass me by—and snatch it away from me, piece by piece!

FOLDAL. Likewise for me.

BORKMAN (*paying him no attention*). Just think. How close I was to my goal! If I'd only had eight days' respite

to cover myself. All the deposits would have been replaced. All the securities I'd used so audaciously would
have been back again, lying in the vault as before. That
entire enormous stock pool was within a hair's breadth of
existence. Nobody would have lost a share—

FOLDAL. My Lord, yes—how incredibly close you were—

BORKMAN (*with stifled fury*). And then I met with
betrayal. Right on the brink of success! (*Looks at him.*)
Do you know what I consider to be the most despicable
crime a man can commit?

FOLDAL. No, tell me.

BORKMAN. It isn't murder. Nor robbery, nor housebreak-
ing. Not even perjury. Most cases of that kind are directed
against people one hates or is indifferent to, people of no
concern.

FOLDAL. But the most despicable crime, John Gabriel—?

BORKMAN (*emphatically*). Is to abuse the trust of a
friend.

FOLDAL (*somewhat skeptically*). Yes, but listen—

BORKMAN (*bristling*). What are you getting at! I can
read it in your face. But it's not true. The investors who
kept their securities in the bank would have gotten them
all back. To the last decimal point! No, I'm telling you—
the most despicable crime a man can commit is to betray
a friend's correspondence—to publish to the whole wide
world what was entrusted to one single person only, in
confidence, like a whisper in an empty, dark, locked
room. The man who can resort to such means is cankered
and poisoned to the core with the morality of a loan
shark. And I had that sort of friend. And he's the one who
ruined me.

FOLDAL. I can guess who you mean.

BORKMAN. There wasn't one facet of my business affairs
that I didn't lay open to him. And then the moment
arrived when he turned the weapons against me that I'd
put in his hands myself.

FOLDAL. I never could understand why he— Well, there
were a lot of various rumors at the time, of course.

BORKMAN. What rumors? What were they? Tell me. I

didn't hear anything. I went right away into—into isolation. What were they gossiping about, Vilhelm?

FOLDAL. You were supposed to be made a cabinet minister, they said.

BORKMAN. They offered me a post. But I turned it down.

FOLDAL. So you weren't blocking him there.

BORKMAN. Oh no; that's not why he betrayed me.

FOLDAL. Well, then I simply can't understand—

BORKMAN. I might as well tell you, Vilhelm.

FOLDAL. Yes?

BORKMAN. You see, there was—a woman involved.

FOLDAL. A woman? But, John Gabriel—?

BORKMAN (*breaking off*). Oh, never mind—enough of these old, idiotic stories— Well, neither of us made the cabinet.

FOLDAL. But he rose to the heights.

BORKMAN. And I went to the depths.

FOLDAL. Oh, it's a terrible tragedy—

BORKMAN (*nodding to him*). I guess, almost as terrible as yours, when I stop to think of it.

FOLDAL (*innocently*). Yes, at least as terrible.

BORKMAN (*with a quiet laugh*). But from another perspective, it's really a kind of comedy, too.

FOLDAL. A comedy? This?

BORKMAN. Yes, the way it seems to be developing now. No, this really is something—

FOLDAL. What?

BORKMAN. You say you didn't meet Frida when you came?

FOLDAL. No.

BORKMAN. While the two of us sit here, she's sitting down there playing dances for the man that betrayed and ruined me.

FOLDAL. I hadn't any inkling of that.

BORKMAN. Yes, she took her music and went straight from me to—to that mansion.

FOLDAL (*apologetically*). Ah yes, poor child—

BORKMAN. And can you guess whom she's playing for—among others?

FOLDAL. Who?

BORKMAN. My son.

FOLDAL. What!

BORKMAN. Yes, what do you make of it, Vilhelm? My son down there in the throngs of dancers tonight. Isn't that, just as I say, a comedy?

FOLDAL. Well, but he certainly doesn't know any of this.

BORKMAN. Of what?

FOLDAL. He certainly doesn't know how *he*—this, uh—

BORKMAN. You can say the name. I can stand hearing it now.

FOLDAL. I'm sure your son doesn't realize the connection, John Gabriel.

BORKMAN (*grimly, drumming on the table*). He knows it—as sure as I'm sitting here.

FOLDAL. But can you conceive, then, his *ever* wanting to enter that house!

BORKMAN (*shaking his head*). My son, I suppose, doesn't see things the way I do. I'm willing to swear that he sides with my enemies! Undoubtedly he thinks, as they do, that Hinkel only acted damn well as a responsible attorney when he went and betrayed me.

FOLDAL. But—who could have given him that idea?

BORKMAN. Who? Are you forgetting who brought him up? First his aunt—from when he was six, seven years old. And since then—his mother!

FOLDAL. I think you're being unfair to them.

BORKMAN (*heatedly*). I'm never unfair to anyone! Those two have incited him against me, I'm telling you!

FOLDAL (*indulgently*). Yes, of course, I guess they have.

BORKMAN (*full of indignation*). Oh, these women! They corrupt and distort our lives! They completely botch up our destinies—our paths to glory.

FOLDAL. Not all of them!

BORKMAN. Really? Name me one single one who's any good!

FOLDAL. No, that's the problem. The ones I know— they're just no good.

BORKMAN (*snorts scornfully*). Well, then what's the point! So good women exist—but you never know them!

FOLDAL (*with warmth*). Yes, but, John Gabriel, all the same there *is* a point. It's such a blessed and consoling thought to realize that somewhere, out there around us, far away—*there* the true woman is waiting to be found.

BORKMAN (*shifting restlessly on the sofa*). Oh, cut that poetical rot!

FOLDAL (*looks at him, deeply wounded*). You call my most sacred faith poetical rot?

BORKMAN (*curtly*). I do, yes! It's the cause of your never having gotten anywhere in life. If you could only rinse your mind of all that, I could still help you get on your feet—and to move ahead.

FOLDAL (*smoldering inwardly*). Ah, you can't do that.

BORKMAN. I *can*, when I come back in power again.

FOLDAL. But that's an awfully remote possibility.

BORKMAN (*vehemently*). Maybe you think the time will never come? I want an answer!

FOLDAL. I don't know how to answer you.

BORKMAN (*rises, cold and imposing, and motions toward the door*). Then I no longer have any use for you.

FOLDAL (*springing up from his chair*). No use—!

BORKMAN. If you don't believe that my fate will change—

FOLDAL. But I can't believe against all reason! You're asking for full restitution—

BORKMAN. Go on! Go on!

FOLDAL. I know I never took my degree, but I've read *that* much law in my day—

BORKMAN (*quickly*). You mean it's impossible?

FOLDAL. There's no precedent for it.

BORKMAN. There *are* no precedents for exceptional men.

FOLDAL. The law doesn't make such allowances.

BORKMAN (*caustically*). You're no poet, Vilhelm.

FOLDAL (*impulsively clasping his hands*). You say that in all seriousness?

BORKMAN (*dismissing the matter*). We're only wasting each other's time. You better not come again.

FOLDAL. Then you want me to leave you alone.

BORKMAN (*without looking at him*). I've no more use for you.

FOLDAL (*gently*). No, no, no; I guess not.

BORKMAN. All this time, you've been lying to me.

FOLDAL (*shaking his head*). I never lied, John Gabriel.

BORKMAN. Haven't you sat here, lying hope and faith and trust into me?

FOLDAL. Those weren't lies as long as you believed in my talent. As long as you believed in me, I believed in you.

BORKMAN. Then we've practiced mutual deception on each other. And perhaps deceived ourselves—both of us.

FOLDAL. But isn't that the very basis of friendship, John Gabriel?

BORKMAN (*smiles wryly*). Quite so. To deceive—is friendship. You're right. I've had the experience once already.

FOLDAL (*looking at him*). No talent for poetry. And you could say that to me so callously.

BORKMAN (*tempering his voice*). Well, I'm no specialist in that field.

FOLDAL. More perhaps than you realize.

BORKMAN. I?

FOLDAL (*quietly*). Yes, you. Because I've had my own doubts from time to time, you know. The dreadful doubt—that I've botched my whole life up for the sake of a fantasy.

BORKMAN. When you doubt yourself, then you've lost your footing.

FOLDAL. That's why it was so heartening to come here for your support, because you believed. (*Taking his hat.*) But now you seem like a stranger to me.

BORKMAN. As you seem to me.

FOLDAL. Good night, John Gabriel.

BORKMAN. Good night, Vilhelm.

(FOLDAL *goes out to the left.* BORKMAN *stands for some moments and gazes at the closed door; he makes a gesture as if he would call* FOLDAL *back, but then reconsiders and begins to walk up and down the floor, his hands behind his back. He then stops at the sofa table and puts out the lamp. The salon now is in semidarkness. Shortly thereafter, a knock is heard on the tapestry door.*)

BORKMAN (*by the table, starts, turns and asks loudly*). Who's knocking?

(*No answer. Another knock.*)

BORKMAN (*frozen in place*). Who is that? Come in!

(ELLA RENTHEIM, *with a lighted candle in her hand, appears in the doorway. She is wearing a black dress as before, with her coat thrown loosely over her shoulders.*)

BORKMAN (*staring at her*). Who are you? What do you want with me?

ELLA (*shutting the door after her and coming closer*). It's me, John Gabriel. (*She sets down the candle on the piano and remains beside it.*)

BORKMAN (*stands and gazes at her as if thunderstruck; in a faint whisper*). Is that—is it Ella? Ella Rentheim?

ELLA. Yes—it's "your" Ella—as you used to call me. Once. So many—so many years ago.

BORKMAN (*as before*). Yes, it's you, Ella—I see that now.

ELLA. You still recognize me?

BORKMAN. Yes, I'm beginning to now—

ELLA. The years have worn and withered me, Borkman. Don't you think so?

BORKMAN (*uneasily*). You're somewhat changed. At first glance, anyway—

ELLA. I don't have the dark curls tumbling down my back anymore. Those curls you once liked to wind around your fingers.

BORKMAN (*briskly*). Right! Now I see, Ella. You've changed your hair style.

ELLA (*with a sad smile*). Exactly. It's the hair style that does it.

BORKMAN (*changing the subject*). I never knew you were here, in this part of the country.

ELLA. I've only just arrived.

BORKMAN. Why did you make that trip—now, in winter?

ELLA. You're going to hear why.

BORKMAN. Is it something you want from *me*?

ELLA. You, as well. But if we're going to talk about that, I'll have to begin far back.

BORKMAN. You must be tired.

ELLA. Yes, tired.

BORKMAN. Won't you sit? There—on the sofa.

ELLA. Yes, thank you. I need to.

(*She goes over to the right and seats herself in the near corner of the sofa.* BORKMAN *stands by the table, his hands behind his back, and studies her. Short silence.*)

ELLA. It's ages since the two of us met face to face, John Gabriel.

BORKMAN (*somberly*). A long, long time. With all that wretchedness in between.

ELLA. A whole lifetime between. A lifetime wasted.

BORKMAN (*looks sharply at her*). Wasted!

ELLA. Yes, just that. For us both.

BORKMAN (*in a cold, businesslike tone*). I don't rate my life wasted as yet.

ELLA. Well, what about *mine?*

BORKMAN. There you can only blame yourself, Ella.

ELLA (*with a tremor*). And *you* can say *that!*

BORKMAN. You could very well have been happy without me.

ELLA. You think so?

BORKMAN. If you'd resolved to.

ELLA (*bitterly*). Yes, I'm perfectly aware that there was someone else waiting to marry me—

BORKMAN. But you turned him away—

ELLA. Yes, I did.

BORKMAN. Time after time you turned him away. Year after year—

ELLA (*scornfully*). You mean, year after year I turned away from my happiness?

BORKMAN. You could just as well have been happy with him. And *I* would have been saved, then.

ELLA. You—?

BORKMAN. Yes. Then you would have saved me, Ella.

ELLA. How do you mean?

BORKMAN. He thought I was behind your refusals—your constant rejection. So he took revenge. He could do that so easily—since he had all those ill-considered, confidential letters of mine in his possession. He used them—and that put an end to me, for a time, at least. You see, all that was your doing, Ella!

ELLA. That's right, John Gabriel—if we really get down to cases, it seems *I* owe a debt to *you.*

BORKMAN. You can take it that way. I know thoroughly well how much I need to thank you for. You bought the estate, this entire property, at the auction, and turned it completely over to me and—your sister. You took in Erhart—and cared for him in every way—

ELLA. As long as I was allowed to—

BORKMAN. By your sister, yes. I've never intruded in these domestic questions. As I was saying, I know what you've sacrificed for me and for your sister. But then, you were *able* to. And you have to remember that *I* was the one who put you in that position.

ELLA (*heatedly*). You're enormously mistaken, John Gabriel! It was the deep warmth of my feeling for Erhart—and for you, too—it was *that* alone that moved me.

BORKMAN (*interrupting*). My dear, let's not get into feelings and such. I only mean that, if you acted the way you did, I was the one who gave you the power to do so.

ELLA (*smiles*). Hm, the power, the power—

BORKMAN (*incensed*). Yes, the power, exactly! When the great, decisive blow was poised to fall—when I couldn't spare friends or family—when I had to take, and did take, the millions that were entrusted to me—then I spared everything of yours, everything you owned and held—although I could have borrowed it, and used it, like all the rest.

ELLA (*with icy calm*). That's undoubtedly true, John Gabriel.

BORKMAN. It is. And that's why, when they came and took me, they found all your securities undisturbed in the bank vault.

ELLA (*scrutinizing him*). I've many times thought about that. Just why did you spare my holdings? And only mine?

BORKMAN. Why?

ELLA. Yes, why? Tell me.

BORKMAN (*with harsh disdain*). I suppose you think it was so I could have something to fall back on—if anything went wrong?

ELLA. Oh, no—you didn't think that way in those days, I'm sure.

BORKMAN. Never! I was so utterly confident of victory.

ELLA. Yes, but why then—?

BORKMAN (*shrugging his shoulders*). Good Lord, Ella—it's not so easy to remember motives from twenty years ago. I only remember that when I was alone then, struggling in silence with all the vast projects that would be set in motion, it seemed to me almost as if I were a voyager in the air. I walked the sleepless nights, inflating a huge balloon that would sail out over a shadowy, perilous ocean.

ELLA (*smiling*). You, who never doubted your victory.

BORKMAN (*impatiently*). Men are like that, Ella. They both doubt and believe at the same time. (*Gazing into space.*) And that's probably why I didn't want you and what you owned with me in the balloon.

ELLA (*intently*). Why? Tell me why?

BORKMAN (*not looking at her*). One doesn't care to take all that's dearest along on a journey like that.

ELLA. You had what was dearest to you on board. Your own future life.

BORKMAN. One's life isn't always what's dearest.

ELLA (*breathlessly*). Was that how you felt then?

BORKMAN. I think so.

ELLA. That *I* was dearest of all to you?

BORKMAN. Yes, I have—something of that impression.

ELLA. And yet that was years after you'd abandoned me—and married—someone else!

BORKMAN. You say I abandoned you? You know well enough there were higher incentives—well, *other* incentives—that impelled me. Without his aid, I would have gotten nowhere.

ELLA (*controlling herself*). So you abandoned me for—higher incentives.

BORKMAN. I couldn't get on without his help. And he set *you* as his price.

ELLA. And you paid the price. In full. Without a murmur.

BORKMAN. I had no choice. It was win or go under.

ELLA (*her voice trembling, as she looks at him*). Is it really true what you say—that I was dearest in this world to you then?

BORKMAN. Both then and after—long, long after.

ELLA. And still you traded me away. Bargained your rightful love to another man. Sold my love for a—for a bank presidency.

BORKMAN (*somberly, bowed down*). The necessity was overwhelming, Ella.

ELLA (*rises from the sofa, quivering with passion*). Criminal!

BORKMAN (*starting, then recovering his composure*). I've heard the word before.

ELLA. Oh, don't think I mean any law of the land you've broken! The use you made of all these stocks and bonds, or whatever—what do you think I care about that! If I could have been standing beside you when everything went to pieces—

BORKMAN (*tensely*). Then what, Ella?

ELLA. Believe me, I would have borne it so gladly with you. The shame, the ruin—all of it I would have helped you bear—

BORKMAN. Would you have had the will to? And the courage?

ELLA. The will and the courage both. Because then, you see, I knew nothing about your great, intolerable crime—

BORKMAN. Which? What do you mean?

ELLA. I mean the crime that's beyond all forgiveness—

BORKMAN (*staring at her*). You're out of your senses.

ELLA (*advancing on him*). You're a murderer! You've committed the supreme, mortal sin!

BORKMAN (*backing toward the piano*). You're raving, Ella!

ELLA. You've killed the capacity to love in me. (*Approaching him.*) Can you understand what that means? In the Bible it speaks of a mysterious sin for which there *is* no forgiveness. I've never known before what that could be. Now I know. The great unforgivable sin is—to murder the love in a human being.

BORKMAN. And that's what you say I've done?

ELLA. You've done that. I've never truly realized before this evening exactly what it was that happened to me. That you abandoned me and turned instead to Gunhild—I took that as no more than a simple lack of constancy on your part, and the result of heartless calculation on hers. I almost think I despised you a little—in spite of everything. But *now* I see it! You abandoned the woman you *loved!* Me, me, me! The dearest that you had in this world you were ready to sign away for profit. It's a double murder you're guilty of! Murder of your own soul, and of mine!

BORKMAN (*with cold self-control*). How well I recognize that overbearing passion in you, Ella. I suppose it's very natural for you to see this the way you do. You're a woman. And so it seems, to your mind, that nothing else in the world exists or matters.

ELLA. Yes, nothing else.

BORKMAN. Only what touches your own heart.

ELLA. Only that! Only that! Yes.

BORKMAN. But you have to remember that I'm a man. As a woman, to me you were the dearest in the world. But in the last analysis, any woman can be replaced by another.

ELLA (*regarding him with a smile*). Was that your experience when you took Gunhild to marry?

BORKMAN. No. But my life's work helped me to bear *that*, too. All the sources of power in this country I wanted at my command. The earth, the mountains, the forests, the sea—I wanted to subjugate all the riches they held, and carve out a kingdom for myself, and use it to further the well-being of so many thousands of others.

ELLA (*lost in memory*). I know. All those many evenings that we talked about your plans—

BORKMAN. Yes, I could talk with you, Ella.

ELLA. I used to joke about your projects and ask if you wanted to wake all the slumbering spirits of the gold.

BORKMAN (*nods*). I remember the phrase. (*Slowly.*) All the slumbering spirits of the gold.

ELLA. But you didn't take it for a joke. You said: "Yes, yes, Ella; that's exactly what I want."

BORKMAN. And it was. If only I once could get my foot in the stirrup—and that depended then on this one man. He was able and willing to ensure my control of the bank—if, in return—

ELLA. Yes! If, in return, you gave up the woman you loved—and who loved you beyond expression—

BORKMAN. I knew his unbounded passion for you—and that no other condition would satisfy his—

ELLA. So you came to terms.

BORKMAN (*fervently*). Yes, Ella, I did! Because the rage for power was so relentless in me, don't you see? I came to terms. I *had* to. And he helped me halfway up toward the enticing heights I longed for. I climbed and climbed. Year upon year, I climbed—

ELLA. And I was erased from your life.

BORKMAN. But even so, he toppled me into the abyss. Because of you, Ella.

ELLA (*after a brief, reflective silence*). John Gabriel—doesn't it seem to you as if there's been a kind of curse on our whole relationship?

BORKMAN (*looks at her*). A curse?

ELLA. Yes. Don't you think so?

BORKMAN (*uneasily*). Yes. But why, really—? (*In an outburst.*) Oh, Ella—I scarcely know any longer who's right—you or I!

ELLA. You're the guilty one. You put to death all the natural joy in me.

BORKMAN (*anxiously*). Don't say that, Ella.

ELLA. All the joy a woman should know, at least. From the time your image began to fade in me, I've lived as if under an eclipse. Through all those years it's grown harder and harder—and finally impossible—for me to love any living creature. Not people, nor animals, nor plants. Only that one—

BORKMAN. Which one?

ELLA. Erhart, of course.

BORKMAN. Erhart—?

ELLA. Your son, John Gabriel.

BORKMAN. Has he meant all that to you, actually?

ELLA. Why else do you think I took him in, and kept him as long as I could? Why?

BORKMAN. I thought it was out of compassion. Like all the rest you've done.

ELLA (*reflecting powerful inner feeling*). Compassion, you say! (*With a laugh.*) I've never known any compassion—since you left me. I'm wholly incapable of that. If a poor, starving child came into my kitchen, freezing and weeping, and begged for a little food, then I left it up to my cook. I never felt any urge to take the child in myself, warm it at my own hearth, and enjoy sitting by, watching it eat its fill. And I was never like that in my youth; I remember so clearly. It's you who've made this sterile, empty desert within me—and around me, too.

BORKMAN. Except for Erhart.

ELLA. Yes, except for your son. But for all else, all that lives and moves. You've cheated me of a mother's joy and happiness in life. And of a mother's cares and tears as well. And maybe that's been the hardest loss.

BORKMAN. You'd say so, Ella?

ELLA. Who knows? A mother's cares and tears are perhaps what I've needed most. (*With still stronger feeling.*) But I couldn't reconcile myself to that loss. And that's why I took Erhart in. Won him completely. Won all of the warm, trusting heart of a child—until—oh!

BORKMAN. Until what?

ELLA. Until his mother—his physical mother, I mean—took him from me.

BORKMAN. He had to leave you, to live here in town.

ELLA (*wringing her hands*). Yes, but I can't stand the desolation! The emptiness! The loss of your son's heart!

BORKMAN (*a malignant look in his eyes*). Hm—I'm sure you haven't lost it, Ella. It's not easy to lose one's heart to anyone down below—on the ground floor.

ELLA. I've lost Erhart here. And *she's* won him back. Or

someone else has. That's clear enough from the letters he
writes to me now and then.

BORKMAN. Are you here, then, to take him home with
you?

ELLA. If that were only possible—!

BORKMAN. It's perfectly possible, if it's really what you
want. You *do* have the first and greatest claim on him.

ELLA. Oh, claim, claim! What does a claim mean here?
If he's not mine by his own free will, then I can't have him.
And I must! I must have my child's heart now—whole
and intact!

BORKMAN. You have to remember that Erhart's into his
twenties. You could hardly figure on retaining his heart
intact, as you put it, for very long.

ELLA (*with a sad smile*). It wouldn't have to be for very
long.

BORKMAN. No? I would have thought, if you wanted
something, you'd want it to the end of your days.

ELLA. I do. But that's why I say it wouldn't have to be
for long.

BORKMAN (*startled*). What does that mean?

ELLA. You knew, of course, that I've been ill for the
past few years?

BORKMAN. You have?

ELLA. You didn't know?

BORKMAN. No, actually not—

ELLA (*looks at him, surprised*). Erhart hasn't told you
that?

BORKMAN. I honestly can't remember at the moment.

ELLA. Perhaps he's never mentioned me at all?

BORKMAN. Oh, I know he's talked about you. But the
fact is, it's so seldom I see anything of him. Hardly ever.
There's someone down below who keeps him away from
me. Far away, you understand.

ELLA. You're positive of that?

BORKMAN. I know it for certain. (*Changing his tone.*) But Ella—you say you've been ill!

ELLA. Yes, I have. This past autumn it got so much worse, I decided I'd better come in and see some specialists.

BORKMAN. And have you seen them already?

ELLA. Yes, this morning.

BORKMAN. What did they say?

ELLA. They gave complete confirmation of what I'd long suspected—

BORKMAN. Well?

ELLA (*in a calm monotone*). The illness I have is terminal.

BORKMAN. Oh, you mustn't believe anything of the kind!

ELLA. It's an illness for which there's no help or cure. The doctors don't know any treatment. They just let it run its course. There's nothing they can do to arrest it. Just alleviate the pain a little, perhaps. And, of course, that's always something.

BORKMAN. But it can last for a long time still, believe me.

ELLA. It might possibly last out the winter, I've been told.

BORKMAN (*without thinking*). Well—the winters here are long.

ELLA (*quietly*). In any case, long enough for *me*.

BORKMAN (*animatedly, avoiding the subject*). But what on earth could have caused this illness? You've lived such a healthy, regular life—? What could have caused it?

ELLA (*looking at him*). The doctors concluded that perhaps, at some time, I'd undergone a severe emotional upheaval.

BORKMAN (*flaring up*). Emotional upheaval! Ah yes, I understand. It has to be *me* that's to blame!

ELLA (*with rising inner agitation*). It's too late to argue that now. But I *must* have the child of my heart, my one and only again, before I go! It's too inexpressibly mourn-

ful to think that I have to leave all that life is—leave the
sun, the light, and the air, without leaving here behind me
one single person who'll think of me and remember me
warmly and tenderly—the way a son thinks, remembering
the mother he's lost.

BORKMAN (*after a short pause*). Take him, Ella—if you
can win him.

ELLA (*exhilarated*). You'll consent to it? *Can* you?

BORKMAN (*somberly*). Yes. It isn't much of a sacrifice.
Because he's really not mine to give.

ELLA. Thank you, thank you for the sacrifice, even so!
But then I've just one thing more to ask you for. Something big for me, John Gabriel.

BORKMAN. Well then, tell me.

ELLA. You may find it childish of me—and won't understand—

BORKMAN. Go on—tell me!

ELLA. Soon now, when I'm gone, there'll be a considerable inheritance—

BORKMAN. Yes, I would guess so.

ELLA. It's my intention to let it all go to Erhart.

BORKMAN. Well, you really have no one who's closer.

ELLA (*with warmth*). No, certainly no one closer than
he.

BORKMAN. No one of your own family. You're the last
of the line.

ELLA (*nodding slowly*). Yes, that's it, exactly. When I
die, the Rentheim name dies as well. And to me, that's a
torturing thought. To be erased from existence—even to
one's very name—

BORKMAN (*incensed*). Ah—I see what you're after!

ELLA (*passionately*). Don't let it happen! Let Erhart
carry on the name!

BORKMAN (*looking fiercely at her*). I quite understand.
You want to spare my son the weight of his father's
name. So that's it.

ELLA. No, never! I would have borne your name myself
gladly, with pride, together with you! But a mother who's
about to die— A name binds more than you could believe, John Gabriel.

BORKMAN (*coldly and proudly*). All right, Ella. I'll be
man enough to bear my name alone.

ELLA (*grasping and pressing his hands*). Thank you,
thank you! Now everything's made up between us. Yes,
yes, I hope that's so! You've redeemed as much as you
could. For when I'm gone, Erhart Rentheim will live on
after me.

(*The tapestry door is thrown open.* MRS. BORKMAN, *with
her large shawl over her head, stands in the doorway.*)

MRS. BORKMAN (*convulsively agitated*). Never in all
eternity will Erhart take that name!

ELLA (*shrinking back*). Gunhild!

BORKMAN (*grimly threatening*). No one's permitted to
come up here to me!

MRS. BORKMAN (*advancing a step*). I permit myself
that.

BORKMAN (*moving toward her*). What do you want of
me?

MRS. BORKMAN. I want to fight for you. Protect you
from the evil powers.

BORKMAN. The worst of those powers are in yourself,
Gunhild.

MRS. BORKMAN (*harshly*). Whatever you say. (*Menacingly.*) But *I* say, he'll carry on his father's name—and
bear it high again, in honor. And I'll be his mother—I
alone! My son's heart will belong to me. To me, and no
one else.

(*She leaves through the tapestry door, closing it behind
her.*)

ELLA (*shaken and distraught*). John Gabriel—Erhart's
bound to go down in this storm. There's got to be some
understanding between you and Gunhild. We must go
down to her at once.

BORKMAN (*looks at her*). We? I, as well, you mean?

ELLA. You and I both.

BORKMAN (*shaking his head*). She's hard, Ella. Hard as the metal I once dreamed of tunneling out of the mountains.

ELLA. Then try—just try, now!

(BORKMAN *does not answer, as he stands looking at her, full of doubt.*)

⟨ ACT THREE ⟩

MRS. BORKMAN'S *living room. The lamp is still burning on the table by the sofa. The garden room to the rear is now dark.* MRS. BORKMAN, *with the shawl over her head, enters through the hall door, profoundly shaken. She goes to the window and draws the curtain aside slightly; then she crosses over to sit in the armchair by the stove, but immediately springs to her feet again and goes to the bellpull and rings. For a moment she stands, waiting by the sofa. No one comes. She rings again, this time more violently. After some moments the* MAID *enters from the hall. She looks sleepy and ill-tempered and appears to have dressed in haste.*

MRS. BORKMAN (*impatiently*). What's become of you, Malene? I had to ring twice!

MAID. Yes, ma'am, I heard you.

MRS. BORKMAN. And still you didn't come.

MAID (*petulantly*). Well, I had to throw on a few clothes first, I guess.

MRS. BORKMAN. Yes, you dress yourself up properly. And then you've got to run over right away and fetch my son.

MAID (*staring at her in amazement*). Me—fetch Mr. Erhart?

MRS. BORKMAN. Yes. Just tell him he has to come home to me at once. That I have to speak with him.

378

MAID (*sullenly*). Then I guess I better go wake the coachman in the annex.

MRS. BORKMAN. Why?

MAID. So he can harness the sleigh. It's been an awful snowstorm tonight.

MRS. BORKMAN. Oh, that's nothing. Hurry up and go! It's only around the corner.

MAID. No, but, ma'am, that's not just around the corner.

MRS. BORKMAN. Why, of course it is. Don't you know where Mr. Hinkel's place is?

MAID (*sarcastically*). Oh, I see—is *that* where Mr. Erhart is tonight?

MRS. BORKMAN (*puzzled*). Where else would he be?

MAID (*suppressing a smile*). Oh, I only thought he was over where he usually is.

MRS. BORKMAN. Where do you mean?

MAID. At that Mrs. Wilton's, as they call her.

MRS. BORKMAN. Mrs. Wilton's? My son isn't there so often.

MAID (*under her breath*). There's some say he's there every day.

MRS. BORKMAN. That's a pack of nonsense, Malene. Now go over to Mr. Hinkel's and see that you get hold of him.

MAID (*tossing her head*). Oh, all right; I'm going.

(*She is on the verge of going out down the hall, when at that instant the hall door opens, and* ELLA RENTHEIM *and* BORKMAN *appear on the threshold.*)

MRS. BORKMAN (*recoils a step*). What does this mean?

MAID (*terrified, impulsively clasping her hands*). In Jesus' name!

MRS. BORKMAN (*whispering to her*). Tell him to come directly, at once!

MAID (*quietly*). Yes, ma'am.

(ELLA *and, behind her,* BORKMAN *come into the room. The*

MAID *steals around in back of them and out the door, shutting it after her. A brief silence.)*

MRS. BORKMAN (*again controlled, turning to* ELLA). What does he want in my room down here?

ELLA. He wants to try and reach some understanding with you, Gunhild.

MRS. BORKMAN. He's never tried to before.

ELLA. He wants to this evening.

MRS. BORKMAN. The last time we faced each other— was in court. When I was summoned to give an explanation—

BORKMAN (*approaching closer*). And tonight I'm the one who'll give an explanation.

MRS. BORKMAN (*looking at him*). You!

BORKMAN. Not about my offense. The whole world knows about that.

MRS. BORKMAN (*with a bitter sigh*). Yes, how true. The whole world knows.

BORKMAN. But it doesn't know why I committed it. Why I *had* to commit it. People don't understand that I had to because I was myself—John Gabriel Borkman—and no one else. That's what I want to try and explain to you.

MRS. BORKMAN (*shaking her head*). It's no use. Intentions acquit no one. Nor impulses, either.

BORKMAN. They can acquit a man in his own eyes.

MRS. BORKMAN (*with a gesture of dismissal*). Oh, let's be done with all this! I've pondered all those dark dealings of yours to the limit.

BORKMAN. So have I. Through five endless years in my cell—and elsewhere—I've had time enough for that. And with eight years in the salon upstairs, I've had more than enough time. I've retried the whole case—all to myself. I've reopened the proceedings again and again. I've been my own prosecutor, my own defender, and my own judge. More impartially than anybody else would be—that I'll wager. I've walked the floor up there, turning every detail of my actions over and over in my mind. I've scrutinized them backward and forward just as unsparingly and remorselessly as any lawyer. And the verdict I continually arrive at is this: that the only one I've committed an offense against—is myself.

MRS. BORKMAN. Not against me? Or your son?

BORKMAN. You and he are included in what I mean by myself.

MRS. BORKMAN. And what of those hundreds of others— the ones they say you ruined?

BORKMAN (*more intensely*). I had the power! And the relentless voices within me! The buried millions lay everywhere, deep in the mountains, all over the country, crying out to me, crying out to be freed! But not one of all the others heard. Only I, alone.

MRS. BORKMAN. Yes, to brand the name Borkman with dishonor.

BORKMAN. Who knows, if the others had had the power, whether they wouldn't have acted just as I did?

MRS. BORKMAN. No one, no one besides you could have done the same.

BORKMAN. Maybe not. But then that was because they lacked my abilities. And if they *had* done it, they couldn't have done it with *my* vision. The action would have to be different. In short, I've acquitted myself.

ELLA (*in a softly appealing tone*). Oh, how can you speak so surely, John Gabriel?

BORKMAN (*nodding*). Acquitted myself to *that* extent. But then comes the great, crushing self-accusation.

MRS. BORKMAN. What's that?

BORKMAN. I've holed myself away up there and wasted eight priceless years of my life! The very day I was released, I should have moved out into reality—iron-hard, dreamless reality! I should have begun at the bottom and raised myself up to the heights again—higher than ever before—in spite of what intervened.

MRS. BORKMAN. Oh, it would just be the same life all over again—believe me.

BORKMAN (*shakes his head and regards her with a didactic air*). Nothing new ever happens. But whatever has happened never repeats itself, either. It's the eye that transforms the action. The newborn eye transforms the old action. (*Breaking off.*) Ahh, you don't understand that.

MRS. BORKMAN (*brusquely*). No, I don't understand it.

BORKMAN. Yes, that's the curse, exactly: that I've never found understanding in any human soul.

ELLA (*looking at him*). Never, John Gabriel?

BORKMAN. With one exception—perhaps. Long, long ago, in the days when I didn't think I needed understanding. But since then, never, with anyone! I've had no one attentive enough to be near at hand, encouraging me— rousing me like a morning bell—urging me on once more to do inspired work. And confirming to me that I've done nothing irretrievable.

MRS. BORKMAN (*laughs contemptuously*). So—you need outside confirmation of that?

BORKMAN (*with gathering resentment*). Yes, when the whole world hisses in unison that I'm a man lost beyond recall, then I have moments when I'm almost ready to believe it myself. (*Lifting his head.*) But then my inner- most consciousness rises triumphant again. And that ac- quits me!

MRS. BORKMAN (*regarding him bitterly*). Why did you never come and ask me for what you call understanding?

BORKMAN. What use would it have been—coming to you!

MRS. BORKMAN (*with a gesture of dismissal*). You've never loved anything outside yourself—and that's the es- sence of it.

BORKMAN (*with pride*). I've loved power—

MRS. BORKMAN. Power, yes!

BORKMAN. The power to create human happiness for vast multitudes around me.

MRS. BORKMAN. You once had the power to make *me* happy. Have you used it for that?

BORKMAN (*not looking at her*). Someone very often has to go down—in a shipwreck.

MRS. BORKMAN. And your own son! Have you used your power, have you lived and labored, to make *him* happy?

BORKMAN. I don't know him.

MRS. BORKMAN. Yes, that's true. You don't even know him.

BORKMAN (*harshly*). You—you, his mother, took care of that.

MRS. BORKMAN (*regards him with an imperious air*). Oh, you have no idea what I've taken care of!

BORKMAN. You?

MRS. BORKMAN. Yes, I—I alone.

BORKMAN. Tell me.

MRS. BORKMAN. I've shaped your final reputation.

BORKMAN (*with a short, dry laugh*). My final reputation? Come now! That sounds as though I were already dead.

MRS. BORKMAN (*stressing her words*). And you are.

BORKMAN (*slowly*). Yes, maybe you're right. (*Flaring up.*) But no, no! Not yet! I've come so close, so close to it. But now I'm awake. Revived again. Life still reaches ahead of me. I can see that new and radiant life still waits there, beckoning. And you'll see it as well. You, too.

MRS. BORKMAN (*raising her hand*). No more dreams of life! Rest quietly where you lie.

ELLA (*appalled*). Gunhild! Gunhild, how could you—!

MRS. BORKMAN (*not listening to her*). I'll raise a monument over your grave.

BORKMAN. A memorial to shame, I suppose?

MRS. BORKMAN (*with swelling emotion*). Oh no, it won't be a marker of stone or metal. And no one will have a chance to carve a slurring inscription on the monument I'll raise. It will be as if a living fence, a woven hedge of trees and bushes was planted thick, thick around your buried life. All the dark of the past will be screened away; and all remembrance of John Gabriel Borkman will vanish into oblivion.

BORKMAN (*hoarsely and cuttingly*). And *that* work of love you'll carry out?

MRS. BORKMAN. Not through my own efforts. That's beyond me. But I've trained an assistant who'll focus his life on this one thing. His life will be so pure and brilliant and exalted that all your own grubbing in the dark will be wiped from this earth!

BORKMAN (*in grim warning*). If it's Erhart you mean, you better say so right now.

MRS. BORKMAN (*looking him straight in the eye*). Yes, it's Erhart. My son, that you're willing to relinquish—in penance for your failings.

BORKMAN (*with a glance at* ELLA). In penance for my greatest sin.

MRS. BORKMAN (*dismissing the thought*). A sin only against a stranger. Remember the sin against *me!* (*Looking exultantly at them both.*) But he won't listen to you! When I cry out to him in my need, then he'll come! For it's with *me* he wants to be! With me, and nobody else— (*Abruptly listens, then cries.*) There, I hear him! He's here—he's here! Erhart!

(ERHART BORKMAN *bursts open the hall door and comes into the room. He is wearing an overcoat and a hat on his head.*)

ERHART (*pale and anxious*). Mother—what in God's name—! (*He sees* BORKMAN, *standing by the doorway to the garden room, starts, and takes off his hat. A brief pause.*) What do you want me for, Mother? What happened?

MRS. BORKMAN (*stretching out her arms toward him*). I want to see you, Erhart! I want to have you with me— always!

ERHART (*stammering*). Have me—? Always! What do you mean?

MRS. BORKMAN. To have you! I want to have you— because there's someone trying to take you from me!

ERHART (*falls back a step*). Ah—then you know?

MRS. BORKMAN. Yes. But *you* know, too?

ERHART (*surprised, looking at her*). Do *I* know? Why, naturally—

MRS. BORKMAN. So! Plotting—behind my back! Erhart, Erhart!

ERHART (*quickly*). Mother, tell me, what is it you know?

MRS. BORKMAN. I know everything. I know that your aunt's come here to take you away from me.

ERHART. Aunt Ella!

ELLA. Oh, listen to *me* a while first, Erhart!

MRS. BORKMAN (*continuing*). She wants me to give you over to her. She wants to assume your mother's place, Erhart! She wants you to be her son hereafter, and not mine. She wants you to inherit everything she owns, and to drop your own name for hers instead!

ERHART. Aunt Ella, is all this true?

ELLA. Yes, it's true.

ERHART. I didn't know any of this till now. Why do you want me back with you?

ELLA. Because I feel I'm losing you here.

MRS. BORKMAN (*harshly*). Losing him to me—yes! And that's just as it ought to be.

ELLA (*looks imploringly at him*). Erhart, I can't afford to lose you. You must be aware that I'm a lonely—dying woman.

ERHART. Dying—?

ELLA. Yes, dying. Will you stay with me to the end? Commit yourself wholly to me—as if you were my own child—?

MRS. BORKMAN (*breaking in*). And abandon your mother and perhaps your mission in life as well? Do you want that, Erhart?

ELLA. I'm condemned to die. Answer me, Erhart.

ERHART (*warmly, moved*). Aunt Ella—you've been good to me beyond words. With you I was able to grow up in as much carefree happiness as I think any child could have known—

MRS. BORKMAN. Erhart, Erhart!

ELLA. What a blessing that you still feel that way!

ERHART. But I can't sacrifice myself for you now. It's impossible for me simply to give myself over to being a son to you—

MRS. BORKMAN (*triumphantly*). Ah, I knew it! You won't get him! You won't get him, Ella!

ELLA (*heavily*). I see. You *have* won him back.

MRS. BORKMAN. Yes, yes—he's mine, and he'll stay mine! It's true, isn't it, Erhart—the two of us still have a long way to go together?

ERHART (*struggling with himself*). Mother—I might just as well tell you right now—

MRS. BORKMAN (*tensely*). Yes?

ERHART. It's only a short distance more we'll be going together, you and I.

MRS. BORKMAN (*as if physically struck*). What does *that* mean?

ERHART (*mustering his courage*). My God, Mother— I'm young! The air here in this room—I feel it's going to smother me completely.

MRS. BORKMAN. Here—with me!

ERHART. Yes, here with you, Mother!

ELLA. Then come with me, Erhart!

ERHART. Oh, Aunt Ella, it's not one shade better with you. It would be different there. But not better. Not for me. It's roses and lavender—stale indoor air, exactly like here.

MRS. BORKMAN (*shaken, but with composure reestablished*). The air is stale here, you say?

ERHART (*with mounting impatience*). Oh, I don't know what else to call it. All this morbid concern about me, this—this idolatry, or whatever it is. I can't take it any longer!

MRS. BORKMAN (*with a look of profound solemnity*). Are you forgetting what you've dedicated your life to, Erhart?

ERHART (*vehemently*). Oh, you mean what *you've* dedicated my life to! You've been my will! I've never been allowed to have one of my own. But I won't wear these chains any longer! I'm young! You've got to remember that, Mother. (*With a polite, respectful glance at* BORKMAN.) I can't dedicate my life to someone else's atonement—no matter who that someone may be.

MRS. BORKMAN (*gripped by a gathering dread*). Who is it that's changed you, Erhart?

ERHART (*caught*). Who—? Couldn't it be that, all on my own, I—

MRS. BORKMAN. No, no, no! There's some strange power that's over you. You're not under your mother's influence anymore. Nor your—your foster mother's, either.

ERHART (*with effortful defiance*). I know my own strength now, Mother. And my own will, too!

BORKMAN (*approaching* ERHART). Then perhaps my time has finally come.

ERHART (*with a distant, formal courtesy*). What—? What do you mean, sir?

MRS. BORKMAN (*contemptuously*). Yes, and I'd certainly like to hear.

BORKMAN (*continues calmly*). Listen, Erhart—would you consider going in with your father? No man can find restitution through somebody's else's career. That's just an empty dream that's been spun for you here—down in this stale indoor air. Even if you could manage to live a life like all the saints put together, it wouldn't help me one particle.

ERHART (*deferentially*). That's just as you say.

BORKMAN. Yes, it is. And it wouldn't help either if I let myself wilt away in penance and contrition. I've tried to nurse myself along through all these years on hopes and dreams; but they've done me no earthly good. And now I want to shed my dreams.

ERHART (*bowing slightly*). And what—what will you do, sir?

BORKMAN. Reestablish myself, that's what. Begin from the bottom again. It's only by his present and his future that a man can expiate the past. By work—by unremitting work for everything that, in my youth, meant more to me than life itself. And that means now a thousand times more. Erhart—would you go in with your father and help me win this new life?

MRS. BORKMAN (*raising her hand in warning*). Don't do it, Erhart!

ELLA (*warmly*). Yes, yes, do it! Oh, help him, Erhart!

MRS. BORKMAN. And that's *your* advice? You—alone and dying—

ELLA. It doesn't matter about me.

MRS. BORKMAN. Yes, just so *I'm* not the one who takes him from you.

ELLA. Precisely, Gunhild.

BORKMAN (*to* ERHART). What do you say?

ERHART (*painfully distressed*). Father, I can't, not now. It's totally impossible.

BORKMAN. Well, what *do* you want then?

ERHART (*in a blaze of emotion*). I'm young! I want my chance to live, for once! I want to live my own life!

ELLA. But not to give up a few short months to lighten the last days of an unhappy life.

ERHART. As much as I wish to, Aunt Ella, I can't.

ELLA. Not for someone who loves you beyond words?

ERHART. As I live and breathe, I tell you—I can't.

MRS. BORKMAN (*looking intensely at him*). And your mother can't hold you now, either?

ERHART. Mother, I'll always love you. But I can't continue living for you alone. Because that isn't life for me.

BORKMAN. Then why not come in with me! Because life is work, Erhart. Come, let's the two of us take life on and work together!

ERHART (*passionately*). Yes, but I don't *want* to work now! Because I'm young! I've never known what that meant before, but now I feel it surging through every fiber of me. I *will* not work! Just live, live, live!

MRS. BORKMAN (*with a cry of premonition*). Erhart—what will you live for?

ERHART (*his eyes kindling*). For happiness, Mother!

MRS. BORKMAN. And where do you think you can find *that*?

ERHART. I've found it already!

MRS. BORKMAN (*in a shriek*). Erhart—!

(ERHART *strides quickly over to the hall door and opens it.*)

ERHART (*calls*). Fanny—you can come in now.

(MRS. WILTON, *in her winter coat, appears in the doorway.*)

MRS. BORKMAN (*her hands upraised*). Mrs. Wilton—!

MRS. WILTON (*rather shyly, with a questioning glance at* ERHART). Can I then—?

ERHART. Yes, now you can. I've said everything.

(MRS. WILTON *enters the room,* ERHART *closing the door after her. She bows politely to* BORKMAN, *who silently returns the greeting. A brief pause.*)

MRS. WILTON (*in a subdued, but firm voice*). So the words have been said. Then I guess I stand here as someone who's inflicted a great catastrophe on this house.

MRS. BORKMAN (*slowly, looking rigidly at her*). You've shattered the last remnants of what I had to live for. (*In an outburst.*) But this—this is all so utterly impossible!

MRS. WILTON. I understand very well, Mrs. Borkman, that this must seem impossible to you.

MRS. BORKMAN. Yes, you must be able to see that yourself, that it's impossible.

MRS. WILTON. Implausible, utterly implausible—I'd prefer to call it that. But, nevertheless, it *is*.

MRS. BORKMAN (*turning*). Are you completely serious about this, Erhart?

ERHART. This is happiness to me, Mother. The greatest, loveliest happiness of life. I can't tell you more than that.

MRS. BORKMAN (*to* MRS. WILTON, *wringing her hands*).

Oh, the way you've inveigled and seduced my unfortunate son!

MRS. WILTON (*tossing her head proudly*). I've done nothing of the kind.

MRS. BORKMAN. Oh, haven't you!

MRS. WILTON. No. Neither inveigled nor seduced him. Erhart's come to me of his own free will. And I've met him freely halfway.

MRS. BORKMAN (*eyeing her up and down with contempt*). Yes! Oh yes, that I can well believe!

MRS. WILTON (*restraining herself*). Mrs. Borkman— there are forces in human life that you seem to know singularly little of.

MRS. BORKMAN. What forces, might I ask?

MRS. WILTON. The forces that impel two people to unite their lives indissolubly—without fearing the consequences.

MRS. BORKMAN (*smiles*). I thought you were already indissolubly united—to someone else.

MRS. WILTON (*curtly*). That someone deserted me.

MRS. BORKMAN. But he's still living, they say.

MRS. WILTON. He's dead to *me*.

ERHART (*incisively*). Yes, Mother, for Fanny he's dead. Moreover, this other man has nothing to do with me.

MRS. BORKMAN (*looking severely at him*). You know about him, then—this other man.

ERHART. Yes, I know. I know all about it, completely!

MRS. BORKMAN. And even so, you say it has nothing to do with you?

ERHART (*with airy disdain*). I can only tell you, it's happiness I want! I'm young! I want to live, live, live!

MRS. BORKMAN. Yes, you're young, Erhart. Much too young for this.

MRS. WILTON. Don't think, Mrs. Borkman, I haven't told him just that. I've laid out my whole life story for him. I've reminded him repeatedly that I'm a full seven years older than he—

ERHART (*interrupting*). Oh, look, Fanny—I knew that at the start.

MRS. WILTON. But nothing, nothing does any good.

MRS. BORKMAN. Really? Not at all? Then why didn't you dismiss him flat? Close your house to him? You know, you could have done that in good time.

MRS. WILTON (*looks at her and says softly*). I simply couldn't, Mrs. Borkman.

MRS. BORKMAN. Why not?

MRS. WILTON. Because my happiness was at stake in him, too.

MRS. BORKMAN (*scornfully*). Hm—happiness, happiness—

MRS. WILTON. I've never before known what happiness is in life. And I can't possibly turn it away, just because it came so late.

MRS. BORKMAN. And how long do you think this happiness will endure?

ERHART (*interrupting*). Short or long, Mother—what's the difference?

MRS. BORKMAN (*furious*). What a blind fool you are! Can't you see where all this is leading?

ERHART. I don't want to consider the future. Or be farsighted in any direction! I just want the chance to live my own life for once!

MRS. BORKMAN (*pained*). And you call that life, Erhart!

ERHART. Yes, don't you see how lovely she is?

MRS. BORKMAN (*clenching her fists*). And *this* burden of shame, then, I'll have to bear, too.

BORKMAN (*from the back of the room, brusquely incisive*). Ha! You're well practiced in that sort of thing, Gunhild!

ELLA (*imploringly*). John Gabriel—!

ERHART (*similarly*). Father—!

MRS. BORKMAN. Here I'm condemned to go on day by day, seeing my son with a—a—

ERHART (*breaking in fiercely*). You'll see nothing like that, Mother—rest assured! I'm not staying here any longer.

MRS. WILTON (*briskly and decisively*). We're going away, Mrs. Borkman.

MRS. BORKMAN (*turning pale*). Going away! Together, I suppose?

MRS. WILTON (*nods*). I'm traveling south, yes. Abroad. Together with a young girl. And Erhart's going with us.

MRS. BORKMAN. With you—and a young girl?

MRS. WILTON. Yes. It's that little Frida Foldal that I took into my house. I want her to go abroad and develop her music.

MRS. BORKMAN. So you're taking her with you.

MRS. WILTON. Yes. I could hardly send the child down there all on her own.

MRS. BORKMAN (*suppressing a smile*). What do *you* say to *that*, Erhart?

ERHART (*somewhat ill at ease, with a shrug*). Well, Mother—if that's how Fanny wants it to be, then—

MRS. BORKMAN (*coldly*). When will this entourage be leaving, might I ask?

MRS. WILTON. We're departing immediately, ·tonight. My sleigh is waiting—over at the Hinkels'.

MRS. BORKMAN (*scanning her*). I see—so that was the evening party.

MRS. WILTON (*smiling*). Yes, no one but Erhart and me. And Frida, of course.

MRS. BORKMAN. And where is she now?

MRS. WILTON. Sitting in the sleigh, waiting.

ERHART (*painfully embarrassed*). Mother—I hope you understand—? I wanted to spare you—spare everyone—all of this.

MRS. BORKMAN (*looks at him, deeply injured*). You would have left me without saying good-bye?

ERHART. Yes. I thought it was best that way. Best on

both sides. Everything was ready to go. Our bags were packed. But then when you sent that message for me, well— (*Reaches his hands out toward her.*) Good-bye then, Mother.

MRS. BORKMAN (*averting herself, with a gesture of repulsion*). Don't touch me!

ERHART (*gently*). Is that your last word?

MRS. BORKMAN (*austerely*). Yes.

ERHART (*turning*). And good-bye to you, Aunt Ella.

ELLA (*pressing his hands*). Good-bye, Erhart! Live your life—and be as happy—just as happy as you can!

ERHART. Thanks, Aunt Ella. (*Bows to* BORKMAN.) Good-bye, Father. (*Whispers to* MRS. WILTON.) Let's get away now, the quicker the better.

MRS. WILTON (*softly*). Yes, let's.

MRS. BORKMAN (*with a malevolent smile*). Mrs. Wilton —do you think you're very wise, taking that young girl along with you?

MRS. WILTON (*returns the smile, half ironically, half seriously*). Men are so variable, Mrs. Borkman. And women likewise. When Erhart is finished with me—and I with him—then it'll be good for both of us that he, poor boy, has someone to fall back on.

MRS. BORKMAN. But you yourself?

MRS. WILTON. Oh, I'll arrange for myself, don't worry. Good-bye, all of you!

(*She bows slightly and goes out the hall door.* ERHART *stands a moment as though faltering; then he turns and follows her.*)

MRS. BORKMAN (*her folded hands dropping*). Childless.

BORKMAN (*as if awakening into resolution*). Out into the storm alone then! My hat! My coat! (*He moves rapidly toward the door.*)

ELLA (*in terror, stopping him*). John Gabriel, where are you going?

BORKMAN. Out in the storm of life, you hear. Let go, Ella!

ELLA (*gripping him tightly*). No, no, I won't let you go out. You're ill. I can see that.

BORKMAN. I said, let me go! (*He tears himself loose and goes out down the hall.*)

ELLA (*in the doorway*). Help me to hold him, Gunhild!

MRS. BORKMAN (*remains standing in the middle of the room; cold and hard*). There's nobody in this world that I'm going to hold. Let them all leave me. This one and that. As far—as far as ever they want. (*Suddenly, with a rending cry.*) Erhart, don't go!

(*She rushes with outstretched arms toward the door. ELLA RENTHEIM stops her.*)

ACT FOUR

A stretch of open ground outside the main building, which lies to the right. One of its corners, including a flight of stone steps leading to the entrance door, projects out. Extending across the background near the edge of the open land, steep slopes covered with fir trees. To the left, scattered trees, the beginnings of a small woods. The snowstorm has ended, but the earth is deeply buried under the new-fallen snow. The fir branches hang heavy under its weight. The night is dark with scudding clouds. Occasionally a pale glimmer of the moon shines through. The surroundings are visible only in the faint light reflected by the snow.

BORKMAN, MRS. BORKMAN, *and* ELLA RENTHEIM *are standing on the steps.* BORKMAN *leans wearily against the wall of the house. He has an old-fashioned cape thrown over his shoulders and holds a soft gray felt hat in one hand, a thick, gnarled walking stick in the other.* ELLA *carries her coat on her arm.* MRS. BORKMAN'S *large shawl has slipped down about her neck, leaving her hair uncovered.*

ELLA (*barring* MRS. BORKMAN'S *path*). Don't go after him, Gunhild!

MRS. BORKMAN (*panic-stricken*). Out of my way, you! He mustn't leave me!

ELLA. I tell you, it's totally useless! You'll never catch up to him.

MRS. BORKMAN. I don't care; let me go, Ella! I'll scream

after him down the road. He's got to hear his mother's cry!

ELLA. He can't hear you. He's already sitting in the sleigh—

MRS. BORKMAN. No, no—he couldn't have reached the sleigh!

ELLA. He's been in the sleigh for some time, believe me!

MRS. BORKMAN (*in desperation*). If he's in the sleigh, then he's sitting by her, by her—her!

BORKMAN (*laughs darkly*). Then he won't likely hear his mother scream.

MRS. BORKMAN. No—then he won't hear. (*Listens.*) Shh! What's that?

ELLA (*also listening*). That sounds like sleigh bells—

MRS. BORKMAN (*with a stifled moan*). It's *her* sleigh!

ELLA. It could be somebody else's—

MRS. BORKMAN. No, no, it's Mrs. Wilton's sleigh! Those silver bells, I know them. Listen! Now they're driving right past us—at the foot of the hill.

ELLA (*hurriedly*). Gunhild, if you want to call to him, do it *now!* Maybe he still might— (*The sleigh bells sound close at hand within the woods.*) Quick, Gunhild! They're down there below us right now!

MRS. BORKMAN (*stands indecisively a moment; then stiffens, hard and cold*). No, I won't cry after him. Let Erhart Borkman go from me—far, far off into what he now calls life and happiness.

(*The sound fades in the distance.*)

ELLA (*after a moment*). You can't hear them anymore.

MRS. BORKMAN. To me they sounded like funeral bells.

BORKMAN (*with dry, hushed laughter*). Ah—they're not ringing for *me* yet.

MRS. BORKMAN. But for *me.* And for him that left me.

ELLA (*nodding pensively*). Who knows, Gunhild—they could be ringing in life and happiness for him, after all.

MRS. BORKMAN (*with a start; stares at her*). Life and happiness—?

ELLA. For a brief while, anyway.

MRS. BORKMAN. Would you wish him life and happiness
—with *her*?

ELLA (*fervently*). Yes, I would, from the bottom of my
heart!

MRS. BORKMAN (*coldly*). You must be richer than I,
then, in the power to love.

ELLA (*looking far off*). Maybe it's lack of love that
nourishes the power.

MRS. BORKMAN (*fastens her eyes on her*). If that's so,
Ella—then I'll soon be as rich as you.

(*She turns and goes into the house.* ELLA *stands a moment,
looking with concern at* BORKMAN; *then she lays her hand
lightly on his shoulder.*)

ELLA. John, do come inside. You, too.

BORKMAN (*as if awakening*). I?

ELLA. Yes. You can't take this raw winter air—you're
showing the cold, John. Come on now; go in with me.
Inside, where it's warm.

BORKMAN (*angrily*). You mean, up in that salon again?

ELLA. No, downstairs instead, with her.

BORKMAN (*seething with rage*). I'll never set foot under
that roof again.

ELLA. But where will you go then? It's late in the night,
John.

BORKMAN (*puts on his hat*). First of all, I want to go
out and have a look at my buried treasures.

ELLA (*regarding him anxiously*). John—I don't understand you!

BORKMAN (*with a coughing laugh*). Oh, I don't mean
any stowed-away embezzlings. Don't worry about that,
Ella. (*Stops and points.*) Look, a man, *there!* Who *is* it?

(VILHELM FOLDAL, *in an old, snow-spattered greatcoat,
with his hat-brim turned down and a large umbrella in his
hand, appears, making his way with difficulty toward the
corner of the house. He limps markedly on his left foot.*)

BORKMAN. Vilhelm! What are you doing back here?

FOLDAL (*looks up*). Good Lord—you're out on the steps, John Gabriel? (*Bows.*) And Mrs. Borkman, too, I see.

BORKMAN (*curtly*). This isn't my wife.

FOLDAL. Oh, excuse me. The thing is, I lost my glasses in the snow. But what's brought you, who never go out of doors—?

BORKMAN (*with a careless gaiety*). It's about time I became an outdoorsman again, don't you think? Nearly three years in detention; five years in the cell; eight years in that salon up there—

ELLA (*with concern*). John Gabriel—please—!

FOLDAL. Ah me, yes, yes—

BORKMAN. But what do you want of me?

FOLDAL (*remains standing at the foot of the steps*). I wanted to see you, John Gabriel. I felt I *had* to come up and see you in the salon. Dear me, that salon—!

BORKMAN. Wanted to see me, after I showed you the door?

FOLDAL. Good Lord, that's not important.

BORKMAN. What did you do to your foot? You were limping.

FOLDAL. Yes, you know what—I was run over.

ELLA. Run over!

FOLDAL. Yes, by a sleigh.

BORKMAN. Aha!

FOLDAL. With two horses. They came sweeping down the hill. I couldn't get out of the way fast enough, and so—

ELLA. So they ran over you.

FOLDAL. They bore right down on me, Mrs.—or Miss. Right down on me, so that I rolled in the snow and lost my glasses and got my umbrella broken— (*Rubs his leg.*) —and injured my foot a bit, too.

BORKMAN (*laughs silently*). You know who was in that sleigh, Vilhelm?

FOLDAL. No, how could I see? It was a closed sleigh, and the curtains were drawn. And the coachman didn't slow one iota when I went spinning. But what's the difference, because— (*Impulsively.*) Oh, I'm so wonderfully happy!

BORKMAN. Happy?

FOLDAL. Well, I really don't know what to call it. But the nearest word for it is happy. Because something so extraordinary has happened! And that's why I *couldn't* resist—why I simply *had* to come back and share my joy with you, John Gabriel.

BORKMAN (*gruffly*). Well, let's have my share, then.

ELLA. Invite your friend in with you first, John Gabriel.

BORKMAN (*adamantly*). I told you, I'm not going into that house.

ELLA. But you heard that he's been run over!

BORKMAN. Oh, we all get run over—sometime in life. But then you have to pick yourself up. And pretend it was nothing.

FOLDAL. Those were deep words, John Gabriel. But I can just as well tell you quickly out here.

BORKMAN (*more gently*). Yes, if you'd be so kind, Vilhelm.

FOLDAL. Well, listen to this! When I got home this evening from your place—would you believe it?—I found a letter. Can you guess who it was from?

BORKMAN. From your little Frida perhaps?

FOLDAL. Exactly! To think, you guessed it right off! Yes, it was a long—a fairly long letter from Frida. A servant had brought it. And can you imagine what she wrote?

BORKMAN. Was it possibly a farewell message to her parents?

FOLDAL. Precisely! It's incredible the way you can guess, John Gabriel! Yes, she wrote that Mrs. Wilton had taken such a great liking for her. And now she wants to travel abroad with her. So Frida can study more music, she writes. And Mrs. Wilton's arranged for a highly capable tutor to go along to give Frida private instruction. Because, unfortunately, she's fallen behind a bit in some of her subjects, you see.

BORKMAN (*shaking with silent laughter*). Why, yes, yes, I see the whole thing amazingly well.

FOLDAL (*continues enthusiastically*). And just think, she only found out about the trip this evening. That was at the party that you know—uh, hm! And still she took time to write. And the letter's so warm and so beautiful and so heartfelt; it really is. Not a trace of contempt for her father. And what a thoughtful gesture, her wanting to say good-bye to us in writing—before she went. (*Laughs.*) But we can't have anything like *that*!

BORKMAN (*looks inquiringly at him*). Like what?

FOLDAL. She writes that they're leaving tomorrow, quite early.

BORKMAN. I see, I see—tomorrow. She writes that?

FOLDAL (*laughs and rubs his hands*). Yes, but I'm the sly one, see! I'm on my way right now to Mrs. Wilton's—

BORKMAN. Tonight?

FOLDAL. My goodness, yes. It still isn't so very late. And if the house is dark, I'll ring. Without hesitation. For I will and I must see Frida before she leaves. Good night, good night! (*He starts off.*)

BORKMAN. Vilhelm, listen—you can save yourself that hard piece of road.

FOLDAL. Oh, you mean my foot—

BORKMAN. Yes, and you'll never get in anyway at Mrs. Wilton's.

FOLDAL. Oh, I will definitely. I'll keep on ringing and ringing till somebody comes and opens up. Because I simply have to see Frida.

ELLA. Your daughter's already left, Mr. Foldal.

FOLDAL (*thunderstruck*). Frida's left, already! Are you positive? Who told you that?

BORKMAN. Her future tutor.

FOLDAL. Oh? And who's he?

BORKMAN. A student named Erhart Borkman.

FOLDAL (*radiant with delight*). Your son, John Gabriel! Is *he* going with them?

BORKMAN. That's right. He's the one who'll help Mrs. Wilton with your little Frida's education.

FOLDAL. Well, thank God! Then the child's in the best of hands. But is it really for certain that they've left already with her?

BORKMAN. They drove off in the sleigh that ran you down.

FOLDAL (*clasps his hands*). Imagine, my little Frida in that elegant sleigh!

BORKMAN (*nods*). Oh yes, Vilhelm—your daughter's riding high these days. And son Erhart as well. Did you notice those silver bells?

FOLDAL. Well, now—silver bells, you say. Were they silver bells? Genuine, solid silver?

BORKMAN. You can bet your life they were. Everything was solid. Both outside and—and in.

FOLDAL (*with quiet feeling*). Isn't it curious, the way good fortune can unfold for a person? It's my—my frail talent for poetry that's transformed itself to music in Frida. So really, it hasn't come to nothing that I've been a poet. For now she has her chance to go out in the great, wide world that I once dreamed so hopefully of seeing. Little Frida, riding in a closed sleigh. And with silver bells on the harness—

BORKMAN. And riding down her father—

FOLDAL (*joyously*). Oh, now! What's that to me—as long as the child— Well, so I did come too late, after all. I'd better go home then and comfort her mother, who's sitting in the kitchen, crying.

BORKMAN. She's crying?

FOLDAL. Yes, can you imagine? She was crying as if her heart would break when I left.

BORKMAN. And you laugh, Vilhelm.

FOLDAL. Quite so, I do! But she, poor thing, she doesn't know any better, you see. Well, good-bye. It's lucky I have the streetcar so near. Good-bye, good-bye, John Gabriel! Good-bye, miss! (*He bows and hobbles back the same way he came.*)

BORKMAN (*stands silently a moment, gazing into space*). Good-bye, Vilhelm! It's not the first time in life you've been run over, old friend.

ELLA (*looks at him with suppressed anxiety*). You're so pale, so pale, John—

BORKMAN. That's from the prison air upstairs.

ELLA. I've never seen you like this before.

BORKMAN. Probably because you've never seen an escaped convict before.

ELLA. Oh, please, John, come in with me now!

BORKMAN. You can drop the cajoling voice. I've already told you—

(*The MAID appears out on the steps.*)

MAID. Begging your pardon, but Madam has said I should lock up the front door now.

BORKMAN (*in an undertone to ELLA*). Hear that! Now they want to lock me in again.

ELLA (*to the MAID*). The master isn't too well. He'd like a little fresh air first.

MAID. Yes, but Madam said to me herself—

ELLA. I'll lock up the door. Just leave the key in it—

MAID. Oh, all right then; that's what I'll do. (*She goes back into the house.*)

BORKMAN (*stands quietly a moment, listening, then goes hurriedly down onto the open ground*). Now I'm outside the walls, Ella. They'll never get me again!

ELLA (*going down beside him*). But you're a free man in there, too, John. You can come and go as you will.

BORKMAN (*hushed, as if in fright*). Under a roof for the last time! It's so good being out here in the night. If I went up in the salon now, the ceiling and walls would close in and crush me—grind me flat as a fly—

ELLA. But where will you go?

BORKMAN. Just walk and walk and walk. See if I can

win my way through to freedom, and life, and people again. Will you go with me, Ella?

ELLA. I? Now?

BORKMAN. Yes, yes—at once!

ELLA. But how far?

BORKMAN. As far as I can manage.

ELLA. Oh, but what are you thinking! Out in this wet, cold winter night—

BORKMAN (*in a hoarse, rasping voice*). Aha—the lady's worried about her health? Yes, of course—it *is* fragile.

ELLA. It's *your* health I'm worried about.

BORKMAN (*with a laugh*). A dead man's health! I have to laugh at you, Ella! (*He walks farther on.*)

ELLA (*follows him and holds him back*). What did you say you were?

BORKMAN. I said, a dead man. Don't you remember Gunhild telling me to rest quietly where I lay?

ELLA (*decisively, throwing her coat about her*). I'll go with you, John.

BORKMAN. Yes, we two, we really belong together, Ella. (*Proceeds farther.*) Come on!

(*Little by little they enter the low trees to the left, which increasingly conceal them until they disappear from sight. The house and the open land are lost to view. The landscape, with its slopes and ridges, alters slowly and becomes wilder and wilder.*)

ELLA'S VOICE (*heard from within the trees, right*). Where are we going, John? I don't know where this is.

BORKMAN'S VOICE (*higher up*). Keep following my footprints in the snow.

ELLA'S VOICE. But why do we need to climb so high?

BORKMAN'S VOICE (*nearer*). We have to go up the winding path.

ELLA (*still hidden*). Oh, I'm not good for much more.

BORKMAN (*at the edge of the forest, right*). Come on!

We're not far now from the view. There used to be a
bench here once—

ELLA (*becoming visible through the trees*). You remember that?

BORKMAN. You can rest yourself there.

(*They have emerged in a small clearing, high in the
woods. The slope rises sharply behind them. To the left,
far below, is an expansive landscape, with fjords and high,
distant mountain ranges towering one after another. In the
clearing at the left is a dead fir-tree, with a bench beneath
it. The snow lies deep on the ground.* BORKMAN *and, behind him,* ELLA *struggle across from the right through the
snow.*)

BORKMAN (*stops where the clearing falls off at the left*).
Come here, Ella, so you can see.

ELLA (*joining him*). What do you want to show me,
John?

BORKMAN (*pointing out*). You see how the land lies
before us, free and open—all the way out.

ELLA. We often used to sit on that bench—and look
even farther still.

BORKMAN. It was a dreamland we were seeing then.

ELLA. The dreamland of our lives, yes. And now it's a
land of snow. And the old tree is dead.

BORKMAN (*not hearing her*). Can you see the smoke
from the great steamers out on the fjord?

ELLA. No.

BORKMAN. I can. They come and they go. They make
this whole round earth into one community. They spread
light and warmth into human hearts in countless thousands
of homes. *That's* the thing I dreamed of doing.

ELLA (*softly*). And it stayed a dream.

BORKMAN. It stayed a dream, yes. (*Listening.*) Hear
that? Down by the river, the factories whirring! *My* factories! All the ones *I* would have built! Can you hear how
they're going? It's the night shift. Night and day they're
working. Listen, listen! The wheels are spinning, and the

gears are gleaming—around and around! Don't you hear them, Ella?

ELLA. No.

BORKMAN. *I* hear them.

ELLA (*fearfully*). I think you're mistaken, John.

BORKMAN (*more and more exhilarated*). Oh, but all this—it's only a kind of outworks enclosing the kingdom, you know!

ELLA. The kingdom? What kingdom?

BORKMAN. My kingdom, of course! The kingdom I was on the verge of possessing when I—when I died.

ELLA (*quietly shaken*). Oh, John, John!

BORKMAN. And now it lies there—defenseless, leaderless—exposed to the rape and plunder of thieves—! Ella! Do you see those mountain ranges *there*—far off. One after another. They leap skyward. They tower in space. That's my deep, my endless, inexhaustible kingdom!

ELLA. Yes, but John, the wind blows ice-cold from that kingdom!

BORKMAN. That wind works on me like the breath of life. It comes to me like a greeting from captive spirits. I can sense them, the buried millions. I feel the veins of metal, reaching their curving, branching, beckoning arms out to me. I saw them before me like living shadows—the night I stood in the bank vault with a lantern in my hand. You wanted your freedom then—and I tried to set you free. But I lacked the strength for it. Your treasures sank back in the depths. (*His hands outstretched.*) But I'll whisper to you here in the silence of the night. I love you, lying there unconscious in the depths and the darkness! I love you, your riches straining to be born—with all your shining aura of power and glory! I love you, love you, love you!

ELLA (*with constrained but mounting agitation*). Yes, your love is still down there, John. That's where it's always been. But up here in the daylight—here there was a warm, living human heart that beat for you. And this heart you crushed. Oh, more than that! Ten times worse! You *sold* it for—for—

BORKMAN (*a cold tremor seems to go through him*). For the kingdom—and the power—and the glory—you mean?

ELLA. Yes, it's what I mean. I said it once before to you this evening: you've murdered the capacity to love in the woman that loved you. And that you loved in return—as far as you *could* love anyone. (*Her arm upraised.*) And so I prophesy this for you, John Gabriel Borkman—you'll never win the prize you murdered for. You'll never ride in triumph into your cold, dark kingdom!

BORKMAN (*falters over to the bench and sinks down heavily*). I'm almost afraid your prophecy is right, Ella.

ELLA (*over beside him*). It's nothing to be afraid of, John. It would be exactly the best that could ever happen to you.

BORKMAN (*with a cry, clutches his chest*). Ah—! (*Faintly.*) There it let me go.

ELLA (*shaking him*). What was it, John?

BORKMAN (*slumps against the back of the bench*). A hand of ice—that choked my heart.

ELLA. John! Now you feel it, the ice hand!

BORKMAN (*murmurs*). No—no ice hand. It was a hand of metal. (*He slides down upon the bench.*)

ELLA (*tearing her coat off and spreading it over him*). Lie still and rest quietly! I'll go for help. (*She moves several steps to the right, then stops, returns, and feels his pulse and his face for a long moment.*) No. It's best, John Borkman. Best like this for you. (*She tucks the coat more tightly around him and sits down in the snow in front of the bench.*)

(*After a short silence,* MRS. BORKMAN, *wrapped in her overcoat, comes through the snow from the right. The* MAID *goes ahead of her with a lit lantern.*)

MAID (*shining the light on the snow*). Oh, yes, ma'am. It's their footprints here—

MRS. BORKMAN (*peering about*). Yes, there they are! Over there on the bench. (*Calls.*) Ella!

ELLA (*getting up*). Are you searching for us?

MRS. BORKMAN (*acidly*). Yes, I thought I'd better.

ELLA (*pointing*). See, there he lies, Gunhild.

MRS. BORKMAN. Sleeping!

ELLA (*nods*). A deep sleep and a long one, I think.

MRS. BORKMAN (*in an outburst*). Ella! (*Controls herself and asks in a whisper.*) Did it happen—deliberately?

ELLA. No.

MRS. BORKMAN (*relieved*). Not by his own hand, then?

ELLA. No. It was a freezing hand of metal that seized his heart.

MRS. BORKMAN (*to the* MAID). Get some help. Some people from the farm.

MAID. Yes, of course, ma'am. (*Softly.*) In Jesus' name— (*She goes off through the trees to the right.*)

MRS. BORKMAN (*standing behind the bench*). Then the night air killed him—

ELLA. I suppose so.

MRS. BORKMAN. He, that strong man.

ELLA (*moving in front of the bench*). Won't you look at him, Gunhild?

MRS. BORKMAN (*with a gesture of aversion*). No, no, no. (*Lowers her voice.*) He was a miner's son—Borkman, the bank president. He couldn't survive in the fresh air.

ELLA. It was more probably the cold that killed him.

MRS. BORKMAN (*shaking her head*). You say, the cold? The cold—that killed him a long time back.

ELLA (*nodding to her*). And turned the two of us into shadows.

MRS. BORKMAN. You're right about that.

ELLA (*with a painful smile*). A dead man and two shadows—that's what the cold has made.

MRS. BORKMAN. Yes, a coldness in the heart. And so, at last, we two might reach our hands out to each other.

ELLA. Now I think we can.

MRS. BORKMAN. We two twin sisters—over him we both once loved.

ELLA. We two shadows—over the dead man.

(MRS. BORKMAN, *behind the bench, and* ELLA RENTHEIM, *in front of it, reach across and take each other's hands.*)

AFTERWORD

It seems hardly necessary to argue the contemporaneity of Henrik Ibsen. His long shadow, like that of his near contemporary Joyce, has extended across more than a century and remains a constant presence even in the postmodern world of the past half century and into the new millennium. Perhaps no dramatist, save Shakespeare, has been produced more persistently on the worldwide stage, exerted more influence, or provided the inspiration for more playwrights. As Rolf Fjelde writes in his 1970 foreword to this text, we merely await new actors to seize Ibsen's "multidimensional life . . . liberate it, and make it their own." Yet, as with any works in the established canon, Ibsen's dramas have sometimes been diminished by critical clichés, and certain of his texts have been ignored according to the dictates of current literary theory. Furthermore, in an age of deconstruction, feminist criticism, performance theory, and various other versions of postmodern theory, Ibsen's dramaturgy and themes have sometimes been dismissed as worn-out or passé. Of course nothing could be farther from the truth. The four plays reprinted here in the superb Fjelde translations bear witness to the enduring relevance of Ibsen's vision.

The female protagonists in *Ghosts* and *The Lady from the Sea* form part of Ibsen's remarkable set of portraits of women on the threshold of the modern age: Dina Dorf, Nora Helmers, Helene Alving, Hedda Gabler, Rebecca West—all seek freedom from social and psychological repression in an age of heightened self-consciousness. It is no wonder that, at a time when our own awareness of women's issues has been dramatically raised, Ibsen's depiction of both their social and psychological lives maintains a remarkable currency, despite his claim that he never wrote any play for a social purpose. *Ghosts,* as many have noted, is a retelling of *A Doll House* from the perspective of a woman who opts to remain in a loveless marriage rather than escape her socially defined doll house. In creating Nora Helmer two years earlier, Ibsen avoided the facile view that Nora is merely the victim of the patriarchal society and suggested that she is essentially enslaved by her own willful, if largely unconscious, acceptance of conventional morality. He recognized that the most powerful chains are, in Blake's phrase, "mind-forg'd manacles." In *Ghosts,* he portrays Nora as an older woman still struggling to free herself from the code of social morality and the past. He emphasizes Helene Alving's female nature by featuring her relationship with her symbolically diseased only child, upon whom she has placed the burden of her own redemption. Ibsen employs the "child" as a symbol in most of his plays. Though some of Ibsen's child characters are literally illegitimate, more often than not they are psychologically and spiritually orphaned—and they are everywhere. Many are the issue of what Margot Norris calls "spiritual adultery." Children of mismatched pairs, they haunt the plays from *The Vikings at Helgeland* to *When We Dead Awaken.* Many endure physical deformities that expose the flawed relationships of their parents—Osvald Alving's syphilitic condition, Hedvig Ekdal's encroaching blindness, and Eyolf Allmer's crippled body. So also the deaths of Ulf Brand, Ellida Wangel's sickly infant, and Aline Solness's poisoned twins give testimony of illicit unions. In addition, such figurative progeny as Eilert Løvborg's manuscript in *Hedda Gabler,* Rebecca West's fraudulent child in *Rosmersholm,* and the violated statue-child in *When We Dead Awaken* bear witness to deficient relationships and spiritual failure. In an age of rampant child abuse such as our own, these characters speak to us with extraordinary power.

Like *A Doll House, Ghosts* is often reduced by a too simplistic characterization of the protagonist as victim of the external forces exposed in Ibsen's realistic depiction of culture forces—a domineering husband, the mores of the patriarchal society, Pastor Manders' moral absolutism and lack of courage—but Ibsen's vision goes well beyond the dictates of the conventional problem play in its characterization of Mrs. Alving. For Ibsen understands that the real enemy of Mrs. Alving, as of Nora Helmer, is the self; by remaining in a loveless marriage, Mrs. Alving is an unwitting coconspirator in her own defeat. Rejecting the seductive appeal of victimization, Ibsen grants Mrs. Alving tragic stature by showing that she has chosen—and so must bear responsibility for the consequences of choice. As Osvald reminds her when Mrs. Alving ironically claims a mother's right to possess him even as he regresses into childhood in the terminal stages of syphilis, she is "the obvious choice" to assume responsibility for his fate: "What more obvious choice than you?" In surely one of the most ironic lines in modern drama, she responds, "My child has his mother to nurse him." In reclaiming her "child," she comes face-to-face with the potential cost of "freedom" as tragically as any "new woman" on the modern stage. And the way Ibsen ends—or perhaps more accurately does not end—the play bespeaks its modernity as well. Often accused of writing melodramatic rather than meaningful endings (Nora slamming the door, Hedda Gabler shooting herself, Hedvig Ekdal sacrificing herself, Rosmer and Rebecca jumping into the mill-race, Solness falling from the tower, John Gabriel Borkman being reclaimed by "the icy hand," Arnold Rubek leaping into the avalanche), Ibsen also brings down the curtain in *Ghosts* with a sensational ending as Osvald slips into childish madness; but he keeps it open-ended, nonetheless, in anticipation of so much of modern drama in its apparent lack of closure. In the play's stunning *incompletion*, Ibsen makes clear that Mrs. Alving must indeed define herself as woman, as the "mother" in whose hands the choice of life and death remains. Though *Kindermord* occurs frequently in Ibsen, it carries extraordinary power here. Having committed the crime of innocence under Manders' influence by accommodating the social code, Helene Alving has again become the "mother" to the diseased child she has been killing all along. Now she is at last free, however ironically, to choose independent of any external control, and it really does not matter what she chooses, only *that* she chooses—and she *must* choose. Avoiding the superficial, Ibsen gives mythic dimension to the spiritual and existential crisis in the play, portraying in Mrs. Alving's unresolvable dilemma the contesting Apollonian and Dionysion forces doing battle in the guise of social propriety and the will to freedom.

A product of Ibsen's later career, *The Lady from the Sea* explores the dark recesses of the psyche even more deeply and, like the plays to follow, presents a penetrating study of an individual suffering from the disease of modern life. A combination of powerful mythical and psychological impulses, Ellida Wangel is among the playwright's most complex and enigmatic figures. Trapped, like Nora, Mrs. Alving, and Hedda, in an enclosed social and psychic world (represented by the confines of the summerhouse), Ellida tells her husband, Wangel, "The plain, simple truth is that you came out there and—and bought me." What Nora discovers and Hedda already painfully realizes, Ellida confesses: "I met your offer—and sold myself to you." Ibsen again exposes the corrupt bourgeois capitalism in which women are barter; but he moves from the meticulously furnished middle-class rooms in *A Doll House* and the pretentious mausoleum where Hedda Gabler is entombed to a richly primal setting on the edge of the water, where land and sea assume archetypal meaning as projections of the elemental counterforces operating in Ellida.

Called "The Heathen" ten years earlier when the then-youthful Arnholm proposed to her, Ellida was "married" to a mysterious seaman in a ritual ceremony when they exchanged rings and threw them into the water, vowing to "marry themselves to the sea"—"just as binding as a marriage license" (an interesting echo of Rebecca and Rosmer's ritual marriage at the end of *Rosmersholm*). Now seemingly resurrected from the sea, the universal symbol of the unconscious, the supposedly dead seaman returns to lay claim to his "Lady from the Sea." As in other plays of Ibsen's later period, the action depends on extremely taut dialogue with very limited action (one thinks of *Little Eyolf* in which the only real action occurs at the end of act one, and the two acts following constitute a lengthy and compelling denouement).

Reflections of earlier plays surface as well. Another orphan figure like Peer Gynt's "ugly brat," Nora, Hedda, Mrs. Alving, Dina Dorf, Rebecca West, Hilda Wangel, and Asta Allmers, Ellida is spiritually disenfranchised. Even the theme of incest resurfaces here as it does spectacularly in *Ghosts* and *Rosmersholm.* Ellida lived alone with her father at his lighthouse, an obvious phallic symbol like General Gabler's pistols. Ibsen also again addresses the role of women as wives and mothers in distinctly modern terms. Ellida and Wangel's only child died at age two-and-a-half, five months before the play opens, another illegitimate child victimized by his mother's guilt. Nor can Ellida serve as stepmother to Wangel's daughters, who are approximately her own age. Unfulfilled as wife or mother, she sees her guilt as an "unfaithful wife" in her dead infant's eyes that "changed with the sea," a mirror of her spiritual husband associated with the sea, and a voice rising from her own unconscious like the judgmental eyes of Little Eyolf that stare up from the sea and penetrate the soul of Rita Allmers.

Another play of retribution, of the persistence of the past, *The Lady from the Sea* juxtaposes Apollonian and Dionysian powers vying in Ellida Wangel's psyche. Here, however, Ibsen offers a resolution. With the resurrection of the seaman and his claim on her, Ellida confronts the psychic forces that bind her. By allowing Ellida to choose, Wangel places the full weight of choice onto her, dissolving "the contract" that legally binds them—and as in all Ibsen's plays, "freedom . . . transforms everything!" Ellida can now *choose* to be wife and mother. And even though we are perhaps no more certain what the future holds here than we are at the end of *Little Eyolf* when Rita welcomes her supposed stepsister Asta, Ellida embraces her stepdaughter Hilda at the end of the play, symbolically attesting, at least momentarily, to her motherhood and her new sense of self.

The earlier and more polemical *An Enemy of the People* exceeds as well the limitations of a simple protest play, though it too is often reductively misread. When Arthur Miller early in his career adapted Ibsen's text for a 1950 restaging in the shadow of the McCarthy hearings, he followed the error of many by transforming it into "a teaching play." Although he rightly claimed in his essay "Ibsen's Warning" that *An Enemy of the People* "is far more applicable to our nature-despoiling societies than to even turn-of-the-century capitalism, untrammelled and raw as Ibsen knew it to be," he largely ignored Ibsen's irony and the comic incongruity with which Ibsen often undercuts his idealistic protagonist Dr. Stockmann. Contrary to Ibsen, Miller makes Stockmann into what David Bronson calls "a mouthpiece" and "a package of virtue." In fact Stockmann assumes the guise of a modern antihero as much as the pose of a hero in Ibsen's hands, even though Stanislavsky considered Stockmann his favorite role. As Professor Fjelde notes, Ibsen complicates the nature of the play, showing that the liberals are every bit as dangerous and hypocritical as the conservatives who target Stockmann, neither possessing the vision to bring about the "Third Kingdom." Professor Fjelde aptly identifies Stockmann as one of the new revolutionaries, "the prime agent of revolt against the tyranny of fixed abstractions . . . and of constricting naturalistic circumstances." But Ibsen intentionally mutes his protagonist's heroism, exposing him as driven as much by egotism as by principle. The self-absorbed doctor seeks his twelve disciples at the end and never questions his own motives. Neither a ninny nor a true idealist, he emerges as an ambiguous modern figure. Far from being the pat hero projected in superficial readings of the text, the naive, proud, and often petty Stockmann remains ignorant of himself and suspect as a moral figure even though, as Professor Fjelde proposes, he seems "the bearer of the new conception of revolution." Ibsen invites a far more cynical, postmodern evaluation of him than the view afforded by those seeking a full-blooded, conventional hero.

The other male protagonist included here provides one of the first full portraits of the modern capitalist financier, a sort of bourgeois Faust driven by the counterimperatives of acquiring wealth and power and benefiting humanity. On one hand a visionary like Brand and Julian (in *Emperor and Galilean*), John Gabriel Borkman is also as ruthless as any tycoon of the Gilded Age or current Wall Street investor. In this late play, Ibsen probes his protagonist far more deeply than he does his earlier, much more polemical "enemy of the people." As he generally does, Ibsen constructs a triangular relationship to characterize his central character and develop his themes. The two sisters, Ella and Gunhild, establish the internal dialectic that propels Borkman. Here Ibsen brings to bear the themes and dramatic strategies that are his signature. Merging myth and realism, he portrays his capitalist overreacher as sacrificing love for power, just as Rubek denies love for art in Ibsen's last great play, *When We Dead Awaken*. Another orphaned child, Erhart is alienated from his parents. Gunhild welcomes him only as the instrument of revenge, and Borkman sees him as the agent of his dream of unparalleled economic might. Gunhild's sister, Ella, his true spiritual mother, claims him as a substitute for her failed life. In consequence of these specious claims, Erhart is utterly deprived of will.

Interestingly, almost alone among Ibsen's orphaned children, Erhart is rescued. Irene declares that she should have killed her and Rubek's spurious child-statue, and Aline remorselessly recalls in *The Master Builder* how she poisoned her infants even as she mourns the loss of her nine dolls— "Just like unborn children"; but Erhart is spared by Fanny Wilton's determination to take him away, even if their love proves temporary. Gunhild's last word as Fanny and Erhart

depart defines the cost of all their freedom—"Childless."
Typically Ibsen retains a certain ambiguity at the ends of
his plays, and here too we are left to wonder if Fanny has
merely seduced the naive Erhart like the troll-like Hilda
Wangel tempts Solness to climb the tower. Regardless, as
Professor Fjelde concludes, "it is now up to the new generation to revise and improve or to reject the sum of their
parents' lives."

All these plays illustrate the sustaining vision of Ibsen's
art. In his aligning of the mythic with the psychological— of
"retribution" with the inexorable presentness of the past—
in his portrayal of the conflicting imperatives of self and
society in the emerging culture, in his conception of tragedy
in a world with neither God nor a moral center in which
determinism and free will do constant battle, in his compelling use of symbolism, in his Freudian sensitivity to the counterforces of Eros and Thanatos, and in his profound
awareness of spiritual alienation and ambiguity in a world
peopled by orphans, Ibsen provides an enduring portrait of
the human condition in the modern age.

TERRY OTTEN
Wittenberg University

READ THE TOP 25 SIGNET CLASSICS

❏ ANIMAL FARM BY GEORGE ORWELL   0-451-52634-1 $6.95

❏ 1984 BY GEORGE ORWELL   0-451-52493-4 $6.95

❏ HAMLET BY WILLIAM SHAKESPEARE   0-451-52692-9 $3.95

❏ GREAT EXPECTATIONS BY CHARLES DICKENS   0-451-52671-6 $4.95

❏ ADVENTURES OF HUCKLEBERRY FINN BY MARK TWAIN   0-451-52650-3 $4.95

❏ NARRATIVE OF THE LIFE OF FREDERICK DOUGLASS
     BY FREDERICK DOUGLASS   0-451-52673-2 $4.95

❏ HEART OF DARKNESS & THE SECRET SHARER
     BY JOSEPH CONRAD   0-451-52657-0 $4.95

❏ JANE EYRE BY CHARLOTTE BRONTE   0-451-52655-4 $4.95

❏ A TALE OF TWO CITIES BY CHARLES DICKENS   0-451-52656-2 $4.95

❏ THE ODYSSEY (W.H.D. ROUSE, TRANSLATOR)   0-451-52736-4 $5.95

❏ A MIDSUMMER NIGHT'S DREAM BY W. SHAKESPEARE   0-451-52696-1 $3.95

❏ MACBETH BY WILLIAM SHAKESPEARE   0-451-52677-5 $3.95

❏ OTHELLO BY WILLIAM SHAKESPEARE   0-451-52685-6 $3.95

❏ ROMEO AND JULIET BY WILLIAM SHAKESPEARE   0-451-52686-4 $3.95

❏ THE JUNGLE BY UPTON SINCLAIR   0-451-52420-9 $5.95

❏ PRIDE AND PREJUDICE BY JANE AUSTEN   0-451-52588-4 $4.95

❏ LES MISERABLES BY VICTOR HUGO   0-451-52526-4 $7.95

❏ WUTHERING HEIGHTS BY EMILY BRONTE   0-451-52338-5 $4.95

❏ ONE DAY IN THE LIFE OF IVAN DENISOVICH
     BY ALEXANDER SOLZHENITSYN   0-451-52709-7 $4.95

❏ THE SCARLET LETTER BY NATHANIEL HAWTHORNE   0-451-52608-2 $3.95

❏ BEOWULF (B. RAFFEL, TRANSLATOR)   0-451-52740-2 $4.95

❏ THE COUNT OF MONTE CRISTO BY ALEXANDER DUMAS   0-451-52195-1 $6.95

❏ KING LEAR BY WILLIAM SHAKESPEARE   0-451-52693-7 $3.95

❏ GULLIVER'S TRAVELS BY JONATHON SWIFT   0-451-52732-1 $3.95

❏ THE ADVENTURES OF TOM SAWYER BY MARK TWAIN   0-451-52653-8 $4.95

TO ORDER CALL: 1-800-788-6262